MW00462709

An Introduction to

EDUCATIONAL RESEARCH

An Introduction to

EDUCATIONAL RESEARCH

Connecting Methods to Practice

Chad R. Lochmiller
Indiana University

Jessica N. Lester
Indiana University

Los Angeles | London | New Delhi
Singapore | Washington DC

Los Angeles | London | New Delhi
Singapore | Washington DC

FOR INFORMATION:

SAGE Publications, Inc.
2455 Teller Road
Thousand Oaks, California 91320
E-mail: order@sagepub.com

SAGE Publications Ltd.
1 Oliver's Yard
55 City Road
London EC1Y 1SP
United Kingdom

SAGE Publications India Pvt. Ltd.
B 1/I 1 Mohan Cooperative Industrial Area
Mathura Road, New Delhi 110 044
India

SAGE Publications Asia-Pacific Pte. Ltd.
3 Church Street
#10-04 Samsung Hub
Singapore 049483

Copyright © 2017 by SAGE Publications, Inc.

All rights reserved. No part of this book may be reproduced or utilized in any form or by any means, electronic or mechanical, including photocopying, recording, or by any information storage and retrieval system, without permission in writing from the publisher.

Printed in the United States of America

ISBN 978-1-4833-1950-6

Acquisitions Editor: Theresa Accomazzo
Associate Editor: Jessica Miller
Editorial Assistant: Georgia McLaughlin
eLearning Editor: Katie Bierach
Production Editor: Libby Larson
Copy Editor: Catherine Forrest
Typesetter: C&M Digitals (P) Ltd.
Proofreader: Laura Webb
Indexer: Joan Shapiro
Cover Designer: Karine Hovsepian
Marketing Manager: Ashlee Blunk

This book is printed on acid-free paper.

SFI Certified Sourcing
www.sfiprogram.org
SFI-00453

15 16 17 18 19 10 9 8 7 6 5 4 3 2 1

BRIEF CONTENTS

TABLE OF CONTENTS

PREFACE

AIMS OF THE TEXTBOOK

There are many introductory educational research textbooks available. The majority of these textbooks provide a balanced discussion of qualitative, quantitative, and mixed methods approaches to research and discuss the basics of how to conduct educational research and evaluate published research studies. Similarly, this textbook offers a balanced discussion across research methodologies and presents the basics of the research process. However, when we set out to write this textbook, we wanted to take a slightly different approach to the discussion of educational research. The majority of research textbooks present research in a *research-first* manner, with research methodologies and methods as the prime focus and implications for practice dealt with last or as separate "case studies." While this approach is useful for many students, in our own teaching we have found that students who are currently immersed in professional practice often struggle to see the connection between learning about the details and language of evaluating and conducting educational research and their own professional practice. Further, many students find *research-first* discussions of educational research intimidating or simply disconnected from their daily lives. As such, we wanted to write a book for practitioners who inherently strive to understand their professional work in more detail and who may also seek to improve schools, districts, and educational organizations by conducting research within these contexts. We refer to these individuals—indeed, to you—as practitioner-scholars because we believe that it captures the nature of your work and the strength of your interest in improving schools. More specifically, we wrote this book for classroom teachers, teacher leaders, school and district administrators—those who individually and collectively act as leaders in schools and districts.

The students we have worked with come from a diverse array of professional experiences, many of which uniquely equip them to understand research through the lens of a practitioner-scholar. Many of these practitioner-scholars enter our research methods classrooms with a comprehensive understanding of the work that takes place on a daily basis in their schools, districts, and educational organizations. They ask compelling and interesting questions related to the problems of practice that they face each day. Many of these same problems are found in the annals of educational research and are the focus of scholars' lives and careers. Recognizing the relationship between problems of practice and educational research, in *An Introduction to Educational Research: Connecting Methods to Practice*, we adopt a *practice-first* orientation. We aim to provide the reader with an introduction to educational research in a way that aligns with their professional experiences and illuminates the ever-present connections between these experiences and educational research. Throughout the textbook, we incorporate problems of practice, linking these problems to particular steps of the research process, theoretical perspectives, research methodologies, and methods. In addition, we present links to specific research practices throughout the textbook to highlight how practitioner-scholars undertake research and, in practical terms, what that undertaking involves.

More particularly, this book serves five purposes. First, we provide you with a broad introduction to the research process. Second, we assist you in becoming conversant in the language of research, which will support you as you develop abilities related to the critical consumption of research and the process of conducting research. Third, we offer illustrative problems of practice that illuminate the connections between research and your practice as a practitioner-scholar. Fourth, in exposing you to these problems of practice, we hope to prepare you to identify research topics and ideas that you might study independently or with your colleagues. Fifth, through reflective opportunities staged throughout the book, we assist you in considering your identity as a researcher, identifying your assumptions about responsibly conducting research, and weighing various approaches to research given your particular interests and values.

It is important to keep in mind that the purpose of this textbook is not to introduce you to *all* research methodologies and methods equally. Rather, the purpose is to prepare you to connect specific research methodologies and methods with common problems of practice. In orienting to the textbook this way, we acknowledge that some topics will not be covered in depth or with sufficient breadth. Instead, we focus on those topics that we believe are most essential to helping you develop the skills you need to think as a researcher would in your own area of professional practice.

We thus strongly encourage you to see this book as a starting point in your learning process—one that provides you with *some* useful tools for thinking critically about educational research. Yet, we recognize that you will not become a practitioner-scholar simply by reading this textbook. Rather, we invite you to view this textbook as one step in the process toward an improved understanding of research, deeper appreciation for professional practice, and a more compelling grasp of the connections between these two worlds. Further, we invite you to begin thinking about how you might engage in the *practice of research* in relation to your current work, as any textbook or methods course can only take you so far. There will come a point at which you will need to go out and *do* what you are reading about.

ORGANIZATION OF THE TEXTBOOK

This textbook is organized in three parts. In Part I, we establish a broad context for educational research methodologies (for example, qualitative and quantitative) and their related methods (that is, procedures used to carry out a research study). We use contemporary problems of practice (for example, the achievement gap) to orient you to problems that can be explored through various research methodologies, while introducing you to the varied purposes and definitions of educational research. In Part I, we also review four broad approaches to educational research (qualitative, quantitative, mixed methods, and action research) and associate these research methodologies with specific problems of practice. We also consider the process of searching for relevant literature and evaluating the quality of a published research study. We end the first section by considering the foundational role of ethics in conducting research.

In Part II, we focus on the data collection and analysis processes, while also providing you with an opportunity to consider some of the common approaches to qualitative and quantitative research. In addition, we discuss mixed methods approaches to research and analysis, as well as action research. Throughout, we highlight various technologies that can support the data collection and analysis process.

In Part III, we provide a focused discussion around the process of writing and presenting research findings for key stakeholders. We give particular attention to emergent practices for disseminating research findings, particularly to groups of people who are engaged in the work of schools, districts, and educational organizations. We conclude the textbook by returning to the problems of practice to highlight the various ways in which research methodologies can be used to understand, examine, critique, and address these problems. We use this discussion as a springboard to encourage you to begin identifying, defining, and carrying out a research study of your own.

TEXTBOOK FEATURES TO SUPPORT LEARNING

Throughout the textbook, we have included several features aimed at supporting your learning. Each chapter begins by listing the key learning objectives. These objectives point toward central ideas to consider and come back to as you read and study a particular chapter. To support this feature, we provide Reflective Opportunities in each chapter, which are invitations for you to think more deeply about a concept, and, at times, make personal connections to your practice. These Reflective Opportunities are intended to help you identify your own assumptions as a researcher, clarify your beliefs about responsibly conducting research, and consider various strategies for carrying out research. We also include Links to Practice in many of the chapters, which illustrate in practical terms various steps in the research process, as well as how you might approach the research process. As a complement to the Links to Practice, most of the chapters include From the Field boxes, which provide illustrative examples drawn directly from published literature. After each chapter's summary, we list key terms with abbreviated definitions. These defined concepts are intended to revisit the language of research and reinforce your current understanding of the material presented in a given chapter. Following the key terms, we provide Questions to Consider designed to facilitate individual reflection, as well as small and large group discussions. If you are reading this book independent of a class or without a group of colleagues, these questions might serve as a way for you to check and extend your understanding. At the end of each chapter, four chapter exercises are included that provide you with tasks designed to encourage you to apply what you have read within a given chapter. We also offer recommended readings, which we refer to as Learning Extensions. Because we assume that this textbook is only one component of your learning process as a practitioner-scholar, we believe it is important to provide you with suggested readings that may deepen your understanding and future practice. Finally, there are several ancillaries available with this textbook. A student study site is available that provides Student Quizzes, eFlashcards, and Multimedia Resources. There is also a password-protected instructor site including a Word and Respondus Test Bank, PowerPoint Slides, Lecture Notes, and Multimedia Resources for each chapter.

$SAGE edge™

SAGE edge offers a robust online environment you can access anytime, anywhere, and features an impressive array of free tools and resources to keep you on the cutting edge of your learning experience.

SAGE edge for Students provides a personalized approach to help you accomplish your coursework goals in an easy-to-use learning environment.

- Mobile-friendly eFlashcards strengthen your understanding of key terms and concepts

- Mobile-friendly practice quizzes allow you to independently assess your mastery of course material

- A complete online action plan includes tips and feedback on your progress and allows you to individualize your learning experience

- Chapter summaries with learning objectives reinforce the most important material

- Interactive exercises and meaningful web links make it easy to mine internet resources, further explore topics, and answer critical thinking questions

SAGE edge for Instructors, supports your teaching by making it easy to integrate quality content and create a rich learning environment for students.

- Test banks provide a diverse range of pre-written options as well as the opportunity to edit any question and/or insert your own personalized questions to effectively assess students' progress and understanding

- Sample course syllabi for semester and quarter courses provide suggested models for structuring your courses

- Editable, chapter-specific PowerPoint® slides offer complete flexibility for creating a multimedia presentation for your course.

- EXCLUSIVE! Access to full-text SAGE journal articles that have been carefully selected to support and expand on the concepts presented in each chapter

- Multimedia content includes original SAGE videos that appeal to students with different learning styles

- Lecture notes summarize key concepts by chapter to help you prepare for lectures and class discussions

- Course cartridge for easy LMS integration

ACKNOWLEDGMENTS

We are grateful to several individuals who have been integral to the development of this textbook. First, we thank the SAGE editorial team who provided us with ongoing feedback and support throughout the writing process. We are particularly grateful to our editor, Theresa Accomazzo, who offered us meaningful feedback and support as this project unfolded. We are also thankful for the ongoing assistance provided by Jessica Miller and Georgia McLaughlin. This textbook would not have been possible without the efforts and commitment of the SAGE team.

We also acknowledge the many reviewers who devoted their time and efforts to shaping this textbook. In particular, we thank:

Dr. Diane P. Bagwell, University of West Florida

Ruth Ban, Barry University

Steven R. Banks, University of Tennessee at Chattanooga

Valerie Beltran, University of La Verne

James A. Bernauer, Robert Morris University

Denise A. Boldman, PhD, Urbana University

Jill Bradley-Levine, University of Indianapolis

Mary (Rina) M. Chittooran, PhD, Saint Louis University

Harriett Gaddy, PhD, Centenary College

Gerard Giordano, University of North Florida

Dr. Marlene Gombach, Cleveland State University

Dr. Darrell L. Groves, Clark Atlanta University

Nataliya V. Ivankova, University of Alabama at Birmingham

Cynthia L. Jew, PhD, California Lutheran University

Rosalind Latiner Raby, California State University, Northridge

Dr. Maura Martindale, LSLS Cert. AVEd., California Lutheran University

Keli Mu, PhD, OTR/L, Creighton University

Benjamin Ngwudike, Jackson State University

Eucabeth Odhiambo, Shippensburg University

Arturo Olivarez, Jr., University of Texas at El Passo

Dr. Edward Schultz, Midwestern State University

John D. Tiller, EdD, Tennessee State University

Wendy G. Troxel, Illinois State University

We also thank our students—many of whom are practitioner-scholars in their own right—for providing feedback and suggestions on early iterations of this textbook. We are particularly grateful to the many students enrolled in Strategies for Educational Inquiry (Y520) and Data-Driven Decision Making (A629) at Indiana University who read portions of the textbook and whose reflections and writing assignments served as a catalyst for the textbook's development. In addition, we acknowledge our former doctoral students in the Statewide Educational Leadership Program at Washington State University whose experience conducting their own research greatly informed our understanding of practitioner-scholarship and honed our skills as methods instructors. Finally, we thank Dr. Colleen Chesnut and Ms. Gina Mosier for their assistance preparing the instructional materials for this textbook.

ABOUT THE AUTHORS

Chad R. Lochmiller is Assistant Professor in Educational Leadership & Policy Studies in the School of Education at Indiana University where he teaches courses on data-driven decision-making, school finance, and research methods for practitioners. Dr. Lochmiller received his Ph.D. in Education with a specific focus on leadership, policy, and organizations from the University of Washington in 2010 and received his Master's of Educational Administration from Gonzaga University in 2005. His research focuses on contemporary education policy issues, specifically those related to school finance and human resources. He is particularly interested in the ways in which finance and personnel issues influence leaders' ability to enact meaningful reforms at the school and district level. He is also interested in issues related to leadership development and preparation. His research has been recently published in journals such as *Educational Administration Quarterly*, *Education Policy Analysis Archives*, *Journal of School Leadership*, *Journal of Research on Leadership Education*, and *Journal of Cases in Educational Leadership*.

Jessica Nina Lester is Assistant Professor in the Inquiry Methodology program in the School of Education at Indiana University where she teaches courses focused on introductory research methods and qualitative research methodologies, with a particular focus on discourse and conversation analysis. Dr. Lester received her Ph.D. in Educational Psychology and Research, along with a graduate certificate in Qualitative Research Methods in Education, from the University of Tennessee in 2011. She received her Master's of Education in 2005 from the University of Mary. Her research activities lie at the intersection of disability studies, discourse studies, and critical/social theory. Dr. Lester recently coedited a book focused on performance ethnographies and coauthored a book focused on the use of digital tools across the qualitative research process. She is currently the coeditor of *The Palgrave Handbook of Child Mental Health: Discourse and Conversation Studies* and *The Palgrave Handbook of Adult Mental Health: Discourse and Conversation Studies*. She most recently published in journals such as *Qualitative Inquiry*, *Discourse Studies*, and *The International Journal of Qualitative Studies*.

PART I

EXAMINING
THE FOUNDATIONS OF
EDUCATIONAL RESEARCH

The first part of the textbook broadly introduces you to the concept of educational research in relation to practitioner-scholars and problems of practice. The primary purpose of Part I is to orient you to the underlying research concepts and practices that you need to know to critically consume and carry out a research study. There is an explicit focus on defining research and considering the practice of research in light of various research paradigms, research methodologies, and research methods. Further, this section introduces the overall research process, including designing a research study, developing a literature review, and identifying some of the salient differences and similarities between qualitative, quantitative, mixed methods, and action research approaches to research. Foundational to these considerations is a focused discussion around research ethics, which is at the core of any research endeavor.

1

STUDYING EDUCATION PRACTICE WITH RESEARCH

CONSIDERING THE VALUE OF RESEARCH

As you sit in your first (or perhaps last) research class, you may wonder how research relates to your work as a classroom teacher, teacher leader, school administrator, or district leader. Research is often filled with terms, concepts, and ideas that may seem foreign or unrelated to your daily work. And yet, as you have undoubtedly heard, research informs your practice. But how? What do you need to know about research to use it in your practice? What do you need to know in order to undertake your own research study?

INTRODUCTION

As illustrated in the opening vignette, in this chapter we invite you to begin learning some of the key concepts related to education research. To some, this invitation may seen daunting, as the technical nature of research and the skills required to carry out a research study may feel beyond their grasp. We argue that practitioner-scholars need *not* maintain this fear. Rather, as we will demonstrate, the research process can be experienced as both straightforward and rewarding.

This chapter aims to provide you with a broad foundation for understanding educational research and also how researchers think about the research process. It may be a chapter you want to return to again and again as you progress in your work as a practitioner-scholar. We begin this chapter by discussing the key assumptions of this textbook and the idea of practitioner-scholars and research more generally. Next, we briefly introduce four problems of practice that are used throughout the textbook. Then, we discuss the various purposes of educational research specifically related to practitioner-scholars, as

By the end of the chapter, you will be able to:

- Define the meaning of *practitioner-scholar*.

- State a working definition of educational research.

- Describe the problems of practice discussed throughout the textbook and their relationship to research.

- Summarize the purposes of educational research.

- Discuss the differences between the dominant research paradigms.

- Describe the meaning and role of ontology and epistemology in the research process.

- Identify and state the differences between research methodology and research method.

- Paraphrase basic definitions of qualitative, quantitative, mixed methods, and action research.

well as the various research paradigms and the meaning of key social science terms such as *research methodologies* and *methods*. Finally, we briefly highlight some of the distinctions between qualitative and quantitative research traditions.

PRACTITIONER-SCHOLARS DEFINED

Despite how research may appear or be presented, we start this textbook with several assumptions about you and the research process. First, we assume that research is connected to your professional practice. Second, we assume that the professional challenges and issues you face can be understood and, in part, addressed through research. Third, we assume that you are likely a consumer of research, meaning that you read, digest, and enact ideas taken directly from research of various kinds. Thus, being familiar with the language and central practices of research are likely important to you. Finally, we assume that through your investment in research training, you will acquire skills that compliment your capacity as a practitioner and thus we position you as a practitioner-scholar. We define a practitioner-scholar as an individual who aspires to study problems of practice in a more comprehensive and systematic way, allowing them to better understand the schools, districts, and other educational organizations within which they work. Practitioner-scholarship is *both* about your practice as an educator and your practice as a researcher.

In preparing this textbook, we reviewed numerous research textbooks that positioned the world of research as being different from the world of practice. Some research textbooks assumed that you, as a practitioner-scholar, aspire only to consume existing research and thus that the primary aim of a research methods textbook is to familiarize you with research terminology, rather than show you how the work that you already do can be understood through research practices. Alternatively, other textbooks assumed that you aspire to be researchers and therefore minimized the connections between research and practice. While we agree that research methods are distinct and require specialized training, we do not believe that research is irrelevant to or disconnected from practice and practitioners. We see practitioner-scholarship and you, as a practitioner-scholar, as simultaneously seeking to understand practice and becoming familiar with and skilled at using research methods. Thus, our task is to show you: (a) how research practices are connected to problems of practice, which we define next, and (b) how your professional work can be better understood through research practice.

USING PROBLEMS OF PRACTICE TO FRAME RESEARCH

In this textbook, we aim to connect some of the contemporary problems of educational practice to research methods. Problems of practice are common, everyday challenges that confront school leaders, teachers, and educators of all stripes in their classrooms, schools, districts, and educational organizations. For you as a practitioner, these are challenges that likely inspire, frustrate, embolden, or drive you to support student learning. You may have already heard the term *problem of practice*, whether working with your colleagues in a professional learning community (PLC), developing a school improvement plan, or discussing how your own challenges as a classroom teacher complicate your work with students. These are problems that shape your work in any number of ways and perhaps lead you to pose questions about how you and others might respond to the challenge. These problems may include things like the achievement gap or educational policies that directly impact your daily practice in the classroom.

As a practitioner-scholar, many of the problems of practice that you encounter are topics that the research community seeks to understand and elaborate on through a systematic investigation, which is often referred to as research. We define research as a systematic investigation designed to make sense of complex, everyday problems that impact your work as a professional educator. In other words, educational research is an intentional practice that typically follows a step-wise process and is designed to identify and understand current problems of practice.

We acknowledge that research, and science for that matter, can be defined in multiple ways. In fact, throughout history there have been varied ways of making sense of the concept of "doing research" or conducting a scientific study (see, for example, Woolgar, 1988 for a discussion of how the idea of science came to be). For instance, when you hear the word *research* you may immediately think of a scientific laboratory where scientists follow the scientific method. In contrast, you may picture an anthropologist studying the cultural practices of a given community, using an ethnographic approach to make sense of the context of interest. Perhaps you picture a group of educators coming together to identify patterns and trends in student achievement data in order to develop interventions to address specific student needs.

Throughout this textbook, we emphasize the importance of thinking about your own assumptions regarding how we come to understand the world; in this case, those problems of practice that are of importance to you. We believe that reflecting upon your assumptions about the world is where the research process must begin. Further, when we think about the different research traditions or approaches to research, such as qualitative, quantitative, mixed methods, or action research, it is important to keep in mind that a given approach to research brings with it a set of assumptions about how the world is ordered and can come to be understood. Perhaps you have read or heard people say that the main difference between quantitative and qualitative research is that one approach uses numbers and the other does not. We beg to differ! The main differences lie not solely in the type of data or procedures used to analyze the data, but in the assumptions the researcher makes about the data and the world more generally. In other words, one's research methods—those procedures that are used to carry out a study—do not alone make a study qualitative, quantitative, or mixed methods. Rather, it is the foundational assumptions of a particular research approach that truly shape it (Willis, 2007).

For now, a few basic distinctions between the three, main research traditions are needed. First, qualitative researchers are typically interested in studying things in their natural environments with a focus on exploring and understanding how people make sense of and experience the world in which they live (Denzin & Lincoln, 2005). Second, quantitative researchers use numeric data to represent individuals, experiences, and outcomes. They study numeric data to identify, understand, and assess the strength of relationships between data points and to make inferences about relationships between data points. Third, mixed methods researchers use both qualitative and quantitative research methods to make sense of a research question and/or problem.

REFLECTIVE OPPORTUNITY 1.1

Take a moment to reflect on your own assumptions. Consider the following questions:

1. When you think about the word *research*, what images come to mind?

2. How do you define research?

3. What is your past experience with research as a consumer of research?

4. What is your past experience with conducting research?

In this textbook, we also give special attention to action research, which seeks to use the systematic process of research to improve practices and/or processes. Action researchers often use qualitative and/or quantitative research strategies, while including an intentional focus on a current problem of practice. For this reason, we view action research as being particularly useful for practitioner-scholars.

Throughout the textbook, we return to the distinctions across the research traditions. At this stage, however, we move to discuss four contemporary problems of practice, all positioned in relationship to particular research traditions.

AN OVERVIEW OF THE PROBLEMS OF PRACTICE

In each of the following sections, we briefly summarize topics that have been studied by researchers and that, we believe, are familiar to you as a practitioner-scholar. We position these research topics as problems of practice, as they are likely closely related to the everyday challenges that you face in your schools. Throughout the textbook, we will refer to these problems of practice to illustrate how you might use them to develop a research study. Here, we provide a brief overview of the topic, describe the commonly used theoretical perspectives, and note how we will treat the topic throughout the textbook. We frame each of these topics in a specific way, but acknowledge upfront that many of the topics we present have been framed in different ways by different researchers. For example, even though we present the challenge related to the achievement gap as one primarily understood through the use of quantitative research, there are numerous studies and numerous researchers who use qualitative approaches to examine the same phenomenon. Similarly, we frame the study of educational organizations as one that might be understood qualitatively, but acknowledge that many researchers use quantitative approaches to investigate the challenges related to educational organizations.

The narrowness of our framing is not to discourage you from considering multiple research methodologies to investigate the same unit of study or phenomenon of interest. Nor should our framing imply that there is one correct way to design research studies around particular topics. Rather, our intent is to provide you with clarity and consistency from which to acquire an understanding of how the research methodologies and methods we describe relate to the problems of practice. Further, in this section, we describe these approaches to research using terminology with which you may not be familiar. These terms will be discussed in more detail. At this stage, your primary task is to familiarize yourself with how we are thinking about these problems of practice and how we will present them to you. As the textbook unfolds, you will have opportunities to become more familiar with these problems of practice and approaches to research.

Problem of Practice 1: Promoting Educational Equity in Student Achievement

For decades, researchers have focused on the persistent differences in student achievement between white and minority students (Lee, 2002), male and female students (Dee, 2007), and English-speaking and non-native English-speaking students (Rumberger & Willms, 1992). Much of the research focused on these differences has discussed an achievement gap. Researchers have attempted to identify the underlying causes of differing achievement levels (Howard, 2010), including the impact of school and non-school factors on student achievement (Desimone & Long, 2010).

Theoretically, researchers have used numerous perspectives to explain why differences in student achievement exist. For example, researchers have used economic perspectives to explain how a child's socioeconomic status influences their achievement (Orr, 2003). Some researchers have used theories of motivation and engagement to explain why students may disconnect from the learning environment and thus achieve at lower levels (Brophy, 1987). Researchers have also used critical theories to explain unspoken biases in instructional practices that reflect how educators view students or assess their potential for success (Anyon, 2005).

Many researchers have used numerical data to identify and explain differences in student achievement based on gender, race or ethnicity, and socioeconomic status. Researchers have also sought to identify the influence of school conditions (which have principally been described as factors that influence student learning) including the qualifications and practices of classroom teachers, class size, curriculum, instructional strategies, and the allocation of time. Most researchers have assumed that one or many of these factors influence how students perform. The research literature suggests that many of these challenges are best understood through the use of numerical data, such as student test scores. Thus, throughout the textbook, we use this particular problem of practice to introduce you to quantitative research methodologies and methods. We see this topic as an important one for practitioner-scholars, particularly given the increasing pressure to use data to inform decision-making as well as the significant role of achievement in schools and educational practice.

Problem of Practice 2: Implementing Education Policies

Issues related to educational equity are typically related to specific educational policies. Thus, researchers have often invested considerable energies into identifying and exploring problems and challenges in existing education policies. In particular, researchers have examined challenges and opportunities that arise from the development, design, implementation, and evaluation of these policies. From recent policies such as the Obama administration's Race to the Top Initiative to more established policies such as No Child Left Behind, researchers have invested considerable time in developing an understanding of the impact that such policies have on students, teachers, schools, and districts.

These impacts are often studied both quantitatively and qualitatively. Quantitatively, researchers often use student achievement data and survey responses from large samples of teachers, administrators, and stakeholders. Qualitatively, researchers have tended to rely on qualitative data to understand isolated impacts of education policy, such as the impact policies have on individual classroom teachers. They have also focused these qualitative research efforts on understanding the conditions, perspectives, beliefs, values, and thinking of those charged with implementing these policies. For example, a recent qualitative research study included interviews with key stakeholders in state education systems to make sense of the implementation challenges of the Common Core State Standards (McDonnell & Weatherford, 2013). Relatedly, states are increasingly invested in the implementation of new evaluation criteria for classroom teachers and school principals aimed at improving classroom instruction and the quality of instructional leadership. For instance, researchers have used observational data collected from K–12 classrooms to examine the impact of feedback from principals who use performance evaluation models on teachers' instructional practices (Milanowski & Kimball, 2004; Sartain, Stoelinga, & Brown, 2011).

Multiple theoretical perspectives have also been used to ground the interpretation of policy related challenges. Indeed, our review of the literature suggests that researchers have used perspectives broadly related to the policy process (Sabatier, 2007), the arenas and venues where policy decisions are made (Mazzoni, 1991), and the formal legislative or policy-making processes (Wirt & Kirst, 1997). At a local or micro level, researchers have discussed how policy actors make sense of the directives contained in policies and thereby use these directives to shape their work (Honig, 2006; Weatherly & Lipsky, 1977). Thus, many studies examining education policy have drawn on theories of sociocultural learning (Vygotsky, 1978) as well as policy learning (May, 1992).

Given the breadth of policy research, we present policy-related problems of practice as those that often use a mixed methods research approach. Thus, we use this problem of practice to introduce you to the concept of mixed methods research. We highlight how both qualitative and quantitative research approaches can work together to inform studies of educational policy. While as a practitioner-scholar you may not see a direct connection between the development of policies and your daily work, the implementation of various policies likely defines your work in significant ways. Thus, we believe that practitioner-scholars should understand how to conduct research related to policy, as it is yet another way for you to understand your work.

Problem of Practice 3: Reforming and Improving Educational Organizations

Given recent policy changes surrounding educational organizations (for example, Common Core Standards, Next Generation Science Standards, Race To The Top, and so on), another set of challenges confronting practitioner-scholars relates to the task of reforming and improving educational organizations (such as schools, districts, education service agencies, and so on). The literature is filled with examples of school reform dating back to the late 1970s (Edmonds, 1979), district reform dating to the mid-1990s (McLaughlin & Talbert, 2003), and, more recently, central office transformation (Honig, 2012). Within large school district bureaucracies, attention has also been focused at the micro level, where researchers have sought to define and understand specific activities that take place within school districts, such as improving personnel functions (Odden, 2012), enhancing the allocation of resources to support students and teachers equitably (Knapp, Copland, Honig, Plecki, & Portin, 2014), or configuring new programs or services to support teaching and learning (Honig, 2012). Recently, researchers have studied the structures and functions of state education agencies, which parallels previous research focused at the school and district level (Jochim & Murphy, 2013). Given the focus on the conditions, beliefs, behaviors, and actions that individuals take within a broader organizational structure, we use this problem of practice to introduce you to qualitative research methodologies.

There are numerous theoretical perspectives that might be used to understand this problem of practice. Some researchers have used organizational theories to describe the structures, behaviors, and interactions that occur within school districts and schools (Knapp, 2008). For instance, Honig (2003) used sociocultural learning theory (Vygotsky, 1978) to explain how central office administrators supported improvements in teaching and learning. In contrast, other scholars have relied on theories of organizational learning to explain how organizations acquire information, make sense of that information, and then enact it in organizational practice (Senge, Cambron-McCabe, Lucas, & Smith, 2012). Other theoretical perspectives have been used to describe how individuals within organizations behave, and what their role is relative to the organization's mission and functions. Regardless of the school or school district in which you work, the opportunity to study these organizations and the people within them is a valuable one. It provides you with the opportunity to acquire a deeper understanding about the context that shapes your work.

Problem of Practice 4: Improving Instructional and Leadership Practice

Given changes to educational policies and required improvements in educational organizations, researchers have increasingly focused on applying research to practice or adopting research models that allow for connections between research and practice to be made. Research focused on the improvement of practice has been particularly popular in programs preparing classroom teachers (Price, 2001), in studies focused on the preparation of school and district leaders (Osterman, Furman, & Sernak, 2014), and in studies that look specifically at improving practices that lead to school improvement (Calhoun, 2002). These studies often describe how educators of various stripes collect information from their practice, analyze it, and enact improvements that support student learning. Nolen and Vander Putten (2007) described these studies as "practical yet systematic" (p. 401) in that they focus on familiar practices or behaviors, use readily available data, and tend to emphasize immediate implementation. There is a growing body of literature that frames this approach to research as a form of action research (Nolen & Vander Putten, 2007; Stringer, 2007). Given the practical orientation of many of these studies, we use this topic or problem of practice to introduce you to action research.

Here, unlike other problems of practice, the aim is not simply to make sense of the organization, practices, or processes, but to thoughtfully collect information about them and then enact changes to them. Instead of a theoretical perspective guiding the study, action research frequently rests on a process or model (c.f., Stringer, 2007), which we will discuss further in Chapter 11. This final problem of practice and related research approach is perhaps among the most valuable for you as a practitioner-scholar, as it enables you to make immediate changes to your practice, your school, or your school district.

THE PURPOSES AND TYPES OF EDUCATIONAL RESEARCH

Educational research has many purposes and it is beyond the scope of this textbook to identify *all* of these purposes. Nonetheless, in this textbook we suggest that the purpose of educational research is to use a systematic approach to investigate everyday problems that impact students, educators, schools, and districts. This assumes that educational research is inherently practice-focused and that the results/findings of research studies should directly inform the work that happens in schools and school districts.

Researchers often distinguish between two types of, or orientations, to research: basic research and applied research. Basic research is research that aims to generate new knowledge and understanding about a research topic of interest. For example, a qualitative study that focuses on developing a theoretical understanding of the activities that take place in a school district would be considered basic research, as such a study aims to generate new knowledge and may or may not directly inform the daily work of practitioners. Applied research is research that aims to understand a problem of practice and uses this understanding to address the problem. For instance, this type of research might include conducting an action research study of instructional practice in an individual classroom or a grade-level instructional team. The findings of this action research study would have direct application to the daily work of the classroom teacher or grade-level instructional team.

We further delineate these types of research to include descriptive, predictive, and explanatory research. Practitioner-scholars engage in descriptive research for the purpose of describing educational practices, processes, or outcomes. Descriptive research provides important information about "what is" and thus provides opportunities to understand and critique existing practices in the education system. This research, however, does not allow practitioner-scholars to anticipate changes in outcomes. Predictive research is designed to help practitioner-scholars anticipate changes in outcomes, such as student achievement, teacher behavior, or parent relationships. Predictive research anticipates what "could be" given particular changes or alternatives. Some researchers consider predictive research to be more powerful than descriptive research in that it allows researchers to make assumptions and claims about anticipated changes in outcomes. Finally, explanatory research enables researchers to generate theoretical understandings of current practices, programs, processes, and policies. These understandings can be used to explain what is or what could be. And, more important, these explanatory studies seek to provide an answer to "why" practices, policies, programs, and processes interact or act as they do.

A more recent addition to the purposes of educational research involves using research to improve practice, programs, processes, or policies. Indeed, to some extent, we see this purpose underlying

⚓ LINK TO PRACTICE 1.1

CONSIDERING YOUR ORIENTATION FOR YOUR RESEARCH

Let's assume that you are a central office administrator who is interested in studying how the central office supports the implementation of new teacher evaluation criteria. You have seen principals you supervise struggle with the new criteria and realize that this topic is one that interests you and that would make for an interesting thesis or dissertation study. Thinking about the topic, you realize that you are not as interested in the evaluation criteria, per se, as you are interested in the ways that the district supports principals in implementing the criteria. Thus, you are primarily interested in studying this topic from an organizational perspective and now must decide whether you will orient to your research from a descriptive, predictive, or explanatory stance, as well as whether your research will be basic research or applied research.

You first think critically about your interests in completing the research. Do you, for example, want to simply describe the practices or in some way explain the practices using existing organizational theories? After reflecting on this, you decide that the primary goal for your study is to describe the practice and explain it using existing theories, mostly drawn from organizational theory. Thus, you

decide that your research will be both descriptive and explanatory in nature.

Next, you must decide who the research will appeal to. On the one hand, you are interested in writing your research for your colleagues (that is, teachers, principals, and others with whom you work). This interest compels you to write for a practitioner audience and thus aligns your study with applied research. However, for this study, you recognize that the audience with whom you are most interested in communicating are researchers and scholars. You believe that there is an important gap that your study can address. Thus, you ultimately decide to position your study as a basic research study, as it will essentially contribute to the field's understanding of existing theories and perspectives.

Focus Questions

1. How might you decide whether your research study should appeal to a practitioner-scholar audience, a research audience, or both?

2. How might you determine whether your research study should be basic or applied?

each of the three purposes discussed previously. More specifically, however, improvement-oriented research seeks to address practice, as it uses knowledge derived through research. It is concerned with identifying what could be if particular actions or reforms were adopted. Improvement-oriented research may be the most appealing to you as a practitioner-scholar given your work in schools; yet it is important to note that this type of research can be coupled with descriptive, predictive, or explanatory research.

Given the purposes of research, we also think it is important to identify why we conduct research. One of the reasons we conduct educational research is to build knowledge and understanding about practice and the social world more generally. A component of this certainly involves describing practice, but it also involves evaluating practice with the intent to improve it. More broadly, practitioner-scholars also conduct research to contribute to the

As you consider the purposes of educational research as related to practitioner-scholarship, consider the following questions:

1. From the perspective of a practitioner-scholar, what are the primary purposes of research?

2. In what ways do you see educational research informing and/or being disconnected with your work as a practitioner?

3. What can you do to make better connections between educational research and your work as a practitioner?

scholarly conversation about what constitutes good or effective practice, what influences practice, and what aspects of practice can be generalized across types of students, schools, districts, and states.

RESEARCH PARADIGMS

Generally, when people talk about a paradigm they are referring to a way of thinking, with the popular idea of a paradigm shift typically pointing to a change in how someone thinks or makes sense of something. When discussing a research paradigm, it is helpful to think about a paradigm similarly. A research paradigm can be thought of as a way of thinking about and making sense of the world. This way of thinking is centered around a shared set of assumptions about how the world works and how we, as practitioner-scholars, can go about studying the world. A paradigm is somewhat similar to a worldview or a filter that shapes how you interpret life (Saldaña, 2014), and is ultimately associated with your beliefs about how knowledge is gained (that is, the research approach that you use when studying a problem of practice). Kuhn (1970) suggested that paradigms are competing ways of thinking about the world. For instance, what counts as knowledge? Is there only one reality or are there multiple realities? These questions matter to practitioner-scholars, as how we answer them reveals how we assume that the world should be studied and interpreted.

Qualitative and quantitative approaches to research involve very different assumptions about the world, as well as about how research should be conducted and the conclusions that can be drawn from this research. In other words, various research traditions take up different research paradigms. Specifically, these research paradigms include assumptions about what we believe the universe is composed of and how we can come to know the universe (Grix, 2002; Hatch, 2002). Two key concepts related to the idea of research paradigms are ontology and epistemology. Both ontology and epistemology are philosophical concepts of study related to the study of being (ontology) and knowing (epistemology); however, for the purposes of our discussion, we focus on more narrowly defining these concepts as they relate to consuming and carrying out research.

Ontology refers to the nature of reality and some scholars suggest that this is the starting point for all research (Grix, 2002). Essentially, ontology refers to claims and assumptions that are made about the nature of social reality, claims about what exists, what it looks like, what units make it up and how these units interact with each other. In short, ontological assumptions are concerned with what we believe constitutes social reality. (Blaikie, 2000, p. 8)

Your ontological position or assumptions can be better understood by answering the question: "what is the nature of social and political reality" (Hay, 2002, p. 63)? Some people might suggest that reality is driven by universal, natural laws and distinct from social actors, while others would counter that an absolute reality is unknowable as it is made up of individual perspectives and always being reconstituted. These two perspectives are an example of two different ontological assumptions, which are associated with particular research paradigms.

Epistemology refers to the idea of knowledge construction and centers around what we know and how we go about knowing. More specifically, epistemology is a branch of philosophy that is particularly interested in making sense of the methods and practices used to gain knowledge about social reality. Your epistemological position or assumptions can be better understood by answering the question: "What can be known, and what is the relationship of the knower to the known" (Hatch, 2002, p. 14)? Some people would argue that knowledge is a human construction and therefore a practitioner-scholar goes about co-constructing their understanding of the world with their research participants. Other people would suggest that the world has order and this order can be discovered; therefore, the task of the practitioner-scholar is the "capture" the "immutable truth" of the world that they study (Hatch, 2002, p. 14).

Unpacking Five Research Paradigms

There are a number of research paradigms. While limited in scope, we center this brief discussion around five research paradigms, drawing upon Hatch's (2002) organization. The paradigms we discuss are: positivist, postpositivist, constructivist, critical/feminist, and poststructuralist. Table 1.1 provides a description of the ontological and epistemological assumptions associated with these research paradigms, with the next five paragraphs offering brief descriptions of each of the paradigms in turn.

Within a positivist paradigm, a practitioner-scholar assumes that his or her research can identify a single truth about the phenomenon that they are studying. For example, if you are studying differences in student achievement as measured by student learning assessments, a positivistic paradigm assumes that differences in achievement can be known and explained objectively. In other words, truth is objectively known. This assumption allows you to generalize your findings to a much broader population. This is often the paradigm that is adopted in quantitative research.

On the other hand, a post-positivist paradigm assumes that a reality exists (similar to a positivist perspective), but acknowledges that the reality must be interpreted and thus can only be approximated because of our own limitations as researchers. The aim of a post-positivist paradigm is to develop through the research the best possible approximation of the reality that they are observing. For example, if you were to conduct a qualitative study of a classroom in your school, you would likely develop a description of the classroom, the activities adopted by the teacher, and

Table 1.1 Research Paradigms

Research Paradigm	Ontology (What is the nature of reality?)	Epistemology (What can be known?)
Positivist	Reality is out there to be captured	How the world is really ordered can be known
Postpositivist	Reality exists but can only be approximated	Approximation of how the world is really ordered can be known
Constructivist	Multiple realities exist and are constructed	Knowledge is a human construction
Critical/Feminist	There is a reality, which has been shaped by economic, social, cultural, and political forces	Knowledge is subjective and political
Poststructuralist	There are multiple realities that individuals construct to give meaning to the universe	There is no truth with a capital T to be known

Source: Adapted from Hatch, 2002, p. 13.

the reactions of the students through your observations of the environment. Your observations and the interpretation that you apply to them thus approximates what you presume you are actually seeing.

A constructivist paradigm assumes that there are multiple realities that can be studied and that the researcher derives his or her understanding of these realities by working with and through the participants' perspectives of a given phenomenon or problem of practice. In other words, if you conducted a qualitative study in your school related to the community's current needs, you would derive your understanding by asking the teachers, staff, parents, and other community members about their needs. The assumption that you would make is that the needs of your school are unique and thus your aim is to use research to construct an in-depth, contextually detailed understanding of the needs of your school. This understanding, though, might not apply to another school and thus would likely not be generalizable.

A critical/feminist paradigm raises questions about the power bases and inherent inequities that exist across race, gender, social class, sexual orientation, ethnicity, and language. The critical/feminist seeks to question these power bases and inherent inequities. The perspective that a researcher takes is thus not objective but intentionally grounded in their understanding of the world, their lived experience, and their identity as a researcher. As an example, if you conducted a qualitative study in a school to examine the experiences of LGBTQ-identified high school students, a critical perspective might serve as a lens to challenge what had previously been characterized as traditional or customary practices. As Hatch (2002) suggested, the purpose of critical/feminist perspectives is to "reveal for others the kinds and extent of oppression that are being experienced by those studied" (p. 17). Thus, one of purposes of research grounded in this paradigm is to summon the reader to act in response to the inequities.

As a practitioner-scholar it is important to spend time thinking through your own assumptions about the world, as this shapes how you conduct your own research and interpret research results/findings. Take a few moments to consider the following questions:

1. Which research paradigm(s) is most aligned or consistent with your beliefs?

2. Considering the research paradigm you most align with, what are your ontological and epistemological beliefs?

3. How might your ontological and epistemological beliefs relate to the way you go about conducting and evaluating research?

A poststructuralist paradigm includes multiple perspectives and is therefore a bit difficult to unpack within the confines of a paragraph. Nonetheless, individuals who align with this paradigm generally assume that there is no single truth to be known. In other words, they claim that truth with a capital T does not exist. So, poststructuralists often begin their qualitative research by critiquing the notion of a universal truth (that is, statements or views that have historically been unchallenged and assumed to be fact). Their analyses often reveal how larger social narratives support these truths and how power structures benefit from particular social narratives. For instance, a researcher might study how students with disabilities have been historically described in the language adopted in special education policies. The aim of their qualitative study might be to highlight the ways in which the language of special education policies have historically defined the identities of students with disabilities as incapable of academic achievement or independent living. Quite often, one of the purposes of research grounded within this paradigm is to offer a counter-narrative that challenges what we have traditionally assumed to be true.

As you likely noted, particular paradigms are typically aligned with particular research traditions (qualitative or quantitative). As such, when you are conducting or consuming research, it is important to consider whether there is alignment between one's paradigm (including one's ontological and epistemological assumptions) and one's research methodology and methods. These concepts are all tightly linked.

DEFINING RESEARCH METHODOLOGIES AND RESEARCH METHODS

Research methodology and research method are two different, but interrelated concepts (Maxwell, 2013). Your research methodology (for example, ethnography, survey, grounded theory, and so on) is the stance or perspective that you adopt in order to understand a particular problem of practice. In other words, your methodology is how you frame your study, which brings with it particular ontological and epistemological assumptions. Your methodology will typically be defined as either qualitative or quantitative.

Historically, there have been two broad methodological approaches to the study of human life and social experience: qualitative methodologies and quantitative methodologies. Figure 1.1 illustrates

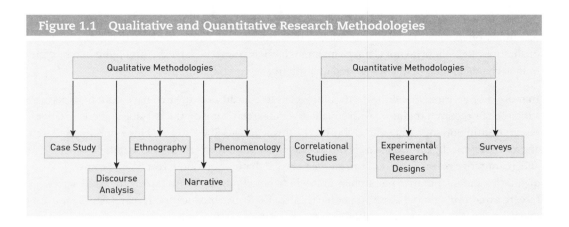

Figure 1.1 Qualitative and Quantitative Research Methodologies

how both qualitative and quantitative methodologies can be thought of as umbrella terms that capture a variety of unique, empirical approaches to the study of problems of practice.

Qualitative methodologies represent a variety of interpretative, inductive approaches to the study of human experience. These methodologies are inherently exploratory, with the qualitative researcher being positioned as the primary research instrument. As such, even though two researchers may use the same qualitative methodology to study the same research phenomena, the iterative and emergent nature of qualitative research will likely lead the two researchers to different (but likely related) conclusions. Some qualitative methodologies include: case study, discourse analysis, ethnography, narrative, phenomenology, and many more. So, the term qualitative methodologies is an umbrella term that brings together methodologies that share *some* assumptions about how to make sense of the world and the types of data that help a researcher interpret the world. In Chapter 5, we discuss some of these qualitative methodologies in greater detail.

Quantitative methodologies represent a variety of deductive approaches to the study of human experience typically represented by numerical data. Much like qualitative methodologies, quantitative methodologies encompass a variety of approaches, many of which share similar ontological and epistemological assumptions about making sense of the world. These methodologies are typically presumed to follow a positivist paradigm, meaning that the purpose of the research is intended to uncover the truth rather than construct truth, as in qualitative research, through the interpretation of data. Some of these quantitative methodologies include: correlational studies, experimental research designs, surveys, and many more. In Chapter 6, we discuss some of these quantitative methodologies in greater detail.

While both qualitative and quantitative researchers attempt to make warranted claims about the social world (Johnson & Onwuegbuzie, 2004), there are important distinctions between these two research traditions. These distinctions relate to paradigmatic differences, as quantitative methodologies typically take up a more positivistic paradigm whereas qualitative methodologies take up paradigms that range from postpositivism to poststructuralism. In addition, the very language that a qualitative researcher uses to write up their research study is unique from a quantitative researcher, with the researcher's language often marking their article or book as being either qualitative or quantitative in scope. For instance, many qualitative researchers write in the first person, as they are making explicit that they are the primary research instrument and the (subjective) interpreter of the phenomenon they study. On the other hand, a quantitative researcher often writes in a way that conveys their objective stance, something that many qualitative researchers do not claim to maintain in their research. Table 1.2 highlights some of the unique characteristics of qualitative and quantitative research traditions.

In more recent years, mixed methods approaches to educational research have been heralded as a third-chair research tradition, with "qualitative research sitting on the left side and quantitative research sitting on the right side" (Johnson & Onwuegbuzie, 2004, p. 15). This emerging research approach is typically positioned as pragmatic, as a mixed-methods researcher combines qualitative and quantitative research methods to answer a research question of interest. While some qualitative and quantitative researchers argue for a purist position, with mixing methods across research traditions viewed as incompatible (Howe, 1988), other education researchers suggest that mixed methods approaches allow you to pragmatically understand contemporary problems of practice and further unbind researchers from purist positions, which may have in the past prevented researchers from having a comprehensive understanding of everyday challenges. The advantage to mixed methods research is that these mixed methods allow researchers to generate a comprehensive understanding rather than an understanding that is potentially limited by methodological traditions (Johnson & Onwuegbuzie, 2004). We view mixed methods research as less of a methodology and more of a set of methods, which we discuss further in Chapter 10.

In contrast to research methodologies, research methods are those specific tools and procedures used to complete the research study. For instance, quantitative methods may include carrying out statistical tests on large quantities of numeric achievement data or developing an instrument to survey a large population of students about their experiences in school. Alternatively, qualitative methods may include conducting interviews with a small population of students about their experiences in school or entail making observations of classroom teachers in professional development settings. Quite often, there are particular methods associated with particular

Table 1.2 Distinctive Characteristics of Qualitative and Quantitative Research Traditions

	Research Tradition	
	Qualitative	Quantitative
Purpose	Explore, understand, and discover human behavior	Describe, explain, and predict patterns of human behavior
Research Paradigm(s)	Postpositivist, Constructivist, Critical/Feminist, and/or Poststructuralist (among others)	Positivist
Analytic Approach	Inductive	Deductive
Types of Data	Uses contextual details, words, and narratives to generate meaning	Uses numeric data to generate understanding
Research Role	Subjective stance; primary research instrument	Objective stance; formal instruments used

CONSIDERING RESEARCH PARADIGMS AND RESEARCH METHODOLOGIES

After deciding that your research will be a basic research study designed to both describe and explain how district central offices support principals in implementing new teacher evaluation criteria, your next consideration is how a given research paradigm influences your selection of a methodology. For this study, your instinct tells you there is unlikely to be a single explanation for the way(s) that the district has supported principals in implementing new teacher evaluation criteria. Rather, you recognize that there are likely multiple interpretations and thus your interpretation will be only one of many that might be offered. Thus, as you consider the various research paradigms, you quickly realize that you will likely be constructing an interpretation of the support provided and that this ultimately means you will be adopting a constructivist paradigm in your research. As you reflect on this, you realize that you will be relying on what other people in the district (for example, principals and central office staff) tell you about their work and the support provided.

Continuing to reflect, you also realize that your interests are primarily exploratory and you are most interested in the perceptions of the people involved in supporting principals in implementing the new teacher evaluation criteria. While it would be nice to confirm that supports for principals exist and/or that specific types of assistance are provided, you realize that what is more important to you (at least right now) is to explore how principals think about and experience the support they receive, and what support ultimately means to them. Thus, recognizing that you have adopted a constructivist paradigm, you also believe that a qualitative methodology is the best approach for understanding support.

Focus Questions

1. What should inform how you choose to align with a particular research paradigm?

2. How might the research paradigm(s) that you align with inform the methodology that you ultimately use?

---

methodologies. Ideally, the methods that you choose to complete your study should align with your methodology, as this will create consistency in your research design.

A research design is your overall plan to study a problem of practice. It articulates your research methodology, the research methods that you will use, the research questions you will pose, and your approach to the analysis of the data. Other aspects of the research process include practices such as conducting a literature review, carrying out the research study, and reporting your findings.

SUMMARY

We began this chapter by discussing one of the core concepts of this textbook—practitioner-scholarship—which both informed how we developed the book and

informed how we orient to you as a reader. We also used this chapter as an opportunity to introduce four problems of practice that, throughout the textbook, we use to inform and illustrate the research process, as well as highlight the underlying steps involved in carrying out a research study. Finally, we focused on distinguishing between research paradigms, research methodologies, and research methods. Throughout the discussion, we operationalized key concepts, such as ontology and epistemology, using Links to Practice to illustrate some of these big ideas.

KEY TERMS

Action Research 5

Applied Research 9

Basic Research 9

Constructivist Paradigm 13

Critical/Feminist Paradigm 13

Descriptive Research 9

Epistemology 12

Explanatory Research 9

Improvement-Oriented
   Research 10

Mixed Methods 16

Mixed Methods Researchers 4

Ontology 11

Positivist Paradigm 12

Post-Positivist Paradigm 12

Poststructuralist Paradigm 14

Practitioner-Scholar 3

Predictive Research 9

Problems of Practice 3

Qualitative Methodologies 15

Qualitative Researchers 4

Quantitative Methodologies 15

Quantitative Researchers 4

Research 4

Research Design 17

Research Methodology 14

Research Methods 16

Research Paradigm 11

QUESTIONS TO CONSIDER

1. How would you define what it means to be a practitioner-scholar?

2. How do you define research?

3. How might the four problems of practice presented in this chapter relate to your work as a practitioner-scholar?

4. What are the purposes of educational research?

5. What are some of the primary distinctions across the various research paradigms?

6. How do one's ontological and epistemological assumptions shape the research process?

7. What is the relationship between a research methodology and a research method?

8. What are the basic characteristics of qualitative, quantitative, and mixed methods research?

CHAPTER EXERCISES

1. Make a list of the various ways in which you use research in your daily work.

2. As a practitioner-scholar, you likely have multiple topics of interest (for example student motivation) that you want to explore further. List several of the topics that you would be interested in

exploring further and share why you think these topics are of interest to you.

3. Based on your current understanding, develop a T-chart that lists out the distinctions between qualitative and quantitative approaches to research.

4. Find two to three articles in a journal within your field (such as the *Journal of Research in Leadership Education* or the *American Educational Research Journal*). Read the articles you identified and determine: (1) what methodology (that is, qualitative, quantitative, mixed methods, or action research) was used, and (2) what research methods were used (for example, data collection, data analysis, and so forth).

LEARNING EXTENSIONS

To further your understanding of the four problems of practice, we encourage you to review the following articles. First, Desimone and Long's (2010) discussion of the effects that teachers and teaching quality have on persistent inequities in student achievement serves as a useful article to understand how you might present a study examining the achievement gap that relies on a primarily quantitative design. Second, McDonnell and Weatherford's (2013) discussion of the development and subsequent unraveling of the Common Core State Standards offers an intriguing example of a qualitative study focused on the difficulties of implementing educational policies. Third, Honig's (2003) analysis of central office administrators' work in Oakland depicts how you might examine issues related to the improvement of educational organizations by drawing upon existing theoretical perspectives of organizational theory. Finally, Calhoun's (2002) action research study demonstrates how research can be used to directly inform and improve school practices, particularly among classroom teachers, teacher leaders, and school principals.

Sharpen your skills with SAGE edge!

edge.sagepub.com/lochmiller

SAGE edge for Students provides a personalized approach to help you accomplish your coursework goals in an easy-to-use learning environment. You'll find action plans, mobile-friendly eFlashcards, and quizzes as well as videos, web resources, and links to SAGE journal articles to support and expand on the concepts presented in this chapter.

2

DESIGNING A RESEARCH STUDY

DEVELOPING A RESEARCH STUDY

As a classroom teacher, you are keenly aware that improving practice in your classroom is a high priority for you and your school. Being able to reach all of your students in a meaningful way is essential to improving the outcomes that you see them achieve on state and district assessments, as well as in their daily lives. Thus, you are interested in designing a research study that will help you understand how your practice (and that of your colleagues) impacts students in your school. But where should you start this study? What questions should you ask? What research design do you need to develop? These are some of the questions that you must ask as you begin designing your research study.

INTRODUCTION

As illustrated in the introductory vignette, this chapter positions the research process as being fundamentally about making sense of, informing, and/or improving practice. As a practitioner-scholar, we believe that this is an appropriate starting point for most research studies. In Chapter 1, we described problems of practice that can be used as a basis for your research, as well as how various research paradigms shape your thinking about research and inform your approach to research. In this chapter, we begin to operationalize the research process, specifically the process of designing a research study.

As such, this chapter walks you through the development of a research study. Specifically, we provide you with an opportunity to weigh the various options available, consider the strengths and weaknesses of each research design, and learn the process—a process

Learning Objectives

By the end of the chapter, you will be able to:

- Discuss the cyclical research process.

- Summarize how to design a qualitative and quantitative research study.

- Construct a research problem statement for a qualitative and quantitative study.

- Illustrate the process of creating and evaluating research questions.

- Describe the differences between a theoretical and conceptual framework.

- Explain the general considerations for selecting a research methodology.

- Identify common research methods associated with particular research methodologies.

- Paraphrase the procedures for carrying out a qualitative or a quantitative data analysis.

- Describe the various data sources that might be included in a qualitative and quantitative study.

that we describe as cyclical and iterative. We highlight specifically the process for selecting a research design that is theoretically grounded, developing well-constructed research questions, and engaging in rigorous analysis. While in this chapter we focus on qualitative and quantitative research studies, in Chapter 10 we discuss the process of designing a mixed methods study. Further, in Chapter 11 we highlight the process of designing an action research study.

THE OVERARCHING RESEARCH PROCESS

Regardless of the research methodology that you select, there are some overarching steps within the research process to consider. Many researchers describe the research process as a cycle that begins with the formulation of a research question and concludes with the dissemination of your research results/findings. We agree with this description, as it generally conveys how researchers approach their work. However, we think it is important to highlight the nuances of each step in this process, while recognizing that the process itself is messy and less than sequential at times. Broadly, we suggest that the research process involves: identifying a problem of practice that you want to study and problematizing it so that it can be studied; designing a study that allows you to explore the problem in greater detail; analyzing your data (discussed further in Chapters 8 and 9); and writing up and sharing your results/findings (discussed further in Chapters 12 and 13). This cyclical process is illustrated in Figure 2.1.

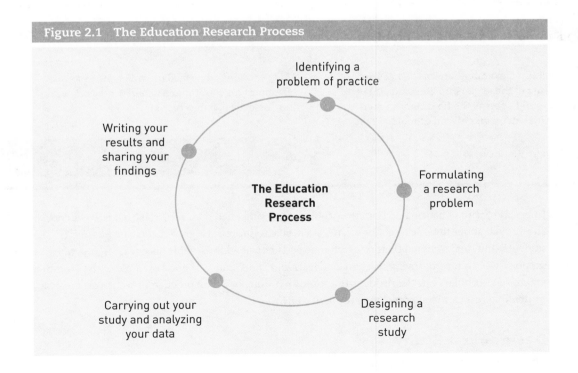

Figure 2.1   The Education Research Process

Identifying a Problem of Practice and Formulating It as a Research Problem

The first step is to identify a problem of practice that you want to study further and to then formulate it as a research problem. We suggest that your daily work serves as fertile ground for the identification of a potential research topic that is suitable for investigation, using qualitative, quantitative, and mixed methods approaches to research. For instance, you may be a classroom teacher who is interested in studying what motivates your students to become independent readers. Similarly, you may be a teacher leader interested in understanding your colleagues' perspectives on collaboration or the reasons why some colleagues may collaborate more frequently or effectively than others. In either case, these are research problems linked to contemporary problems of practice that you are able to examine through systematic exploration.

Many times practitioner-scholars think that all they need to do is identify a research topic (for instance, instructional leadership); yet, a research topic is not specific enough to conduct an entire study. Rather, you must formulate your research topic so that it can be studied empirically, which requires that you formulate the research topic as a research problem. A research problem describes what you are actually studying and is typically formulated in relationship to what we already know about the particular topic, thereby being tightly connected to your familiarity with the literature. Consider From the Field 2.1, for example, where Elfers and Stritikus (2014) describe a problem that compels their research.

FROM THE FIELD 2.1

An Example of a Research Problem

Despite limited examinations of the needs of EL students in the leadership literature, there is much to build upon as the field comes to terms with shifting demographics in schools. . . This study examines how leaders can create systems of support for classroom teachers who work with linguistically diverse students.

Source: Elfers & Stritikus, 2014, p. 307

 Read the full article at: www.sagepub.com/lochmiller

Elfers and Stritikus articulated both the problem that compelled their research (that is, we do not know much about the role or actions that leaders take to support English-Language Learner (ELL) students) and then oriented their research to explain how it addresses this need (that is, describes support systems for improving teaching and learning). This study is a good example of the ways that practitioner-scholars can clearly identify a topic for a study based on practice, as well as articulate a compelling reason to undertake the proposed study.

Designing a Study

After selecting a research topic and developing a research problem, your next task is to design a research study. As noted previously, there are numerous considerations for this process that go well

REFLECTIVE OPPORTUNITY 2.1

1. Return to the problems of practice that you
   identified as central to your work in Chapter 1
   and formulate a research problem.

beyond simply selecting a research methodology or research method. Indeed, it is imperative that you consider the research paradigm that you will adopt and the ontology and epistemology that underpin this paradigm, as discussed in Chapter 1. With these considerations in mind, your next step is to determine whether you will undertake a qualitative or quantitative study. Some will argue that this determination is based solely on your research questions. We suggest that this decision is also based on the research paradigm and its underlying ontological and epistemological assumptions, as well as your own assumptions about the world. It is essential to ensure congruence between these factors so that your study proceeds from a clear conceptual, methodological, and analytical perspective. Identifying how you will undertake the study (methodology) and what you will do to collect your data (method) are more appropriately considered after achieving conceptual, methodological, and analytical clarity.

As you design your study, it is also appropriate to consider who you will include in your study and where your study will take place, as well as what type(s) of data you will collect. Additionally, it is important to determine how you will analyze your data. This, too, should be informed by your research paradigm and research methodology. Once you have established a clear plan for your study, it is then appropriate to begin gathering data and ultimately moving into your analysis. Finally, while research ethics are important to consider across the research process, they are especially important to keep in mind as you design your study. We discuss the role of ethics in research in greater detail in Chapter 4.

Carrying Out Your Study and Analyzing Your Data

After establishing a plan to conduct your research, the rewarding work of data collection begins. What data you collect depends entirely on the nature of your study (whether it is qualitative or quantitative), as well as what questions you are attempting to explore. For now, however, it is important to understand that the data collection process is vital to carrying out a good study and setting yourself up for successful analysis of your data.

After your data collection is complete (and in some cases before), you begin the process of analyzing your data. How you analyze your data depends entirely on the research methodology and type of research you are conducting. For now, what is important to understand is that the data you are analyzing should be congruent with the selected research methodology, and that the analytic process takes place before you begin writing your results/findings. While you may have hunches about what your data tells you, it is important to verify these hunches through the analysis process and avoid jumping to conclusions.

REFLECTIVE OPPORTUNITY 2.2

1. As you think about your own research problem of interest, what are some of the ethical dilemmas that you need to consider as you design your study, particularly as you think about collecting data?

Writing and Sharing Your Results/Findings

The final step in the research process involves writing up your results (more commonly referred to as findings in qualitative research) and sharing them with the broader research community. For many practitioner-scholars this stage is rife with challenges, as they are unaccustomed to writing up research. Indeed, writing research is never easy and we all struggle at times to find meaningful ways to convey our results/findings to individuals who may not be familiar with the purposes of the research study. For instance, as a writer of research, you must become familiar not only with the differences between writing up a qualitative, quantitative, mixed methods, and action research study, but also with how to write for particular audiences. At this stage, what is important to keep in mind is that across the various research methodologies your aim is to write a coherent manuscript for a specific audience that contains a compelling argument. Developing a coherent argument is at the heart of academic writing, which is something we explore more specifically in Chapter 12.

DESIGNING A RESEARCH STUDY

While the research process described above characterizes how practitioner-scholars approach their work in broad strokes, the process of designing a research study and carrying it out requires more specificity. In this section, we offer greater detail about particular steps that practitioner-scholars take when designing a study. These steps include: (1) formulating a research problem, (2) developing research questions, (3) identifying a conceptual or theoretical framework, (4) selecting a research methodology, (5) selecting research methods, and (6) determining an approach to data analysis. Underlying each of these steps is the assumption that you have completed a thorough review of the existing literature. While we do not give attention to this important step in this chapter, we discuss the process of conducting a literature review in detail in Chapter 3. Further, while sharing or disseminating your research results/findings is an important part of the process, we do not give this topic substantial detail here either. Rather we focus on writing in more detail in Chapter 12.

Formulating a Research Problem

It is important to understand that all quality research studies include a clearly defined research topic and a well-formulated research problem statement. A research problem statement is simply a statement that describes what your study will investigate. As such, the problem statement should refer in some way to the problem of practice that you will investigate. A problem statement is similar to a thesis statement in that it states the purpose of the research study, as well as identifies the primary issue that the study will examine. As Kilbourn (2006) asserted, "An educational problem gets translated into a research problem (1) when it is couched in an argument . . . that illustrates its educational significance and (2) when it explicitly refers to existing research" (p. 541). A problem statement is not simply a statement which says, "this study is about"; rather, it formulates the research topic in a way that the reader can understand *why* the research is needed and *what* the research will seek to accomplish. From the Field 2.2 provides an example of a problem statement from a quantitative study of the costs associated with leadership coaching for school administrators.

As the statement in From the Field 2.2 illustrates, the problem that motivated the study was both an absence of research regarding the cost of coaching support, as well as the limitations that an absence of such information has for the development of policy. Thus, as illustrated, a well-developed problem statement includes both a strong rationale for a study and a clear articulation of the study topic.

It is important to note that qualitative and quantitative problem statements are formulated in slightly different ways. In a quantitative study, the emphasis of the problem statement is "on the need to explain, predict, or statistically describe some outcome or event" (Johnson & Christensen, 2010, p. 71). Research problems in quantitative research are often formulated as a hypothesis, which is a theory-based prediction about the phenomenon you are studying. There are two types of hypotheses in quantitative research: experimental and null. An experimental hypothesis describes the anticipated effect of an intervention on a specified outcome. Practitioner-scholars formulate their experimental hypothesis based on existing published research and theory. An experimental hypothesis should directly connect to and build from the literature review. Alternatively, a null hypothesis states that the intervention will not have any effect.

It is helpful to illustrate this concept with a recent example from the literature. In a study of professional development for school administrators, Grissom and Harrington (2010) drew upon published research about principal preparation programs to establish a series of hypotheses regarding effective and ineffective forms of principal professional development. In particular, their study examined the connection between administrator professional development and

FROM THE FIELD 2.2

An Example of a Problem Statement in a Quantitative Study

Given the absence of information regarding the cost of coaching and the implications that these limitations have in terms of policy development, in this paper, I draw upon administrative personnel data from Washington State to estimate the cost to provide one year of leadership support to novice school administrators across a state education system.

Source: Lochmiller, 2014, p. 3

school performance in a national sample of schools. The authors cited existing research on principal professional development to formulate the following hypotheses. First, drawing upon their review of literature related to university principal preparation activities, the authors hypothesized that, "Participation in university courses as an administrator professional development activity will be negatively associated with principal performance" (p. 587). Second, drawing upon recent research related to the importance and impact of mentoring for school principals, they further hypothesized that, "Participation in administrator mentoring or coaching will be positively associated with principal performance" (p. 589). Finally, summarizing research regarding principal networks, they hypothesized that, "Participation in principal networks will be positively associated with principal performance" (p. 589). Taken together, the authors assumed that university coursework will not impact principal performance, but mentoring and professional networks will. The authors thus undertook a quantitative study to examine whether these hypotheses were true.

The formulation of a research problem statement is also essential when determining whether you will undertake a qualitative or quantitative research study. Indeed, how a practitioner-scholar formulates their problem statement often informs whether their research design will be qualitative or quantitative. The formulation of a quantitative problem statement reflects the view that all events can be attributed to a few causes (Salmon, 2007). Moreover, a quantitative research problem tends to adopt what has been called a "narrow-angle lens" (Johnson & Christensen, 2010, p. 35), in that quantitative research studies tend to focus on only a few of the potential factors that explain the outcome or result that is being investigated. Quantitative research studies also seek to control for extraneous factors that may influence or skew the results. Thus, a problem statement for a quantitative study is usually constructed so that it narrows the focus of the study to a specific relationship or interaction. For example, Hill, Rowan, and Ball (2005) studied the effect of teachers' mathematical content knowledge on student achievement. They stated that, " . . . an important purpose of our study was to demonstrate the independent contribution of teachers' mathematical knowledge for teaching to student achievement, net of other possible measures of teacher quality such as teacher certification, educational coursework, and experience" (p. 373). As this problem statement illustrates, the study looked narrowly at the relationship between a teacher's understanding of math content and the impact that such an understanding had on student achievement. Consistent with a quantitative design, their study controlled for teacher characteristics such as certification, coursework, and years of experience.

In contrast, qualitative problem statements tend to situate the research problem within a particular societal, organizational, cultural, relational, intellectual, or theoretical setting. Merriam (1998) suggested that it is "the thing you are curious about" that "forms the core of the research problem, or the problem statement" in qualitative research studies (p. 58). The problem statement is typically linked to your theoretical and/or conceptual framework (discussed below) and the broader literature. As a practitioner-scholar, you must attempt to outline the logic of your study, moving from broader understandings drawn from the literature toward a very narrow focus centered on particular questions. From the Field 2.3 provides an example of how a problem statement was developed across several paragraphs in a qualitative study.

As illustrated in From the Field 2.3, in qualitative research, a problem statement is something that is initially developed broadly in relationship to the literature. We picture the development

An Example of a Problem Statement in a Qualitative Study

This study examines one strategy for improving instruction: the development of instructional teacher leader roles, sometimes referred to as instructional coaches. These school-based, nonsupervisory roles are intended to be an onsite resource for teachers. Although there is no known research that demonstrates a causal link between instructional teacher leader roles and student achievement, the development of these roles is predicated on their potential for facilitating effective professional development. By providing sustained and context-specific professional development to teachers, instructional teacher leaders can improve instruction and thereby increase student achievement (Cohen & Hill, 2001; Garet, Porter, Desimone, Birman, & Yoon, 2001; Loucks-Horsley, Love, Stiles, Mundry, & Hewson, 2003). Based on this potential benefit, instructional teacher leader roles have become a core component of large-scale school improvement initiatives (for example, the federal Reading First program) as well as a growing component of localized efforts to improve instruction (see Mangin, 2005).

Much of the research on the role of the instructional teacher leader focuses on school-level enactment. These studies investigate how various coach and teacher leader configurations influence instruction, the kinds of tasks performed, and the sources of support and constraint (see Camburn, Rowan, &

Taylor, 2003; Datnow & Castellano, 2001; Mangin, 2005, 2006, 2007; Mangin & Stoelinga, 2008). Although these studies provide useful information about how existing roles function, they provide little information about the origin of these positions. What prompts districts to implement instructional teacher leaders? And are some districts more likely than others to implement these roles? To date, no known research has been conducted on the district-level implementation of instructional teacher leaders—that is, the kinds of contexts that influence implementation and how those contexts are influential.

In response to this gap in the literature, I examined the implementation of literacy coach roles—one kind of instructional teacher leader—in 20 school districts that composed one regional intermediate school district (ISD). The ISD provided a literacy coach training program that was intended to facilitate but not mandate the implementation of literacy coach initiatives. Through interviews with district leaders, I examined (A) the extent to which each district implemented formal literacy coach roles and (B) the contextual factors that influenced implementation. Findings from this study indicate that variations in districts' contexts were associated with differences in the implementation of literacy coach roles.

Source: Mangin, 2009, pp. 760–761

---

of a research problem in qualitative research to be similar to a funnel or upside-down pyramid, as illustrated in Figure 2.2, wherein at the top you simply identify the general area of interest or focus for your study. Then, you gradually begin to present a more refined focus as you move toward your specific problem statement.

In the example in From the Field 2.3, the narrowest statement, "we looked for patterns in leaders' emphases on internal expertise such as the practical insights of fellow faculty relative to external expertise such as university-designed staff development" (p. 520), highlighted the researchers' problem statement. However, they did not begin here. Rather, they began with a broad angle view of the literature, highlighting also the gaps in the literature that justified the need for their study.

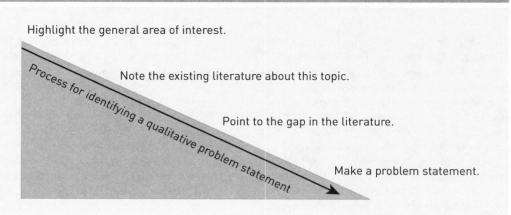

Figure 2.2 The Narrowing Process for Identifying and Developing a Qualitative Research Statement

Highlight the general area of interest.

Process for identifying a qualitative problem statement

Note the existing literature about this topic.

Point to the gap in the literature.

Make a problem statement.

Developing Research Questions

After you have identified your research topic and formulated a research problem statement, then you are likely ready to begin thinking about your research questions. We think about your initial research questions as being similar to hunches that help guide you to the event, topic, and/or question that you will examine. We thus recommend waiting to develop your initial research questions until after you have reviewed the literature and formulated a problem statement. This allows for you to establish greater congruence between your problem statement, theoretical or conceptual framework, and your research questions. Well-designed research studies demonstrate considerable alignment between these facets.

Many of our students ask, "What is a good research question?" This question has many different answers. Indeed, there is no single guide for developing research questions. What we do know, however, is that effectively crafted research questions make or break your research study. Research questions that are biased, for example, unnecessarily skew your study and thus interfere with your interpretation of the data. Vague or poorly defined research questions lead to a lack of clarity both in how you collect your data, as well as what your study seeks to address. Finally, research questions that are too narrow might make it difficult to conduct your study given unexpected results/findings.

Wallen and Fraenkel (2001) suggested that research questions should be clearly stated, ethical, feasible, and significant. Clarity implies that your research questions should be easily understood by an uninformed reader. Terms should be explicitly defined and the relationship between the concepts in your study should be made clear. There are three ways to clarify terms in your research questions. First, you can define terms using a constitutive definition, which is akin to using the dictionary definition of the term. For example, if your study examines teacher collaboration, you could use the dictionary definition of collaboration rather than applying a theoretically or conceptually driven definition to the term. While this approach may help the reader understand the terms, it may impede your ability to fully explain the relationships or interactions between factors being considered in your study. Thus, a second approach to defining terms in your research question(s) is to define by example. For example, if you are interested in teacher collaboration you might include an example in your research question to

FORMULATING A PROBLEM STATEMENT

As a classroom teacher, you enjoy watching your students become confident, independent readers. Your desire to study the factors that influence their motivation to read thus emerges from this perspective. More specifically, you are interested in exploring how students describe the impact that your classroom instruction has on their motivation to read. As you begin reading the literature, however, you begin to see that simply asking students will likely not result in the kind of data that you need. Instead, you find that researchers tend to rely on various proxies to study reading motivation. In the literature, these proxies were defined either by interviewing students about their reading behaviors or by surveying them to determine what factors potentially influence them. Thus, you find yourself struggling with how to formulate your problem statement.

Your primary interest is in the impact that your instruction has on students' interest in reading; thus, you initially assume that your problem statement could state just that. For example, you could control for differences in student characteristics that likely explain why your instruction impacts students' motivation differently. This would require formulating a series of hypotheses about the impact that various factors have on the students' motivation. Yet, this approach feels limiting in that you are not sure that your instruction actually does impact student achievement. Thus, you feel more inclined to examine how students' experiences of your instruction impact their self-efficacy. Given this interest, you see your study as being uniquely situated in the students' experience in your classroom and thus see that your instruction may not directly impact the students.

Focus Questions

1. What might a problem statement be for the study described above?

2. What role does the literature review play in the development of a problem statement?

highlight or signal the specific type of collaboration that you are interested in studying. For instance, you might ask, "How do classroom teachers perceive that informal collaboration (for example, working together without compensation or dedicated time) impacts their instructional practice?" As illustrated, the definition of informal collaboration is clarified using the example provided in the question. Finally, a third approach to ensuring that your research question is clear relies on an operational definition, which effectively highlights in specific terms the various components of the phenomenon that you are studying. For example, as Wallen and Fraenkel (2001) suggested, you might be interested in studying open classrooms. The concept of an open classroom is likely not clear to an uninformed reader. Thus, an operational definition provides clarity. Wallen and Fraenkel (2001) offered the following as an example of an operational definition of an open classroom:

1. Any classroom judged (by an observer spending at least 1 day per week in the classroom for 4 to 5 weeks) to possess the following attributes:

   a. No more than three children work with the same materials at the same time.

   b. The teacher never spends more than 20 minutes per day addressing the class as a group.

c. At least half of every class period is open for students to work on projects of their own choosing at their own pace.

d. Several (more than three) sets of different kinds of educational materials are available for every student in the class to use.

e. One third of all objects in the classroom have been made by the students in the class.

f. The classroom uses nontraditional seating—students sit in circles, in small groupings, or even on the floor to work on their projects. (pp. 16–17)

As this example highlights, the operational definition specifies the various characteristics that are essential to the research study. Indeed, "One strength of operational definitions is that their focus on specifying the identification or measurement process can help in developing constitutive definitions" (Wallen & Fraenkel, 2001, p. 17).

Research questions should also be ethically stated, such that they are unbiased and that the execution of the research question does not lead to unintended harm of the research participants. For example, the question "Why do students taking Advanced Placement or Honors classes always succeed in life?" is stated in a way that the outcome of the study is pre-determined because the question is framed in a biased manner. Further, the question is unethical because it implies that students who do not take these classes are potentially *not* likely to succeed. Thus, when presenting research questions, it is imperative that you pose the question in an unbiased manner, aiming not to implicate the success or failure of participants outside the scope of your study.

Further, research questions should be feasible. This is particularly important for practitioner-scholars setting out to conduct their very first research study. It may be all too tempting to propose a study that examines *everything*. For example, the question "How does high school course placement effect student persistence to graduate?" is so broad that it is likely not a feasible research question. First, the question lacks definition. Which high schools are being considered? How is persistence defined? Second, the question does not specify which high school students might be impacted. Thus, as stated, the question would imply that the researcher is collecting data for *all* high school students *everywhere*. In contrast, a feasible research question allows the researcher to collect data needed for the study with "relatively modest expenditure of time, money, and energy" (Wallen & Fraenkel, 2001, p. 15).

Finally, research questions should be significant. Significance is a relative concept that only you, in consultation with your review of the literature, can define. Generally speaking, however, practitioner-scholars should strive to pose research questions aligned with contemporary problems of practice; that is, something that is meaningful today and will be meaningful tomorrow. More important, your research questions should seek to make a contribution to the field. For example, if you are studying the ways that classroom teachers use data to inform their decision-making about classroom instruction, you will want to ensure that your research in some way contributes to and expands upon the existing research about data-driven decision-making (see Wayman, 2005).

Identifying a Conceptual or Theoretical Framework

An integral part of developing your research study is to determine what conceptual or theoretical framework you will use to inform your study. Merriam (1998) described a framework as "the orientation or stance that you bring to your study" (p. 45). Put another way, the theoretical or conceptual framework provides an explanation to your audience about the way that you made sense of the relationships and interactions in your study. While many scholars interchange the terms theoretical framework and conceptual framework, we see them operating in slightly different but related ways.

A theoretical framework serves as the foundation for your research study. It is founded on established theoretical perspectives that refer to broad theoretical perspectives, including, for example, transformational learning and adult development (Mezirow, 1991), sociocultural theory (Vygotsky, 1978), or organizational learning theory (Senge, 1990). There are countless other theoretical perspectives that can be used to inform education research. Nonetheless, the basic function of the theoretical perspective or framework you select is to convey to the reader the stance or position that you take relative to your research design. Theoretical perspectives ultimately help you explain how you make sense of the world and also inform your interpretations. To a certain extent, they embody particular epistemological assumptions about the phenomenon being studied. More important, though, they provide the reader with a concrete way to understand how you approached your study.

A conceptual framework builds from a theoretical framework, but explains narratively or graphically "the key factors, variables, or constructs and their presumed interrelationships that are central to your study" (Miles, Huberman & Saldaña, 2014, p. 20). This framework can be "simple or complex" as well as "descriptive or causal" (p. 20). More succinctly, a conceptual framework serves as "the researcher's map of the territory being investigated" (p. 20). In many education research publications, researchers include their conceptual framework as a diagram that illustrates the relationships between key variables or components in their study. For example, Huberman and Miles (1984) studied the school improvement process, and offered a model to describe the relationships between the various components of that process. The diagram they presented is an excellent illustration of a conceptual framework for a qualitative research study. As illustrated in Figure 2.3, the conceptual framework highlights various bins that relate to steps or stages in the school improvement process, as well as various factors that impede or support the process. While this represents an initial depiction of the final conceptual framework, it serves as a useful example in that your own conceptual framework might begin this broad and then become narrower over the course of your study.

What are the key differences between a theoretical and conceptual framework? First, a theoretical framework serves as a broad lens for your research study. It provides a theoretical rationale for the approach you have taken in your study. And, most important, it provides an anchor for your study relative to the larger literature base. A conceptual framework, on the other hand, serves as a more fine-grained lens that operationalizes and explains relationships between theoretical concepts. As such, a conceptual framework both situates your study within the literature and elaborates on the key connections between concepts that you feel are important.

Figure 2.3   An Example of a Conceptual Framework

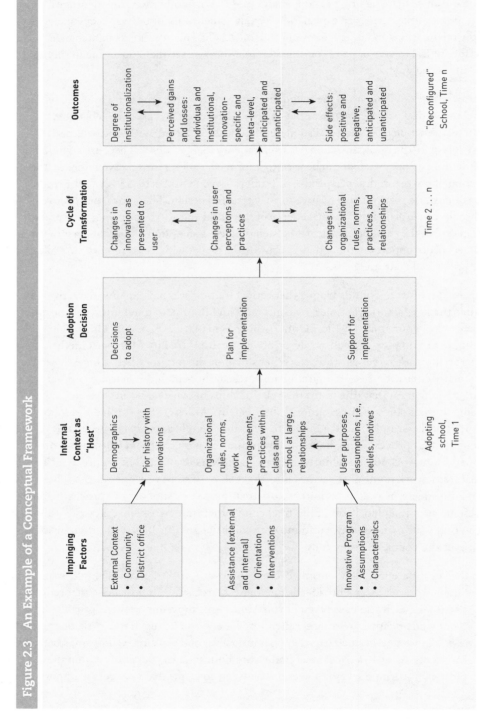

Source: Springer, Environment, Development, and Public Policy, Innovation up Close: How School Improvent Works, 1984, Huberman & Miles, reprinted with permission of Springer Science + Business Media

Thus, a conceptual framework is as much a lens as it is a statement of understanding of the conceptual relationships that exist in your study.

Second, a theoretical framework is often selected *prior* to your analysis and remains consistent throughout the analytic process. As such, it serves as a guide for your analysis. A conceptual framework, on the other hand, may be initially stated at the outset of the study but revised and adjusted as the data analysis unfolds. We see a conceptual framework as being both a guide for analysis, as well as a product of the analysis. While these distinctions are based largely on our own experiences, we think they serve as an important factor for you as you develop your study. If you plan to select a theoretical framework, then this selection will likely guide your analytic strategy to the point that it might also shape which statistical analyses you select in a quantitative study, and perhaps which codes you apply in a qualitative study.

Regardless of whether you use a theoretical or conceptual framework to guide your study, the framework should build from your literature review and inform both your research questions and your overall research design. In qualitative research, alignment between your theoretical or conceptual framework, study design, and analysis is key to ensuring that the study is well conducted. Likewise, in quantitative research, the theoretical or conceptual framework ultimately determines how you anticipate the variables you are studying will interact or relate. It should also be intimately tied to your hypotheses.

Selecting a Methodology: A Decision-Making Process

After clarifying the purpose of the study and defining your research questions, it is appropriate to select a research methodology. Selecting a research methodology is not a linear decision-making process, but something that requires flexible thinking and a willingness to explore alternative possibilities. While some authors have argued that your research question is the driving force behind the selection of your methodology, we suggest that a research question is only one aspect to consider during your decision-making process. Your aim is to assure that there is congruence between the research paradigm(s), methodology, and the research questions being posed.

As such, there are several questions to consider when selecting a methodology. We see these questions as part of a larger decision-making process about your research. In this section of Chapter 2, we focus specifically on critical questions that are designed to help you determine whether your methodology will be primarily qualitative or quantitative. We do not, however, present the nuances of each individual qualitative methodology (case study) or individual quantitative methodology (survey). Rather, we encourage you to explore these individual differences in Chapters 5 and 6, wherein particular methodologies are presented in greater detail.

Some of the key questions to consider when selecting your methodology are:

- *How many participants will be included in your study?* Quantitative studies tend to rely on a larger number of participants or participant observations, while qualitative studies typically rely on a smaller number of participants while studying these participants in much greater depth.

⚓ LINK TO PRACTICE 2.2

SELECTING A THEORETICAL FRAMEWORK

Given your interest in improving student achievement in reading, you decide to focus your study on the relationship between classroom instruction and students' interest in reading chapter books versus other publications. In order to explain how instruction impacts student reading behaviors, you realize that your study will need to be framed with motivational theories associated with reading. You select Bandura's (1986) theory of self-efficacy as one theoretical explanation for the factors that motivate students to read. In reading Bandura's research, you determine that your study must explore the way instruction impacts student's beliefs about themselves as readers. Bandura's theory will serve as the theoretical framework for your study. You will use the framework to broadly situate your study and eventually offer a discussion of your findings.

Focus Questions

1. What is one factor that should guide the selection of a theoretical/conceptual framework?

2. What is the primary purpose of a theoretical/conceptual framework?

- *Do you primarily want to report your results/findings as being derived from the participants' experience or based on independent observations of individual data points?* Qualitative studies rely heavily on the participants' experiences to generate findings. Qualitative studies utilize these experiences to inform a broader understanding of the individual, group, or phenomenon being studied. Quantitative studies tend to rely on independent observations that are not directly associated with the participants' experiences. For example, a quantitative study that seeks to examine the impact of socioeconomic status on student achievement would not consider how an individual's life history or personal story may have contributed to their achievement. Rather, a quantitative study would look narrowly at the relationship between the student's socioeconomic status and student achievement and seek to control for variables that may obscure that relationship.

- *Will your approach be primarily inductive or deductive?* If your approach to the research process will be primarily inductive (that is, moving from localized understandings to broader interpretations) then you would likely want to employ a qualitative methodology. Qualitative methodologies rely heavily on inductive approaches to analysis. Alternatively, if you adopt a primarily deductive approach (that is, moving from broader interpretations to localized understandings), then you would likely employ a quantitative methodology, as this type of research relies heavily on deductive approaches to analysis.

Your answers to these questions should ultimately help you to position your study as qualitative or quantitative. However, we emphasize that these questions are meant as general guidelines and that it is ultimately up to you to select the methodology which best supports your research interest. Moreover, it is important to understand that responses to these questions are not entirely exclusive.

Selecting the Research Methods

For both qualitative and quantitative methodologies, specific research methods (that is, procedures) and the given methodology should be well aligned. These are closely connected constructs and nothing raises questions about a study's design more quickly than misalignment between research methods and research methodology. For example, if you undertook a discourse analysis study you would not use a survey as your primary research method. Likewise, you would not collect and analyze interview data if your primary research methodology is an experimental research design. These methods are incongruent with the methodology that you have selected and ultimately the research question(s) you pose. Thus, an important question for you to consider as a practitioner-scholar is what research method is best aligned with the methodology you have selected. Table 2.1 provides a general overview of data sources that are commonly associated with particular qualitative methodologies.

Unlike qualitative research methods, which encompass an array of data types, there is considerably more uniformity in terms of the type of data that is used in quantitative research. For the most part, quantitative research includes numeric data drawn from administrative data systems, surveys, and questionnaires. Thus, as illustrated in Table 2.2, it becomes important in quantitative research to carefully identify which variables you are most interested in studying. Variables are simply

Table 2.1 Qualitative Methodologies and Commonly Associated Data Types	Case Study	Grounded Theory	Narrative	Phenomenology	Ethnography	Discourse Analysis
Interviews	✓	✓	✓	✓	✓	✓
Focus groups	✓				✓	✓
Observations	✓	✓			✓	
Documents	✓				✓	
Everyday conversations or interactions						✓
Images or photographs			✓		✓	
Journals or diary entries			✓		✓	
Field notes	✓				✓	
Online data					✓	✓

Table 2.2 Examples of Quantitative Variables by Source of Data

Source of Data	Examples of Variables That Could Be Studied in Quantitative Research
Student data	<ul><li>Age</li><li>Height</li><li>Weight</li><li>Gender</li><li>Race/ethnicity</li><li>Language status</li><li>Free or reduced-price lunch eligibility</li><li>Test scores</li><li>Number of minutes spent in class</li></ul>
Teacher data	<ul><li>Years of experience</li><li>Number of minutes spent in class</li><li>Number of minutes for preparation</li><li>Number of hours of professional development completed</li><li>Teacher evaluation score</li></ul>
Classroom data	<ul><li>Number of students enrolled</li><li>Percentage of students who receive special education services</li><li>Percentage of students who are eligible for free or reduced-price lunch</li><li>Number of computers per student</li></ul>
School and district data	<ul><li>Number of teachers employed at the school</li><li>Number and percentage of students by race/ethnicity</li><li>Number and percentage of students who are eligible for free or reduced-price lunch</li><li>Number and percentage of students who transfer to school from another school</li><li>Amount of school funding per pupil</li></ul>
Community data	<ul><li>Percentage of families living below federal poverty line</li><li>Percentage of families where one parent works outside the home</li><li>Number of children born each year</li><li>Percentage of families owning their home</li></ul>

expressions of a construct. For example, age or experience both relate to the construct of time. Similarly, the free or reduced-price lunch eligibility is often included in studies to represent the construct of poverty.

Determining the Approach to Data Analysis

After you have selected the data that you will include in your study, the next step involves determining how you will approach your data analysis. The process is slightly different for qualitative and quantitative research studies. Yet, there is a common element in the process that

SELECTING YOUR RESEARCH METHODOLOGY AND RESEARCH METHODS

After selecting your research topic, you begin considering whether you will use a quantitative or qualitative methodology. You want to focus on a small number of students who have had difficulty maintaining their interest in reading chapter books. Further, you seek to generate themes/findings from your interpretation of their experiences. You think this approach is feasible given the time and resources you have to complete the study. Further, it serves your primary aim of looking at these students' experiences to determine what, if anything, classroom instruction may be doing to impact their motivation to read. Thus, given these considerations as well as the theoretical framework that you plan to use in your study, you decide that you will use a qualitative research methodology to complete your research.

You realize that selecting this methodology limits the types of data you will use in your analysis. For example, you will not spend a great deal of time reviewing test scores or assessment data. Instead, you will focus on qualitative data, such as interviews or focus groups, observations, and samples of student work that allow you to understand the students' experience as a reader in the classroom, as well as the ways that instruction impacts their motivation to read.

Focus Questions

1. What are two potential considerations that you might make when deciding to use a qualitative study?

2. What are two potential considerations that you might make when deciding to use a quantitative study?

is important to highlight. Regardless of whether you are conducting a qualitative or quantitative study, your analytic approach should be congruent with your theoretical or conceptual framework, aligned with your research questions, and directly tied to the methodology and the type of data that you collect. For example, you would not conduct a statistical analysis on interview transcripts nor would you attempt to carry out a thematic analysis of salary data downloaded from a state data system. These approaches are not congruent with the type of data that you collected. Thus, it is especially important when selecting an approach to data analysis to select the approach that best fits the data that you are working with, and that is most closely aligned with the traditions/ assumptions that guide your study. In the next two sections, we highlight the big considerations that often guide data analysis decisions related to qualitative and quantitative data. We discuss data analysis in much greater detail in Chapters 8 and 9.

QUALITATIVE DATA ANALYSIS. The data analysis process in qualitative research is often uniquely influenced by the qualitative methodology selected, as well as the theoretical and/ or conceptual frameworks that frame your study. The foundation for many approaches to qualitative data analysis involves coding data in order to assign meaning to those data. Coding is referred to as the process of applying " . . . a word or short phrase that symbolically assigns a summative, salient, essence-capturing, and/or evocative attribute [to] a portion of language-based or visual data (Saldaña, 2009, p. 3). Put another way, a code is simply a flag or label that you, as the practitioner-scholar, apply to the text to associate it with a particular meaning. Coding is thus the basis for many forms of qualitative analysis.

Miles, Huberman, and Saldaña (2014) broadly characterized the qualitative analysis process in this way:

- Assigning codes or themes to a set of field notes, interview transcripts, or documents

- Sorting and sifting through these coded materials to identify similar phrases, relationships between variables, patterns, themes, categories, distinct differences between subgroups, and common sequences

- Isolating these patterns and processes, and commonalities and differences, and taking them out to the field in the next wave of data collection

- Noting reflections or other remarks in jottings, journals, and analytic memos

- Gradually elaborating a small set of assertions, propositions, and generalizations that cover the consistencies discerned in the database

- Comparing those generalizations with a formalized body of knowledge in the form of constructs or theories. (p. 10)

The codes you apply to your data are often directly informed by the theoretical or conceptual frameworks you selected for your study. These frameworks serve as a road map for you as you review, code, and interpret the qualitative data you have collected. These frameworks, moreover, highlight or make significant particular statements, views, beliefs, or experiences raised by your study participants.

Another important aspect of the qualitative analysis process is that it often involves moving from coded statements to broader categories that more generally describe what the coded passages refer to. For example, if you are conducting a study that examines teacher perceptions of the school improvement planning process and you find that teachers consistently refer to the support of their department chair, you might categorize these comments as being related to the "support of the department chair in the school improvement process." The categories you establish in your study set the stage for the next step of your analysis, which is to generate themes or findings. Themes generally refer to the relationships, interactions, similarities, or differences between the categories you construct. For example, if you found that teachers generally viewed the support of their department chair as important, but placed different values on specific types of support that the department chair provided, you might develop a theme that broadly describes the importance of differentiated support provided by department chairs as an enabling factor in the school improvement planning process.

A final step in the qualitative data analysis process often involves identifying illustrative or representative quotes from the coded data that help you to substantiate the findings or themes that you have generated. For example, you might wish to include comments from teachers who described the support of the department chair as being primarily about securing resources that enable them to engage more deeply in collaborative opportunities about school improvement. Likewise, you might want to highlight passages of text that illustrate how teachers describe their department chairs engaging in or facilitating the school improvement process. Ultimately, you will include these representative quotes within your final report/paper and offer explicit interpretations of them. A common mistake is to include quotes without providing adequate interpretations. It is critical to keep in mind that quotes do not stand alone, as in qualitative analysis your interpretation is central to the process.

QUANTITATIVE DATA ANALYSIS. Unlike qualitative data analysis, it is important to understand that quantitative data analysis involves using either descriptive or inferential statistics and is thus a process of applying different statistical tests or procedures to identify meaning in the data. Descriptive statistics describe the distribution of the scores/values in a particular dataset. Inferential statistics, alternatively, allow you to describe relationships, predict outcomes, or make associations between variables in the dataset. Whether you conduct a statistical analysis using descriptive or inferential statistics depends on the type of data that you are using in your study, the aims of your study, and your desire to explain or predict a particular outcome.

When selecting an analytic strategy for a quantitative study, there are three questions you must ask: (a) What type of data are you using? (b) Are you primarily interested in describing the data or identifying/exploring relationships within the dataset? (c) Are you interested in testing for or identifying a specific outcome? The type of data, and more specifically the type of variables, that you use in your quantitative study will influence how you approach your analysis. There are three types of variables in quantitative research, which we describe in greater detail in Chapter 9. Categorical variables refer to a category (for example, male or female). These variables are often used to group participants together or to define a particular participant characteristic. Interval or ratio variables are numeric variables that are equally situated on some type of scale. The primary difference between an interval and ratio variable is that an interval variable does not have an absolute zero, while a ratio variable does. For example, height would be considered an interval variable because it is impossible to be zero inches tall. Alternatively, dollars spent per pupil would be considered a ratio variable, because it is possible to spend absolutely no money to educate an individual student. Finally, ordinal variables describe the rank of an individual or score relative to other scores. An ordinal variable is thus equivalent to a first-, second-, or third-place ranking.

Second, if you are primarily interested in describing the data, then it is most appropriate to use a descriptive analysis in your study. Such an analysis effectively summarizes the distribution of the data and thus presents to your reader a picture of what the data say. Alternatively, if you are primarily interested in understanding or identifying potential relationships among variables or in some way associating the variables with one another, then it is most appropriate to use a statistical analysis that includes inferential statistics.

Third, if the aim of your study is to test for or identify a specific outcome, then you are most likely to conduct an analysis using inferential statistics. Inferential statistics allow you to predict outcomes or associate. For example, you could explore the influence of a student's socioeconomic status on achievement using inferential statistics. This analysis would allow you to identify the extent to which the student's socioeconomic status predicts, explains, or can be associated with differences in the students' achievement.

As we mentioned previously, it is beyond the scope of this textbook to describe all of the ways that qualitative and quantitative data analysis can be conducted. For now, it is important that you have a general understanding of the differences between these analytic approaches and the overarching factors that prompt you to select specific approaches given the goals of your study.

PLANNING YOUR ANALYSIS

After deciding upon your research methodology, as well as the type of data that you will use in your study, you realize that your next task is to plan your analysis. The analytic process for a qualitative or quantitative study is different and thus what you would plan for a qualitative study would not necessarily apply if you undertake a quantitative study. Recognizing this, however, you begin thinking through the various aspects of your qualitative analysis. First, what types of data are most appropriate given your methodology? Qualitative methodologies tend to rely on textual materials as well as visual materials. Thus, you will want to select an analysis approach that allows you to fully examine these types of data. Second, how does the specific methodology you selected limit the types of data that can be or should be included in your analysis? You know, for example, that a case study often includes interviews, observations, and documents. Alternatively, you know that grounded theory tends to privilege interview data. Thus, the methodology you select will determine, to some extent, which types of data you include in your study and thus include in your analysis. Third, based on your review of the methodological literature related to your study, how has that methodology traditionally defined the analytic process? For example, some qualitative methodologies tend to rely on an analysis that results in the identification of specific themes, whereas other qualitative methodologies tend to examine the function of language choices in your participants' conversations. Fourth, what are the potential ethical considerations that will arise as you begin analyzing your data? For example, if you are working with student data obtained directly from your classroom, you will need to de-identify or make confidential the data you are including in your study. Additionally, it will require that you to consider how your knowledge of the students potentially influences your interpretation of the data.

Focus Questions:

1. What questions should you ask when determining how you will analyze your data?

2. What are the primary differences between qualitative and quantitative data analysis?

CARRYING OUT THE STUDY

Beyond considering how you will design your study, it is important to give ample consideration to the way that you will actually carry out your research study. In particular, you must consider how you will get access to the data that you need to complete your analysis, how you will engage or recruit participants for your study, and what steps you must take to ensure that your study conforms to ethical guidelines.

After determining what your study will entail, one of the first questions you should ask yourself is how you will get access to the data you need to complete the study. For example, if you are conducting a quantitative study, how will you get access to the quantitative data that will be required to complete your analysis? Will you need to, for example, contact the school district or state department of education to file a formal data request? Will you need to develop a survey to collect participant perspectives? If you are conducting a qualitative study, how will you recruit participants? How will you gain access to a research site? Not accounting for these steps can introduce significant delays in starting your research study. For example, a data request to a state agency for student achievement data can take more than three months to complete.

Thus, we encourage you to consider what you must do to acquire the data needed to complete the study as part of the process of designing your study.

Further, while it may be tempting to assume that all of your colleagues will want to participate in your study or that you will have unlimited access to participants for you research, the more likely scenario is that you will need to invest substantial time engaging and recruiting prospective participants. We suggest identifying the strategies you will employ to recruit participants as part of your research study design, and, as part of that consideration, give yourself sufficient time to meet with prospective participants, and inform them about the study and their rights as potential research participants. Additionally, as the informed consent process will result in some participants choosing not to participate in your study, a critical consideration involves identifying alternative participants. We discuss sampling procedures in greater detail in Chapter 7.

Finally, we recommend including additional time in your study plans to allow your study to be fully reviewed by the Institutional Review Board at your college/university, as well as to be reviewed by the research ethics committee at the school or school district where you plan to complete your research. We discuss the Institutional Review Board process and other ethical considerations in Chapter 4.

REFLECTIVE OPPORTUNITY 2.3

You perhaps noted that the research cycle did not explicitly include a separate component related to research ethics. Generally, research ethics are thought to be important *throughout* the research process. However, there are certain steps wherein you may need to consider ethical concerns more carefully.

1. Considering the processes described earlier, what aspects of the research process do you believe are linked most closely to ethical considerations?

2. Why do you believe this to be the case?

SUMMARY

In this chapter, we provided you with an overview of the process for designing a research study. We highlighted some of the differences between qualitative and quantitative research designs, while also pointing out the similarities. Throughout, we noted the importance of developing coherence between your research problem statement, research questions, research methodology, and research methods. Finally, we emphasized the importance of anchoring your research study to your theoretical or conceptual framework.

KEY TERMS

Categorical Variables 39

Code 37

Conceptual Framework 31

Descriptive Analysis 39

Descriptive Statistics 39

Experimental Hypothesis 25

Hypothesis 25

Inferential Statistics 39

Interval or Ratio Variables 39

Null Hypothesis 25

Ordinal Variables 39

Research Problem 22

Research Problem Statement 24

Theoretical Framework 31

Variables 35

QUESTIONS TO CONSIDER

1. What are some of the key steps to consider when designing a qualitative or quantitative research study?

2. What are the characteristics of a qualitative and a quantitative research problem statement?

3. What are some of the key considerations for developing research questions?

4. What are the similarities and differences between a theoretical and conceptual framework?

5. How might you determine which methodology is best for your research study?

6. What are the ways to decide which research methods are most appropriate for your research study?

7. What are some of the central procedures for conducting qualitative data analysis? What are some of the central procedures for conducting quantitative data analysis?

8. What are the various types of data that might be collected in a qualitative or quantitative research study?

CHAPTER EXERCISES

1. Gather 12 to 15 research articles related to a topic that interests you. Identify the salient points within these articles. Using these articles, practice developing a research problem statement. Share this statement with others to acquire critical feedback and suggestions for improvement.

2. Working with the research problem statement you developed in the first chapter exercise, develop six research questions that you could use to study the topic in greater detail. Formulate three of the research questions as though you were conducting a qualitative study and three of the research questions as though you were conducting a quantitative study.

3. Given the research questions you developed in the second chapter exercise, consider how you would carry out the study. Specifically, what data would you need to collect? How might you collect them? Who might your research participants be? Develop a simple table that describes the data that you hope to collect and link it to the research questions you think the data address.

4. Given the research questions you developed in the second chapter exercise and the data you identified in the third chapter exercise, consider how you might analyze the information you gathered. Write a short paragraph that succinctly describes your analytic approach and explains how you will move from the data you collected to an interpretation of the information.

Kilbourn's (2006) article offers a clear and concise description of how to move from a research interest to a problem statement to research questions when designing a qualitative research study. It provides several helpful examples of how to narrow your research focus, while situating your qualitative research study in the larger body of literature.

Vogt, Gardner, and Haeffele's (2012) book, *When to Use What Research Design*, is a useful text for considering various research designs. While the book includes some discussion of qualitative and mixed methods research designs, it is particularly helpful for thinking through how to design a quantitative study.

Sharpen your skills with SAGE edge!

edge.sagepub.com/lochmiller

SAGE edge for Students provides a personalized approach to help you accomplish your coursework goals in an easy-to-use learning environment. You'll find action plans, mobile-friendly eFlashcards, and quizzes as well as videos, web resources, and links to SAGE journal articles to support and expand on the concepts presented in this chapter.

3

REVIEWING THE LITERATURE

FIGURING OUT WHERE TO BEGIN YOUR REVIEW OF THE LITERATURE

As a school principal, you are constantly perplexed by the differences in students' achievement on standardized tests. You are interested in exploring what other researchers have written about this topic. You begin with a simple Google search and discover that there are a variety of research and non-research articles written on this topic. In fact, there are thousands of results from your search and you are now not sure where to begin. You begin to ask yourself many questions. Should you trust and therefore read all of the results? Should you focus only on those articles with titles that sound like research? Is a Google search rigorous enough or is there a search engine that is more comprehensive? These are only some of the questions that you face as you begin to review the literature.

INTRODUCTION

As illustrated in the opening vignette, the literature review process can sometimes be overwhelming for practitioner-scholars and therefore requires careful consideration to be successful. In this chapter, we focus on the process of conducting a literature review. We, like many of our colleagues, see this as a key starting point for scholarly work. For many practitioner-scholars, however, reviewing educational literature can be a challenging endeavor. The educational literature base is vast and frequently written for researchers as opposed to practitioners. Thus, practitioner-scholars must learn to conduct a literature review as well as become familiar with the language, format, and organization of research articles.

In this chapter, we provide you with a straightforward approach to reviewing the literature and building a literature review

Learning Objectives

By the end of the chapter, you will be able to:

- Describe the role and purposes of the literature review in the research process.

- Discuss the various sections of a literature review.

- Compare and contrast the role of a literature review for qualitative and quantitative research studies.

- Develop a literature review in a step-wise fashion.

- Assess the various types of sources.

- Analyze literature for quality.

- Identify technological tools to support the literature review process.

that ultimately supports your research study and broader interests. First, we discuss the importance of conducting a literature review. Second, we share how the literature review process is positioned in relation to the larger research study. Third, we focus a great deal of our discussion around the actual process of carrying out a literature review, including how to identify, access, and assess resources. Fourth, we present some of the distinctions between the various types of literature resources (for example, primary versus secondary). Finally, we introduce a few of the technologies that can support you in organizing, annotating, and evaluating your selected literature.

THE IMPORTANCE OF THE LITERATURE REVIEW

Research studies often begin with a thorough literature review. As Boote and Beile (2005) claimed, "A thorough, sophisticated literature review is the foundation and inspiration for substantial, useful research" (p. 3). Despite its importance, practitioner-scholars with whom we have worked have regularly expressed some variation of this sentiment: "Why do I need to review the literature when I'm trying to create something new?" While we empathize with these practitioner-scholars, we recognize that research without substantive connections to the existing literature base cannot be fully integrated or used by a field of study. Understanding what has been previously written about a particular research topic is essential to ensuring that a research study contributes new ideas to the field.

We see the literature review as having three distinct roles in educational research. First, the literature review provides the practitioner-scholar with an opportunity to examine previous research findings and identify salient opportunities for new research. Second, the literature review provides the practitioner-scholar with an opportunity to ground their study in a substantive understanding of the existing literature so that their findings and interpretations link to the existing scholarly discussion. This is how you become a part of the broader conversation that is already happening in a field. Third, the literature review provides the practitioner-scholar with a resource from which to frame their analysis. Past research findings provide you with valuable clues about previous interpretations that shape current understandings, as well as ideas related to how a particular problem of practice might be studied.

REFLECTIVE OPPORTUNITY 3.1

Hart (1998, p. 27) suggested that there are many reasons for conducting a literature review. These reasons might range from determining what has been done from what needs to be done next to gaining a new perspective on a topic to identifying relationships between ideas and practices.

1. As you think about your own goals, what are some of the reasons that you will review the literature?

UNPACKING THE LITERATURE REVIEW

Before we describe the process of conducting a literature review, it is helpful to understand the basic structure of a literature review. It should be noted, however, that there is no single way to approach a literature review, nor a single format to write a literature review.

While authors frequently adapt the literature review zstructure to fit their own style, most literature reviews begin with an introductory section that describes the focus of the literature that was reviewed, explains the procedures that were used to identify specific resources, and states clearly how the literature review is organized. From the Field 3.1 provides an example of how one group of researchers discussed the procedures they used for conducting a literature review of school climate research (Thapa, Cohen, Guffey, & Higgins-D'Allessandro, 2013).

The introductory section of a literature review should also state the purpose of the review. For example, you might wish to say that "The purpose of this literature review is to summarize existing research that I later use to inform my interpretation of the results." Similarly, you may want to suggest that "The purpose of this literature review is to review theoretical perspectives that define how I made sense of the data I collected." You may also offer a more generic introductory statement that highlights the literature base(s) that you focused on, thereby implicitly pointing to the purpose of your literature review. From the Field 3.2 provides an example of how Lochmiller, Huggins, and Acker-Hocevar (2012) introduced the literature review in a study that examined different approaches to preparing principals for leadership in math and science.

FROM THE FIELD 3.1

Description of the Procedures Used to Conduct a Literature Review

To conduct this literature review we adopted the following method. First, we consulted a group of experts in the field of school climate research and gathered their feedback on dimensions and subdimensions on which this review should be grounded. As a result, we finalized five dimensions of school climate listed previously. Second, with helpful feedback from those experts, we collected all papers, books, and reports they recommended that relate to school climate research from 1970 to date. Once we had a list of these resources, we examined all the citations used in those studies and then compiled a list of studies that were relevant to school climate research. In addition, we also focused on literature reviews and meta-analyses on school climate research and cross-examined them for relevant citations. Third, we conducted a comprehensive search for papers, articles, and reports on school climate on Google Scholar. This search was conducted for (A) school climate in general, (B) each of the five major dimensions of school climate listed previously, and (C) other related areas of school climate. To conclude, we then finalized a list of more than 200 references relevant for this review. Out of these citations, approximately 5 percent are experimental studies, 45 percent are correlational studies, 25 percent are literature reviews, and 25 percent are other descriptive studies, including qualitative studies, mostly published in peer-reviewed journals.

Source: Thapa et al., 2013, p. 359

 Read the full article at:
www.sagepub.com/lochmiller

Introducing a Literature Review

In preparing this article, we reviewed literature broadly related to student achievement in math and science, research about principals' instructional leadership, and existing discussions of the strengths and weaknesses of principal preparations.

Source: Lochmiller et al., 2012, p. 200

Following this introductory section, the literature review often begins by reviewing the literature that is the most tangentially related to the topic that you will study. In effect, you are using the literature review to move the reader toward a specific understanding of the research you reviewed, as well as setting the stage for the reader to understand why your research study is important and needed. If, for example, you are planning to conduct a quantitative study that describes differences in high school graduation rates by student race or ethnicity, you might begin by describing the research studies that relate to graduation rates more generally. As part of your discussion, you may also highlight whether or not this problem is of growing concern to policymakers, educators, and others who may read your study. This gives your study relevance and motivates the reader to continue reading. From the Field 3.3 provides an example of how Lochmiller (2012) linked the purpose of his literature review to the broader context surrounding principal leadership, in particular, the resource challenges facing principals following the great recession of 2008–2010 in the United States.

Setting a Context for a Literature Review

School districts throughout the United States currently face unprecedented fiscal challenges caused by the worst national recession since the Great Depression. The federal government has provided roughly $100 billion to help school districts close the budget gaps, retain classroom teachers, and preserve education programs (Ellerson, 2009; Mead, Vaishnav, Porter, & Rotherham, 2010). Despite this federal assistance, school districts continue to face significant budget challenges. Several organizations have taken an interest in the fiscal challenges facing school districts in the United States. The American Association for School Administrators (AASA), for example, has surveyed district administrators throughout the recession to document the effects that the recession is having on school districts and individual schools. Their survey research revealed that the current crisis has had an unprecedented impact on schools and school districts. Two-thirds (66%) of the respondents to a December 2010 survey indicated that their school district was preparing to lay off additional employees to compensate for declining state resources (Ellerson, 2010a). At one point, the AASA projected that as many as 275,000 classroom teachers could be laid off (Ellerson, 2010b). The situation facing school districts is nothing short of a "fiscal tsunami" that threatens to upend decades of stable education funding (Guthrie & Peng, 2011, p. 19).

Source: Lochmiller, 2012, p. 166

In the next portion of your literature review, you should focus on the literature that directly relates to your research study. In this section, you want to highlight research studies that are the most similar to your work and thus have the greatest potential to inform how you approach your research study. Of particular interest, you should highlight studies that have reached similar and/ or different conclusions. While you typically complete your literature review prior to conducting your study, this is also a section that you may want to return to and adjust once you have completed your study and established or produced your results/findings.

Before moving to the next section of the literature review, you should provide the reader with a succinct summary of the main points. This summary section is designed to assist the reader in recalling key ideas, research studies, and/or research results/findings that influence how you set up your research study. Quite often, you will provide a reader with multiple summary sections or paragraphs throughout your literature review, incorporating a summary section after the review of each conceptually related set of publications. The inclusion of multiple summary sections is more common when writing a thesis or dissertation chapter focused on the literature review. From the Field 3.4 provides an example of how Patall, Cooper, and Allen (2010) concluded a section of their literature review focused on summarizing the research around extended time in school and academic achievement.

The final section of the literature review is often devoted to reviewing theoretical perspectives or presenting a conceptual model that will guide the research study. Some researchers embed this section within their literature review, while others develop it as a separate section entitled "Theoretical Frameworks" and/or "Conceptual Frameworks/Conceptual Models." Here, as in the previous sections, your task is not simply to summarize the theories or concepts. Rather, it is to demonstrate how you see these perspectives linking to the previous research you reviewed, as well as setting the stage for your own study. From the Field 3.5 provides an example of how this section of a literature discussion might be started. Gallucci (2008), who conducted a qualitative study of instructional reform and professional learning communities, provides a useful example of how you might include a discussion of the literature surrounding your theoretical perspective.

The section focused on theories and conceptual perspectives is the place where you make explicit the links between concepts and ideas that will inform your interpretation of the data. Regardless

FROM THE FIELD 3.4

Making the Literature Review Relevant

Of the three studies examining the relationship between ED [Extended Day] and academic achievement, all found some evidence that ED led to improvements in academic achievement, although rarely was the relationship significant across all grade levels, SES groups, or for all outcomes. Furthermore, one study suggested that the effect of ED on achievement may be particularly pronounced for at-risk students.

Source: Patall et al., 2010, p. 423

Discussing Theoretical Perspectives in the Literature

I explore theories about how organizations learn (that is, how they learn to support the growth of professionals within the organization) and propose a framework based on sociocultural views of learning that is useful for exploring the questions about capacity building posed earlier in the article.

Source: Gallucci, 2008, p. 546

of whether your study is qualitative or quantitative, we see this section as critical to your work. Without it, the reader is unable to see how you connect theoretical concepts to the design of your study and the interpretation of the data.

DIFFERENCE BETWEEN QUALITATIVE AND QUANTITATIVE LITERATURE REVIEWS

While both qualitative and quantitative research requires you to review the existing literature, the purposes of the literature review in both of these traditions is slightly different. Paulus, Lester, and Dempster (2014) noted that because qualitative research is often "emergent (starting with a context of interest rather than with a predetermined hypothesis)" (p. 49), the literature review for a qualitative research study serves a slightly different purpose than it does for a quantitative research study. For example, in quantitative research, the purpose of the literature review is to summarize existing information so that you can clearly demonstrate how your findings both extend on and relate to what has already been studied. This reflects the confirmatory nature of quantitative research studies.

In qualitative research, the purpose of the literature review is often to situate your study more broadly in the current discourse, as well as to disclose to your reader how you will interpret the data you collect. As such, the nature of the qualitative literature review tends to be more exploratory in that it links concepts and ideas together in a way that supports your interpretation of the data. While we treat the literature review as a separate section, you should note that many qualitative researchers blend their literature review and their discussion of findings. For example, qualitative researchers who use a discourse analysis methodology may incorporate literature around particular conversational features (for example, the function or purpose of silences or pauses in classroom talk) into their discussion of the findings, using this literature to build their narrative. From the Field 3.6 provides an example of this from Lester's (2012) research article illustrating how previous literature was woven into the presentation of research findings.

Regardless of whether you are conducting a qualitative or quantitative research study, the literature review serves to situate your research in a broader, scholarly conversation and can also serve to guide you as you develop your research design (Paulus, Lester, & Dempster, 2014).

Framing Findings With Literature

Nicole began by stating that she "hates" to call autism a disability, implying that to be named disabled is undesirable. Edwards (1999) noted that it is particularly relevant to consider how emotions are used in discourse to link specific ideas together. Everyday understandings and uses of emotions do not simply reflect mental states, but instead point to the "cultural values and the prerogatives of power that some members of this society currently hold" (Lutz, 1990, p. 204). So, it is particularly telling to consider how in the above excerpt, the word "hate" is deployed in relation to disability. Historically, being named disabled has been linked to social exclusion, stigma, and deficits (Braddock, & Parish, 2001) and has rarely functioned as a desired social category.

Source: Lester, 2012, Art. 1

THE PROCESS OF CONDUCTING A LITERATURE REVIEW

While practitioner-scholars may approach qualitative and quantitative literature reviews differently, the process of conducting a literature review is essentially the same. As Machi and McEvoy (2009) proposed, the literature review process is a cycle that moves from the identification of a particular research topic to the development of an argument that elaborates on and provides support for your interpretation of that topic. As illustrated in Figure 3.1, the literature review process involves six steps.

First, you select a research topic that will become the focus of the literature review. As we noted in the discussion of the research process in Chapter 2, we suggest that this topic be aligned with a problem of practice that you would like to study in more detail. Second, you search the literature to identify salient resources that relate to your topic or the problem of practice that you will study. It is imperative that, at this stage, you catalog and document your resources so that you are able to retrieve them later. Third, after you have collected the literature, you need to develop an argument that relates to your topic and supports (justifies) the need for your study. Although many practitioner-scholars assume that the purpose of the literature review is only to summarize the existing research, an equally important purpose is to develop an argument for your study. Thus, beyond summarizing, your literature review should also discuss strengths and weaknesses of the literature, and identify potential gaps in the literature base that provide justification for your study. Fourth, after constructing an argument, you next survey the literature you have collected to identify specific resources that support your argument. At this stage, you begin summarizing, analyzing, and synthesizing the literature. Relatedly, the fifth step in the literature review process involves critiquing the literature to identify weaknesses or gaps that your study can address. Your critique might be framed on substantive, conceptual, theoretical, methodological, or practical grounds. For instance, in Lochmiller's (2012) literature review, he critiqued the literature on substantive grounds, stating: "The existing literature provides very few clues about the actions principals might take to prepare their schools for budget reductions or what decisions they may make" (p. 169). Finally, after developing your

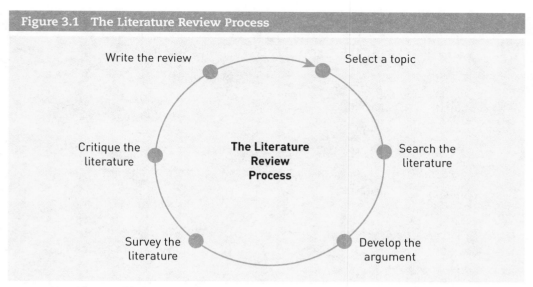

Figure 3.1   The Literature Review Process

Write the review

Select a topic

The Literature Review Process

Critique the literature

Search the literature

Survey the literature

Develop the argument

Source: Adapted from Machi & McEvoy, 2009, p. 5

argument and identifying relevant resources, you write the literature review so that it addresses your research topic and builds support for your study.

Identifying a Topic for the Literature Review

An effective literature review begins with a clearly defined research topic. As Machi and McEvoy (2009) suggested, "Most applied research begins when you select an everyday problem, interest, or concern for further study. Selecting an interest for study needs great care and forethought" (p. 16). The second part of this quote, regarding the need for care and forethought in selecting a research topic, is essential. All too frequently, practitioner-scholars begin their research with a topic that is too broad to be studied. While we suggest that research ideas be drawn from problems of practice, we also acknowledge that these problems often must be reframed to be an appropriate research topic. Researchers rarely study problems of practice in their entirety. Rather, they focus on some aspect of a problem of practice and attempt to explain or examine that aspect in greater detail. For example, it would be unwise to attempt a study about the differences in student achievement without specifically identifying the aspect of these differences or the causes for these differences that you are most interested in understanding.

Beginning a literature review with a topic that is too broad will result in many unproductive resources being retrieved and make it difficult to develop a coherent argument from the literature review. Moreover, a topic that is too broad may well overwhelm you given the sheer breadth and diversity of published resources. Similarly, beginning a literature review with a topic that is too narrow will unnecessarily eliminate potentially valuable resources that might inform your argument.

Accessing Resources

Assuming that you have selected a research topic that can be used for the basis of a literature review, your next task is to begin searching for resources. College and university libraries have invested substantially in electronic resources that are designed to make it easier for you to locate

DEVELOPING A TOPIC FOR A LITERATURE REVIEW

Let's assume you are a school principal who is interested in studying differences in student achievement on state assessments. You have met with your master's adviser or dissertation chair and have been told by them that your topic needs to be narrowed. You originally proposed a study that would look at differences in student achievement among elementary school students. Your adviser indicated that this topic is interesting but requires further narrowing. She suggested looking at some aspect of achievement or at a specific cause for differences in student achievement. Upon reflecting on the data from your school, you recognize that students who perform at lower levels on the state assessment do so when they are instructed in classrooms that use

less small-group instruction. Thinking about this difference, you decide that your interest is less about the differences in achievement than about the effect of specific types of instruction on achievement. You reformulate the focus of your literature review to be: "The effect of elementary instructional strategies on student achievement, as measured by state assessments of student learning."

Focus Questions

1. How did the principal go about narrowing the topic of the literature review?

2. What might the principal need to do next in order to determine whether this topic is viable?

information within the university's library catalogue, as well as to identify resources online. While these resources make reviewing the literature easier, we suggest that you meet with an education librarian at your college or university to identify the tools that are available to you and will provide you with the most valuable information. Throughout the process, we also encourage you to meet with your faculty adviser to ask them for guidance in selecting resources that support your particular research interest. Faculty advisers can assist you in identifying specific search terms, relevant databases, and may even be able to suggest specific journals that you should consult throughout your literature review. In our experience, the advice obtained from advisers and education librarians proves invaluable for finding relevant resources.

Searching the Literature and Identifying Resources

After identifying the research topic and selecting search terms or keywords, we recommend using one or more of the online search engines or databases maintained by your college or university. A database is simply a repository of information that can be accessed using queries. In particular, we have found that Academic Search Premier, Dissertation Abstracts, EBSCO, ERIC, Education Full Text, JSTOR, and PsychInfo provide the best access to education-related resources. This list is not exhaustive and an education librarian at your college or university can assist you in determining whether additional databases may be useful in your search.

One resource that we strongly encourage you to use is the Education Resources Information Center (ERIC) administered by the Institute of Education Sciences at the U.S. Department of Education. ERIC provides researchers with a convenient portal to identify resources, as well as to

REFLECTIVE OPPORTUNITY 3.2

As you consider your interests and the problem(s) of practice that is most relevant to you, list out some of your broad topics of interest. After doing so, consider the following questions:

1. Are your current topics too broad or too narrow?

2. What are some of the practical ways that you can determine whether your topic is too broad or too narrow?

identify search terms that can be used in most education databases. The ERIC Thesaurus helps you to develop a comprehensive list of search terms, keywords, and in some cases, the timeframe when these terms were most prevalent in publications. This service allows you to quickly narrow your search to relevant search terms that can be used in any electronic search database. Given the evolving nature of education research, this resource can help you identify the terms that will be most helpful in identifying resources that will support your work and save you significant time.

Most databases involve using a combination of keywords or search terms to identify information. Library databases typically use Boolean Logic to structure the database search. According to Machi and McEvoy (2009), a Boolean query uses keywords (for example, academic achievement) that are then linked to "logical operators," including AND, OR, and NOT to define and narrow the search (p. 41). For example, you might use the Education Full Text database to retrieve articles related to the effect of instructional method on student achievement. To enter this as a Boolean query, you might type "instructional method" AND "student achievement" in order to narrow the search to include only resources related both to instructional method and student achievement. Similarly, you might type "student achievement" NOT "instructional method" in order to exclude any work that references instructional method. Finally, you might use "instructional method" OR "student achievement" to include any references that expand the search to include more information. While no single expression may produce all of the results you need, our recommendation is to use multiple expressions or keyword variations to determine which provides you with the most useful resources. Table 3.1 provides a summary of the Boolean operators and their function.

Table 3.1 Boolean Operators and Their Effect on a Search

Boolean Operator	Effect on Search	Descriptor Use
and	*Narrows*	*Links descriptors*
not	*Excludes*	*Qualifies descriptors*
or	*Broadens*	*Adds descriptors*

Source: Adapted from Machi & McEvoy, 2009, p. 42

Assessing the Types of Resources Available

While search services are invaluable to you as you conduct a literature review, the breadth of resources contained in these databases also requires that you become more discerning about the kind of information that you include in your literature review. For example, the online resources at your university may include books, edited books, journal articles, reports, monographs, and periodicals. However, not all of these resources have equal weight when considered in the context of a literature review.

One way to differentiate between the types of resources you use is to distinguish between primary and secondary resources, as well as peer-reviewed and non–peer-reviewed sources. Primary sources report the results of an original research study. Gall, Gall, and Borg (2007) described primary sources as "a document (for example, journal article or dissertation) that was written by the individual who actually conducted the research study or who formulated the theory or opinions that are described in the document" (p. 98). For example, Cozza and Oreshkina (2013) conducted a qualitative study that examined the problem-solving discourses of ten-year-old students in math classes in Russia, Spain, Hungary, and the United States. This study would be considered a primary source as Cozza and Oreshkina were the principal investigators, conducted the analysis, and reported on their findings in the published article. A secondary source is a "publication written by authors who were not direct observers of, or participants in, the events being described" (Gall, Gall, & Borg, 2007, p. 107). Thus, published literature reviews summarizing the work of Cozza and Oreshkina would be considered a secondary source, as the author was not directly involved in the completion of the original study. The *Review of Educational Research*, a journal of the American Educational Research Association, is a particularly valuable secondary source because it focuses on publishing literature reviews that are peer-reviewed and does not publish original research.

Beyond considering primary versus secondary sources, scholar-practitioners should also consider whether a journal article has been peer-reviewed or refereed. Peer-reviewed journal articles are typically considered the most authoritative research publications, as they have undergone review by experts in the field. This process ensures that the content of the research article adheres to the standards of the profession, and that the study was ethically conducted and included a rigorous and accurate application of research methodology and methods. Further, a peer-reviewed journal article is typically presumed to be making a substantive contribution to the field. While many peer-reviewed journal articles are considered authoritative, the simple fact that an article has been peer-reviewed does not mean that you should simply accept the claims or findings it presents. Rather, much like any other resource, you should review the claims and findings with a critical perspective.

You should also be mindful when reviewing publications that have undergone editorial review. An editorially reviewed publication is not the same as a peer-reviewed publication. An editorially reviewed publication has typically been reviewed by an editor for its substance and style, but may not have undergone rigorous review in terms of its research method, data analysis, or research design. Many popular publications in the field of education are editorially reviewed. For example, *Phi Delta Kappan*, *Educational Leadership*, and *School Administrator* are editorially reviewed publications. While these journals publish valuable and informative articles, the substance of the articles has not undergone peer review and therefore should not be treated in the same way that you might treat a peer-reviewed article.

Non–peer-reviewed articles, including those presented in newspapers and periodicals, often report opinions or perspectives that do not have an empirical or theoretical basis.

Practitioner-scholars must be careful not to rely on non–peer-reviewed sources to construct a scholarly argument. Rather, if you decide to use non–peer-reviewed sources in your literature review, we recommend using them only to augment and/or highlight key perspectives in your literature review. For example, if you develop a literature review about high school graduation rates, you might consider including an exposé published in a periodical (such as *Education Week*) that described the experience of a student who had or was considering dropping out of school. Though blogs and online communications have become increasingly popular forms of informal communication, they have not yet been recognized by many researchers as legitimate sources to convey empirical research. Thus, while it may be tempting to summarize or include research presented in a blog post or to highlight information obtained from a news outlet, you should always keep in mind that others may discount the findings you present from these sources, as they do not typically undergo rigorous review. We suggest that your literature review primarily includes peer-reviewed articles, edited book chapters, academic books (many of which are peer-reviewed), conference papers (to some extent), and research or technical reports from respected research organizations (for example, the National Center for Education Statistics, the Institute for Education Sciences, and so on). In general, literature reviews should *not* primarily rely on web pages, blogs, newspapers, or periodicals, as these publications are not peer-reviewed and frequently express an opinion or advocate for a position that may or may not be theoretically substantiated or empirically based.

As illustrated in Figure 3.2, we envision the sources you use in your literature review as a pyramid, with the base of the literature review, and thus the basis for your argument, resting on peer-reviewed journal articles. The body of the literature, then, is primarily based on peer-reviewed journal articles, books, edited book chapters, technical reports, conference papers, and conference proceedings. Within this pyramid, newspapers, periodicals, websites, and blogs should only be used sparingly to highlight key points or to add emphasis drawn from current, popular discussions.

Figure 3.2 Body of the Literature Review and Its Relation to Different Sources

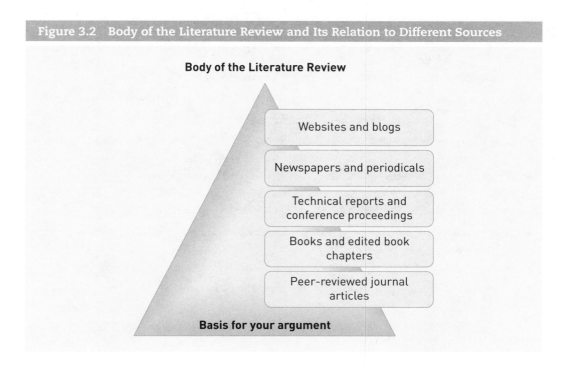

Body of the Literature Review

- Websites and blogs
- Newspapers and periodicals
- Technical reports and conference proceedings
- Books and edited book chapters
- Peer-reviewed journal articles

Basis for your argument

Identifying and Evaluating Research as Good or Reputable

Assuming you have identified your primary and secondary sources, another challenge related to assessing the literature involves determining whether the literature is good or reputable, and whether the findings presented can be trusted. Unfortunately, there is not a single model for assessing the quality of a research study, nor is there a specific test that accurately determines whether the research is good or bad. If research has undergone some type of peer-review, it is generally thought to have been conducted in accordance with the traditions of that discipline. However, this does not mean that the research presented is necessarily the best research available given the problem of practice you are seeking to explore.

Rather than offering a decision-making model for evaluating the quality of a primary or secondary source, we provide you with a series of questions to consider when evaluating whether to include a published research study in your literature review. As illustrated in Table 3.2, these questions are not exhaustive. Rather, they are specific and mostly aimed at helping you decide whether the study supports the needs of your literature review.

While the questions in Table 3.2 might also be used as a beginning point for evaluating and critiquing the selected literature, we suggest that a more intensive evaluation process is

Table 3.2 Questions to Consider When Evaluating the Literature

Consideration	Questions to Ask
Research Topic	• Is the topic related to the problem of practice you are interested in examining?
	• Can you make a connection between the topic presented and the problem of practice you are studying?
Research Question	• Does the question posed by the study relate to your problem of practice?
	• Does the question posed by the study justify further study of your problem of practice?
	• Is the question presented in a clear and unbiased manner?
Epistemology, Methodology, and Method	• Has the author made clear her/his epistemological perspective(s)?
	• Does the methodology align with the epistemological considerations?
	• Do the research methods presented in the study align with (or support) the research questions?
Results/Findings	• Has the author(s) fully described the results/findings?
	• In the case of qualitative study, has the author explained how she/he moved from data sources to themes or conclusions?
	• In the case of a quantitative study, has the author explained how she/he arrived at the results and which statistical tests were used?
	• Does the author provide sufficient detail or depth to support her/his findings?
Conclusions or Implications	• Does the author link or make connections to the existing literature in interpreting her/his results/findings?
	• Do the results/findings presented have clear or compelling connections to theory, research, or practice?
	• Has the author(s) developed implications that expand on existing research or improve existing practice?

CARRYING OUT A LITERATURE REVIEW

Let's assume that you want to focus on the differences in student achievement, particularly reading achievement. Your interest is primarily to understand these differences, particularly why some students perform better in reading than others. Clearly, searching the literature to identify what prompts or causes differences in reading achievement is too broad. You will receive countless hits with this topic, but few may be directly aligned with your topic. Thus, you narrow the topic to something more manageable. For example, you consider differences in third grade reading achievement based on the instructional method used (such as direct instruction, shared reading, guided reading, or literature discussion circles).

After identifying the topic, you begin by identifying possible search terms. These search terms include, "reading achievement" and "reading assessments," which identify broadly that you are interested in reading achievement. However, connecting these terms with the instructional method using Boolean operators seems to provide you with results that directly relate to your study. For example, "reading achievement" AND "instructional method" or "reading achievement" AND "direct instruction" provide you with fewer results, but results that more directly aligned with your study. When you are unsure about which search terms to use, you consult with ERIC, as it provides a thesaurus that helps you to identify terms to use in the search engine. Next, you set up a spreadsheet or list of the search terms, as well as the combinations of search terms you intend to use. It is important to recognize that this list will grow and change throughout your literature search. Moreover, you realize that the search terms you selected originally do not produce the results that you

need and thus you need to select new search terms altogether. Next, you select a search engine to begin identifying specific references or studies that relate to your topic. You select a search engine with your librarian's assistance, deciding to use Education Full Text, ERIC, and JSTOR.

As you begin searching, you recognize that many of the results do not relate to your study. Thus, you have to identify only those studies that do relate and that potentially help you build an argument in your literature review. You specifically consider three things. First, does the topic or focus of the article align with your topic? Second, does the methodology or method align with your methodology or method? You consider methodology and method because you know that the literature frequently serves as a powerful source of models for your own research study. Third, what do the results/findings suggest about the need for your study? At this stage, you determine whether past research has studied your research topic extensively.

In reviewing the articles that are returned, you do not begin by reading every article. Rather, you want to work smarter and focus only on getting a general sense of the articles. You decide to only read those articles that relate to your study in greater depth once you have reviewed the literature and begun identifying key ideas. Thus, you focus on reading each article's **abstract**, which is a brief summary of the contents of the article, typically placed at the beginning of an article. You read these abstracts to determine whether the study fits and should be read in greater depth. As you read the abstract, you take note of the methodology and methods used, key

(Continued)

(Continued)

results/findings, and conclusions. After reading the abstract, you ask yourself whether the article fits with the focus of your literature review. If it does, you include it! If it does not, you exclude it. While it is tempting to continue searching the literature to discover every reference that exists, the likelihood of doing this successfully is small. Instead, you decide to work strategically and identify only those articles that support the argument that you are trying to make or that provide justification for the study that you are trying to complete.

You begin writing your literature review while still reviewing the literature. Thus, at this early stage, you begin building an outline for your literature review. While you plan to review the literature more closely as you construct your specific argument, you've found it helpful to begin adding references to specific sections of your literature review outline to ensure that you have sufficiently covered the literature. Also, you find that this helps you begin to see how your argument might unfold. You continually remind yourself of Rudestam and Newton's (1992) words, "Build an argument not a library" (p. 49).

Once you have begun outlining your literature review, you return to read the included articles in greater depth. Not only does this familiarize you with the research in this area, but it also provides you with an opportunity to see which references other researchers have identified and thus other references you may want to include in your argument. While it may be tempting to simply construct a literature review using the references identified in other research articles, you resist the temptation and consult the original articles to determine what the actual interpretation of the data was and how the original author made the claim.

You now begin the work of evaluating the articles in detail. You create a table that highlights both a summary and critique of each article. You then incorporate your summary and critique of each article into your literature review outline and begin the work of writing up your literature review. You realize that this process goes far beyond simply summarizing what previous authors have written. Instead, it involves summarizing previous research results/findings, analyzing or interpreting the results/findings within the context of your research topic, and synthesizing the results/findings so that it is clear how they relate to your study and how past findings relate to each other. You remind yourself again and again that effectively written literature reviews have a balance of summary, analysis, and synthesis.

Focus Questions

1. How might you make decisions around which articles to include and exclude in the literature review?

2. How would you decide which articles to elaborate upon in greater depth within your literature review?

needed. This is particularly true in that a central task of the literature review is to critically evaluate the literature, not simply summarize it. Johnson and Christensen (2010) suggested that, "To be an effective consumer of research, you should not consider the results of any one study to be conclusive. You need to look across multiple studies to see whether the findings are repeatedly confirmed" (p. 78). As such, determining whether the research presented in a published article or book is good research involves asking additional questions. This evaluation process involves looking specifically at the basic structure of the research study (that is, its introduction, methodology, methods, results/findings, and discussion/implications) to determine what each study reported and whether the study's results/findings are consistent with or different from past research. As illustrated in Table 3.3, the analysis of the literature involves asking questions of a specific nature unlike the more general questions proposed in Table 3.2.

We suggest that you keep clear records of your answers to each of the questions above as related to a given published source, as this can become the basis for the writing up your literature review.

Table 3.3 Questions to Consider When Evaluating Quantitative and Qualitative Studies

	Quantitative Studies	Qualitative Studies
Introduction	• Is the research topic clearly stated?	• Is the research topic clearly stated?
	• Is the research problem defined clearly?	• Is the research problem defined clearly?
	• Is the purpose of the study clearly defined?	• Is the purpose of the study clearly stated?
	• Are the research questions posed in an unbiased manner?	• Are the research questions presented clearly?
	• Has the author identified clear research hypotheses?	• Is the methodology and method clearly stated?
	• Is the theory from which the hypotheses derived clearly stated?	• Has the theoretical perspective or lens been introduced?
Method	• Are the demographics of the study participants or sample population stated clearly?	• Have the research setting and participants been described in detail?
	• Have sampling procedures been clearly articulated?	• Has the sampling procedure been described in detail?
	• Have the research instruments been described in sufficient detail?	• Have the methods used to collect the data been described in detail?
	• Have the procedures used been described?	• Have limitations of the analysis been explained?
	• Have the statistical tests used in the analysis been described?	• Has the analytic approach been explained in detail?
	• Were limitations explained in sufficient detail?	• Does the researcher make clear how she/he triangulated or checked findings across multiple data sources?

(Continued)

Table 3.3	(Continued)	
	Quantitative Studies	**Qualitative Studies**
Results/ Findings	• Were appropriate statistical tests used to analyze the data? • Were the results presented clearly and with appropriate annotation? • Was any part of the data ignored, such as some participants being excluded? • Can the results be generalized?	• Were the findings presented with sufficient detail and depth? • Did the author interpret the quotes and/or statements? • Were competing or contrasting views presented throughout the findings? • Did the author use multiple sources of evidence to support her/his findings? • Does the author present her/his findings in a manner that is consistent with their analytic approach (i.e., thematic analysis is presented as themes)?
Discussion	• Do the researchers clearly explain the meaning and significance of the results of the study? • Are the findings discussed in relation to the theoretical framework and/or previous literature? • Are alternative explanations for the study results presented and/or evaluated? • Are limitations of the study discussed?	• Does the researcher connect her/his findings with previous research? • Are the findings discussed in relation to the theoretical or conceptual framework? • Are limitations noted and/or described?

Source: Adapted from Johnson & Christensen, 2010, pp. 79–80

REFLECTIVE OPPORTUNITY 3.3

As you begin to summarize, analyze, and synthesize the literature, it is important to consider how you will give proper credit to ideas that were originally presented in the literature. This is particularly important when you are not directly quoting, but instead paraphrasing big ideas from your literature review.

1. What might be some strategies that you can use to ensure that you give proper credit and do not plagiarize?

STAYING ORGANIZED AND UPDATED: A FEW REMINDERS

While it is beyond the scope of this textbook to provide you with a complete set of tools to conduct the literature review, we can offer you the following suggestions (some of which we mentioned above) to make the process more manageable.

First, be diligent about keeping track of your references, article downloads, and search terms. Both in our own research and our students' research, we often hear the question, "Where did I find that reference?" This question is frustrating to answer, particularly if articles are hidden in cryptic file names or buried in a stack of freshly printed paper. It is important to develop a straightforward labeling system for your files (for example, author-year), and to commit to keeping track of your references and article downloads as you are reviewing the literature. Using a simple Microsoft Excel spreadsheet, Word document, Google document, Pages, or Numbers spreadsheet to record the references as you search for them will assist you in preparing your reference list at the end of your project. More important, by keeping track of your search terms and the number of results derived, you will prevent yourself from duplicating searches, expanding rather than narrowing your search range, and in the process wasting rather than saving time.

Second, take notes as you are reading and be prepared to construct an annotated bibliography. Whether using a citation management software tool (such as Mendeley) or simply noting key points in the margins of printed articles, we cannot stress enough the importance of taking notes as you read. As you begin writing your literature review, consult these notes to identify key points or salient themes to discuss.

Third, use technology as much as possible, particularly as you work to stay organized. For instance, it is helpful to store your files in more than one place, avoiding the possibility of losing your files in a computer crash. You may want to store your files on a jump drive, hard drive, and/or cloud-based storage system (such as Dropbox). Also, there are a number of citation management tools available (for example, Mendeley, RefWorks, Zotero, or Endnote) that can assist you in cataloging the references you gather, as well as offering features to assist you in noting key points, methodological considerations, or limitations that you can then integrate into your literature review. Combined with file storing and sharing tools (such as Dropbox or Google Drive), citation management tools allow you to maintain your reference library across multiple computers or devices and ensure that your quick search at work during a free moment does not result in duplicate references and confusion or misdirection when you begin searching again at home.

USING TECHNOLOGY TO COMPLETE THE LITERATURE REVIEW

Literature reviews need not result in stacks of paper and piles of books. Technology has increasingly made reviewing the literature something that can be an electronic and even paperless endeavor (Paulus, Lester, & Dempster, 2014). Most peer-reviewed research journals now publish their articles online in the form of easily downloadable Adobe PDFs. Further, the availability of scanners and other digitization tools enables many students to convert sections of books and book chapters to an electronic format, if such materials are not already in electronic form. In this section, we offer a few practical suggestions with which to organize and manage the information you gather from your literature reviews. We focus specifically on how citation management systems, such as Mendeley, RefWorks, Zotero, or Endnote, are useful tools for practitioner-scholars during the literature review process. We also highlight how tools that support annotation or note-taking directly to electronic files allow for you to begin the important process of analyzing your literature, including computer-assisted qualitative data analysis software packages.

Citation Management Systems

There are a variety of citation management systems available, including Mendeley, RefWorks, Zotero, and Endnote. These citation management systems can be used to efficiently store and manage your electronic documents. Many of these systems can also be used within academic databases to directly download articles, while also extracting the article's details (author, title, journal, and so on) for use in generating a bibliography. While many of these citation management systems offer similar features, we focus more specifically on Mendeley.

Mendeley is a particularly useful citation management system, with some describing it as "the next generation of citation management software" (Hensley, 2011, p. 207). Mendeley is free (up to 1 GB) software that is platform and browser agnostic and includes a desktop, web, and mobile version. You can therefore easily synchronize your literature database across multiple machines and even share it with colleagues. For instance, you could access an article from your smartphone that you downloaded at your home computer earlier in the day. Mendeley also allows you to collaborate with others, developing "groups" around a particular literature base. Further, Mendeley is structured like a social networking site, allowing you to set up a profile page with contacts. This feature may be particularly useful for staying up-to-date on literature, as you can keep in contact with other practitoner-scholars and view the literature that they are uploading and/or sharing. Figure 3.3 shows the Mendeley desktop library interface, with folders and collaborative groups on the left, documents listed in the middle, and bibliographic information listed on the right (for example, author, year of publication, and so on).

Figure 3.3   An Example of a Mendeley Library

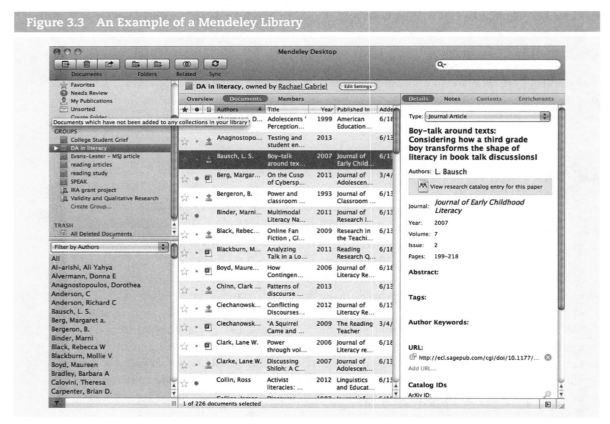

Source: Mendeley.com

Many people use citation management systems, such as Mendeley, with the hopes of automatically generating a reference list using a particular citation style (such as APA or MLA) and/or more easily creating in-text citations. However, at this stage of development, many of the citation management systems available require you to spend a great deal of time editing the metadata or bibliographic data (author, year, and so on) extracted from the database in order to have an accurately formatted bibliography. If an automatically generated reference list is appealing to you, it may be worth the energy and time required to carefully edit and maintain the metadata so that accurate citations are included in your research.

Annotation Tools

During a literature review, taking notes while reading is important, whether you are working with paper copies or have decided to go paperless. Many of the citation management systems not only support storing and organizing files, but also support you in reading and annotating your files. Annotating your files involves highlighting sections of text and applying comments ("sticky notes") to important passages. Even if you do not use an application such as Mendeley, it is helpful to use a tool that allows you to highlight key passages and make notes relevant to your literature review. As you begin developing key understandings across the literature, you will return to these notes again and again. Mendeley, like other annotation tools, even allows you to export your annotated files and share them with others. Figure 3.4 provides an example of an annotated and highlighted article within Mendeley.

Figure 3.4   An Example of Annotating in Mendeley

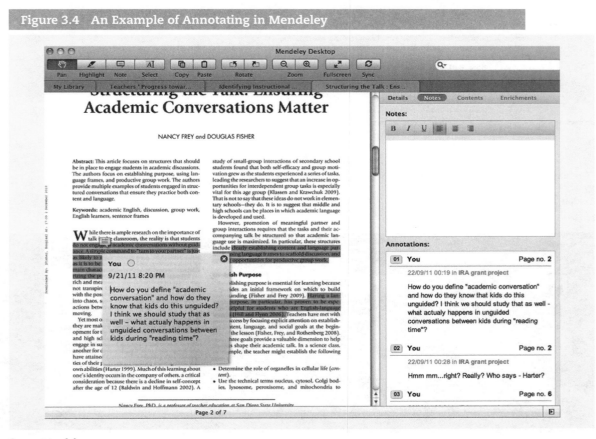

Source: Mendeley.com

Onwuegbuzie, Leech, and Collins (2012) suggested that analyzing literature is somewhat analogous to analyzing qualitative data, something we discuss in detail in Chapter 7. As such, many people are beginning to use computer-assisted qualitative data analysis software (CAQDAS) packages to support the analysis of their literature. CAQDAS packages are comprehensive data analysis software packages that support researchers engaged in qualitative data analysis. Many of these packages, such as NVivo and ATLAS.ti, provide you with a way to systematize your literature review process, while supporting you as you engage in analyzing and synthesizing your literature. Figure 3.5 illustrates how you might use the memoing (or note-taking) feature in ATLAS.ti to make notes attached to a segment of an article or to the entire article.

Figure 3.5   An Example of Using ATLAS.ti for Annotating and Analyzing the Literature

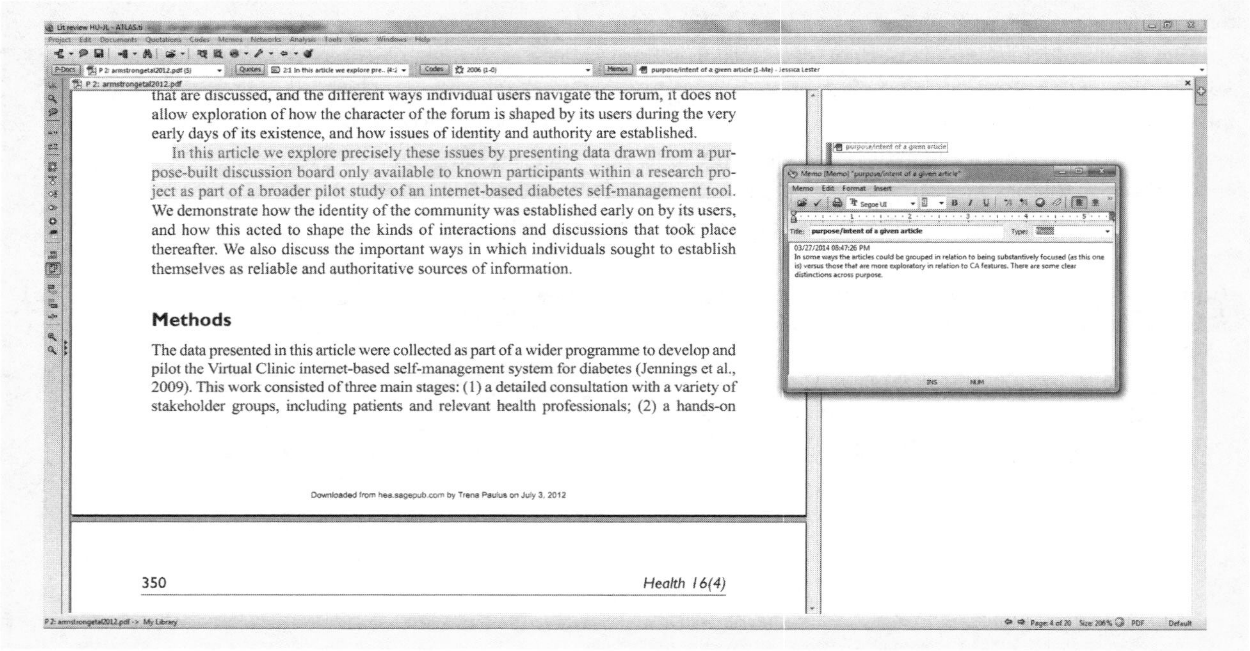

Source: ATLAS.ti

REFLECTIVE OPPORTUNITY 3.4

As you explore the potential use of a citation management software package, consider the following questions:

1. Despite the conveniences of using citation management software, what might be some of the limitations of these technological tools?

2. Why might some researchers choose not to invest time learning how to use a citation management software package such as Mendeley or Zotero?

SUMMARY

In this chapter, we focused on the process of conducting a literature review. We began by highlighting differences in the types of resources that you might use in your literature review. We specifically noted the importance of using peer-reviewed sources to construct or frame your literature review. We also presented an overarching process for conducting the literature review. We concluded by discussing some of the ways that technology, particularly citation management systems, can be used throughout the literature review process.

KEY TERMS

Abstract 59

Citation Management System 61

Computer-Assisted Qualitative
  Data Analysis Software
  (CAQDAS) 63

Database 53

Editorially Reviewed Source 54

Mendeley 62

Non–Peer-Reviewed
  Source 55

Peer-Reviewed Source 54

Primary Source 54

Secondary Source 54

QUESTIONS TO CONSIDER

1. What is the purpose(s) of the literature review in the research process?

2. How might the various sections of a literature review be organized?

3. How is a literature review different for a qualitative and quantitative research study?

4. What are different strategies that you can use to search the literature?

5. What are the different types of literature and which type(s) of the literature should you primarily include in your literature review?

6. What are some of the distinguishing characteristics of "quality" literature?

7. How might technology support your literature review?

CHAPTER EXERCISES

1. Select one of the databases listed above (such as Academic Search Premier) and carry out a literature search related to your research topic. What strategies did you use? Did you retrieve the types of articles you were expecting?

2. Returning to your research topic, spend some time carrying out some initial searches. As you do so, develop a systematic approach for recording your search terms/keywords and the Boolean Operators that you use within your search.

After completing an initial search, consider the following questions:

a. How did your results differ as you used different Boolean Operators?

b. As you carried out your initial search, did you identify a need to adjust your keywords/search terms?

c. If you made an adjustment, what led you to make the change?

3. Return to some of the literature that you retrieved from the search you conducted in the second chapter exercise. Spend time distinguishing between the types of sources you retrieved, reflecting on the following questions:

   a. Identify the types of resources that your search retrieved. What were the primary types of sources retrieved?

   b. How might your evaluation of the type of sources retrieved impact whether you incorporate these sources into your literature review?

4. Download one of the citation management systems (such as Mendeley or Zotero) and explore the features that might be useful to your own literature review. Consider the price, ability to synchronize across mobile devices, annotation features, and citation format support.

LEARNING EXTENSIONS

To further your understanding of the literature review process, consider reading the following two publications. For an excellent discussion of how to go about critiquing the literature, consult Boote and Beile's (2005) article in *Educational Researcher*.

For a useful guide for how to conduct a literature review, with a particular focus on analyzing literature, consider Hart's (1998) book entitled *Doing a Literature Review: Releasing the Social Science Research Imagination*.

Sharpen your skills with SAGE edge!

edge.sagepub.com/lochmiller

SAGE edge for Students provides a personalized approach to help you accomplish your coursework goals in an easy-to-use learning environment. You'll find action plans, mobile-friendly eFlashcards, and quizzes as well as videos, web resources, and links to SAGE journal articles to support and expand on the concepts presented in this chapter.

4

CONSIDERING RESEARCH ETHICS

FACING ETHICAL CHALLENGES

Let's imagine that you are a school principal who is interested in studying teacher professional development in your school. You want to know what classroom teachers think about the professional development they are currently receiving, as well as the professional development that they need to become more effective at teaching the district's new math curriculum. As you consider your study, you begin realizing that many of the questions that you would like to ask teachers potentially place them in an awkward situation. For example, you would like to know whether teachers think the professional development they are currently receiving is helping them to be more successful. However, as the primary professional development provider in the school and the teachers' supervisor, you realize that asking teachers to critique the professional development they receive may make them uncomfortable or provide you with information that may bias your future evaluation of the teachers. Thus, you begin considering the ethical challenges associated with your study's design and how these challenges can be dealt with as you conduct your research.

INTRODUCTION

As illustrated in the opening vignette, the research process is a complex endeavor that typically involves a practitioner-scholar interacting with people in their everyday environments. Not surprisingly, the human aspect of the research process demands that we think carefully about how we interact with others and the consequences of our interactions. Central to these interactions is the need to make ethical decisions, many of which are not black and white and require critical thinking and reflection.

In this chapter, we focus on the role of ethics in the research process. We first provide a general overview of why ethics is important to

Learning Objectives

By the end of the chapter, you will be able to:

- Summarize the role of ethics in the research process.

- Discuss the role of institutional regulations and policies in research ethics.

- Identify the purposes and procedures common to Institutional Review Boards (IRB).

- Report ethical considerations for managing research relationships with schools and districts.

- Explain key ethical considerations when planning, designing, carrying out, and reporting research.

- Define the unique ethical considerations inherent to particular research approaches (for example, qualitative versus quantitative research methodologies).

- Construct examples of ethical issues that you might encounter when engaging in educational research.

the research process. Then, we discuss the legal and institutional requirements, such as the Institutional Review Board, that shape how research is and should be carried out in relationship to ethical decision-making. Finally, we discuss more specifically the role of ethics across the research process and highlight some of the unique considerations for practitioner-scholars engaged in qualitative versus quantitative research studies. We also give particular attention to practitioner-scholars who carry out action research studies, as this particular approach to research brings with it some unique ethical dilemmas.

ETHICS AND EDUCATIONAL RESEARCH

In this textbook, we position ethics as being foundational to the entire research process. As such, before we discuss the details of particular research methodologies or methods, we believe it is critical to consider the ethical challenges and commitments that should undergird any sound research study. Other writers have noted, however, that research ethics becomes more "practically relevant *after*" you have made decisions around your research methodology, methods, and overall research design (Vogt, Gardner, & Haeffele, 2012, p. 228). We recognize this reality and thus throughout the textbook, you will find that many of the Reflective Opportunities focus on thinking about how ethical issues may arise in relationship to a particular methodology or approach to data analysis. Nonetheless, we suggest that before we discuss specific methodologies further, it is important to make sense of the role and impact of research ethics for you, as a practitioner-scholar.

To begin, how should we think about research ethics? At the core, research ethics involves practitioner-scholars acting in a responsible and fair way, while continually keeping in mind the interests, needs, and protection of current and/or future research participants. In general, ethical responsibilities are based on a set of norms or rules that have been established by a particular discipline, field, and/or legal body. For instance, the American Educational Research Association (AERA) has developed ethical standards for educational researchers. Within their ethical standards, AERA (2002) noted that:

> It is of paramount importance that educational researchers respect the rights, privacy, dignity, and sensitivities of their research populations and also the integrity of the institutions within which the research occurs. Educational researchers should be especially careful in working with children and other vulnerable populations. (p. 3)

This statement is an example of how one disciplinary body, in this case AERA, describes the ethical responsibilities of educational researchers. The broader AERA guidelines, which are frequently updated, offer even more specific suggestions and are an important resource for practitioner-scholars to review (see Table 4.1).

Other disciplinary bodies, such as those focused on school psychology, have established ethical standards (see, for example, Jacob, Decker, & Hartshorne, 2011) that continually change, particularly as researchers begin exploring new types of data (such as online data). As you embark on the research process, it is therefore important to identify whether there are ethical guidelines that your field has established, as these guidelines may help you think carefully about your ethical responsibilities.

Table 4.1 Illustrative Ethical Principles

	AERA's Ethical Principles Guiding Research Practices
Principle A: Professional Competence	Education researchers strive to maintain the highest level of competence in their work; recognize the limitations of their expertise; and they undertake only those tasks for which they are qualified by education, training, or experience. They recognize the need for ongoing education in order to remain professionally competent; and they utilize the appropriate scientific, scholarly, professional, technical, and administrative resources needed to ensure competence in their professional activities. They consult with other professionals when necessary for the benefit of their students, research participants, and clients.
Principle B: Integrity	Education researchers are honest, fair, and respectful of others in their professional activities—in research, teaching, practice, and service. Education researchers do not knowingly act in ways that jeopardize the welfare of others. Education researchers conduct their professional activities in ways that are worthy of trust and confidence.
Principle C: Professional, Scientific, and Scholarly Responsibility	Education researchers adhere to the highest scientific and professional standards and accept responsibility for their work. Education researchers value the public trust in research and are concerned about their ethical behavior and behavior of other education researchers that might compromise that trust. Education researchers understand that they form a community and show respect for other education researchers even when they disagree on theoretical, methodological, or personal approaches to professional activities. While endeavoring always to be collegial, education researchers must never let the desire to be collegial outweigh their shared responsibility for ethical behavior. When appropriate, they consult with colleagues in order to prevent or avoid unethical conduct.
Principle D: Respect for People's Rights, Dignity, and Diversity	Education researchers respect the rights, dignity, and worth of all people and take care to do no harm in the conduct of their work. In their research, they have a special obligation to protect the rights, welfare, and dignity of research participants. They are sensitive to cultural, individual, and role differences in teaching, studying, and providing service to groups of people with distinctive characteristics. They strive to eliminate bias in their professional activities, and they do not tolerate any forms of discrimination based on race; ethnicity; culture; national origin; gender; sexual orientation; gender identity; age; religion; language; disability; health conditions; socioeconomic status; or marital, domestic, or parental status. In all of their work-related activities, education researchers acknowledge the rights of others to hold values, attitudes, and opinions that differ from their own, and they treat others with dignity and respect.
Principle E: Social Responsibility	Education researchers are aware of their professional and scientific responsibility to the communities and societies in which they live and work. They apply and make public their knowledge in order to contribute to the public good. When undertaking research, they strive to advance scientific and scholarly knowledge and to serve the public good.

Source: Drawn from AERA's Code of Ethics (2011, pp. 146–147)

Legal bodies and regulations also inform how practitioner-scholars should make sense of what research ethics entails. For instance, the U.S. Government Office for Human Research Protections provides definitions and guidelines related to what practitioner-scholars need to consider from a legal standpoint when conducting a research study. These ethical guidelines require that any institution that conducts research funded by a U.S. government agency must have an Institutional Review Board or ethics board. We discuss the Institutional Review Board and your responsibilities related to it later in this chapter.

Beyond established codes of ethics, standards, and legal guidelines, ethical responsibilities are often linked to a practitioner-scholar's views on notions of morality and what they conceive as being their moral responsibility during the research process. In our society, there is indeed some overlap between legal and moral responsibilities. Vogt et al. (2012) described a researcher's ethical responsibilities as being divided into three groups, including the research participants, other researchers (that is, our colleagues), and society more generally. Figure 4.1 illustrates this.

Ultimately, your commitment to research participants is to protect them from any harm (that is, an intentional or unintentional experience or event that adversely impacts the research participant or a group of participants), ensure that everything you learn about and from them remains confidential, and that you do not do anything without their consent. Your commitment to your colleagues is to keep in mind that the education research community is built on a foundation of trust and openness (Vogt et al., 2012). It is expected that you remain transparent about your research practices, avoid dishonesty, and abide by the established ethical standards for your field or research discipline.

One of the ethical standards assumed in educational research is that you will disclose any potential conflict(s) of interest. A conflict of interest occurs when a researcher may benefit financially from the research that she or he is conducting. For instance, a practitioner-scholar who studies the effectiveness of a curriculum developed by a company in which they hold stock has a conflict of interest in that she or he may benefit financially from research findings that indicate the curriculum is effective. It is therefore important to think through potential conflicts of interest when both designing and carrying out your study.

As the AERA (2011) ethical standards highlighted, one of our responsibilities is to "value the public trust in research" and be "concerned about . . . ethical behavior and behavior of other education researchers that might compromise that trust" (p. 146). Thus, beyond ethical responsibilities to colleagues, practitioner-scholars who conduct education research must recognize that their actions as researchers impact society in some way. Thus, ethical responsibilities must be considered in light of how research conduct and misconduct ultimately breaks public trust and may have a deleterious effect on society and the individual research participants. To this end, it is particularly important to always *invite* rather than *demand* the consent of participants, something that we discuss in greater detail next.

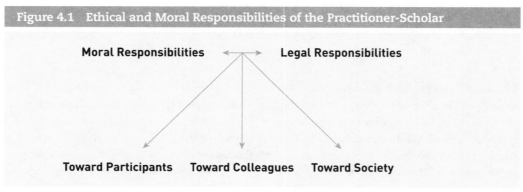

Figure 4.1   Ethical and Moral Responsibilities of the Practitioner-Scholar

Moral Responsibilities ← → Legal Responsibilities

Toward Participants   Toward Colleagues   Toward Society

Source: Adapted from Vogt et al., 2012, p. 229

Inviting Participants' Consent and Assent

At the most basic level, ethics in educational research involves: (a) inviting the consent of participants, (b) ensuring no harm is done, and (c) protecting the identity of participants. Consent is the process of informing and getting agreement from a research participant to participate in the study. Technically, there are two types of consent: direct consent and third-party consent. Direct consent, which is preferred, occurs when the individual being asked to participate in a research study gives their consent directly to the researcher. Alternatively, third-party consent occurs when someone other than the individual being asked to participate in the study gives consent on the participant's behalf. This type of consent may be necessary at times. For example, third-party consent is required when working with minors or may be required when working with people with cognitive or emotional disabilities.

Informed consent is the process of informing the participant about his or her rights as a research participant. This includes discussing with the participant the purpose of your research study, as well as the types of activities that they will be asked to complete as a research participant. In this process, you should also inform the participant about the potential risks that may arise during their participation and the way that you, as the practitioner-scholar, will handle these risks should they arise. A particularly important part of the informed consent process is to explain to the participant that their participation is *completely voluntary* and that they are free to withdraw from the study at any time without penalty. It is important to understand that informed consent applies to individuals who are 18 years of age. When a study deals with minors (individuals who are younger than 18 years of age), the informed consent process also includes the child's parent or guardian, as they must provide their consent prior to the study beginning. In addition, the child must offer their assent to participate in the study. Assent refers to the process wherein a minor agrees to participate in a research study.

It is essential that you remember that a participant's consent is *always* voluntary and may not be permanent. At any time before, during, or after the start or completion of a study, a participant has the right to withdraw their consent to participate. In this way, it is helpful to think about acquiring consent as a process—one that you will likely need to revisit throughout the course of your study. Why does this matter? If at any time during a study, there is an adverse event, such as a research participant feeling stressed during an interview or a researcher discovering a previously unknown condition, you must respond to these needs and reaffirm to the participant that they are not obligated to participate in the study.

In addition, participants may grant their consent in a variety of ways, including signing a paper, offering verbal consent, and so on. You should consult your institution's guidelines, specifically the Institutional Review Board, as you develop the best way to invite and record the informed consent of your participants. Your Institutional Review Board will likely have samples available of how to structure your informed consent and assent forms. Figure 4.2 provides an example of an informed consent document, and Figure 4.3 provides an example of an assent statement.

In the example provided in Figure 4.3, you may have noted that the assent statement invited the children to write their names, acknowledging that they understood the nature of the study and agreed to participate. Depending upon the age of the children and what is believed to be the most thoughtful and meaningful way to invite assent, a researcher might invite their verbal assent, using a statement such as Figure 4.4, for instance.

Figure 4.2   Parent or Guardian Informed Consent

Informed Consent Letter

Your child is being invited to take part in a project designed to explore the use of a method of psychoeducational assessment, called dynamic assessment, in which there is teaching within the test. Its primary goal is to identify barriers to effective learning and to test various ways of overcoming those barriers, thus getting at "unobstructed" learning potential. The tasks used in DA are usually interesting to children: puzzle-type problems, some computer-based tasks, but all are tasks that require conscious logical thought. In dynamic assessment, failure is not allowed; the children are given all the help they need to complete the tasks, so the children usually find it rewarding, especially when they are helped to succeed at tasks that might have seemed initially too challenging. The outcomes are often used to help teachers and parents construct classroom and home-based approaches and strategies that lead to more effective learning and intervention for children with autism spectrum disorders (ASD).

INFORMATION ABOUT PARTICIPANTS' INVOLVEMENT IN THE STUDY

The assessment will range from 30 minutes to three hours, although it is unlikely that any child's assessment would continue significantly longer than one hour. We will not keep your child at the tasks beyond his or her tolerance. Your child will participate in either an individual dynamic assessment or a group dynamic assessment with a small number of other children. You may be asked to allow your child to participate in both individual and group dynamic assessment. For the purposes of this study, the examiners will establish a working rapport, capitalizing on something your child already knows how to do or is known to enjoy. A series of tasks will then be presented with help given where needed. Possible tasks in the present case include: estimating the passage of time in a computer-based clock task; determining which two of five words do not belong (i.e., are not members of a class); drawing model designs both from visible models and from memory; constructing designs by imagining the sequential stacking of patterned stencils; remembering the positions of buttons in successive presentations of 3 × 3 arrangements; connecting dots to form geometric figures; some verbal tasks if appropriate—and possibly others as we begin to observe abilities and obstacles to learning your child displays. Your decision to allow your child to take part in the study is voluntary. You and your child are free to choose for him or her to not to take part in the study or to stop taking part in the study at any time without any penalty. Further, your decision for your child to participate or not participate in this study has no effect on present or future treatment provided by The Testing Place's professional affiliates or any other practitioner who may have told you about this opportunity. If you choose to allow your child to participate, your child must be between the ages of 7–16 at the time that the study is to begin. In addition, your child must have either a school or clinical diagnosis consistent with the Diagnostic and Statistical Manual of Mental Disorders-IV for ASD (American Psychiatric Association, 2000). Your child cannot participate in this study if he or she has any genetic conditions often associated with ASD, such as Fragile X, uncorrected vision/hearing impairments, and uncontrolled seizure disorders. This assessment will last from 30 minutes up to three hours. We may also ask you a few questions regarding your child's developmental history and background.

If your child meets the inclusion criteria as stated above, he or she will be invited to participate in the dynamic assessment. If you subsequently choose to have your child participate:

***Your child will participate in the individual and/or group dynamic assessment for up to three hours per session.

***There will only be one individual session and one group session. You may be asked to consider having your child participate in both an individual and group session.

***You will allow your child's strengths and weaknesses to be assessed with dynamic assessment tests.

***Throughout the study, we will provide you with copies of any assessment results, as well as oral descriptions.

RISKS

Though there do not appear to be any risks related to your child's participation in the study, the researchers will tell your child that he or she may withdraw from the study at anytime without any penalties.

BENEFITS

Participating in this study may provide promising benefits; your child will receive free dynamic assessment, which includes his or her engagement in tasks independently and with assistance as needed. In addition, you will be contributing to future interventions and assessment procedures of other students with ASD.

CONFIDENTIALITY

All information acquired in this study, including, but not limited to, answers to questionnaires, history, and results of assessments, will be kept strictly confidential. Data will be stored securely in a locked office at The University of Southeast and will be made available only to persons conducting the study unless participants specifically give permission in writing to do otherwise. Data stored digitally will be stored in a password protected file. It will be securely stored for a 10-year period, after which time it will be permanently destroyed. Data derived from this research could be used in reports, presentations, and publications but your child will not be individually identified. No reference will be made in oral or written reports that could link participants to the study. Pseudonyms will be assigned to each participant and real names will be known only by the researchers. Any information with your child's name attached will not be shared with anyone outside the research team. Further, if you choose to share any developmental or academic history reports with the research team, we will delete all references to your child, replacing them with a pseudonym. Further, as soon as the researchers have completed reviewing the academic histories, we will destroy (shred) the documents. Until then, they will be stored in a locked file cabinet in the School of Education.

CONTACT INFORMATION

If you have questions at any time about the study or the procedures (or your child experiences adverse effects as a result of participating in this study) you may contact the researcher. If you have questions about your rights as a participant, contact the Office of Research Compliance Officer at (xxx) xxx-xxxx.

(Continued)

Figure 4.2 (Continued)

PARTICIPATION

Your child's participation in this study is voluntary; you may decline participation without penalty. If you decide to consent to your child's participation, you may withdraw your child from the study at anytime without penalty and without loss of benefits to which your child is otherwise entitled. Testing will occur at The Testing Place, located at 1111 Testing Place.

CONSENT

I understand the procedures described above. My questions have been answered to my satisfaction, and I agree to allow my child _____to participate in this study.

☐ I have been provided a copy of this form.
    Parent's signature _____ Date
    Researcher's signature _____ Date

☐ My child may participate in individual dynamic assessment.
    Parent's signature _____ Date
    Researcher's signature _____ Date

☐ My child may participate in group dynamic assessment.
    Parent's signature _____ Date
    Researcher's signature_____Date

Figure 4.3 Assent for Study

Assent Form for a Study of African Refugee Children at the Nexus of Home and School: Implications for Policy and Practice

I am doing a research study. A research study is a special way to learn about something. I am doing this research study because we are trying to find out more about what it's like for Burundian children to live in the United States and learn in the schools here. I would like to ask you to be in this research study.

Why am I being asked to be in this research study?

You are being asked to be in this research study because you recently came to the United States and have been going to school here.

What will happen during this research study?

I want to tell you about some things that might happen if you are in the study. This study will take place at your home and in your neighborhood. I will meet with you four times a year to interview you at your house. Then, twice a year, we'll walk around the neighborhood and talk about things that you like to do in your neighborhood. We'll do this for two years. Also, I'll spend time in your neighborhood, observing what it's like to live here.

If you want to be in this study, here are the things that I will ask you about. I'll ask how things are going at school and what you like or don't like about school. I'll also ask you to show me the places you like to hang out in the neighborhood and share what you do there.

Are there any bad things that might happen during the research study?

Sometimes bad things happen to people who are in research studies. These bad things are called "risks." The risks of being in this study might be that someone might know that it is you telling me things about the neighborhood. Also, sometimes it might be hard to talk about some of your experiences. Not all of these things may happen to you. None of them may happen. Things may happen that the researchers don't know about yet. If they do, I will make sure that you get help to deal with anything bad that might happen.

Are there any good things that might happen during the research study?

Sometimes good things happen to people who are in research studies. These good things are called "benefits." The benefits of being in this study might be that you help others better understand how they can support children who come to live in a new country. We don't know for sure if you will have any benefits. We hope to learn something that will help other people some day.

Will I get money or payment for being in this research study?

You will not get any money for being in this research study.

Who can I ask if I have any questions?

If you have any questions about this study, you can ask your parents or guardians or the researcher. Also, if you have any questions that you didn't think of now, you can ask later. You can ask me your questions the next time we meet.

What if I don't want to be in the study?

If you don't want to be in this study, you don't have to. It's up to you. If you say you want to be in it and then change your mind, that's okay. All you have to do is tell us that you don't want to be in it anymore. No one will be mad at you or upset with you if you don't want to be in it.

My choice:

If I write my name on the line below, it means that I agree to be in this research study.

_____   _____
Participant's Signature   Date

_____
Participant's Name

_____   _____
Signature of person obtaining assent   Date

_____
Name of person obtaining assent

Source: Adapted from Indiana University, Institutional Review Board

Figure 4.4 Acquiring Verbal Assent From a Child Participant

Hello, (name of participant).

Your guardian said that you are willing to help me in my project by letting me videotape all that you do when you are in class . You can help me by just doing what you always do when you are here. I think that I will learn lots from you. Are you willing to help with this project? (Child's response). Great! So, is it okay if I watch and type out the videotapes from your time in class after you finish today? (Child's response). Thanks! Is it okay if I record what you are doing/saying? (Child's response). Thanks! Also, is it okay if I observe? (Child's response). Great! If you decide that you don't want me to record or observe you anymore, you can just say, "I don't want you to record me anymore" or "I don't want you to observe/watch me anymore." Okay? (Child's response). I will do my best to protect your identity and keep your sessions private. I will change your name when I type up all that you say and do in your sessions. Do you have any questions? (Child's response). Thanks!

Source: Adapted from Lester & Barouch, 2013, p. 69

In Figure 4.4, the child is invited to offer their verbal agreement, which a researcher would need to systematically record (for example, make an audio recording or maintain record of the day, time, and place that assent was given). Ultimately, decisions around the design of the informed consent and assent process will certainly be related to both your institutional requirements and the age and unique needs of your participants. Regardless of the design of the process, your goal is to assure that your participants fully understand the nature of your study and that their participation is 100 percent voluntary, which relates to capacity.

Capacity refers to an individual's ability to understand and retain information, which becomes particularly important when sharing the purpose of a study with a potential participant. As a practitioner-scholar, you need to know that a research participant has the capacity to evaluate information about a research study as they decide whether or not they are willing to participate. In general, an individual's capacity is determined by a few factors, including age and whether an individual identifies or has been identified as having a cognitive disability. For instance, as noted above, if your potential research participants are students who are younger than 18 years of age, you cannot include them in your research study unless their parents or guardians have consented to them participating. A child's interests as a research participant are believed to be protected when the individual granting consent (such as a parent) makes the child's needs their primary interest (Field & Behrman, 2004).

Beyond age, capability is also determined by one's ability to understand the nature of a given study and the consequences for their participation in it. While this notion of understanding fundamentally applies to children, it also applies to research participants who may have a cognitive or emotional disability. However, it is important to keep in mind that simply because an individual identifies as having a disability, they are not presumed to be incompetent. In contrast, even when an individual is deemed legally competent by the court system, a practitioner-scholar must still work to ensure that the participant understands the information. In other words, determining a potential research participant's capability is not a simple task and requires care, sensitivity, and thoughtfulness on the part of the practitioner-scholar.

While much practitioner-scholarship involves students, parents, and other educators, it is important to know whether your participants are considered a vulnerable population. A

IDENTIFYING PARTICIPANTS

One of the first ethical challenges you face in designing your study about teachers' perspectives of the professional development you provide is to consider who you want to participate in the study.

Given the study is about your school's professional development program, you think it is best that the study include classroom teachers who work in your school. However, you recognize that this could be challenging as these teachers all report to you as a supervisor and you are responsible for evaluating their practice. Thus, you wonder whether these teachers would be willing to share openly about the professional development they receive. When you present this idea to your graduate adviser, she questions whether it is ethical for you to interview classroom teachers who you supervise. She notes that your responsibility as a supervisor makes these teachers vulnerable. Further, she worries that selecting only teachers in your school could skew your data in ways that favor your current work in the building. Your graduate adviser asks, "Would you feel comfortable telling the full truth to your supervisor?" You are hesitant in your response and this makes you worry about the potential ethical challenges that you might face. Despite these worries, you decide that you should include these teachers and that you can mitigate your adviser's concerns about having them participate by fully explaining to each participant their rights and responsibilities, as well as by making clear that their participation in the study is voluntary and that you are not approaching them as their supervisor but as a researcher interested in studying their views about professional development.

Focus Questions

1. How might the initial discussion of your research study with the teachers inform how they view your research and their participation in it?

2. What steps might you take to assure teachers that both their positive and negative responses will not influence how you evaluate them in the future?

vulnerable population includes anyone that could be rendered powerless because of their current age, disability, or situation, and thereby potentially less capable of understanding the potential risks of participating in a research study. Individuals who are institutionalized, incarcerated, or have significant disabilities are typically described as vulnerable populations. There are unfortunately many examples of vulnerable participants being taken advantage of and made to believe that a research study will benefit them when in fact they will accrue no benefits; thus, typically, extra caution needs to be taken when including vulnerable populations in your research studies. This cautionary stance does not mean that you should not conduct research with populations deemed vulnerable; rather, it highlights the need to be thoughtful, reflective, and purposeful in the way you design and carry out your research study.

LEGAL AND INSTITUTIONAL ETHICAL REQUIREMENTS

As previously noted, there are ethical codes and statements that professional associations, such as AERA, have developed that guide education researchers. In addition, there are ethical standards

REFLECTIVE OPPORTUNITY 4.1

Ethics is both a product of our past and the anticipation of the future.

1. How do the experiences from the Nuremberg Trials, the Tuskegee experiment, and other events shape your understanding of what ethics is today?

that have been established by governmental agencies. Many of these legally binding regulations came about after World War II and the atrocities that occurred via what the Nazi regime called "medical research." The Nuremberg Code, a set of research ethics, was developed after the Nuremberg trial in which 23 Nazi doctors who conducted "human experimentation" were tried for crimes against humanity. The Nuremberg Code centered on ten principles or practices that were designed to guide medical ethics. These ten principles included a focus on voluntary consent of all human participants and the suggestion to avoid all medical experimentation that does not directly benefit society, among other points (see the National Institutes of Health's description at: http://history.nih.gov/research/downloads/nuremberg.pdf).

Beyond the Nuremberg trials, the "Tuskegee Study of Untreated Syphilis in the Negro Male," which took place from 1932 to 1972, led to the establishment of the government-based Office for Human Research Protections, the 1979 Belmont Report, and related federal regulations requiring Institutional Review Boards. The Tuskegee study was a 40-year-long study in which researchers hoped to study the progression of untreated syphilis. What were the problems with this study? First, no informed consent was acquired from the 600 African American men enrolled in the study. Second, researchers simply told the men that they were being treated for "bad blood" when in fact they were not receiving the treatment they needed to cure their illness. In this way, the research led to harm being done to the participants. The fallout from this study was extensive and led to the establishment of greater governmental regulations and several reports. In the United States, the Belmont Report was released in 1979 and outlined three basic research practices for biomedical and behavioral science research, including the need to: (a) protect the autonomy of participants through an informed consent process; (b) minimize harm and maximize benefits to research participants; and (c) carry out non-exploitative research.

Following the Tuskegee study, an Institutional Review Board (IRB) became a requirement for any institution conducting research funded by the U.S. government. An IRB is a group of individuals who are authorized by an institution, such as a university, to determine whether a proposed research study complies with federal and institutional research regulations and ethical professional standards. These boards are now required to review all human research protocols prior to studies being conducted. At the most basic level, the IRB is meant to assure that any research conducted abides by the Code of Federal Regulations for the Protection of Human Subjects. By design, they are not intended to offer advice on your methodology or theoretical framework. Rather, the IRB focuses on assuring that the research you plan to carry out will abide by established ethical principles. Typically, if your study qualifies for IRB review, you will submit a research protocol that includes statements related to the:

- Purpose of the research;

- Rationale for the study;

- Research design;

- All methods, such as where and how data will be collected and later securely stored;

- Participant population;

- Participant recruitment and sampling procedures;

- How informed consent or assent will be acquired prior to the start of the study;

- Incentives being offered (or not) to the participants;

- Risk and benefit ratios; and

- Procedures for assuring privacy and confidentiality before, during, and after the study.

FROM THE FIELD 4.1

An Example of Making IRB Approval Explicit in a Published Article

Following Institutional Review Board approval, I collected a corpus of data for a larger ethnography, which included (a) 175 hrs of conversations that occurred in the clinic's waiting room and in therapy sessions with participating therapists, children with autism, and other caretakers; (b) interview data with participating parents, therapists, and a state disability advocate; (c) observational field notes, totaling 650 pages of written text focused on the institutional goals of the clinic; and (d) documents used within the therapy sessions.

Source: Lester, 2014, p. 181

Given that IRB protocols are often unique to a particular institution, you should consult with your adviser or local research administrator to determine what forms to submit. Further, in the write-up of your research study, it is often appropriate to include reference to whether your study has been approved by your IRB. For instance, From the Field 4.1 provides an example of a researcher referencing that prior to beginning their study, they received approval from the IRB.

As you likely noted, many of the ethical guidelines and regulations have been shaped by medical research. So, it may not be surprising to discover that some educational studies are considered to be of minimal risk for participants and therefore are either considered exempt or will be expedited for IRB review. Nonetheless, it is important that you find out how your institution interprets the federal regulations, keeping in mind that the goal of an IRB is to protect participants from harm.

⚓ LINK TO PRACTICE 4.2

DEALING WITH PARTICIPANTS WHO OPT OUT

After receiving IRB approval for your study, you recruit classroom teachers in your school to participate. You meet with each classroom teacher who you would like to include in the study and explain the purpose of your study to them. The teachers agree to participate in your study. As part of the informed consent process, you plan to remind teachers throughout your study that they are free to leave the study at any time without penalty. This, you feel, will allow them to participate freely and keep them informed about their rights and responsibilities as research participants.

As your study continues you sense that teachers are enjoying their participation in the study. Many teachers have explained that they appreciate the opportunity to reflect on their practice and especially enjoy the opportunity to share their appreciation for the professional development you have provided. These statements affirm your views that the schools' professional development strategy is on the right track. Further, they provide evidence that teachers are satisfied with your leadership for the professional development.

All appears to be going well until one of the teachers approaches you on the day of her final interview and asks to withdraw from your study. She explains that she is very busy and has been feeling increasingly overwhelmed with the requirements of the study. At first you are confused. How could she reach this stage and drop out? How could she not finish the study after spending so much time participating? While you respect the teacher's decision, you also grapple with how you will now interact with the teacher who, while initially participating in the study, has chosen to leave. After all, the teacher may no longer be a participant in your study but she will still work with you at your school. You realize that you will have to determine how to set aside your disappointment and continue to interact professionally.

Focus Questions

1. Why is it important to view the informed consent process as an ongoing process?

2. What challenges to your research study may emerge when participants opt out of a study?

MANAGING RESEARCH RELATIONSHIPS WITH SCHOOLS AND DISTRICTS

While thus far we have described research ethics within the context of the university setting, we also note that ethics applies to the relationships you cultivate with your research sites, in particular how you acquire access to the classroom, school, or district you want to study. For practitioner-scholars, this often means completing an additional IRB application that is specific to the school or school district where your research will take place. The application often mirrors the form you complete for your college or university in that it describes the research you will conduct and the potential risks and benefits to your research participants. It is, therefore, essential that you consider what steps you must take to gain access to the classroom, school, or district as part of your overall research plan.

Although each school or district will differ, we suggest that at a minimum you complete the following steps before you begin your research study. First, contact the principal or central office administrator who oversees staff who may participate in your study to schedule a meeting with them to discuss the research project. Second, determine whether the district requires a research application, and prepare the necessary paperwork. Finally, meet with the principal and (virgule) or central office administrator following receipt of the approval from the district to explain the study timeline. At this meeting, you should provide the administrators with whatever materials (recruitment e-mails, informed consent forms, and so on) that are needed so that they can help you launch your study.

CONSIDERING ETHICS ACROSS THE RESEARCH PROCESS

Research ethics is not something that you should consider simply while you are collecting or analyzing your data. Rather, it is something that *must* be considered *across* the research process. As illustrated in Table 4.2, we suggest that the best way to approach the potential ethical challenges that arise is to carefully reflect on and consider key ethical questions *before* and *during* your research study. There will not always be black and white answers, as research ethics is full of ambiguity. The challenges may change or evolve and thus your response to these challenges may

Table 4.2 Ethical Questions to Consider When Engaging in Education Research		
Planning and Designing the Study	**Carrying Out the Study**	**Reporting the Research Results/Findings**
• Is my proposed research topic one that can be ethically studied? • Have I disclosed my conflicts of interest and might these conflicts exclude me from carrying out the study? • What are the ethical considerations unique to the research design of my study (e.g., an experimental design may require you to think carefully about whether it is ethical for only some participants to receive an intervention)? • How will I contact the research site? • How will I invite individuals to participate in the study? • What procedures will I put into place to assure the anonymity of the participants and the confidentiality of the data collected?	• What will I do if a participant withdraws from the study? How will I handle the data associated with this participant? • How will I maintain positive relations with a research site? • What procedures will/ did I use to assure the anonymity of the participants and confidentiality of all data collected? • How will I store data in a secure way? • If I am collaborating, how will I share data securely? • How will I ensure that I do not generate inaccurate findings?	• Have I transparently reported all research procedures (i.e., methods) that were used? • Did I write the research report/paper in such a way that the participants' identities are protected? • Did I use pseudonyms throughout the research report/paper? • Did I assure that no plagiarism or self-plagiarism is included in the research report/ paper? • Have all the authors of the research report/ paper made a substantial contribution to the research study?

differ from day to day. It is therefore critical to continuously reflect on the ethical concerns you may face as you carry out your research. It is equally important to consider these questions when you critique research. As consumers of research, we have a responsibility to consider whether a research study was ethical and how ethical responsibilities were carried out.

The Role of Ethics in Planning and Designing a Study

Ethics is something that you should consider long before you even begin your study. We suggest that you should begin thinking about research ethics even as you review the literature and identify a research problem. Ethics should be central to how you go about planning for your study. We highlight three key things to consider: (a) determining whether a research topic should be studied; (b) identifying and disclosing conflicts of interest; and (c) recognizing and exploring ethical challenges specific to your selected methodology.

First, an important question is: Is it ethical to explore this topic? For example, a practitioner-scholar may be interested in studying the impact of high-stakes testing on students' performance when told that they will not graduate if they perform poorly on a test. In actuality, however, the test that the practitioner-scholar uses has no bearing on the students' graduation, but the students do not know this. While the study of high-stakes testing is rich with potential for deeper understanding, there are obvious ethical concerns related to a study that intentionally deceives students and may cause them unnecessary harm, anxiety, or stress. Decisions around whether the study of a particular topic is ethical or not are not black and white, as we will all likely have different perspectives. Nonetheless, it is the responsibility of the researcher to assure that their proposed research topic results in knowledge that contributes ". . . to the public good" (AERA, 2011, p. 147).

Second, as you plan for your study, it is always important to determine whether you may have conflicts of interest. While a conflict of interest does not automatically mean that you cannot carry out the study, it does mean that you need to disclose this conflict and carefully reflect upon its implications. Talking to colleagues about the impact of your conflict of interest is a good place to start. In addition, your IRB will likely require that you disclose this conflict, as they will want to evaluate the consequences of this conflict. In the end, you may come to realize, however, that your conflict of interest creates an ethical challenge that requires you to remove yourself from a study. This is particularly true when you stand to benefit financially from a study.

Finally, as you design your study and determine the methodology that you will use, you need to give attention to how particular methodologies introduce unique ethical challenges. Vogt and colleagues (2012) provided a few suggestions for thinking about potential ethical considerations in relation to particular research methodologies. While we will discuss many of these concerns in greater detail in the upcoming chapters focused on specific methodologies, it is helpful to begin thinking about them now. Table 4.3 highlights some of the unique ethical challenges associated with specific methodologies—challenges that you should consider while you are designing and planning for your study.

At all costs, you want to avoid bumping into these challenges unexpectedly while in the midst of collecting your data. However, we do not intend to suggest that by considering such challenges up front you will avoid facing any ethical dilemmas while carrying out your research. Rather, we suggest your primary aim is to minimize the unexpected.

Table 4.3   Ethical Challenges Specific to Particular Methodologies Discussed in This Textbook

Chapter Where Discussed in Greater Detail	Methodology	Research Ethics Considerations

5	Qualitative Methodologies	• Interview Methods:
		  o Confidentiality of the interviews
		  o Protection from harm that may result from probing questions
		• Observational Methods
		  o Maintaining the anonymity of individuals and organizations observed, particularly those who happen to enter the environment being observed
		  o Covert observation
		• Archival Methods
		• Privacy of data in records

6	Quantitative— Survey Design	• Anonymity of the respondents and their responses • Informed consent procedures, particularly when online surveys are administered
6	Quantitative— Experimental Design	• Deceptive practices (e.g., not telling students that they are receiving a modified curriculum) • Accounting for potential psychological harm • Impact of not receiving an intervention or treatment
10	Mixed Methods	• Tension between aggregate reporting of quantitative data versus individual qualitative responses
11	Action Research	• Close relationships between the practitioner-scholar and the research participants (e.g., colleagues, students, employees, etc.) • Personal investment in the practice(s) or program(s) being studied

Source: Adapted from Vogt et al., 2012

The Role of Ethics in Carrying Out a Study

As you carry out your research study, you will need to consider the ethical questions and concerns highlighted in Tables 4.2 and 4.3. The issues you face will range from navigating the often challenging process of recruiting participants for your study to developing positive relationships with a research site to thinking carefully about how you will anonymize your dataset to being thoughtful about the analysis of your data. We highlight here two of the central issues to consider when carrying out your study: (a) maintaining a secure dataset, and (b) ethical and thoughtful handling of data.

First, it is important to view your data as something that you *must* keep secure and confidential. Part of this process includes thinking about where you might safely store the data (for example, on a password protected computer or hard drive) and how and when you will anonymize your data. Anonymizing data involves removing any identifiable characteristics from the dataset

REFLECTIVE OPPORTUNITY 4.2

Ideally, you want to plan for the potential ethical challenges that you will encounter in your study. However, it is unlikely that you will foresee all of the ethical dilemmas you may encounter.

1. As such, what are some of the strategies you might use to remain aware of ethical challenges as you carry out your study.

2. What are some strategies you might use to account for the decisions that you make along the way?

that could potentially (if the data were disclosed publicly) identify the participants in your study. Anonymizing your data is one way that you can assure participants of their confidentiality, which is a promise to the participant that any information they share will not be disclosed in a way that could potentially identify them. Confidentiality is not the same as guaranteeing anonymity. When you guarantee anonymity, the dataset you receive cannot contain any identifiable information that could potentially identify the individuals who you are studying. For example, an anonymous survey guarantees anonymity because it does not collect any identifiable information for the survey respondents (such as their name, IP address, or e-mail address). In contrast, a confidential survey might collect the participant's IP address or e-mail address, but the researcher might delete this information upon closing the survey administration to ensure participant confidentiality. The primary difference between anonymized and confidential data is thus that confidential data permits the researcher to know some aspect of the participant's identity while anonymized data does not.

Your approach to anonymizing your data will certainly depend on many factors, including the type of data you collect. For instance, you may be working with survey responses in which the data does not include any identifying characteristics (for example, student name). On the other hand, you might be working with interview data in which a participant's name, as well as their hometown and the names of their close friends, were mentioned. When and how should you anonymize this interview data? Should you apply pseudonyms or participant IDs while you transcribe the recorded data or while writing up your research report? There are no clear-cut answers to these questions; however, at some point, you are expected to assure that the identities of your participants are protected.

Second, ethical misconduct in the form of massaging or fabricating data has been known to occur and is something to be avoided. Massaging a dataset occurs when a practitioner-scholar intentionally or unintentionally misrepresents their dataset. At times, massaging the data may occur naively, such as when a practitioner-scholar mistakenly or inaccurately analyzes data. For instance, a practitioner-scholar incorrectly attributes a meaning to a quotation from a classroom teacher, and later discovers that the teacher actually meant something remarkably different. As we discuss in Chapter 8, when conducting a qualitative analysis there are many procedures that can be used to avoid this mistake. In contrast, massaging the data may occur intentionally when a practitioner-scholar unethically alters or excludes data that appears to be an anomaly (Kromrey, 1993). For example, a practitioner-scholar may be concerned that

ENSURING UNBIASED DATA COLLECTION AND INTERPRETATION

After concluding your interviews with teachers in your school, you begin your analysis of the data that you collected. As you examine the data you begin realizing that the teachers in your school were overwhelmingly positive about the professional development that you provided to them. Their statements are glowing and their compliments are plentiful. While these comments fuel your sense of pride, you begin worrying about whether the data are so positive that they will be unbelievable. Further, you worry that you have unintentionally skewed your data by interviewing classroom teachers in your school who report directly to you. You share your findings with your adviser and she questions whether you have fully examined the data you collected. Moreover, she asks you to identify counterexamples that highlight how teachers felt the professional development could be improved. You explain to your adviser that your data does not reference potential improvements. In fact, all of the teachers who participated in the study expressed that the professional development they received was rewarding and helpful. Your adviser encourages you to consider collecting additional data to highlight ways that the professional development

in your school could be improved. How should you do this, you think to yourself, when you know that the participating teachers have not responded in this way? How should you handle the overwhelmingly positive responses that your teachers provided? What should you do now that your study has concluded? Should you massage the quotes so that they are not as positive? Should you collect more data even though your study has now concluded? Should you have a colleague collect additional data so that you have a more neutral interview process? At this stage, you realize that you will need to enlist the help of a colleague with experience in research to conduct additional interviews. You realize that your adviser's concern about interviewing teachers who you supervise has, indeed, biased your study and raised serious ethical concerns.

Focus Questions

1. What might be some of the unforeseen challenges of enlisting a colleague to assist with additional data collection?

2. What would you share with your participants as the reason(s) for why additional data is needed?

negative survey responses might raise concerns about the quality of their leadership practice and thus exclude all negative responses from their study. It is important to understand that an ethical practitioner-scholar is one who refuses to "bury" data that did not support their research aims (Kromrey, p. 25).

Fabricating data occurs when a practitioner-scholar makes up or creates data in order to support their results/findings. For example, a practitioner-scholar who conducts a case study of a district's implementation of a new teacher evaluation system claims to have observed 20 professional development sessions over the course of a school year. However, in reality, the practitioner-scholar only went to one meeting and fabricated their field notes for the other 19 meetings. Fabrication is a gross abuse of the practitioner-scholar's role as a researcher and results in a serious erosion of trust in the researcher and the research process.

The Role of Ethics in Reporting Research Findings

The need to consider research ethics does not end with the collection and analysis of your data. Rather, it remains central to the process of writing up your research report/paper. There are many issues to consider when you write up your research report/paper, including avoiding plagiarism, determining authorship on collaborative projects, and assuring that all identifying participant information has been excluded, as discussed earlier. We focus here on: (a) determining authorship, and (b) avoiding plagiarism.

First, as a practitioner-scholar, you may or may not be researching alone. If you are working collaboratively, you will have to navigate issues around authorship. There are several established guidelines regarding who qualifies to be an author on a research report (see, for example, AERA, 2011). Table 4.4 provides a framework for making decisions around authorship. As Table 4.4 illustrates, determining authorship involves differentiating among various researchers' contributions to the research product. It should not be surprising that contributions relating to the conceptualization of a research project, the collection or preparation of data for analysis, or the development of a first draft all weigh heavily when determining who should be listed as the study's first author. First, authorship implies that the contributor made significant contributions to the conceptualization of the study and was actively involved in the collection of data and the writing of the results/findings. In general, we think it is important to have early conversations with your colleagues around authorship, as you want to avoid any dilemmas around what justifies being an author.

Second, while plagiarism is a commonly discussed topic in K–12 contexts, it is also one that we must think about when writing up our research report/paper. Plagiarism is the use of someone else's words, ideas, or thoughts. It has become an increasingly common issue in academic writing, as more publications are digitized and becoming electronically available (Paulus, Lester, &

Table 4.4 Framework for Decision-Making Around Authorship				
	To what extent did you contribute to the project?			
	Significantly	Moderately	Limited	Not at all
1. Conceptualizing and refining the research idea				
2. Reviewing literature relevant to the study				
3. Selecting or developing research instruments and protocols				
4. Collecting and preparing data for analysis				
5. Analyzing data				
6. Writing the first draft of the report/paper				
7. Writing the second and subsequent drafts of the report/paper				
8. Editing the report/paper				

Source: Adapted from Winston, 1985

Note: If you indicated that you were a significant contributor to 1, 4, or 6, you should be entitled to authorship.

Dempster, 2014). For instance, it is now far easier to simply copy and paste direct quotes into your research report/paper from digitized sources. Because of the ease with which plagiarism can occur, intentionally or unintentionally, it is important to be thoughtful about how you include the ideas and words of others into your report/paper. Citing the ideas of others is expected, as well as using quotation marks or a blocked text when directly quoting an individual. We suggest that the best approach to take when writing is to assume that credit is warranted and thus a citation is needed.

EMERGING ETHICAL CHALLENGES

With the rise of new technologies, such as the Internet, there are opportunities to carry out research in novel ways. For example, some researchers are now studying online discussions that take place in blogs or twitter feeds. Furthermore, researchers have been exploring how the Internet might be used as both a tool for data collection (for example, conducting online surveys and online interviews) and as a research site in and of itself (for instance, studying how online professional development programs support, or do not support, teachers' growth) (Markham, 2006). While it is beyond the scope of this textbook to fully discuss ethics in relation to emergent technologies, it is important to keep in mind that collecting data via the Internet or using the Internet as a research site brings with it many ethical challenges. For instance, the Internet poses new challenges for gaining informed consent from research participants and guaranteeing the privacy of individuals who decide to participate in a study. Beyond this, there is an ongoing debate regarding whether online data are, by their very nature, public or private. Some researchers argue that these data are public and therefore do not require a researcher to acquire a participant's consent, while others view the data as private and therefore require participant consent (McKee & Porter, 2009). If you decide to use the Internet for your research, it is important that you become familiar with the challenges unique to this context, as well as weigh carefully the ethical dilemmas that you will inevitably encounter.

REFLECTIVE OPPORTUNITY 4.3

1. How might social media sites, such as Facebook, influence your current understanding of what

research ethics is and entails given the public nature of such sites?

SUMMARY

As discussed in this chapter, research ethics is an expansive concept that relates both to the rights of individual research participants and to designing and carrying out a research study. Research ethics should not be viewed as a static concept. Instead, research ethics should have a significant and ongoing influence on your research study. Further, as research methodologies continue to evolve and new data sources emerge, we anticipate that research ethics will also change.

Anonymizing 83

Assent 71

Capacity 76

Conflict of Interest 70

Consent 71

Direct Consent 71

Fabricating 84

Informed Consent 71

Institutional Review Board
(IRB) 78

Massaging 84

Plagiarism 86

Third-party Consent 71

Vulnerable Population 77

QUESTIONS TO CONSIDER

1. What is the role of ethics in the research process?

2. What are the various functions of the ethical regulations associated with the Institutional Review Board?

3. During a research study, how might your relationships with schools and districts introduce potential ethical concerns? How might you deal with these ethical concerns?

4. What are some of the unique ethical concerns to consider when planning, designing, carrying out, and reporting research?

5. What are some of the ethical concerns that are uniquely common to qualitative research?

6. What are some of the ethical concerns that are uniquely common to quantitative research?

CHAPTER EXERCISES

1. Obtain a copy of the American Educational Research Association's Ethical Guidelines. Review these guidelines in relation to your identity as a practitioner-scholar. How might these guidelines inform how you will carry out your research? Next, consider these guidelines in relation to your work as a practitioner. How might these guidelines inform your work in schools? Where might there be ethical intersections between your work as a practitioner and your role as a practitioner-scholar? Develop a short, one-page statement that summarizes how you will attend to these intersections.

2. Beyond the American Educational Research Association's ethical guidelines, there are a multitude of professional organizations that distribute and publically share ethical guidelines. Considering the professional organizations that you are a part of, examine whether ethical

guidelines exist and how they might intersect with your work as a practitioner-scholar.

3. Assume you were going to conduct a research study in your school. Make a list of possible data points that you could collect and then consider the possible ethical concerns that might arise should you decide to use the data in a research study. How might you address these ethical concerns? What might you do (given your understanding of research ethics) to mitigate or eliminate the ethical concerns you have identified?

4. Explore the ethical review process that is used at your school or district. After doing so, consider the following: What steps are in place and how might these steps shape how you carry out your research study?

There are an increasing number of books written around research ethics, ranging from a focus on ethics specific to Internet-based data (see McKee & Porter, 2009) to those focused on a particular methodology (see Mauthner, Birch, Jessop, & Miller, 2002, for a discussion of ethics and qualitative research). For a more general discussion of ethics in the social sciences, including the field of education, Israel and Hay's book (2006), *Research Ethics for Social Sciences*, provides a baseline discussion of key concepts to consider when thinking about ethical research practices.

Sharpen your skills with SAGE edge!

edge.sagepub.com/lochmiller

SAGE edge for Students provides a personalized approach to help you accomplish your coursework goals in an easy-to-use learning environment. You'll find action plans, mobile-friendly eFlashcards, and quizzes as well as videos, web resources, and links to SAGE journal articles to support and expand on the concepts presented in this chapter.

PART II

CONSIDERING APPROACHES TO EDUCATIONAL RESEARCH

The second part of this textbook introduces you to qualitative, quantitative, mixed methods, and action research approaches to research. The primary purpose of Part II is to present you with various research methodologies and approaches to data analysis, as well as the process of carrying out your research. Specifically, this section offers a detailed discussion of both qualitative and quantitative methodologies, as well as common considerations for engaging in qualitative and quantitative analyses. Part II of the textbook also introduces you to mixed methods research and analysis, and gives particular attention to the usefulness of action research for practitioner-scholars.

5

INTRODUCING QUALITATIVE RESEARCH

CONDUCTING QUALITATIVE RESEARCH

As a school principal, you face many challenges in your daily work. Many of these challenges are the result of organizational structures and processes that are, to a certain extent, misaligned with your work as an instructional leader. For example, the district central office expects that you are routinely in classrooms observing instruction and yet frequently schedules meetings that take you out of your school and away from the very task that you are expected to perform. This has always frustrated you, and, as a practitioner-scholar, you wonder whether your colleagues in other schools and districts have comparable experiences. How do central office administrators (such as superintendents, deputy superintendents, directors of human resources) define instructional leadership? This question has always fascinated you, particularly given your experience as a building leader. You assume that there are fundamental differences in the ways that central office staff conceive of your work and your colleagues' work. Given these differences, you believe that there may be merit in understanding how central office administrators conceive of the principals' role as an instructional leader. For example, you wonder whether there are specific definitions that administrators have formulated or whether these definitions emerge out of every day practice, culture, or tradition.

INTRODUCTION

As illustrated in the opening vignette, qualitative researchers are most often interested in studying natural environments and focus on understanding how people make sense of and experience the world around them (Denzin & Lincoln, 2005). Indeed, there are fundamental differences between qualitative and quantitative approaches to research, as we highlighted in Table 1.2 in Chapter 1. In this chapter, we present a basic overview of six qualitative methodologies: (a) case study,

Learning Objectives

By the end of the chapter, you will be able to:

- Describe common characteristics of qualitative research.

- Discuss the types of data typically collected in qualitative research studies.

- Summarize why a practitioner-scholar might undertake a qualitative research study.

- Identify what can and cannot be gained from qualitative research findings.

- Explain the basic characteristics and data sources commonly associated with case study, grounded theory, narrative, phenomenology, ethnography, and discourse analysis studies.

(b) grounded theory, (c) narrative, (d) phenomenology, (e) ethnography, and (f) discourse analysis. We selected these methodologies as they are frequently used by practitioner-scholars to examine problems of practice and are thus commonly discussed in educational research. However, it is important to note that there is great variability in qualitative research, and what we share here is only a small sample of the approaches to qualitative research. For instance, even though we discuss phenomenology, we present only a basic overview as there are a multitude of approaches to phenomenology. The same could be said of the other qualitative methodologies discussed. Nonetheless, our hope is that this chapter serves as a foundation for your continued study of qualitative research methodologies, and as a resource for you to consider whether qualitative research methodologies might be appropriate for your own research.

We begin this chapter by revisiting and describing in greater detail some of the basic characteristics of qualitative research. We then share a few of the primary aims and purposes of a qualitative research study, offering examples of the types of research questions you might ask when carrying out this kind of research. We focus much of this discussion on the six qualitative methodologies.

CHARACTERISTICS OF QUALITATIVE RESEARCH

Broadly, qualitative research is an umbrella term that encompasses multiple methodologies and methods that typically seek to understand social life as it unfolds in its natural environment. Polkinghorne (2005) suggested that qualitative research aims ". . . to describe and clarify experiences" (p. 138). These experiences include how we interact, observe, understand, or make sense of the world in which we live. Thus, qualitative research focuses on human experience as it occurs in social life and often seeks to make sense of the social practices (for example, the organizational practices that define instructional leadership in a particular school or district). While there are many different ways to carry out a qualitative research study, there are several shared assumptions about how to conduct a qualitative research study. Patton (2002) has highlighted some of these major assumptions, as illustrated in Table 5.1.

We next discuss five common characteristics of qualitative research in greater detail, including: (a) the researcher as instrument, (b) focus on context, (c) emergent research design, (d) inductive approach, and (e) unique data sources.

Researcher as Instrument

First, qualitative research presumes that the researcher is the research instrument. In quantitative research, a practitioner-scholar may use an instrument to collect data, such as a survey. This creates a degree of distance between the researcher and the data. Furthermore, it creates a sense of objectivity in both the research process and the analysis of the data. In qualitative research, however, practitioner-scholars are assumed to be the primary research instrument, as they are both collecting the data, as well as making sense of the data as they collect and analyze them (Lincoln & Guba, 1985). In qualitative research, there is presumably less distance between the researcher and their data. The process is thus more subjective by design, which is not to say less rigorous.

Table 5.1 Common Characteristics of Qualitative Research

Design Strategies

Naturalistic inquiry	Studying real-world situations as they unfold naturally; non-manipulative and non-controlling; openness to whatever emerges (lack of predetermined constraints on findings).
Emergent design flexibility	Openness to adapting inquiry as understanding deepens and/or situations change; the researcher avoids getting locked into rigid designs that eliminate responsiveness and pursues new paths of discovery as they emerge.
Purposeful sampling	Cases for study (e.g., people, organizations, communities, cultures, events, critical incidences) are selected because they are "information rich" and illuminative; that is, they offer useful manifestations of the phenomenon of interest; sampling, then, is aimed at insight about the phenomenon, not empirical generalization from a sample to a population.

Data-Collection and Fieldwork Strategies

Qualitative data	Observations that yield detailed, thick description; inquiry in depth; interviews that capture direct quotations about people's personal perspectives and experiences; case studies; careful document review.
Personal experience and engagement	The researcher has direct contact with and gets close to the people, situation, and phenomenon under study; the researcher's personal experiences and insights are an important part of the inquiry and critical to understanding the phenomenon.
Empathic neutrality and mindfulness	An empathic stance in interviewing seeks vicarious understanding without judgment (neutrality) by showing openness, sensitivity, respect, awareness, and responsiveness; in observation it means being fully present (mindfulness).
Dynamic systems	Attention to process; assumes change as ongoing whether focus is on an individual, an organization, a community, or an entire culture; therefore, mindful of and attentive to system and situation dynamics.

Analysis Strategies

Unique case orientation	Assumes that each case is special and unique; the first level of analysis is being true to, respecting, and capturing the details of the individual cases being studied; cross-case analysis follows from and depends on the quality of individual case studies.
Inductive analysis and creative synthesis	Immersion in the details and specifics of the data to discover important patterns, themes, and interrelationships; begins by exploring, then confirming, guided by analytical principles rather than rules; ends with a creative synthesis.
Holistic perspective	The whole phenomenon under study is understood as a complex system that is more than the sum of its parts; focus on complex interdependencies and system dynamics that cannot meaningfully be reduced to a few discrete variables and linear, cause-effect relationships.
Context sensitivity	Places findings in a social, historical, and temporal context; careful about, even dubious of, the possibility or meaningfulness of generalizations across time and space; emphasizes instead careful comparative case analyses and extrapolating patterns for possible transferability and adaptation in new settings.
Voice, perspective, and reflexivity	The qualitative analyst owns and is reflective about her or his own voice and perspective; a credible voice conveys authenticity and trustworthiness; complete objectivity being impossible and pure subjectivity undermining credibility, the researcher's focus becomes balance—understanding and depicting the world authentically in all its complexity while being self-analytical, politically aware, and reflexive in consciousness.

Source: Patton, 2002, pp. 40–41

Thus, many qualitative researchers emphasize the importance of being reflexive throughout the research process. Reflexivity is the process of intentionally accounting for your assumptions, biases, experiences, and identities that may impact any aspect of your research study. Understanding the relationship between the researcher, research context, and research participants is a key aspect of the qualitative research process (Watt, 2007). Because the researcher is the research instrument, his or her choices, assumptions, and biases are thought to shape how the research is carried out. It is therefore important for a practitioner-scholar conducting a qualitative research study to take note of how their own perspectives and beliefs may expand or even limit what they come to study and understand. Qualitative researchers work to be transparent about their biases and invite readers to evaluate whether they adequately considered their own subjectivities throughout the research process. In this way, the researcher remains open and honest about how their own beliefs and values shaped the research process, including the research design and the collection and interpretation of the data.

To this end, many practitioner-scholars who complete a qualitative study include a reflexivity statement in their research report/paper that chronicles some of the assumptions and identities (such as gender, ethnicity, sexual orientation, disability status) that are related to their study. They often discuss how these assumptions and identities informed their research study. For instance, in From the Field 5.1, Anders described how her previous research experiences interviewing young men living in prison shaped her current study of the experiences of Burundian children with refugee status living in a new society.

The passage in From the Field 5.1 highlights how Anders' previous experience informed her approach to the current study, as well as the ways in which her own understanding of race and

FROM THE FIELD 5.1

Sharing About Previous Experiences That Shape the Qualitative Research Process

And when I pursued academic work professionally, I did so with explicit commitments to racial and social justice. Most of the students I interviewed in prison believed that there are ways to support and encourage children when they are young that can keep them from making choices the students I had interviewed had made. The students shared with me that they wanted their stories to be heard and that they wanted children in particular to hear them. Indeed, a charge from one of the students, Shoran, carried me to tutoring with Burundian children. Toward the end of our interviews, Shoran, asked me if, when I started my university job, I would sit in "a big office" or continue to work with "kids" (Anders, 2007). Ignoring this charge and escaping

to the comfort that is institutionally and personally available and accessible to me does not feel like an option. Though I am, indeed, saturated with racial and economic privileges as a White scholar at a university, I choose to respond to Shoran's charge and pursue equity in small and local ways even if the acts in that pursuit cannot change the structures of White dominance or dismantle institutionalized racism. This response to Shoran's charge does not disallow the accusation of "White savior" for me as a White individual doing work in targeted spaces with targeted children; at any time others may take up this charge. But Shoran is the one who keeps me company on the most difficult days in South Prairie (public housing project), never believing in a utopia.

Source: Anders & Lester, 2011, p. 227

socioeconomic privilege informed her understanding of the experiences of her participants. As a practitioner-scholar, you would want to explain in a similar way how your own understandings, beliefs, and/or past experiences shape your approach to your research.

In a qualitative thesis or a dissertation, you may include several pages or even a full chapter focused on your assumptions, biases, and identities (see Evans, 2011). Such a section of a research report/paper is often titled with some variation of the following terms: positionality or positionality statement, reflexivity statement, research role(s), or researcher's role. As highlighted in From the Field 5.2, Luter, Lester, and Kronick (2013) included a section titled "Research Roles" in a journal article reporting findings from a qualitative study of the experiences of teachers and staff who participated in a university-assisted community school (UACS). Considering space limitations, they included only brief statements related to their individual and collective assumptions.

In contrast to Anders' example in From the Field 5.1, the example in From the Field 5.2 is written in a much less personalized way and yet continues to make transparent the relationship between the researchers, the research context, and the study participants.

Focus on Context

Another important assumption of qualitative research is an acute focus on a specific context (for example, a particular school or school district, a participant practice, or a community).

FROM THE FIELD 5.2

Description of Research Roles in a Qualitative Research Article

Throughout this research study, we remained cognizant of the ways in which our own participation and beliefs about a UACS in general shaped how we collected data and engaged with the data set. The first author's involvement with this particular UACS afterschool program included his ongoing participation as a volunteer during the course of one year. The second author's involvement included working as a teacher and teaching assistant during the course of one year. The third author was the primary university faculty member who began the university–school partnership. His work around community schools began well over a decade ago, and even today he remains as the primary university member involved in this ongoing work. During the course of this study, each of the authors spent many of their afternoons and evenings at the afterschool program, interacting with the children, their parents, and the school staff. The third author also spent a great deal of time at the school site during the regular school day, working to develop services that spanned across the regular school day and afterschool program. We thus positioned ourselves as quite involved participant-observers, recognizing that we carried with us contextual understandings that we would not have acquired apart from the extensive time we spent at the research/school site. Furthermore, across the research study, we each presumed that the UACS had the potential to provide systemwide services that were responsive to the needs identified by the students, families, and community at large. However, throughout our work, we also assumed that such collaborations require time and patience. As we approached the research process, we recognized that our interpretation was partial and positional (Noblit, 1999), and we invited others to question and critique the interpretations we proffered.

Source: Luter et al., 2013, p. 166, http://www.schoolcommunitynetwork.org/SCJ.aspx

REFLECTIVE OPPORTUNITY 5.1

Thinking about how your personal beliefs and values shape a research study is an important part of the qualitative research process, as such thinking is closely related to the pursuit of research ethics. As you reflect upon your own beliefs and values, consider the following questions:

1. How might your personal beliefs and values influence the way you carry out a qualitative research study?

2. How might the influence of your beliefs and values present a challenge to you as a qualitative researcher?

3. What role might reflexivity play in helping to disclose potential ethical conflicts?

Practitioner-scholars who undertake qualitative research studies become intimately familiar with the research context. Indeed, they recognize that human behaviors and actions are not isolated from their environment; rather, they are considered in relation to their environment. When writing their research report/paper, most qualitative researchers include a thick, rich description of their experiences collecting data, the research site or context, and the research participants to enable their readers to access and assess this acute focus. A thick description is a detailed account of a researcher's experience conducting fieldwork and making sense of local practices (Geertz, 1973). Through this thick description, the researcher makes explicit the cultural and everyday practices that were observed as central within the research site, allowing for a reader to get a clear sense of the context within which the research took place. Minimally, qualitative researchers provide a detailed description of the research site and participants. For instance, From the Field 5.3 illustrates in part how educational researcher Bianca Baldridge (2014) included a detailed description of her research context.

FROM THE FIELD 5.3

An Example of a Research Context Description

Founded in 1989, EE is a college preparatory and completion program situated within a historic urban neighborhood in the northeastern United States, experiencing high levels of gentrification and neoliberal reform. Located just a few feet from one of the busiest streets in the neighborhood, EE occupies a floor in a high-rise building that holds several organizations that provide a variety of services for the surrounding community. In a rather small space for a program that can serve up to 200 students at a time, EE welcomes middle and high school students 5 to 6 days a week for after-school courses and youth development programming. A White multimillionaire with ties to one of the oldest real estate agencies in the Northeast and a history of philanthropy founded EE; at present, he is the largest donor to the organization. In addition to the financial contributions of the founder, EE is supported primarily through individual donors and foundation grants. EE's appointed board of directors, a 23-member group of professionals representing various city, government, and educational agencies, guides EE's finances and mission.

(Continued)

(Continued)

Youth workers at EE who are well versed in the program's history shared that the initial focus of EE was to help Black and Latino/a students access the nation's leading colleges and universities via positive youth-adult relationships in an after-school setting. Under its current leadership, and for the past 10 years, EE has expanded its programming. In addition to academic assistance and college preparation, the organization provides individual counseling, service-learning opportunities both domestic and international, and youth leadership and development courses, such as racial identity development, social awareness, media literacy, sexual health awareness, and research opportunities. After-school programs like EE are unique in their effort to address simultaneously a range of academic, social, cultural, and emotional needs of marginalized youth. With a predominantly Black staff and a race-conscious approach to youth development, EE's attention to an understanding of racially coded rhetoric and the ways it manifests in youth development programs make it a useful site to examine the interaction of race and neoliberalism in after-school community-based programming.

EE is divided into three divisions: Middle School (MS), High School (HS), and Youth Leadership Development (YLD). A director leads each division and supervises a group of youth workers. Students can apply for entry in the fifth grade and are expected and encouraged to remain in the program until they complete college. To be eligible for the program, students must have at least an 80% grade point average and at least a 3 or 4 on state standardized exams. They must write an essay and participate in an interview with the admissions coordinator. Contrary to the eligibility requirements listed on the student application (and mentioned above), some staff members often say that the program serves students in the "forgotten middle"—those who may not be at the top or bottom of their class. It was mentioned often around the program space that the youth development world is "over-saturated" with programming for students excelling academically or for those that are struggling the most but that there are not enough services for those who are barely making it or for those just getting by. As I will discuss, this goal was challenged by the organization's demand to maintain its success, as measured by 100% high school and 95% college completion rates, through the acceptance of "high-performing" students into the program. EE's philosophy rests on an "asset-rich" approach to youth development versus a deficit approach, which means youth workers maintain that students come to their program already possessing strengths and talents that need only be enhanced and nurtured. Fundamentally, EE's philosophy does not consider students to be broken or in need of fixing. To reflect this philosophy, EE avoids using terms like "at risk" or "inner city" and are very critical and skeptical of potential staff members using these terms. Youth workers call student participants "scholars" throughout their tenure in the program. Those looking to be after-school course instructors or part-time or full-time staff members must share an asset-rich imagining and "high expectations" for Black youth for employment at EE.

Source: Baldridge, 2014, pp. 448–449, http://www.schoolcommunitynetwork.org/SCJ.aspx

 Read the full article at: www.sagepub.com/lochmiller

With the acute focus on a particular context, many qualitative researchers are hesitant to claim that their findings are generalizable. Generalizability is the ability to characterize or apply findings from a research study to the larger population. Rather, qualitative research studies frequently focus on context-rich and context-specific phenomena of interest, and describe these phenomena in such detail that a reader can learn from them and come to understand them well. For instance, rather than studying the perspectives of *all* teachers employed in the district toward the district's new reading initiatives, the qualitative researcher might focus on how a *few* teachers

The emergent nature of qualitative research requires that you are both flexible and ready to deal with unexpected ethical dilemmas.

1. What strategies might you use to assure that ethical decision-making is employed throughout the research process, particularly when the process moves in unexpected directions?

make sense of the new reading initiative within the context of their classroom instruction. The assumption here would be that the phenomenon of interest could be made sense of in an in-depth and context-rich way. It is important to note, however, that different qualitative methodologies define and consider context in different ways. While it is beyond the scope of this textbook to consider all of the ways that context might be considered, if you decide to use a particular qualitative methodology, one question you should consider is: How should I deal with context in the collection and analysis of data?

Emergent Research Design

As noted in Chapter 2, qualitative research designs are typically designed in an emergent way. Emergent research designs are those research designs that may adjust their methods even after data collection begins. The emergent nature of qualitative research requires that you are not only flexible with respect to the purposes of your study, but also that you allow for unexpected pathways to appear during the collection and analysis of your data. For instance, if you are conducting a study of a school district's new reading initiative, you may interview the Director of Teaching and Learning about their role in supporting the new initiative. After interviewing the director, however, you might find that you need to interview another staff member who had more direct involvement in the development and implementation of the reading initiative. Though not included in your original research proposal, this individual may prove to be the most valuable informant, providing information both about the development of the initiative as well as the challenges that have arisen.

Inductive Approach

Qualitative research is inherently inductive, meaning that you move from a specific to a broader understanding. For example, you may collect a series of participant-observations of classroom teachers engaged in professional development about the district's new reading initiative in hopes of understanding how they were making sense of the initiative in relation to their practice. Rather than beginning with a particular theoretical perspective, such as sensemaking theory (Weick, 1995), you would begin with the participant-observations, starting with what you observed and working toward more abstract theoretical understandings that may be informed by the theoretical perspective you ultimately select. In From the Field 5.4, Saldaña (2014) provided a useful example of what inductive thinking looks like in qualitative research.

With qualitative research grounded in inductive thinking, many qualitative researchers collect and analyze their data concurrently, making new discoveries along the way.

FROM THE FIELD 5.4

Inductive Thinking in Qualitative Research

You cannot begin fieldwork as a completely blank slate, but you do enter with an open-ended frame of mind in order to learn-as-you-go-along. Thinking inductively is a willingness to have a minimalist agenda beforehand so that the investigative experience itself is like on-the-job training. You observe life unfolding before you and construct meanings as they happen and later during your private reflections and writing. Each successive fieldwork experience, literally day by day, gives you increased awareness of the participants' world and what it's like to live in it. Your cumulative learnings provide evidence and build a case for your abductive thinking and deductive conclusions of "What's happening here?"

Source: Saldaña, 2014, p. 42

Diverse Data Sources

Qualitative research studies often rely on a diverse array of data, which are typically in the form of spoken or written language (Polkinghorne, 2005). For example, a single study may include interview transcripts, samples of student work, videos of classroom instruction, and observations. We caution you not to assume that more types of data are necessarily better or result in a more robust study. Qualitative researchers are very careful about the data that they include in their studies because the ultimate goal is to collect data that are aligned with a given methodology and your research focus, ultimately leading to a rich understanding of the phenomenon of interest.

Generally, the most commonly collected qualitative data sources are interviews, observations, and documents (Patton, 2002). While qualitative researchers may consider some forms of quantitative data as they work to make sense of a given context (for example, achievement scores of students in a given classroom in hopes of better understanding one aspect of the context), the data are by and large considered non-quantitative in scope and include textual materials, such as interview transcripts, documents, archival data, and field notes. They may also include audio or video recordings of everyday interactions (such as classroom talk), visual materials (such as photographs and maps), and/or online communities (such as social networking sites and blogs).

One useful way to think about qualitative data sources is as either being researcher-generated or naturally occurring (Silverman, 2001). Researcher-generated data are data that would not exist apart from the researcher's intervention or effort in generating them. For instance, interview data are only possible because you asked specific questions that resulted in the participant's responses. In contrast, naturally occurring data are data that exist regardless of the presence of a researcher. For example, if you are interested in studying how students navigate conflict in their everyday classroom conversations, you would likely collect naturally occurring classroom talk. This talk would exist regardless of whether you carried out your study. While we have found these two categories particularly useful for making sense of the different types of qualitative data, it is important to keep in mind that they are somewhat blurry distinctions. For instance, when you make participant-observations and record field notes, you are observing an environment that exists regardless of your study. However, you are producing something that is both researcher-generated

Table 5.2 Summary of Common Qualitative Data Sources
Common Qualitative Data Sources
• Documents
• Everyday Conversations/Interactions
• Focus Groups
• Images (for example, photographs generated by the participants with the aim of understanding their perspectives)
• Interviews
• Journal/Diary Entries (generated by participants)
• Observational Field notes
• Online Communities (for example, websites with professional networking components)
• Visual Data (for example, existing photographs and maps)

(the field notes) and naturally occurring (the actual environment). Nonetheless, by and large, you can view the context you are studying as being naturalistic in scope, as it will go on as usual even if you are not taking notes. Table 5.2 provides a summary of some of the more common qualitative data sources, which are discussed in greater detail in Chapter 7.

Taken together, the core assumptions about qualitative research identified thus far should suggest that successful qualitative research studies involve a willingness to fully identify your own biases, live with ambiguity in both the design and completion of your study, and place value on the participants' experiences and/or practices as you record them in your study. In addition, qualitative research involves a diverse array of data sources, which are closely linked to the aims and purposes of qualitative research.

QUALITATIVE METHODOLOGIES

As noted previously, there are common assumptions that underlie qualitative research. Accordingly, the six qualitative research methodologies we discuss here have a great deal in common. However, they also have several unique characteristics, from the type of data commonly collected to the way that findings are written. Table 5.3 shows the broad purpose or focus of each of these methodologies, as well as the type of data that is customarily collected and research questions posed.

While it is beyond the scope of this textbook to discuss all of the differences associated with each methodology, we strive to present a general overview of some of the differences that you should take into consideration when thinking about qualitative methodologies. Therefore, if you choose to carry out a study using one of the methodologies we describe, we strongly encourage you to engage in further reading around the selected methodology and consider taking additional coursework or seminars focused on your selected methodology to ensure that you have a thorough understanding of its unique characteristics.

𝄐 LINK TO PRACTICE 5.1

SETTING THE STAGE FOR A QUALITATIVE STUDY

Given your interest in studying how central office administrators' define instructional leadership, you decide to undertake a qualitative research study that will explore how central office administrators define instructional leadership. As a building principal, you realize that your own experiences will likely influence your thinking about the central office and thus make focusing only on their perspectives difficult. For example, you have often been frustrated that central office staff do not afford you more control over your building. Similarly, you often worry that they attempt to shape your work by introducing new mandates or expectations. Both of these factors have always frustrated you. Further, these factors make you realize that you will need to be especially careful in analyzing your data so as not to import your own biases and beliefs onto the views of the central office administrators you plan to interview.

Your concerns about your positionality also raise important questions about your ability to fully describe the district context so that an uninformed reader can make sense of the setting where the administrators work and thus how that setting may be influencing their definitions of instructional leadership. Unlike many districts, your district is highly centralized and thus the responsibilities held by school principals are somewhat limited compared to those in other settings. Your challenge, then, is to describe this context so that your readers will understand how this setting shapes the central office administrators' understanding of the work of principals.

A final point you consider relates to the data that you will use to complete your research study. While you are most interested in understanding how central office administrators define (and thus think about) instructional leadership at the school level, you realize that interviews will be an important part of your study. But what other sources of data might you use? For example, the job description of the principals in the district might provide some indications about the ways that the central office defines leadership. Likewise, you might be able to "see" how they define instructional leadership by watching their interactions with principals in meetings. Further, you also realize that pictures such as organizational charts might depict how the central office positions principals relative to other leaders in the district. Thus, you realize that your study will likely need to rely on an array of different types of data to fully explain how central office administrators define instructional leadership.

Focus Questions

1. What are the ways in which you can account for your positionality throughout the course of your research study?

2. How might you decide which types of data are most appropriate for your qualitative research study?

Case Study

A case study is an approach to qualitative research in which a practitioner-scholar focuses on a detailed study of one or more cases within a bounded system. Yin (2009) defined a case study as "an empirical inquiry about a contemporary phenomenon (e.g., a "case"), set within its real-world context" (p. 18). A case is thought of as being a bounded system in which there are a set of parts or operations that work together to create the whole. In case study methodology, you are interested in understanding the individual parts, the relationships among them, and how they

Table 5.3   Summary of the Key Characteristics of Selected Qualitative Methodologies

Dimension	Qualitative Methodologies					
	Case Study	Grounded Theory	Narrative	Phenomenology	Ethnography	Discourse Analysis
Research Purpose	To describe one or more cases in depth or to consider how something may be occurring within a given case or cases (e.g., how a school district inducts new teachers)	To generate a grounded theory that describes and/or explains a particular phenomenon (e.g., the process of inducting new teachers)	To understand the life stories and experiences of individuals (e.g., the life stories of novice teachers, particularly as they relate to choosing a teaching career)	To describe one or more individuals' experiences of a phenomenon (e.g., the experience of being a first-year teacher)	To describe, analyze, and interpret the practices, cultural patterns, and perspectives of participants within their natural environment(s) over time (e.g., a study of the everyday practices and perspectives that are central to becoming a teacher during the first five years)	To generate an understanding of the role and function of talk in the production of social practice (e.g., the various versions of "successful teaching" that are produced in the ways that teachers talk about students during team meetings)
Primary Data Collection Method	Multiple data sources, often including interviews, observations, and documents	Interviews and may include observations	Interviews and may include photographs, diaries, and other data sources that might support an understanding of a participants' storied life	In-depth interviews	Participant observations over an extended period of time; interviews; and other relevant documents	Naturally occurring talk (e.g., classroom conversations) or text (e.g., online discussions), interviews, documents, and, depending upon the type of discourse analysis, visual images
Example Research Question	What do central office administrators in an urban school district define as the primary instructional leadership responsibilities for school principals?	What was the process of implementing instructional leadership in an urban school district as perceived by school principals and district administrators?	How do school principals in an urban school district experience instructional leadership responsibilities?	What are the lived experiences of school principals as instructional leaders in an urban school district?	What are the everyday instructional leadership practices of urban school principals?	How do the conversational practices of central office administrators make evident the scope of principals' instructional leadership responsibilities?

Source: Adapted from Johnson & Christensen, 2010, p. 383

function as a whole. Case study methodology is particularly useful when asking certain types of research questions. These questions include "descriptive" questions, such as "what is happening or has happened?" and "explanatory" questions, such as "how or why did something happen?" (Yin, 2012, p. 5). For instance, as a practitioner-scholar, you may be interested in exploring how the human resource department supports principals learning about a new teacher evaluation system. This study could be framed descriptively by asking, "What support does the human resource department provide to principals as they enact a new teacher evaluation system?" It could also be framed as an explanatory study by asking, "How does the human resource department support principals as they enact a new teacher evaluation system?"

Not surprisingly, one of the first steps in case study research is to define your case, which could be a person, organization, event, and so on. The selected case will ultimately serve as your unit of analysis (Yin, 2012). Beyond this, you must determine whether you will focus on a single case or multiple cases, or whether it will be a holistic or an embedded case study, as illustrated in Figure 5.1. A holistic case study focuses on the case as a whole. Thus, if you study what is

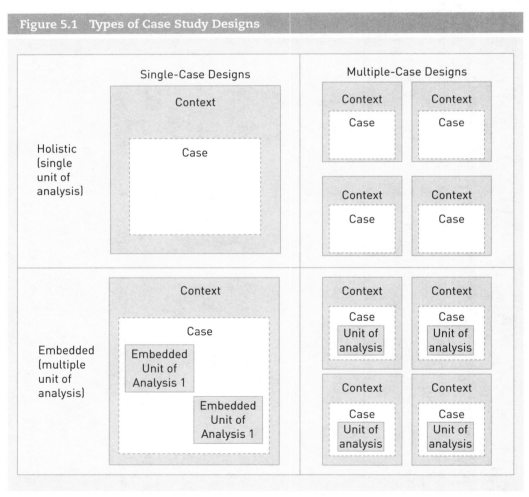

Figure 5.1 Types of Case Study Designs

Source: Adapted from Yin, 2012, p. 8

happening in relation to instruction at a STEM charter school, you would consider all of the parts and perspectives that make up the instructional practices at the school. On the other hand, an embedded case study would focus on some aspect of instruction within the STEM school. For example, you might focus solely on the use of technology to support math instruction in tenth-grade classrooms.

Case study methodology often includes a theoretical framework. A specific theory may be particularly useful in helping you define your case, create research questions, determine the types of data you may collect, and even inform how you analyze your data. For instance, if you are studying professional development learning communities in a school district, you may use the theory of communities of practice (Lave & Wenger, 1991) to inform your case study design. This particular theoretical perspective highlights how a community of individuals with shared goals and knowledge evolve over time and engage in communal practices. This particular theory may be used to help you define your case; perhaps leading you to define your case as one professional learning community within one individual school. As you became more familiar with the theory, it would likely also inform your overarching research questions, the type of data you ultimately collect, and how you make sense of your data. It is thus important to take time up front to become familiar with the literature and those theories previously used to make sense of a particular phenomenon. We see such familiarity as essential, as it can support you in developing a solid case study research design.

While theoretical perspectives may indeed inform the types of data you collect, data collection in a case study typically includes multiple data sources and most commonly includes interviews, observations, and documents. Yin (2012, p. 10) identified six common data sources in case study, as listed here.

1. Direct Observations (e.g., human actions or a physical environment)

2. Interviews (e.g., open-ended conversations with key participants)

3. Archival Records (e.g., student records)

4. Documents (e.g., newspaper articles, letters and e-mails, reports)

5. Participant-Observations (e.g., being identified as a researcher but also filling a real-life role in the scene being studied)

6. Physical Artifacts (e.g., computer downloads of employees' work

These multiple data sources are often discussed in relationship to the concept of triangulation. While there are varied ways to make sense of this concept, triangulation is most often described as a validity procedure wherein a practitioner-scholar seeks to establish evidence across multiple lines of data (Creswell & Miller, 2000). Jink (1979) noted that the term triangulation originated from military operations in which multiple data points were used to identify an object's actual location. Triangulation is thought of as the practice of using multiple data points to build a solid case for the claims you make. Denzin (1979) described triangulation more specifically as including four different types: (a) participant triangulation, (b) researcher triangulation, (c) data triangulation, and (d) theory triangulation. Participant triangulation ensues when a pattern or theme is corroborated across multiple participants. Researcher triangulation occurs when multiple researchers work together to generate a complex understanding of the unit of analysis, with their perspectives converging around a particular pattern and thereby resulting in stronger evidence than a single researcher could produce. Data triangulation, which is frequently highlighted in case study research, is thought to be possible through the use of varied data sources, with evidence being gathered across time and space. Theory triangulation occurs when researchers apply different theories to a dataset to see how various concepts might help them understand their data more fully and increase evidence for the claims they are making.

In case study methodology, and qualitative research more generally, the term triangulation is often used to rationalize why multiple sources of data are used, as multiple data points are believed to allow for a convergence of evidence around a particular pattern or theme. For example, if you were to study the ways in which the human resource department supports principals in implementing a new teacher evaluation system, you would likely include interviews, observations, and documents to substantiate your claims. Interviews would offer first-hand descriptions of the support that was provided. Observations would offer further evidence of the support provided, particularly if the observations focused on information sessions or professional development. Last, documents would offer independent verification of the support provided over time, as well as descriptions of the support.

Finally, it is important to keep in mind that some people view case study as a methodology (Merriam, 1998), while others orient to it as a strategy or choice of how and what is being studied (Stake, 2005). While we view case study as a distinct methodology, we also recognize that case study methodology is versatile and can be combined with other research approaches, some of which we highlight in this chapter. In other words, a case study can be thought of as the Swiss army knife of research designs, as other qualitative methodologies can easily be integrated into the case study. For instance, case study methodology may be combined with grounded theory, which is discussed below, to study the implementation process of a new curriculum in a school. In such a study, the school would be the case (that is, the bounded system), with a specific focus on developing a theory to explain the implementation process (the grounded theory approach).

Grounded Theory

Grounded theory is a qualitative methodology that focuses on the development or construction of a theory that is grounded in a dataset (Charmaz, 2011). This theory or general explanation typically is generated in order to explain a particular process, action, or practice, such as the process of becoming a school administrator. Glaser and Strauss (1967) originally developed grounded theory in contrast to the sociological theories of the day that they felt were being inappropriately applied to research participants. Rather than simply taking a theory from the pages of a book and using it to explain a process or practice, Glaser and Strauss suggested that theories used to explain a particular process should be based on a deep understanding of how people make sense of the process and/or social action under study. Thus, if a practitioner-scholar is interested in studying the process of teachers transitioning through the mid-career hump toward persisting in the field of teaching, they would collect data that allowed them to study this process and eventually develop an explanation or theory that described the process of mid-career teacher development and persistence in the field of teaching. Quite often, grounded theorists will also develop a visual model to represent their theoretical explanations, as illustrated in Figure 5.2.

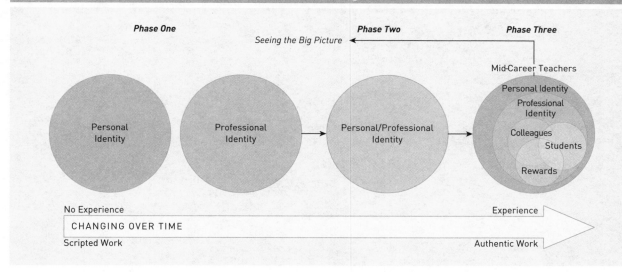

Figure 5.2 An Example of a Grounded Theory Visual Model of the Development of Mid-Career Teacher Identity and Persistence in the Field of Teaching

Source: Coulter & Lester, 2011, p. 19

Like the other qualitative methodologies discussed in this chapter, there are different versions of grounded theory (Corbin, 2009). These versions include constructivist, objectivist, and postpositivist and bring with them very particular assumptions about how to interpret and make sense of a dataset. If you choose to conduct a grounded theory study, it will be important to become familiar with the seminal writings around this approach to research (see Bryant & Charmaz, 2007; Charmaz, 2006; Glaser, 1978, 1998; and Strauss & Corbin, 1998).

Across grounded theory approaches, there is a shared assumption that data collection and analysis occur simultaneously and result in the practitioner-scholar moving from data collection to data analysis in an ongoing fashion. While one of the fundamental assumptions of qualitative research is being inductive, grounded theorists claim to not stop with induction, as they also seek to engage in abductive thinking (Charmaz, 2011). Saldaña (2014) suggested that abductive thinking is focused on considering "multiple possibilities before you reach a deductive conclusion. Abduction also explores the possible links and causation between phenomena—or, what plausibly leads to what" (p. 40). Thus, grounded theorists engage in both inductive and abductive thinking.

In general, grounded theorists collect in-depth interviews, which are often coupled with observations. Within the research process theoretical sampling is used and viewed as central. Charmaz (2011) defined theoretical sampling as occurring "*after* the initial data collection and analysis" as it entails "sampling data to fill out the properties of an emergent conceptual category" (p. 363). Categorical understandings of the data, then, are developed as the grounded theorist eventually moves toward developing a broad explanation or theory.

Narrative

Narrative research or narrative analysis encompasses a wide variety of qualitative approaches to the study of how people make meaning of their life through story (Polkinghorne, 1989).

INTEGRATING OTHER QUALITATIVE METHODOLOGIES INTO A CASE STUDY

As you begin designing your study, you quickly realize that your focus on a single school district makes your study ideal for case study methodology. You plan to bound your case study in your school district, specifically in the Teaching and Learning Department. You have also amassed a number of documents that help to describe the context for your study and thus will enable you to write at length about the unique circumstances of your district. These, you think, will enable you to produce a case study that accurately defines the context and the work of principals in your district and gives meaning to the central office's definition of instructional leadership.

However, as you begin designing your study, you also begin to realize that the case study methodology is versatile and would allow you to integrate other qualitative methodologies into your design. For example, you explicitly consider integrating grounded theory into your case study as an approach to more deeply describe the ways that administrators in the district define instructional leadership. The advantage to grounded theory, of course, is that it allows you to work closely with the data to develop a theoretical explanation for a process. You see the approach as particularly valuable given that your aim is to develop an explanation or definition based on the perspectives of central office administrators in your district.

Yet, as you consider this option, you also see that grounded theory will change your overall approach to the study. You are *not* primarily interested in developing a theory that explains human actions or a process. You are primarily interested in defining what central office administrators think instructional leadership is and using their thoughts to highlight connections with your work as a building principal. Thus, you wonder whether it is appropriate or necessary to integrate such an approach in your study in the first place. You decide that for now you will keep your research study solely positioned as a case study.

Focus Questions

1. How might you determine where and how to bound a case study?

2. What might be some of the inherent challenges of combining qualitative methodologies within one study?

Broadly, narrative research "takes as its object of investigation the story itself" (Riessman, 1993, p. 1). Narrative research has a long history and draws upon a variety of traditions and disciplinary perspectives, ranging from linguistics to anthropology to history to literature to education. Across such fields, stories have been positioned as a site of meaning-making. In education research, narrative research can be used to explore the stories of students, classroom teachers, administrators, and parents. More specifically, narrative research might be used to explore the story of a student who recently immigrated to the United States or was pushed out of school. Likewise, narrative research might focus on the stories of parents living in low-income communities to understand how the barriers of poverty impact their children's access to public education. Regardless of the focus, narrative research seeks to learn from the individual's storied life and thus make meaning from his or her experiences that can be shared and more broadly understood.

Rosenwald and Ochberg (1992) noted that "personal stories are not merely a way of telling someone (or oneself) about one's life; they are the means by which identities may be fashioned" (p. 1). Indeed, storytelling is part of our everyday life. We often tell people about our day by offering a blow-by-blow account of all that happened, including the key actors, plot, and setting. In narrative research, these stories become the site of study, with the narrative presumed to include an ordering of events and some kind of attempt to make sense of the meaning of the experienced event(s). For instance, as a practitioner-scholar you may be interested in better understanding the lives of veteran teachers and all that is entailed in persisting in the field of teaching for decades. This may lead you to collect a series of interviews with several veteran teachers. You would ask open-ended questions and "listen with a minimum of interruptions," tying your questions and responses to the story being told (Bell, 1988).

Narrative research typically involves the collection of in-depth interviews with participants who have experienced the phenomenon of focus. For example, Anders (2011) collected and analyzed the educational narratives of young men who attended college courses while incarcerated in a closed correctional facility. From the Field 5.5 provides an example of the way in which Anders re-storied the lived stories of one participant. Re-storying or re-telling is the analytical process of gathering the stories told and restructuring them in relationship to time, place, plot, and so on. This is a common practice in narrative research.

Narrative research may also include data other than interviews. Narratives can be found in written forms of communication, from diaries to letters, and might even be elicited through photos. For instance, in Bach's (1998) study of girls and school curriculum, she invited four girls to participate in both informal conversations and interviews, as well as the collection of 80 to 120 photographs each documenting their lives inside and outside of school. Both the conversations and the

FROM THE FIELD 5.5

Example of Narrative Re-telling

"Under the Poverty Line"

"I was like eight or nine, when I see my mom lighting candles in the house because we had no lights. So I know it was bad."—Jay 2007

Jay said "under the poverty line" twice, in succession, before I had a chance to ask him what he meant. He said it a second time when he shared that he wore the same pair of pants and two shirts "every day of the week." Yes, it's hard. If you wear the same pair of pants and two shirts every day of the week, that's definitely under the poverty line. I mean, I use that phrase because I feel like that's the only thing that people can comprehend where I'm coming from. . . . You can't come to school smelling a certain way. And kids picking on you. You know what I mean? And you see other kids doing better than you are, you know? Your attention (is) not really up on school or the books or learning or getting an education, so, how can I improve my living? . . . For me, I guess, not for somebody else, but I turned to the streets. You know what I mean? Evidently. Okay, now I'm in prison, but . . . it was all getting a better lifestyle for me and my family.

Source: Anders, 2011, p. 532

photographs were used to develop a visual narrative. Thus, it is possible that different types of data may be included in a narrative study; however, interview data is a mainstay.

Phenomenology

Phenomenology is a qualitative methodology that applies a philosophical perspective to the study of human experience. Polkinghorne (1989) suggested that, "the purpose of phenomenological research is to produce clear, precise, and systematic descriptions of the meaning that constitutes the activity of consciousness" (p. 45). Rather than studying individual experience, the focus is often on describing how a phenomenon is universally experienced. This is often referred to as the essence of the experience (van Manen, 1990). The essence of an experience is that which is universally experienced. For instance, perhaps as a practitioner-scholar you are interested in studying how first-year administrators experience the sense of isolation that often accompanies their first administrative position. To complete this study, you conduct interviews with first-year administrators who have experienced isolation in their first administrative position. Through your analysis, you then develop an understanding of their experience as a first-year administrator who feels isolated in their first administrative position.

Quite often, practitioner-scholars who carry out phenomenological studies will begin their research with what is referred to as a bracketing interview, wherein they will invite a trained colleague to interview them about their own experiences with the phenomenon of interest as a means of identifying their own biases and judgments (Valle, King, & Halling, 1989). Bracketing is defined as a way to suspend your judgment about the phenomenon of interest in order that you might "see the phenomena as it really is" (Laverty, 2003, p. 23). Thus, through the bracketing interview, the practitioner-scholar seeks to make their assumptions explicit and perhaps even suspend judgment in order to be more open to how others experience the phenomenon of interest. In a phenomenological study, this process is essential as it is a form of reflexivity.

A practitioner-scholar who is interested in conducting a phenomenological study would begin with determining whether their research problem is best examined with this methodology. For instance, is their problem one that is best understood through the study of individuals' shared experiences? If so, the practitioner-scholar would proceed by collecting data, which in phenomenology typically includes in-depth interviews with five to 25 participants (Polkinghorne, 1989). Data may also include participants' written responses or accounts of their experience in a different (often textual) format. A phenomenological interview is open ended and typically involves only one to two broad questions and several follow-up questions focused on clarification of meaning. The first question is often focused on the experience of the individual related to the phenomenon, and the second is focused on the contexts wherein the participant has experienced the phenomenon (Moustakas, 1994). For example, Oreshkina (2007) conducted a phenomenological study centered on the following research questions:

1. What is the thematic structure of the experience of expert teachers working with underachieving students in South Africa, Russia, and the United States?

2. What are the differences and similarities in the structures of the experience of expert teachers from South Africa, Russia, and the United States? (p. 20)

DECIDING UPON A METHODOLOGICAL FOCUS

As you consider your study of central office administrators' understanding of instructional leadership, you wonder whether it might be useful to employ either narrative research or phenomenology. Narrative research, you think, would enable you to capture the stories of principals as they have experienced instructional leadership in the district. While interesting, you quickly realize that this would fundamentally shift your study and thus make it less about the central office administrators' definitions of instructional leadership than about the experiences that principals have had as leaders. You also realize that a phenomenology would not align well with your study, as it would focus on the experience of being an instructional leader in an urban school rather than

on the definitions that central office administrators have developed. Taken together, you realize adopting either a narrative or phenomenology approach would require you to focus your study less on central office administrators' definitions than on the actual stories or experiences of principals as instructional leaders.

Focus Questions

1. What strategies might you employ to determine which qualitative methodology you will use?

2. What role do the underlying assumptions of a given methodology play in shaping how you decide which methodology to use?

Oreshkina began each of her 25 interviews with the following request/question: "Tell me about some times when you were teaching students who were not achieving as much as you thought they could" (p. 25). She then asked follow-up questions that invited the participants to give examples or provide stories of when and where this phenomenon was experienced.

Finally, generally, in phenomenology an interpretative approach to data analysis occurs, often with attention being given to common themes across the dataset. Quite often, a "thematic structure" (Oreshkina, p. 20) or essence is developed, offering the reader an understanding of how the phenomenon of focus was universally experienced.

Ethnography

While it has many meanings (Hammersley & Atkinson, 2007), ethnography is a qualitative approach to the study of cultural patterns and everyday practices and perspectives in natural settings. As is true with most qualitative methodologies, there are many approaches to ethnography, ranging from realist ethnography to confessional ethnography to critical ethnography to postcritical ethnography, to name just a few.

Across ethnographic perspectives, however, there are several commonalities related to what ethnographers do. For instance, generally an ethnography involves a practitioner-scholar participating in the everyday lives of people for an extended period of time. Many ethnographers also claim to use an emic approach to the study of cultural patterns and everyday practices. An emic perspective is one that "looks at things through the eyes of members of the culture being studied" (Willis, 2007, p. 100). In other words, an emic perspective provides an insider's perspective and is positioned in contrast to an etic perspective. An etic perspective typically entails a description or an account of cultural patterns and practices that are based on the conceptual perspectives and frameworks of the researcher.

An ethnography also involves a practitioner-scholar collecting a variety of data sources, often including interview and/or focus group data and participant-observations. Generally, an ethnographer will gather all data sources that may provide insight related to their understanding of the practices under study. For instance, in a four-year ethnography of the resettlement experiences of Burundian youth with refugee status living in southern Appalachia, Anders and Lester (2011) conducted multiple interviews and focus groups, participated in cultural events, and completed several hundred hours of participant-observations in the spaces where the children attended school, socialized, and lived.

Hammersley and Atkinson (2007) described five features as being common to the work of those carrying out an ethnography, including:

1. People's actions and accounts are studied in everyday contexts, rather than under conditions created by the research—such as in experimental setups or in highly structured interview situations. In other words, research takes place in the field.

2. Data are gathered from a range of sources, including documentary evidence of various kinds, but participant observation and/or relatively informal conversations are usually the main ones.

3. Data collection is, for the most part, relatively unstructured, in two senses. First, it does not involve following through a fixed and detailed research design specific at the start. Second the categories that are used for interpreting what people say or do are not built into the data collection process through the use of observation schedules or questionnaires. Instead, they are generated out of the process of data analysis.

4. The focus is usually on a few cases, generally fairly small-scale, perhaps a single setting or group of people. This is to facilitate in-depth study.

5. The analysis of data involves interpretation of the meanings, functions, and consequences of human actions and institutional practices, and how these are implicated in local, and perhaps also wider, contexts. What are produced, for the most part, are verbal descriptions, explanations, and theories; quantification and statistical analysis play a subordinate role at most. (p. 3)

These features implicitly highlight the importance of considering time, resources, and access when proposing to carry out an ethnography. Fundamentally, ethnographic research entails a long-term commitment to being in the field and interacting with research participants. As a practitioner-scholar, one of the things you need to consider prior to conducting an ethnography is whether you can devote the time to completing such a study. For example, could you be away from your job for months and/or years? Do you have access to such a

Long-term fieldwork is central to conducting an ethnography.

1. What are some of the ethical challenges that may arise when you are in the field (research site) for an extended period of time, particularly as you develop personal relationships with your participants?

research site? Do you have the resources needed to gather and analyze the data? These are important things to consider at the onset.

Discourse Analysis

Discourse analysis is perhaps best understood as a qualitative methodology that focuses on the study of talk (verbal and nonverbal interactions) and texts (online discussions, documents). It can be broadly characterized as involving the study of talk and text in social practice (Potter, 1997). In other words, there is often a fundamental privileging of data that are naturally occurring, such as everyday conversations in a classroom. There are many approaches to discourse analysis, ranging from critical discourse analysis to poststructural discourse analysis to discursive psychology (Jorgensen & Phillips, 2002). These varied approaches bring with them particular assumptions regarding the very meaning of discourse, the type of data that should be collected, and how the analysis and interpretation should proceed. Nonetheless, across the majority of discourse analysis approaches, there are three common assumptions (Wood & Kroger, 2000).

The first shared assumption is that language always functions to construct something. For example, in talk when someone says, "I was thinking about going to get some pizza. Might you want to come along?" their talk serves to construct an invitation ("might you . . . come along"). The language is not a simple representation of the speaker's inner thoughts; rather, it is being used to produce social action. In this way, discourse analysts view language as action-oriented, as people use it to do many things, such as complain, blame, question, offer advice, create identities, establish expectations and norms, and so on. The action basis of language can be considered in relation to three aspects: (a) what the language utterance is about; (b) what the speaker does with language utterances; and (c) the effects of a language utterance on others. For example, if a student says to a teacher, "you are the reason that I failed the test!" the utterance provides evidence of what the event is about (student failed a test), but it is also doing something. In this case, it is serving to assign blame, as the student positions the teacher (through their language) as the reason for the failure. In a discourse analysis study, we would be equally interested in the next utterance. Does, for instance, the teacher take up the next conversational turn or do other students take it up? What is the function of the next conversational turn? There are indeed many questions that we could ask and consider in great detail.

A second shared assumption about language is that it is also constructed, meaning that there are grammatical devices and linguistic resources that make an utterance possible. Many discourse analysis studies, therefore, give careful attention to the nature of these devices, as these devices are what make the action possible. For instance, in classroom talk, it may be useful to consider pronoun use and how pronoun use might create a sense of teamwork versus working alone. If a teacher says, "Come on everyone—*we* can figure this out together" versus "Come on. *You* need to figure it out" a sense of solidarity versus isolation may be constructed. In fact, research on pronoun use has highlighted how pronouns tend to index solidarity between speakers, while also pointing to power differentials (Ostermann, 2003). In this way, it is important for the discourse analyst to consider the grammatical and linguistic resources used in order to make sense of how the action of the talk is being achieved.

The third and final shared assumption is that discourse is generally understood to be variable. This is an important consideration for discourse analysis, as the assumption is that language likely functions to do different things. Wood and Kroger (2000) suggested that variability is an important thing to understand in discourse analysis research because participants use language in varying ways " . . . to construct their talk for different purposes, for different audiences, and for different occasions" (p. 10). For instance, if you are studying the language that principals use to describe learning improvement challenges, you might observe that they describe these challenges in one way to a district administrator and in another way to a classroom teacher or parent. This variability is of interest within a discourse analysis study.

As highlighted in Table 5.3, a discourse analysis study may include different types of data, ranging from interviews to online discussions to naturally occurring classroom talk. Generally, the type of data that is collected relates to the questions you ask and the discourse analysis tradition that you draw upon. Discourse analysis research uniquely creates opportunities, however, for a practitioner-scholar to study naturally occurring data, as it is often assumed that:

> . . . if we are to understand and analyze participants' own concepts and accounts, then we have to find and analyze them not in response to our research questions, but in the places they ordinarily and functionally occur— "in the activities in which they're employed." (Sacks, 1992, p. 27)

In other words, while you can certainly use interview data in a discourse analysis study, it is often helpful to explore whether you might collect data in the places where they occur regardless of your presence. For instance, Lester and Gabriel (2015) conducted a discourse analysis study of reading comprehension lessons in eight fourth grade classrooms across two states in the United States. Their study considered how the actual interactions of the students and teacher resulted in particular constructions or understandings of what it means to be a good reader. Rather than interviewing the students and teachers and asking them, "what does it mean to be a good reader?" they focused on analyzing how constructions of a good reader were made visible in the actual reading classroom—the place where one might argue it matters most.

⚓ LINK TO PRACTICE 5.4

MAKING A METHODOLOGICAL CHOICE

As you continue thinking through your research study, you also consider whether you might approach your study using an ethnography or discourse analysis. However, you realize that you are not specifically interested in studying the cultural and everyday practices of central office administrators. You decide that an ethnography will be unlikely to serve your needs. Further, the question you are most interested in relates less to the discourse practices of central office administrators and more to the perceptions of central office administrators. You decide, then, that it would not be appropriate to conduct a discourse analysis for your study given your current research interest.

As you reflect on the interests you have, you decide that a case study is most appropriate, as it will enable you to describe the perceptions of the central office

administrators. You will rely primarily on interviews and augment them with observations of meetings, as well as district documents that describe the principal's responsibilities and roles. Yet, even as you make this methodological choice, you realize that the flexibility of qualitative research would have enabled you to take many different paths. Indeed, you see that qualitative research is an umbrella term that characterizes many unique approaches to data collection, analysis, and interpretation.

Focus Questions

1. How might your study be conceived of differently if you pursued an ethnography?

2. How might your study be conceived of differently if you pursued a discourse analysis?

SUMMARY

In this chapter, we presented a general overview of the basic characteristics of qualitative research, noting some of the assumptions that are shared across qualitative methodologies. We also discussed common data sources, as well as some of the ways to think about data types (for example, researcher-generated versus naturally occurring). In addition, we presented a general overview

of six qualitative methodologies, including: (a) case study, (b) grounded theory, (c) narrative, (d) phenomenology, (e) ethnography, and (f) discourse analysis. Throughout the chapter, we noted that there is great variability within qualitative research methodologies. Therefore, there is a need to engage in further study of the qualitative methodology that ultimately frames your research study.

KEY TERMS

Abductive Thinking 107
Bracketing 110
Bracketing Interview 110
Case 102
Case Study 102
Data Triangulation 106
Discourse Analysis 113
Emergent Research Designs 99
Emic Perspective 111

Essence 110
Ethnography 111
Etic Perspective 111
Generalizability 98
Grounded Theory 106
Inductive Thinking 99
Narrative Research 107
Naturally Occurring Data 100
Participant Triangulation 105

Phenomenology 110
Re-storying 109
Reflexivity 95
Researcher-Generated Data 100
Researcher Triangulation 106
Theoretical Sampling 107
Theory Triangulation 106
Thick Description 97
Triangulation 105

QUESTIONS TO CONSIDER

1. What are the common characteristics of qualitative research? How do these characteristics shape the way that you would carry out a qualitative research study?

2. What are the various types of qualitative data and how might they be classified? Provide examples of data types related to your own research topic of interest.

3. What are the reasons that you would carry out a qualitative research study?

4. What types of research questions might you explore when carrying out a qualitative research study?

5. What types of understanding can a qualitative study provide? What types of information does it not provide?

6. What are the basic characteristics of the six qualitative methodologies discussed (case study, grounded theory, narrative, phenomenology, ethnography, and discourse analysis)?

CHAPTER EXERCISES

1. Develop a research study using one of the qualitative methodologies discussed in this chapter. Identify the (1) methodology and (2) overall purpose/scope of your study. Link your discussion to the literature review you began conducting in Chapter 3.

2. Considering the study you developed in the first chapter exercise, write a description of your data sources and consider how these data sources are linked to your methodological choice(s).

3. Develop a series of research questions specific to each of the qualitative methodologies discussed in this chapter. Relate each of these questions to your research topic of interest.

4. As noted above, accounting for your beliefs, biases, and perspectives is an important consideration in qualitative research. Write a positionality or reflexivity statement that is directly linked to your research interests.

LEARNING EXTENSIONS

There are a multitude of qualitative research methods books that may serve as a foundation for your understanding of qualitative methodologies. It is often helpful, however, to begin reading those books that are specifically written for an education audience. As such, Bogdan and Biklen's (2007) introductory qualitative research text, *Qualitative Research for Education: An Introduction to Theories and Methods*, provides a general overview to the qualitative research process, with the discussion situated within the field of education. Similarly, Hatch's (2002) book, *Doing Qualitative Research in Education Settings*, offers a discussion of research paradigms, theories, and qualitative methodologies and methods in relation to educational contexts. Thus, these two books are useful beginning points for those interested in deepening their understanding of qualitative research in education.

Sharpen your skills with SAGE edge!

edge.sagepub.com/lochmiller

SAGE edge for Students provides a personalized approach to help you accomplish your coursework goals in an easy-to-use learning environment. You'll find action plans, mobile-friendly eFlashcards, and quizzes as well as videos, web resources, and links to SAGE journal articles to support and expand on the concepts presented in this chapter.

6

INTRODUCING QUANTITATIVE RESEARCH

CONDUCTING QUANTITATIVE RESEARCH

As a classroom teacher, you have been consistently interested in improving your students' performance in reading and math. You have noted that these subjects are harder for some students and have often wondered why some students struggle more than others. As you consider ways that you could study student performance in these subjects, you quickly find yourself contemplating a quantitative research design. For such a study, you might use your students' recent assessment results or their in-class benchmark tests as a measure of their performance in reading and math. You could, if you wanted to conduct an experiment, change some aspect of your instruction to see if it improved student learning in one or both subjects. Yet, you wonder whether this is feasible. Finally, you might conduct a survey of students to determine what students feel would help them more in these subjects.

INTRODUCTION

As illustrated in the opening vignette, quantitative research almost always focuses on the analysis of numeric data. Unlike qualitative research methodologies, some of which we described in Chapter 5, quantitative research methodologies represent a type of research that relies less on emergent designs than on standardized approaches and measures. Quantitative research has historically been rooted in positivism, which assumes that there is a single, measurable reality (see Chapter 1 for a review of the research paradigms). In this chapter, we present a basic overview of quantitative research, noting its aims and purposes. We focus on the defining characteristics of quantitative research, particularly pointing toward its emphasis on objectivity, positivism, and the management of bias. We then review two types of quantitative research—experimental and non-experimental research.

Learning Objectives

By the end of the chapter, you will be able to:

- Describe the basic characteristics of quantitative research.

- Paraphrase some of the differences between the characteristics of quantitative research and qualitative research.

- Summarize the differences between experimental and non-experimental research.

- Illustrate the basic features of the selected approaches to quantitative research, including: experimental, single-subject, correlational, causal-comparative, secondary data analysis, and survey.

- Explain the various ways in which a selected quantitative research study can be conducted.

As this text is written for practitioner-scholars, we intentionally limit our discussion around experimental research designs, recognizing that experimental designs are unlikely to be completed by a practitioner-scholar. Instead, we focus on non-experimental research designs, in particular correlational, causal-comparative, secondary-data analysis (for instance, data-mining), and surveys. We see practitioner-scholars being more likely to use these quantitative research designs.

We begin this chapter by reviewing the broad characteristics of quantitative research and, where appropriate, note how these characteristics differ from qualitative research. We then review experimental research designs as one type of quantitative research. Next, we review four types of non-experimental research: correlational, causal-comparative, secondary data analysis, and survey research. Throughout our discussion, we highlight the various research questions and considerations that you might ask as you select a quantitative research design.

We intentionally avoid presenting these designs in significant detail. Instead, our aim in this chapter is to broadly familiarize you with the types of quantitative research that exist and what, at a very basic level, you need to know to be able to distinguish among them. It thus bears noting that after this discussion, further reading and preparation are needed to fully understand quantitative research. This chapter serves as a broad overview and a light introduction, which cannot fully prepare you to conduct a quantitative research study. Students with a pronounced interested in quantitative research should work with their adviser to identify basic and intermediate quantitative research courses that will introduce them to the breadth of the methods and analytic techniques that are used.

QUANTITATIVE RESEARCH: AIMS AND PURPOSES

Quantitative research, much like qualitative research, is an umbrella term that encompasses a variety of approaches. Generally, the aim of quantitative research is to describe patterns, trends, and relationships in numeric data. We highlight here some of the general assumptions of quantitative research, recognizing that these assumptions are continually open to critique and further explanation. Nonetheless, it is important to become familiar with some of the widespread assumptions, as they shape how quantitative research studies are designed and results are generated. We highlight next seven characteristics of many of the approaches to quantitative research.

CHARACTERISTICS OF QUANTITATIVE RESEARCH

First, quantitative research has historically been deeply rooted in positivism. It has been noted that, "under the positivist schema, the scientific method" has been presumed to be "the best approach for understanding phenomena in the world around us, and in addition, claims about the world are only meaningful when they can be verified through observation" (O'Dwyer & Bernauer, 2014, p. 45). Thus, quantitative researchers have frequently assumed that there is an objective reality to be known, and that this reality can be known concretely. Unlike some approaches to qualitative research, which presume that knowledge and reality are constructed in and through the research process, quantitative research often emphasizes that through precise measurement and structured analysis research can lead to a full understanding of reality. As such, quantitative research has often been characterized as "top-down," wherein practitioner-scholars develop hypotheses on the basis of theory and then test these hypotheses using data.

Second and relatedly, deductive analysis is central to quantitative research. In deductive analysis, a practitioner-scholar works from a series of premises to formulate a broader understanding or conclusion. In quantitative research studies, practitioner-scholars often construct their analyses based on a series of hypotheses that are typically derived from existing theories. For example, a quantitative researcher might review the educational literature to determine how a student's socioeconomic status is reported to influence their performance on state reading assessments. The practitioner-scholar might determine that socioeconomic status is negatively related to a performance on these assessments, meaning that students from families living in low-income communities will perform at lower levels on the assessment than their peers from higher income communities. The practitioner-scholars would thus seek to confirm or disconfirm this hypothesis through his or her analysis of numerical data. In this way, the practitioner-scholar ". . . starts with a theory and then narrows that theory down to a more specific hypothesis that can be tested empirically using data that have been collected" (O'Dwyer & Bernauer, 2014, p. 46). It is critical that practitioner-scholars think critically about the theories that inform their hypotheses and the constructs that they eventually query. We cannot assume that the literature contains well-grounded assumptions, and thus must be thoughtful about how we engage in deductive analysis.

Third, quantitative researchers typically use numerical data (for example, survey data, student achievement data, and age/demographic data). Unlike qualitative research, which may employ a variety of data types, one of the unique aspects of quantitative research is that it relies almost exclusively on numeric data. While qualitative research may also consider numerical data, it is not considered a mainstay data source and would typically be used in a very different way. In contrast, numerical data could be described as the main data type in quantitative research studies. Such data can be retrieved from a variety of sources ranging from student achievement tests, school information systems, surveys, and other standardized collection measures.

Fourth, it is important to understand that quantitative research is *not* synonymous with statistics. Rather, quantitative researchers *use* statistics as tools to make sense of their data in much the same way that a qualitative researcher uses codes or memos. In a quantitative research study we would expect to see statistics being used, something that we discuss in more detail in Chapter 9.

Fifth, generalizability is a common characteristic of many quantitative studies. Generalizability is the assumption that data from a sample represent the larger population from which the sample is drawn. This concept allows the quantitative researcher to assume that their results represent the broader population on some measure. For example, if you wanted to study the effect of a new reading intervention on students, it would be impractical and potentially damaging to try to administer the new intervention to *all* students. Thus, a practitioner-scholar might collect data about the effect of the reading intervention on a smaller group of students who have characteristics that are similar to the population as a whole. This would allow the practitioner-scholar to assume to some degree that the effect of the intervention on the sample might be observed across the population were the intervention to be administered on a wider scale.

Generalizability requires that all individuals have an equal chance to be included in a study. To achieve this, quantitative researchers typically rely on randomization or random assignment. Random assignment is the process of assigning participants in a way that ensures each participant has an equal chance of being assigned to a group. Randomization is especially important in experimental and survey research designs, designs discussed in more detail later. Some people assume that randomization is simply a haphazard approach to selecting research participants. For example, someone may assume that selecting participants from a list is random. Nothing could be further from the truth. Random participant selection is intentional in that the practitioner-scholar creates conditions so that every possible participant has an equal chance of being included in the study. To ensure this condition is met, the practitioner-scholar must know the characteristics of the population, as well as put in to place procedures to ensure that participants in the sample have an equal chance of being included in the study.

Sixth, another key concern for quantitative researchers relates to the notion of objectivity in the research process. Historically, the notion of objectivity has been linked to the assumption that a truth or reality exists outside of the research process or practitioner-scholar. Under this assumption, the practitioner-scholar is tasked with uncovering an independent truth or reality without contaminating it with his or her biases. In the social sciences, and more particularly educational research, this perspective on objectivity has been increasingly critiqued and even rejected by some. While this critique has been truer of qualitative researchers than quantitative researchers, there is a growing recognition that humans are involved in the doing and making of research (Morgan, 1983). More generally, however, in the quantitative research literature, objectivity has often been discussed in relation to administering exams and defined as being linked to the "extent to which scores on a test are undistorted by the biases of those who administer and score it" (Gall, Gall, & Borg, 2007, p. 646). Within such a definition, the idea of objective knowing is privileged, wherein bias is minimized or managed. Accordingly, quantitative researchers often assume that the biases of the researcher can be minimized and that, unlike qualitative research where the researcher is the instrument of the study, the researcher's role is detached or distanced from the study (O'Dwyer & Bernauer, 2014, p. 47), as she or he takes up an objective stance. Objectivity, then, is frequently assumed to allow quantitative researchers to conduct research in ways that minimize bias and give them confidence that their data accurately reflect the reality of those who were studied.

Seventh and finally, quantitative research is characterized by a strong concern for freedom from bias and measurement error. Quantitative researchers take numerous steps to reduce potential bias and error in their research. Some of these steps have already been discussed (such as pursuing objectivity, randomization, and so on). Bias refers to a practitioner-scholar's or study's tendency to ignore, overlook, or interpret incorrectly data collected in a study. A related concern for quantitative researchers is to design studies that enable them to minimize measurement error, which some have defined as "the difference between an individual's true score on a test and the scores that the individual actually obtains on it [the test] when administered over a variety of conditions" (Gall, Gall, & Borg, 2007, p. 644). Bias and error both undermine the quantitative practitioner-scholar's assurance that what they are observing is an accurate (true) reflection of the world around. Generally, it has been suggested that bias and error both undercut the positivist orientation common to much of quantitative research.

REFLECTIVE OPPORTUNITY 6.1

As you reflect upon the characteristics of quantitative research, you may realize that there are ethical considerations that are particularly pertinent when carrying out a quantitative study. Indeed, each methodological approach brings with it both similar and unique ethical considerations.

1. What might be some of the ethical considerations that may be unique or more relevant to quantitative research designs? Why might this be so?

QUANTITATIVE RESEARCH DESIGNS

Quantitative research rests on a series of established research designs. There are two broad types of quantitative research designs: experimental and non-experimental. Both of these types will be discussed in greater detail below. For now, it is important for you to understand that these designs "function somewhat like templates" and "involve standard nomenclature and procedures for organizing variables, selecting samples, establishing a schedule of data collection, and selecting appropriate techniques for statistical analysis" (Gall, Gall, & Borg, 2007, p. 299). Unlike qualitative research, which values emergent and flexible research designs, quantitative research designs tend to be more heavily standardized and structured.

Experimental Research Designs

Experimental designs seek to identify a cause and effect between an independent and dependent variable. Admittedly, we think it is unlikely that a practitioner-scholar will carry out an experimental research study. Experimental research requires considerable understanding of the research process and frequently involves significant resources (such as people, money, and time) to be completed successfully. While experimental research is not commonly conducted by practitioner-scholars, it is important for practitioner-scholars to understand how experimental research is distinct from other types of research within the quantitative research paradigm.

At their core, experimental research designs enable practitioner-scholars to answer the question, "Does X cause Y?" As such, experimental research designs are often considered the gold standard for research practice because these designs allow practitioner-scholars to determine whether a particular intervention causes a change in behavior or performance (Johnson & Christensen, 2010). More specifically, experimental research rests on the theory of causation (Collingwood, 1940; Cook & Shadish, 1994), which broadly assumes that individuals can manipulate conditions and thus effect changes in individual performance or practice. Experimental research designs involve two types of variables. Independent variables, which do not depend on other factors and are thus manipulated by the researcher to determine whether the variables cause measurable changes in a particular outcome, and dependent variables, which are dependent on other factors and thus thought to influence the outcomes that occur. In an experimental research design, the practitioner-scholar seeks to conclude that the independent variable was the cause of the observed outcomes, performance, or practice. This is illustrated in Figure 6.1.

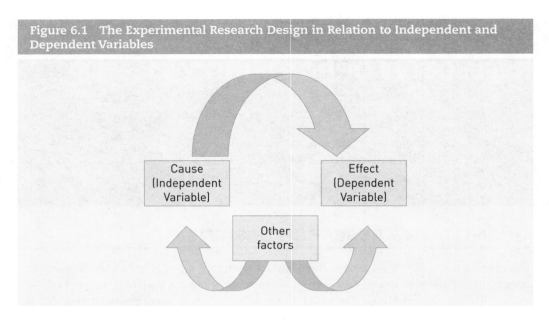

Experimental research typically rests on a hypothesis positing that changes in the independent variables will cause some change in the dependent variables. Further, a true experimental research study involves a treatment and control group. A treatment group receives the intervention from the practitioner-scholar while the control group does not. This allows for the practitioner-scholar to determine whether changes were the direct result of the intervention rather than other conditions.

Quantitative researchers have developed different types of experimental research designs, which allow them to assess the effect of independent variables. The most common experimental research design is the "pre-test/post-test" design, in which the practitioner-scholar assesses research participants *before* applying the intervention and then assesses the same participants *after* the intervention has been applied. Such a design may or may not use a control group, depending on the specific aims of the study. In the most rigorous experimental studies (a *true* experimental study), a control group is almost always used. A "post-test only" design involves assessing performance *after* the intervention has been applied. A limitation of this type of experimental design is that the researcher cannot fully account for the participants' performance before the intervention was applied, but rather assumes that the participants had similar characteristics and thus would be equally impacted by the intervention. A derivative of these designs is the Solomon Four-Group Design (Solomon, 1949), in which a practitioner-scholar uses four groups of participants, with two completing a "pre-test/post-test" design and two completing a "post-test only" design to determine whether the intervention had an effect.

All experimental research designs rely heavily on the researcher's ability to manipulate an independent variable and to control for the influence of extraneous variables. What does manipulation look like in an experimental research study conducted in schools? One possibility might be introducing students to *different* reading or math curricula. In an experimental research study, the practitioner-scholar would intentionally change the conditions that are presented to students to determine whether those conditions (that is, a particular curricula) cause a change in their performance. Relatedly, practitioner-scholars must control for the influence of extraneous variables. Practitioner-scholars exercise control on experiments by structuring specific conditions within the experimental design. For example, if a practitioner-scholar wanted to determine whether a new reading or math curriculum influences student achievement, the researcher would need to control which students were instructed using the new curriculum and which were not. Moreover, they would need to control for the potential impact that students' previous instruction, demographic characteristics, or learning needs might have on the experiment. To this end, the researcher would seek to assign some of the students to a control group, which is the group that does not receive access to the treatment. The control group is intended to provide the researcher with a comparison group. Similarly, the practitioner-scholar might assign students to the treatment and control group so that the students are roughly distributed by ability, background characteristics, and so on. Taken together, these steps allow the researcher to exercise greater control over other, extraneous factors that may unintentionally influence the cause-effect relationship that the practitioner-scholar is interested in studying.

Practitioner-scholars who undertake experimental research designs are particularly concerned with threats to experimental validity. These threats undermine the practitioner-scholar's ability to say with confidence that the independent variable was the cause of the observed effect. Internal validity refers to the practitioner-scholar's ability to say that the independent variable caused the changes in the dependent variable. Experimental studies with a high degree of internal validity allow the researcher to say with confidence that the manipulation of the independent variable caused the changes that they observed in the dependent variable. External validity, on the other hand, refers to the degree to which the results of a study are generalizable. Experimental studies with a high degree of external validity allow the practitioner-scholar to say, with confidence, that their results could be obtained in other settings if the same procedures were used.

What factors influence or potentially undermine internal validity in experimental research studies? This question is one that quantitative researchers have spent considerable time thinking through as they develop their studies. Two sources, Campbell and Stanley (1971) and Cook and Campbell (1979), indicated that internal validity is threatened by history, participant maturation, testing, instrumentation, participant selection, and mortality. History (which we refer to as world events) can affect the experimental research design. These events can be as simple as a fire drill in a school during the experiment to a researcher who ends an experiment prematurely because of the exhaustion of research findings. Experimental research designs are also impacted by the development of research participants—this is particularly true with children. As children age and become more mature, these conditions can impact their participation in an experiment. A child who was selected for an experiment on the basis of some characteristic initially might change by the time the experiment is completed. Testing is also an important consideration for experimental research designs involving children or educators. Pre-tests may influence or shape the child or educator's thinking and thus unintentionally influence their performance on the post-test. Internal validity may also be threatened when the researcher uses instruments that are either not of equal difficulty or that have been constructed in a way that does not allow them to compare the student's or educator's perceptions equally between the administration of the pre-test and post-test. Participant selection also impacts internal validity. Any error in the composition of the control and treatment group, for example, can significantly alter the results achieved in an experimental study. Too many high-ability students in the control group and too few in the treatment group might suggest that the experiment was not effective or successful simply because the control group was improperly weighted. A final consideration related to internal validity is the mortality of participants. This does not refer simply to the death of a research participant, although it certainly could. Rather, mortality refers to research participants who drop out of a research study for any reason. As you'll recall from Chapter 4, the Institutional Review Board requires that participants be allowed to leave a research study at any time without penalty. While this is an important right for research participants, instability in participant groups can decrease the internal validity of experimental studies.

In addition to threats to internal validity, practitioner-scholars who complete experimental research also face threats related to external validity. Bracht and Glass (1968) noted that the threats to external validity can be broken into two categories. The first category relates to the population to which the researcher is attempting to generalize their experimental findings. Practitioner-scholars must recognize that even in the most pristine experimental conditions there is an inherent difficulty in stating that an experiment would produce the same results for all participants. The second category relates to the inherent difficulties in generalizing findings across settings, contexts, and conditions. Indeed, even while experiments can be carefully crafted, practitioner-scholars must acknowledge that slight variations in conditions can meaningfully alter the efficacy of specific interventions. For example, even though many tests are developed using experimental research designs, it is difficult to assure that once the tests are deployed in schools that the conditions will exactly mirror those in the experimental study. Moreover, it also difficult to assure that students will perform exactly as the students who initially participated in the study did. Thus, even though experimental research is considered by some to be the most robust approach for assessing causal effects, there is still a degree of uncertainty once the interventions are deployed in schools, with real students, under real conditions.

Given these various requirements, you may be wondering whether or not experimental studies can occur in schools or district settings. Yes, they can. Johnson and Christensen (2010) noted that experimental research can occur in the field, in a laboratory, or even online. In many experimental studies that examine how curriculum and instructional innovations influence student learning, researchers randomly select students from schools and districts and then work with educators to assign these students to treatment and control groups. These studies often occur as part of large, randomized control trials (RCT). An RCT allows practitioner-scholars to create "experimental conditions" in which they can test the efficacy of a specific educational intervention, curriculum, or program. Indeed, Vogt, Gardner, and Haeffele (2012) noted that RCTs are "a good tool for detecting program outcomes" (p. 49), with this claim being one that has also been critiqued and called into question by some educational researchers.

It bears noting that there has been increasing emphasis in education on the use of experimental research—for good and for bad. Since the passage of the No Child Left Behind Act of 2001, the Institute for Education Sciences at the U.S. Department of Education has increasingly invested in experimental research studies to test the efficacy of educational interventions. Bauer and Brazer (2012) noted that, "In recent years, the U.S. Department of Education has sought to place educational decision-making on a more 'scientific' footing and to provide resources for district and school leaders to use as they address instructional challenges" (p. 5). The What Works Clearinghouse (WWC) is an example of this shift. The WWC provides educators with resources on best-practices and easily read analyses of recent research studies related to specific educational interventions. The WWC also illustrates the degree to which experimental research is permeating more deeply all facets of a practitioner-scholars' work. Of course, such resources hold particular assumptions about which types of research should be considered best, which is certainly up for debate.

While experimental research is frequently cited as the gold standard for research practice, there are concerns about using experimental research designs in schools. Experimental research designs introduce significant ethical concerns. For example, is it ethical to intentionally withhold an educational intervention that may be effective from students? Is it appropriate to change educational programs on the basis of experimental evidence alone? Is this really the gold standard in research practice? Indeed, Vogt, Gardner, and Haeffele (2012) noted that the broader concern regarding experimental research is that it has been elevated to such a degree that other valid and beneficial methodologies are dismissed or unfairly criticized. Researchers and policy makers are "ill advised" to elevate particular methods (Vogt, Gardner, & Haeffele, 2012, p. 49). Indeed, to return to one of the core premises upon which this textbook is based, methodological decisions should not be informed solely on the basis of external standards but instead on the epistemological orientation and research interests that motivate practitioner-scholars to conduct research in the first place. Further, we must always ask: whose interest does our research serve?

SINGLE-SUBJECT EXPERIMENTAL RESEARCH DESIGNS. Of the experimental research designs that are discussed in the literature, the most common design used by practitioners-scholars is a single-subject or single-case experimental research design (Kazdin, 1982). This design allows a practitioner-scholar to test the effect of an intervention on a single individual or a set of individuals who are considered one group. For example, a practitioner-scholar might use a single-subject experimental design to test whether changes in reading instruction affect an individual student's performance on the state reading assessment. Likewise, a practitioner-scholar might use a single-subject research design to test whether changes in reading instruction affect fourth grade student achievement in reading in a single classroom. As illustrated in From the Field 6.1, the abstract drawn from Barnes and Whinnery (2002) study provides an example of a single-case design with repeated measures. Students with a similar disability were introduced to a particular curriculum. The researchers collected measures at different points in time and reported the results.

Single-subject designs often employ some variation of a pre-test/post-test design. These are frequently referred to as ABA or ABAB designs, in which A refers to the baseline condition and B refers to the treatment condition. The primary consideration for a single-subject design is that you are taking multiple measures at different points in time to determine whether the intervention has an effect on the individual or group of individuals being treated. These measures may be taken at different times, across multiple days, or at different stages of a particular program. Collectively, these measures allow you to determine whether the intervention was the cause of the change in the behavior.

Non-Experimental Research Designs

Unlike experimental research designs, non-experimental research designs do not involve any type of manipulation. Kerlinger (1986) defined non-experimental research as a " . . . systematic

⚓ LINK TO PRACTICE 6.1

CHALLENGES OF AN EXPERIMENTAL DESIGN IN SCHOOLS

You and your colleagues have been invited to participate in an RCT that will assess the effectiveness of a new math curriculum on student math achievement. The new curriculum will employ a combination of face-to-face and online instruction designed to improve student achievement. The curriculum is aimed at students who are struggling in math and for whom traditional interventions do not appear to be effective. While you are interested in participating in the study, you are also aware that such studies pose challenges for you as a teacher and raise ethical concerns in relation to your students. Based on the information provided to you, you find that some of the district's students will receive access to a new math curriculum while others will not. This makes you a bit uncomfortable. The students who will receive access will largely come from low-income families and many will have previously taken remedial or learning support classes. Many of these students have already struggled academically. The researchers are focused on these students, as one of their key questions is to determine whether it improves academic outcomes for students from disadvantaged backgrounds, or improves academic outcomes for students who have been primarily enrolled in remedial/learning support classes.

The students who will receive access will be randomly selected and randomly assigned to classes prior to the start of the school year. This means that conversations you had with your colleagues about which classes would be best for particular students will be overruled by the needs of the research study. Three students who were supposed to be in your classroom because of your success working with students who struggle with learning math could be re-assigned to a different classroom. You realize that you might also not know which students you are receiving until a few days before the new school year. Further, you keep coming back to your great worry—that it may be unethical to provide the improved curriculum to some students but not all. Last, you realize that if you are selected as the instructor of the new curriculum, you will be working with a curriculum that is unfamiliar to you. The researchers have offered to provide training but this makes you worry that students who need the support most will not receive it.

Focus Questions

1. What opportunities do experimental studies, such as an RCT, present to educators to improve their educational practice?

2. What are the potential risks that experimental studies pose for students, teachers, schools, and districts? What can be done to minimize these risks?

REFLECTIVE OPPORTUNITY 6.2

1. Considering Link to Practice 6.1. what are the ethical challenges associated with randomized control trials in school settings?

2. How might practitioner-scholars mitigate these ethical challenges?

3. What could practitioner-scholars do to ensure that RCTs do not introduce unintended consequences for students who may not receive the experimental curriculum?

An Abstract From a Single Subject Study

The Mobility Opportunities Via Education (MOVE®) Curriculum is a functional mobility curriculum for individuals with severe disabilities. This study investigated the effects of the MOVE Curriculum on the functional walking skills of five elementary-aged students with severe, multiple disabilities. The MOVE Curriculum was implemented using a multiple baseline across subjects design. Repeated measures were taken during baseline, intervention, and maintenance phases for each participant. All students demonstrated progress in taking reciprocal steps during either intervention or maintenance. Results for each participant are discussed as well as implications and future directions for research.

Source: Barnes & Whinnery, 2002

 Read the full article at:
www.sagepub.com/lochmiller

empirical inquiry in which the scientist does not have direct control of independent variables because their manifestations have already occurred or because they are inherently not manipulable" (p. 348). Put simply, in a non-experimental research design the practitioner-scholar looks at the quantitative data and attempts to make descriptive and inferential claims about the patterns, trends, or relationships within the dataset.

Non-experimental research designs are often used by practitioner-scholars, as such these designs are relatively straightforward. These designs allow practitioner-scholars to work with data that they already have access to or that they collect. Given the relative ease with which non-experimental research designs can be completed, it is far more likely that a practitioner-scholar would undertake a non-experimental research study versus an experimental research study. And, unlike experimental designs, non-experimental designs do not require practitioner-scholar to randomly assign participants to treatment and control groups. Moreover, these designs do not require the practitioner-scholar to take significant steps to control for the influence of extraneous variables. However, non-experimental designs do not allow the practitioner-scholar to make claims about casualty. Indeed, this is a significant limitation of non-experimental research and one that should be weighed carefully when designing research studies.

There are three broad types of non-experimental research approach. These include: (a) descriptive, (b) prediction, and (c) explanatory studies (O'Dwyer & Bernauer, 2014). Descriptive studies are undertaken when the practitioner-scholar wishes to *describe* the characteristics of the data. Such studies are "more interested in *what* the characteristics are rather than in *why* the characteristics are as they are" (p. 154, emphasis in original). For example, if you downloaded recent state assessment data for your students and wished to describe their performance across various attributes, you would be engaging in a descriptive, non-experimental research study. Descriptive studies are often characterized by research questions that begin with "what" (for example, "What proportion of high school students complete the ACT before the end of their junior year?"). Prediction studies may contain a descriptive component but move a step further in that they attempt to make claims about what might happen. In a prediction study, "statistical models are formulated to predict one attribute or behavior (the dependent variable) from another (the independent variable)" (O'Dwyer & Bernauer, 2014, p. 156). For example, a practitioner-scholar undertaking a prediction study might ask, "Does a $1,000 increase in teacher salary increase teacher retention in the Stonebrook School District?" This question would allow you to determine whether the $1,000 increase (the independent variable) predicted an increase in teacher retention (the dependent variable). Finally, practitioner-scholars can undertake an explanatory study to "test theories about how and why some attributes, behaviors, or phenomena are related as they are, or how and why the observed differences between pre-existing groups came to be" (O'Dwyer & Bernauer, 2014, p. 156). The most common prediction study is a causal-comparative design, which is discussed in greater detail later. What is important to understand about prediction studies is that these studies cannot provide support for or make claims about causality between two variables. In other words, a prediction study cannot say that changes in an independent variable *cause* changes in a dependent variable. Only an experimental research design can make these claims. We discuss some of the non-experimental research designs in greater detail in the following sections, including causal-comparative designs, correlational designs, secondary data analysis, and survey research designs.

CAUSAL-COMPARATIVE AND CORRELATIONAL DESIGNS. Causal-comparative designs are used when a practitioner-scholar wants to identify a reason for differences between the outcomes or behaviors of an individual or a group of individuals. Gay, Mills, and Airasian (2012) indicated that, "the basic causal-comparative design involves selecting two groups that differ on some variable of interest and comparing them on some dependent variable" (p. 227). Causal-comparative designs are less about prediction than they are about describing relationships between variables. A causal-comparative study does not allow the practitioner-scholar to determine whether there is a cause-and-effect relationship.

Causal-comparative studies require that the practitioner-scholar selects data from two groups. While these are often referred to as experimental and control groups in an experimental study, they are more accurately referred to as comparison groups in a causal-comparative study. The primary criterion for group selection is, as Gay, Mills, and Airasian (2012) noted, "Either one group possesses a characteristic that the other does not, or both groups have the same characteristic but to differing degrees or amounts" (p. 227). There are two types of causal-comparative studies: a retrospective causal-comparative design or a prospective causal-comparative design. A retrospective casual comparative design "involves starting with effects and investigating causes" (p. 228). In a prospective causal-comparative study, researchers "start with causes and investigate effects" (p. 229). Practitioner-scholars typically rely on retrospective causal-comparative designs.

Causal-comparative designs enable practitioner-scholars to compare a number of individual, family, and school level variables. As illustrated in Table 6.1, a causal-comparative study could be used to explore differences in student achievement based on age or gender. Similarly, a practitioner-scholar could use a comparative study to explore differences in achievement based on family income or socioeconomic status. Finally, a causal-comparative design could also be used to assess differences in achievement based on a student's prior school attendance, the type of school they currently attend, and teacher-level factors (for example, teaching style or years of experience).

In causal-comparative designs, practitioner-scholars often use matching to ensure that participants in comparison groups have similar characteristics. For example, a practitioner-scholar who is interested in comparing student achievement among higher- and lower-performing students

Table 6.1 Examples of Variables Used in a Causal-Comparative Study

Individual Variables	Family Variables	School Variables
Age	Family income	Prior school attendance
Gender	Socioeconomic status	Size of the school
Ethnicity	Parental employment	Type of school
Intelligence	Parental marital status	Per-pupil expenditure
Achievement	Number of siblings	Type of curriculum
Commitment	Homeowner or renter	Teaching experience
Self-esteem		Teaching style
		Classroom size

based on age would ensure that a high-achieving student who is 14 years of age would be matched with a low-achieving student who is 14 years of age. This match ensures that the researcher is comparing comparable students in each group. As illustrated in From the Field 6.2, these types of matched groups provide researchers with opportunities to compare one or more variables. In From the Field 6.2, a group of researchers, for example, used matched groups of students enrolled in full-day or half-day kindergarten to determine whether participation in a full or half-day program influenced reading and mathematics achievement. A key point in this example is that the researchers did not state that participation in a full-day kindergarten program *caused* the students to perform at higher levels.

Correlational studies are similar to causal-comparative designs in that they enable practitioner-scholars to compare variables in two or more groups. As Gay, Mills, and Airasian (2012) explained, "Correlational studies may be designed either to determine whether and how a set of variables are

FROM THE FIELD 6.2

An Abstract From a Causal-Comparative Study

The authors compared the achievement of children who were enrolled in full-day kindergarten (FDK) to a matched sample of students who were enrolled in half-day kindergarten (HDK) on mathematics and reading achievement in Grade 2, 3, and 4 several years after they left kindergarten. Results showed that FDK students demonstrated significantly higher achievement at the end of kindergarten than did their HDK counterparts, but that advantage disappeared quickly by the end of the first grade. Interpretations and implications are given for that finding.

Source: Wolgemuth, Cobb, Winokur, Leech, & Ellerby, 2006, p. 260

related or to test hypothesis regarding expected relationships" (p. 205). Unlike causal-comparative designs, however, correlational designs seek only to determine whether and to what degree a relationship among variables exists and not to explain why variation exists. Correlational research is expressed in terms of a correlation coefficient (Pearson's *r*). The correlation coefficient is a measure that describes the strength and direction of the relationship between two variables. The correlation coefficient is based on a scale ranging from 1.00 to –1.00. A correlation coefficient of 1.00 is considered to be completely, positively related, while a correlation coefficient of –1.00 is said to be completely related but with an inverse relationship. A correlation coefficient equal to 0 indicates that there is no relationship between the variables. Let's illustrate this with a practical example. Assume that you are a physical education teacher interested in exploring the relationship between a student's height and weight. The correlation coefficient for such a study should be close to (if not exactly) 1.00, which means that as height increases so does the student's weight. A correlation coefficient of –1.00 would mean that as a student's height increased their weight decreased. From the Field 6.3 provides an example of an abstract from a correlational study, with a particular focus on the relationship between students' reading achievement and parental involvement.

As is true of all research, the approach used will shape the types of research question being asked. As such, Table 6.2 highlights how the research questions would vary between a causal-comparative and a correlational study.

While many research books present causal-comparative and correlational research designs as unique or different, we encourage you not to overthink these distinctions and to instead recognize that these designs are often quite similar. Correlational studies can be transformed into causal-comparative study simply by categorizing the independent variable. What does this mean in practice? A correlational study that examines the relationship between parental income and student achievement can be transformed into a causal-comparative study by changing parental income to a categorical variable (for example, higher-poverty or lower-poverty; free lunch or paid lunch status) (Johnson & Christensen, 2010).

FROM THE FIELD 6.3

An Abstract From a Correlational Study

The purpose of this study was to determine the relationship between reading achievement and parental involvement for sixth grade middle school students. The participants were forty-eight sixth grade students who completed parental involvement surveys. The parents of these students also completed a parental involvement survey. The results of the surveys were then compared with the students reading level as determined by the McLeod Reading Comprehension Test. The data were then statistically compared to determine a correlation utilizing the Pearson Product Moment Correlation formula. Results of the study indicate a slight positive correlation but failed to reject the null hypothesis that there was no relationship between parental involvement and the reading comprehension and achievement of sixth grade students. Implications for further students are discussed.

Source: Hawes, Carmen Ann; Lee Plourde,. "Parental Involvement and Its Influence on the Reading Achievement of 6th Grade Students." Reading Improvement. Project Innovation. 2005. HighBeam Research. 28 Apr. 2015 <http://www.highbeam.com>.

CONSIDERING CORRELATIONAL STUDIES AND STUDENT ACHIEVEMENT

Given your interest in improving reading achievement in your fourth grade class, you are interested in knowing how the students' characteristics are potentially related to their reading test scores. The characteristics that you are most interested in are students' age, how many hours their parents read with them at home, how many chapter books they read each school year, how many minutes per week they participate in independent reading, and so on. You decide to compile this information for each of the students in the fourth grade level at your school, which will allow you to analyze information for 68 students. With reading achievement as your dependent variable and the students' characteristics as your independent variables, you set out to conduct a correlational study. This study will provide you with Pearson's Correlation, which describes the relationship between reading achievement and these variables. After completing this study, you will not be able to say whether these variables

cause changes in reading achievement, but you will be able to say whether these variables are related to reading achievement. While such a study is limited, it does provide you with an opportunity to describe relationships among variables and thus look for potential changes that you can make in your instruction to better support your students. For example, if you found that reading achievement is positively correlated with the number of minutes a child reads independently, you could then adjust your instruction to increase opportunities for students to engage in independent reading.

Focus Questions

1. As you develop a correlational study, where will you look to determine which variables may be related to student reading achievement?

2. Depending on what you found in your study, how might you integrate this information in your instructional practice?

Table 6.2   Comparison of Research Questions in a Causal-Comparative Study Versus a Correlational Study

Examples of Research Questions	
Causal-Comparative Studies	Correlational Studies
• What differences exist between students enrolled in traditional public schools and charter schools as measured on state math assessments?	• How are the number of hours a parent reads with their child related to the number of books students read outside of school?
• What differences exist between students enrolled in high-poverty and low-poverty schools as measured by the percentage of students who indicate that they will attend college?	• How is a student's family income related to their performance on a state math assessment?

SECONDARY DATA ANALYSIS (OR DATA MINING). Secondary data analysis, or data mining, is another form of non-experimental research. Glass (1976) defined secondary data *analysis* as involving "the re-analysis of data for the purposes of answering the original research question with better statistical techniques, or answering new research questions with old data" (p. 3). Much like correlational or causal-comparative research designs, data mining draws heavily on extant or existing data. Extant data can be obtained from a variety of sources, including student information systems, state departments of education, the National Center for Education Statistics, and data archives. In some cases, the data sets can also be obtained from the original researchers. Data mining is primarily concerned with identifying potential relationships, interactions, or patterns that can be used to inform policy or practice. For practitioner-scholars, data mining provides a convenient way to make use of the abundance of data available in schools and districts. Since teachers and administrators often have access to student information systems and other extant sources, these systems become viable sources of information for potential research studies. While Institutional Review Board approval is required and practitioner-scholars should take care to protect the identity of participants contained in these records, the availability of this information provides a compelling opportunity for practitioner-scholars to engage in meaningful, non-experimental research.

What types of information can be included in this type of research? As illustrated in Table 6.3, practitioner-scholars have the opportunity to study student-, teacher-, school-, and district-level data.

Table 6.3 Level and Type of Data Available to Practitioner-Scholars for Data Mining	
Level of Data	Type of Data Available for Data Mining
Student and class	<ul><li>Demographic information</li><li>Program eligibility data</li><li>Assessment results</li></ul>
Teacher	<ul><li>Demographic information</li><li>Salary information</li><li>Preparation data</li><li>Professional development data</li><li>Aggregate student achievement data</li></ul>
School and district	<ul><li>Demographic information</li><li>Program participation data</li><li>Attendance data</li><li>Aggregate student achievement data</li><li>Aggregate salary data</li><li>Aggregate financial data</li><li>Aggregate program participation data</li></ul>

REFLECTIVE OPPORTUNITY 6.3

Secondary data analysis may involve a practitioner-scholar using a dataset that was used in a previous, published study. It is possible that you may come up with different findings than the original

researchers. When this occurs, you may be faced with an ethical challenge.

1. How do you explain the differences?

2. How do you share your results in an ethical way?

This type of research may be valuable for you as a practitioner-scholar, as it affords an opportunity to analyze information that might not be already analyzed, thereby providing insights about data that can directly inform practice. We see this, more than anything, as one of the key strengths of data mining research and something that you should consider if you are interested in non-experimental research designs.

SURVEY RESEARCH. Survey research designs are one of the most commonly employed quantitative research designs by practitioner-scholars, as they are relatively easy to conduct and the data obtained through a survey are fairly straightforward to analyze. Surveys can be administered on paper, online, and in a telephone format. Survey research is intended to capture the perspectives of participants at a moment in time or changes in their perspectives across a period of time. Surveys can be forward looking ("What will happen?"), focused on the present ("What is happening?"), or retrospective ("What happened?"). The nature of survey research is primarily descriptive, although survey data can be combined with other data sources to allow researchers to predict responses or associate responses with student-, school-, district-, or community-level characteristics. In this regard, surveys are flexible tools from which to infer what a group of individuals thinks, perceives, or feels. Surveys are intended to standardize the collection of information across a group of participants. Survey instruments that are designed to capture information from participants at a single point in time, are referred to as cross-sectional surveys. When surveys collect data at multiple points in time, they are referred to as longitudinal surveys (Babbie, 1998).

There are three types of longitudinal surveys that are commonly used in educational research: (a) trend surveys, (b) cohort surveys, and (c) panel studies. Trend surveys are primarily about the collection of information from a group of participants over time. For example, a practitioner-scholar might be interested in tracking ninth grade perceptions over a period of five years. Each year the practitioner-scholar surveys the ninth grade students to determine how they perceived their transition from middle to high school. This is a trend study as it attempts to track changes in perceptions among ninth grade students over time.

A cohort survey is similar in that it seeks to track changes in perceptions over time. But, unlike a trend study, a cohort survey tracks changes in perceptions for a given group of individuals with similar characteristics. For example, a practitioner-scholar might change his or her trend study to a cohort study simply by surveying all ninth grade students in their district's high schools in their first year of high school and all of the twelfth grade students in their district's high schools in their fourth year of school. In this study, the ninth grade students and twelfth grade students form two cohorts that can be compared. Likewise, a practitioner-scholar might construct a cohort survey based on students who are enrolled in advanced placement classes and those who are enrolled in general education classes to compare the views of students in one cohort with those of another. In both examples, the cohort is defined by the specific characteristics of the students the practitioner-scholar wishes to survey.

A panel study is similar to a cohort study in that it looks at a group of participants; yet, unlike a cohort study, a panel study relies on the same group of participants for multiple survey administrations. Using the same example as before, a panel study would survey all of the district's ninth grade students in their first year of high school and survey the same students' again in twelfth grade. Students who recently entered the district would not be included in this second survey. The primary aim of the panel survey is to compare their perceptions over time. Thus, unlike a cohort study, a panel survey relies on the same participants from one administration to the next, while a cohort survey does not.

It is important to understand that surveys are not simply a list of questions about which you want to gather more information. Rather, surveys are carefully designed, theoretically supported instruments that are used to collect information from participants about a particular experience, phenomenon, policy, program, or perspective. Surveys are extremely purposeful in the questions that they ask. Previous researchers have noted that the effectiveness of a survey depends both on the quality of the survey instrument, as well as the quality of the survey sample (Dillman, Smyth, & Christian, 2014; Fowler, 2013). A poorly designed survey instrument might generate information but not address the research questions. Rea and Parker (2005) indicated that the practitioner-scholars who develop surveys should consider the clarity, comprehensiveness, and acceptability of the questions presented on the survey. Questions should be clearly and simply stated so that the participants are not confused by the purpose of the question. Questions should not include multiple options or unintentionally include two questions instead of one. Surveys should be comprehensive in that they should allow the researcher to proceed with his or her analysis even when one or more questions do not produce the kind of data that were anticipated. Last, surveys should be presented so that they are acceptable to the participant; that is, the survey instrument should be of a reasonable length, in a clear format, and include adequate directions and guidance.

Survey instruments can include a variety of questions, including closed-ended and open-ended questions. Each question type has particular advantages and disadvantages. For example, a practitioner-scholar might include closed-ended questions in her or his survey when the objective is to collect standardized data. A closed-ended question is one that forces the survey participant to select from among a series of pre-determined choices. The data obtained from close-ended questions are uniform, making comparisons among participants reasonably efficient. The disadvantage of closed-ended questions is that participants who would like to offer a response that does not fit within one of the categories cannot offer their response and are thus more likely to skip the question. This is why open-ended questions may also be valuable to include. Open-ended questions offer participants the opportunity to provide a unique response. As such, these questions allow the practitioner-scholar to capture in-depth the participants' thoughts or

DECIDING AMONG AND BETWEEN QUANTITATIVE TRADITIONS

Given your interest in student achievement, you realize that you are likely to conduct a quantitative research study. The nature of the data you hope to collect and use for your study makes this the best choice. Further, the type of questions that you hope to explore also make it clear that a quantitative design is best. Given this recognition, you must decide whether you will undertake an experimental or non-experimental design. While the thought of identifying a specific cause of changes in student achievement appeals to you, the challenge of designing an experiment, as well as the time involved in carrying it out makes it unlikely that you will engage in such a study. You also think it unlikely that you would attempt to survey students about their achievement. Instead, you see a non-experimental design as an appropriate alternative. Your main interest is in describing the factors that are associated with differences in student achievement. On the one hand, a correlational study makes sense in that it would allow you to describe how various

factors relate to student achievement. On the other hand, it seems more valuable to you to use a causal-comparative design that would enable you to explore the underlying factors that potentially explain differences in student achievement. Selecting such a design would also allow you to use existing data from the school district's student information system. This would also lessen the demands on you to collect new data. In the end, you decide that secondary data analysis combined with a causal-comparative design is the best design for you to use given your interests and time.

Focus Questions

1. What are the potential challenges associated with using existing data (that is, data that were not expressly collected for the purpose of your study)?

2. How might you attend to these challenges when completing your study?

opinions. However, open-ended questions are more difficult to analyze quantitatively and do not produce standardized data. Thus, it is often beneficial to include a combination of closed-ended and open-ended survey questions.

Practitioner-scholars often wonder how long a survey should be. The most accurate response is: It depends! Surveys vary in length and complexity, with this length and complexity being dependent upon the research questions and the objectives of the survey itself. Dillman, Smyth, and Christian (2014) noted that survey length is related to survey participant rates—longer, more poorly designed surveys tend to discourage participation, while shorter, well-designed surveys tend to increase participation. As a general guideline, Rea and Parker (2005) suggested that telephone surveys should last between 10 and 12 minutes, mailed or online surveys should take no more than 15 minutes to complete, and in-person surveys should require no more than 30 minutes to complete.

To improve the quality of survey instruments, practitioner-scholars often refine their survey through survey piloting (or simply piloting), which involves presenting a draft survey instrument to prospective participants prior to administering the survey to the entire survey sample. The piloting process is essential for three reasons. First, piloting allows the practitioner-scholar to determine whether the organization and structure of the survey instrument makes sense to the individuals who are likely to take the survey. In the event that the organization of the survey does not make sense, it provides the practitioner-scholar with an opportunity to refine and revise the survey instrument. Second, piloting allows the practitioner-scholar to determine whether the wording of particular questions prompts the kinds of responses that were anticipated. Piloting allows prospective survey participants to offer comments and suggestions for refining the questions, as well as to provide suggestions on specific response options. Finally, piloting allows the practitioner-scholar to test the length and time of the survey instrument. During the piloting process, it is important to ask participants to record how long the survey takes them to complete. Collectively, this information allows the practitioner-scholar to refine the survey instrument and prepare it for full-scale administration.

SUMMARY

In this chapter, we discussed some of the characteristics of quantitative research, and noted several assumptions that shape how quantitative research is carried out and the results are interpreted. We presented the basics of experimental and non-experimental research designs and shared details related to experimental research studies and single-subject experimental research designs. We also offered descriptions and a discussion of the potential applications of non-experimental research designs. We noted the ways in which causal-comparative and correlational studies may be used in practitioner-scholarship, while also pointing to the value of secondary data analysis and survey research. Throughout, we highlighted the importance of considering ethical challenges, and encouraged you to spend further time studying those approaches to quantitative research that may be of interest to you.

KEY TERMS

Bias 121
Causal-Comparative Designs 129
Closed-Ended Question 135
Cohort Survey 134
Control Group 123
Correlation Coefficient 131
Correlational Studies 130
Cross-Sectional Surveys 134
Deductive Analysis 120
Dependent Variable 122
Descriptive Studies 128
Experimental Designs 122

Explanatory Study 129
External Validity 124
Independent Variable 122
Internal Validity 124
Matching 129
Non-Experimental Research 126
Objectivity 121
Open-ended Question 135
Panel Study 135
"Post-test only" Design 123
Prediction Studies 128
"Pre-test/Post-test" Design 123

Random Assignment 121
Randomized Control Trials 125
Secondary Data Analysis 132
Single-Subject or Single-Case
   Experimental Research
   Design 126
Solomon Four-Group Design 123
Survey Piloting 136
Survey Research 134
Treatment Group 123
Trend Surveys 134

QUESTIONS TO CONSIDER

1. What are the basic characteristics of quantitative research?

2. What are some of the assumptions that undergird quantitative research that could be described as being different from qualitative research approaches?

3. What are some of the differences between experimental and non-experimental research?

4. How would you describe the basic features and purposes of the quantitative research designs for your colleagues, including: experimental, single-subject experimental, correlational, causal-comparative, secondary data analysis, and survey?

CHAPTER EXERCISES

1. Develop a research study using one of the quantitative research designs discussed above. Identify the: (1) research design, (2) variables, and (3) overall scope of your proposed study. Link your discussion to the literature review you began conducting in Chapter 3.

2. Develop a series of research questions specific to each of the quantitative research designs discussed in this chapter. Relate each of these questions to your research topic of interest.

3. Go to your state department of education's website and find their public data archive. Identify three potential datasets that you could use within one of the quantitative research designs discussed in this chapter. Develop a rationale for why this dataset could be used, what limitations you might encounter, and the ethical implications for using this dataset for research purposes.

4. Develop a short, five-question survey linked to your area of interest. Send your survey to three colleagues and ask them for feedback on the questions that you included. Using their feedback as a guide, determine how you might modify your survey and how making these changes might impact your response rate, if you were to administer this survey to all of your potential study participants.

LEARNING EXTENSIONS

There are many quantitative research books to explore, with each offering you a foundational understanding of quantitative research designs. We suggest you begin by exploring O'Dwyer and Bernauer's (2014) book entitled *Quantitative Research for the Qualitative Researcher*. This particular book offers an accessible and useful introduction to conducting research from a quantitative perspective. In addition, Dillman, Smyth, and Christian's (2014) book, *Internet, Mail, and Mixed-Mode Surveys: The Tailored Design Method* (4th ed.), is a useful text for those interested in survey research. It provides helpful strategies for designing surveys and includes multiple examples of what different survey designs might look like.

Sharpen your skills with SAGE edge!

edge.sagepub.com/lochmiller

SAGE edge for Students provides a personalized approach to help you accomplish your coursework goals in an easy-to-use learning environment. You'll find action plans, mobile-friendly eFlashcards, and quizzes as well as videos, web resources, and links to SAGE journal articles to support and expand on the concepts presented in this chapter.

7

COLLECTING QUALITATIVE AND QUANTITATIVE DATA

CARRYING OUT YOUR RESEARCH

With your research problem developed and a methodology selected, you are now ready to begin thinking about how to carry out your research. You know this process involves identifying participants, perhaps developing interview questions, and ultimately establishing relationships with research sites. While you understand the basic requirements for your study, you must now decide how you will operationalize your study within the context of your research practice. Where do you begin? What should you do? These are the most pressing questions that seem to shape your thinking about your data collection process.

INTRODUCTION

As illustrated in the opening vignette, one of the major steps in the research process is actually carrying out your study. In Chapters 5, 6, 10, and 11, you learn about some of the underlying characteristics of qualitative, quantitative, mixed methods, and action research studies. In Chapters 7 and 8, we discuss some of the analytic strategies that support your research. In this chapter, we focus on how to actually go about collecting your data. For many practitioner-scholars, it is often rejuvenating to move from designing a research study to actually carrying it out. At this stage, the conceptual ideas seem to become more real.

Whether conducting a qualitative, quantitative, mixed methods, or action research study, the process of actually carrying out your research study includes a number of important considerations. In this chapter, we discuss some of the considerations that prepare you to begin and eventually complete your research. We begin by discussing sampling in both qualitative and quantitative research, and then consider issues related to accessing your research site and participants. Then, we share

Learning Objectives

By the end of the chapter, you will be able to:

- Describe the primary differences between a sample and a population.

- Identify the different qualitative sampling strategies.

- Identify the different quantitative sampling strategies.

- Summarize the considerations for developing an interview, observation, and document collection protocol.

- Paraphrase considerations for using student assessments, research instruments, surveys, and extant data.

- Identify where and how to use technology tools to support the research process.

about preparing to collect qualitative and/or quantitative data. Finally, we conclude by briefly describing how technological tools can support you in carrying out your research.

SAMPLING STRATEGIES

While it may be tempting to say that you will include everyone in your research study or that you will conduct research in every school, it is highly unlikely, and, in many cases, would be very inefficient and unfocused. Accordingly, one of the most important considerations you face when conducting a research study involves determining whether you will attempt to study a population or seek to study a smaller group of individuals that is related to the population. A population is simply a collection of individuals or sites with similar characteristics. A sample refers to the individuals or sites from the population who will be interviewed, observed, surveyed, or otherwise engaged in your research study. As such, a sample is most generally a sub-group of individuals or a subset of sites that you will study in greater detail.

The sampling strategy you use differs depending on whether you are conducting a qualitative or quantitative study. In qualitative research, sampling considerations are less concerned with identifying individuals or sites who represent the population than they are in identifying theoretically important, descriptively valuable perspectives, instances, experiences, or particular individuals. In quantitative research, the aim is to construct a sample that allows the researcher to represent (or approximate) the views, characteristics, experiences, or results of the population as a whole. We discuss some of the different approaches to sampling next.

Sampling in Qualitative Research

One of the most common critiques of qualitative research is that the ways that participants, sites, or experiences are selected do not permit the findings of the study to be generalized to a population. Yet, considering the purpose of qualitative research, we view this critique as ungrounded. The basis for this critique relates to the ways in which practitioner-scholars who are engaged in qualitative research construct their samples. It is important to note that qualitative researchers typically do not seek to generalize their findings to a specific population. Rather, they seek to study experiences, views, and everyday practices in an in-depth manner, frequently with a smaller (compared to many quantitative studies), intentionally selected community or group of individuals, sites, and/or experiences. These communities, individuals, sites, and/or experiences are likely unique and specifically related to the research focus.

Given the flexibility inherent in qualitative sampling strategies, practitioner-scholars may be tempted to think that sample size or even explicitly discussing your sampling approach does not matter in qualitative studies. We beg to differ! As Sandelowski (1995) noted:

> Adequacy of sample size in qualitative research is relative, a matter of judging a sample neither small nor large per se, but rather too small or too large for the intended purposes of sampling and for the intended qualitative product. (p. 179)

As such, the size of the sample in a qualitative research study is inherently rooted in both the qualitative research design and the qualitative methodology that is adopted. Practitioner-scholars must ask themselves whether the sample they propose enables them to address the conceptual, theoretical, or analytic interests of their study. Onwuegbuzie and Leech (2007) noted that the size of the sample in qualitative research " . . . should not be too large that it is difficult to extract thick, rich data," nor should the sample " . . . be too small that it is difficult to achieve data saturation" (p. 242). The ideal sample in a qualitative research study is one that enables researchers to make sound interpretations of the data and to have sufficient data to ground and to produce an in-depth report of their findings.

There are a number of different qualitative sampling strategies (Patton, 2002); however, for most practitioner-scholars three sampling strategies are commonly used in qualitative research, which include: (a) convenience sampling, (b) purposeful sampling, and (c) snowball sampling. We discuss each of these sampling strategies below.

CONVENIENCE SAMPLING. A convenience sample is perhaps the most straightforward approach to sampling in qualitative research, as it involves engaging individuals or research sites that are most accessible to you as a researcher. For example, a practitioner-scholar who is conducting classroom-based research might conduct research in his or her own classroom given it does not require travel to another site, (likely) provides easy access to participants, and creates convenience in completing the research study. As such, the students you may invite to participate in your study are part of a convenience sample, as they are predominately selected based on their proximity and accessibility rather than for specific characteristics. As another example, a practitioner-scholar might conduct research in his or her own school district to determine how the district supported the implementation of new teacher evaluation criteria. As with the classroom research, in this case, the practitioner-scholar might select the site because it makes accessing data and collecting information easier, while still being relevant and closely related to the study's focus.

While convenience sampling is common, it is not without its own problems. First, convenience samples are not typically representative and are often chided by researchers who prefer samples that are selected using specific criteria. Second, convenience samples may be more problematic in terms of research ethics. How, for example, can a practitioner-scholar mitigate the potential differences in power between themselves as a classroom teacher and the students in their class? Will the students feel that they can decline to participate in the study? Will students' responses, for instance, in an interview or on a survey be influenced by the fact that the researcher is also their teacher? These are important considerations when using a convenience sample.

PURPOSEFUL SAMPLING. In contrast to convenience sampling, a purposeful sample is when the researcher selects individuals or sites on the basis of specific criteria. For example, a practitioner-scholar might include individuals with specific characteristics (for example, high school seniors who are English Language Learners) or sites with specific qualities (for example, charter schools within their first year of operation). In both cases, the practitioner-scholar moves away from the selection of individuals and sites purely on the basis of convenience and instead selects individuals and sites on the basis of particular criteria. These criteria are often informed by the practitioner-scholars' research interest, as well as their review of the literature in their field of study.

Although somewhat confusing, a purposeful sampling criteria can be included as part of a broader convenience sampling strategy. For example, a practitioner-scholar might focus on students in his or her school (for convenience), but invite the participation of students who have particular characteristics (such as students who participate in certain classes or have a particular academic trajectory) and thus are sampled purposefully. Any time a practitioner-scholar adopts specific sampling criteria, he or she is engaging in a purposeful sampling strategy. In From the Field 7.1, we highlight a well-developed, purposeful sampling strategy that was used in a case study of ELL students' access to college-preparatory courses.

SNOWBALL SAMPLING. The final type of sampling commonly used in qualitative research is snowball sampling. Snowball sampling (or chain referral sampling) involves identifying one or more participants or sites initially and then allowing recommendations from participants to guide the further development of the sample. Snowball sampling is particularly useful when researching sensitive issues, as people with insider knowledge are likely to know other individuals familiar with the particular issue or matter (Biernacki & Waldork, 1981). For example, assuming you are studying teachers' perspectives of a new curriculum, you might begin by talking with the department chair or teacher leader. In the course of your interview, you might ask who else has had experience with the curriculum. These recommendations thus become the basis for the next participants you invite to participate in your study. Ultimately, your sample develops and evolves as additional participants suggest individuals or sites you should consider including.

FROM THE FIELD 7.1

An Example of a Purposeful Sampling Strategy in a Qualitative Case Study

There were 49 11th-grade ELLs in the 2011–2012 academic year—far too many to follow longitudinally—and thus it was necessary to select a sample of these students for long-term observation (i.e., sampling within the case; Merriam, 2009). Since the larger project was about ELL's transition to collect, the two basic student selection criteria were: (a) that when they entered high school, they were classified as ELLs and (b) that they wanted to go to college. Beyond these basic criteria, the key selection criterion was students' academic performance. In the literature on college access and degree completion (e.g., Adelman, 2006; Cabrera & La Nasa, 2001; Kanno & Cromley, 2013a, 2013b), academic performance has been identified as the most important predictor. Also, since tracking is supposed to group students based on ability (Hallinan, 1994), we reasoned that if tracking was working the way it was supposed to work, high-performing ELLs should be taking significantly different sets of courses than low-performing ELLs. In contrast, if they were all confined to low-track courses regardless of their academic performance, then we would have to assume that a different set of circumstances must be in place for ELLs that keep them in the low track, and it would be our job to investigate what they might be. Thus, we took the utmost care in ensuring that the wide range of academic performance was represented in our sample.

Source: **Kanno & Kangas, 2014, pp. 856–857**

Read the full article at:
www.sagepub.com/lochmiller

SELECTING A SAMPLING APPROACH FOR A QUALITATIVE STUDY

Having decided to conduct a qualitative research study, you must decide which sampling approach to use. The purpose of your study is to determine how central office administrators understand principal instructional leadership. Who you include in your study and why you include them will have a significant impact on the data that you collect and thus the ways that you find that central office administrators make sense of principals' work. On the one hand, it seems appropriate to simply reach out to central office administrators who you know and have a relationship with. This would be rather convenient. As you think about this option, however, you realize that nearly all of the administrators you would contact have had similar experiences. This worries you as it may result in a dataset that reflects only one perspective.

You also think about simply asking administrators in the central office who you should speak with. You consider beginning with administrators who you know and proceeding to other colleagues who they might recommend. This appeals to you as it would likely produce greater diversity in your responses. However, as you consider this option, you realize that this approach would result in you having very little control over the study sample. This worries you as your hope is to be able to explain why you included the participants in your study and how their various background characteristics and experiences shape their understanding of the work of principals. Thus, you decide that the best option for your study is to select participants purposefully.

Focus Questions

1. Thinking about this particular study's focus, what characteristics might you use to construct a purposeful sample?

2. What are the potential drawbacks to purposeful sampling?

While this approach is helpful in that it allows you to contact and potentially include a large number of participants, it also presents some risks. First, as the researcher, you give up control over the final sample. Thus, if your intent is to include individuals who have specific characteristics or to include sites that have certain qualities, a snowball sample might not allow you to ensure that all of your participants or sites have *all* of these qualities. Second, you will need to be thoughtful about confidentiality, as it is possible that all of your participants will know each other and know that they are participating in a study. Finally, it may be difficult to know who to start with for your snowball sampling, particularly when dealing with sensitive matters.

Sampling in Quantitative Research

In quantitative research there are two types of basic sampling strategies: nonprobability sampling and probability sampling. Nonprobability sampling is simply when a practitioner-scholar includes the entire population in their research or selects participants on the basis of non-random characteristics. Probability sampling attempts to construct a sample that includes individuals who *approximate* the population. Probability samples allow you to generalize the results obtained from your sample to the population as a whole. As such, probability sampling is often considered the most powerful type of sampling.

SIMPLE RANDOM SAMPLING. A simple random sample is a sample wherein each participant has an equal chance of being included in the sample. This type of sample is constructed by assigning each individual in the population an identifying number. Then, using a table of random numbers (see Table 7.1), individuals are selected at random for the study on the basis of the numbers they were initially assigned. This process allows each individual in the population to have an equal chance of being included in the sample. For example, let's assume that we wanted to randomly select a sample of 10 students from the 100 third and fourth grade students at your school. First, you would assign each student in the third and fourth grade a number (01 to 100). Next, you would look at a table of random numbers to identify the ten numbers corresponding to the ten students who you would select. As illustrated in Table 7.1, you would select students who you assigned number 52, 13, 44, 91, 39, 85, 22, 33, 04, and 29.

SYSTEMATIC SAMPLING. Systematic sampling is similar to simple random sampling but does not involve using a table of random numbers. Instead, you systematically sample individuals for your study by selecting every nth individual. For example, if you wanted to select a 10-person sample from the 20 fourth grade students in your classroom, you could select every other student on your class roster, as illustrated in Table 7.2. Similarly, if you wanted to select 20 students from the 100 third and fourth grade students in your classroom, you could select every fourth student on the class list. While both will result in a somewhat randomly selected list of potential participants, it bears noting that this approach is not considered as precise as a simple random sampling as it does not involve the use of a table of random numbers.

STRATIFIED SAMPLING. Stratified sampling is used when you want to ensure that the characteristics of the individuals (and potential research sites) included in the sample are representative of the characteristics of the individuals (and sites) in the broader population. For example, if you conducted a survey of classroom teachers across a state education system, it would be important that the characteristics of the teachers in the sample were similar to the entire population of classroom teachers in that state. This would require you to construct a sample that was similar to the entire population in terms of the teachers' gender, years of experience, degree level, type of school, type of students served, and so on. Likewise, if you wanted to ensure that you contained schools or districts with similar characteristics, you would select a sample of schools that had similar characteristics to all schools in the state. For example, you would include schools with similar student enrollment, a similar proportion of students eligible for free-or-reduced-price lunch, and schools with similar achievement characteristics. As illustrated in From the Field 7.2, Elfers, Knapp, and Plecki (2004) developed a stratified random sample of classroom teachers in Washington State. While you might adopt a less

Table 7.1 Illustrative Table of Random Numbers

52	13	44	91	39	85	22	33	04	29
31	52	65	63	88	78	21	35	28	22
91	84	44	38	76	99	38	67	60	95

Source: Kerlinger, 1972, p. 714

Table 7.2 Systematic Sampling Using an Illustrative Classroom Student List

Student's Name	Include	Student's Name	Include
1. Jane	N	11. Stephanie	N
2. Brian	Y	12. Levi	Y
3. Joe	N	13. Martin	N
4. Kelly	Y	14. Dennis	Y
5. Mike	N	15. Tammy	N
6. Liza	Y	16. Jessica	Y
7. Ben	N	17. Denice	N
8. Joel	Y	18. Drew	Y
9. Martha	N	19. Ashley	N
10. Patty	Y	20. Anne	Y

An Example of Stratified, Random Sample From a Survey Study of Classroom Teachers

Teachers were selected based on a stratified random sample of all Washington classroom teachers by region of the state, experience level of the teacher and poverty level of the school in which they teach. The sampling frame was generated by pulling a stratified random sample of the state's teachers using the state's personnel database (S-275) for the 2002–03 school year. The personnel database includes all teachers in the state of Washington. From the database, we identified 57,247 classroom teachers based on duty root (31, 32 or 33), of which we were able to include 54,807 or 95.7% in the sampling frame.

In order to identify teachers by region of the state, teachers were linked to their district's Educational Service District and then grouped in one of three broad regions. The Central Puget Sound is represented by ESD 121. The districts in Western Washington outside of the Central Puget Sound ESD 121 are represented as a group (ESDs 112, 113, 114 and 189). Eastern Washington is represented by the four ESDs which roughly correspond to the eastern side of the state (ESDs 101, 105, 123 and 171) . . . .

Teachers were grouped according to three experience levels: 0–4 years of experience, 5–14 years of experience, and 15 or more years of experience. Additionally, each teacher was linked to his or her school building by a school code. By tagging each school code to the percentage of students enrolled in the Free or Reduced Price Lunch program for the school, a rough indicator of school poverty could be identified. In this way, teachers were grouped into three categories according to school poverty level: low poverty (0–20% students receiving Free or Reduced Price Lunch), moderate poverty (21–50% of students receiving Free or Reduced Price Lunch) or high poverty (51–100% of students receiving Free or Reduced Price Lunch).

A sampling grid containing 27 cells (the total possible combinations of teachers in each of these categories) was generated by the three stratification variables (region, experience level and school poverty level). In order to generate an initial sample of 400 teachers, we randomly selected teachers who fit the appropriate criteria to fill each cell in the sampling grid.

Source: Elfers, Knapp, & Plecki, 2004, pp. 2–3

sophisticated sampling approach for your study, Elfers and her colleagues illustrated well the multi-dimensional, multi-step nature of developing a stratified sample.

Considerations When Sampling Effective Schools or Districts

For many practitioner-scholars, ourselves included, we often seek to include examples of students, schools, districts, programs, or practices that are considered effective. These decisions are frequently based on school or district test scores. Researchers have increasingly cautioned against such measures to represent effective schools and districts. For example, Trujillo (2013) reviewed recent studies that reported results from effective school districts and noted that sampling approaches adopted in these studies were problematic because they over-relied on standardized achievement tests as a measure of effectiveness. Further, the school districts often served predominately white, affluent students, and therefore that did not consider the experiences of students from lower socioeconomic classes nor racial/ethnic minority students. These studies often neglected important factors related to students and classrooms that some scholars would deem as concerning or ineffective. Such concerns have been raised in recent analyses that considered sampling approaches for effective schools, as well (Bowers, 2010; Luyten, Visscher, & Witziers, 2005).

The point of noting these concerns is to remind you that as practitioner-scholars you must think critically about the factors that you use to identify schools and districts for your study. Indeed, it is inappropriate to rely simply on test scores as measures to identify schools and districts to study. Instead, it is imperative that you consider a range of factors in the school. For example, it is entirely appropriate to consider factors that relate to classroom teachers, instructional practice, specific instructional programs, and school-wide initiatives as part of your sampling rationale. As practitioner-scholars, you are uniquely positioned to be aware of these factors and thus weave them into your sampling criteria. Ideally, your sampling criteria should be multifaceted and consider not only the practical nature of your research but also the substantive nature of the research.

SITE ACCESS AND PARTICIPANT RECRUITMENT

Once you have identified your sampling approach, your next step is to determine how you will gain access to your research site(s), as well as how you will recruit participants for your study. Regardless

REFLECTIVE OPPORTUNITY 7.1

Assume you are conducting a qualitative study that will use a purposeful sampling strategy.

1. What are the ethical concerns that might arise if you develop sampling criteria on the basis of the participant's: (a) gender; (b) race/ethnicity; (c) special education status; (d) family income level; and (e) limited English proficiency?

2. For instance, how might you ensure broad representation of perspectives while potentially including a small number of these specific characteristics?

3. How might you respond to these ethical concerns?

of your methodological approach, these are important considerations that are often directly related to the success or failure of your research study. For instance, nothing is more challenging than encountering difficulties in accessing a research site that you based your entire research study upon. Similarly, it is incredibly challenging to go into a study assuming you will get a sufficient number of participants, but encounter difficulty recruiting them. As such, it is important to think about site access and participant recruitment, which of course is part of any quality research proposal and required by Institutional Review Boards. Indeed, gaining access to databases, such as school finance data, requires care as well, which we discuss in Chapter 9.

Acquiring Access to Research Sites

It is especially important that you consider how you will acquire access to your research site, which is often a central concern when carrying out a qualitative research study. If conducting research in your own school or district this may not be as challenging, as you may be quite familiar with the administration, other stakeholders, and internal policies for (dis)approving research studies. However, if you are conducting research in a different school or district from your own, this may create inherent challenges that you as a practitioner-scholar must consider.

We recommend that you treat the process of acquiring access to a research site as a formal invitation to your potential research participants, whether it is a district you are familiar with or not. In effect, you are establishing a partnership with the school or district that will allow you to complete your research study. This requires that you respect the practices of the school or district and acknowledge key 'gatekeepers' in the process. Depending on the location of your research study, key 'gatekeepers' might include the superintendent, central office administrators, school principals, department chairs, or teacher leaders. The following list highlights some of the key considerations and steps to consider when recruiting the participation of research sites and participants.

1. Determine whether you need to acquire district-level approval to carry out your research.

2. Send an initial e-mail to the principal or administrator (or key gatekeeper) with basic descriptive information about your study.

3. Request a meeting with the principal or administrator to discuss your study and formally invite the school or district to participate.

4. Explain to the principal or administrator how you will recruit participants within the school or district and what role, if any, they will have in the recruitment process.

5. Prepare any e-mails, memos, letters, or other recruitment materials for the administrator and provide them with electronic copies that can be sent to potential participants. If you are studying or working within a university, these materials, of course, must also be approved by your Institutional Review Board (see Chapter 4 for further explanation of the ethics process).

6. Once approved, give the principal or administrator specific dates to send the information to participants and ask to be copied on any correspondence.

7. If recommended by the principal or administrator, plan to prepare a short presentation to the school or district impacted by the research that will help inform them about the research study that you are planning to conduct.

8. Complete your recruitment by reaching out to participants only after securing permission from the school or district administrator.

9. Obtain informed consent from participants before conducting any research.

Recruiting Participants for Your Research Study

Much like acquiring access to a research site, we encourage you to approach the process of recruiting research participants for your study formally. Participant recruitment should occur *after* obtaining access to a research site, and, of course, after having acquired approval from your Institutional Review Board. Recruiting research participants differs depending on the nature of your study. If you are conducting a quantitative study, particularly one that involves the use of a survey, you may not recruit participants face to face; rather, you may recruit them online using e-mail invitations, via letters mailed through the postal service, or by asking administrators to distribute invitations during professional development activities, school meetings, parent nights, or other venues. Typically, your recruitment will involve some type of letter, e-mail, or other communication that might accompany or precede the actual survey instrument.

For most qualitative research studies, as well as some quantitative studies (for example, an experimental study), however, your recruitment of participants will most likely occur face to face. Of course, there are exceptions (such as a study of Internet-based discussion groups), and thus you should remain flexible and reflective throughout your recruitment process.

Generally, for practitioner-scholars, the recruitment process is facilitated by school principals, department chairs, teacher leaders, or other gatekeepers who can help you acquire access to participants who fit your sampling criteria. When recruiting participants for a research study, it is especially important to understand that your prospective participants are potentially nervous or hesitant to participate in your research study. Thus, as you invite them, it is critical to keep their concerns in mind and understand that not all participants may be willing to participate in your study. The following list highlights some considerations for recruiting participants to a research study.

1. Prior to recruiting participants for your study, ensure that you have permission from your university's Institutional Review Board to conduct the study and that you have secured the necessary permission(s) from the school or district.

2. If needed, work with the principal and/or other administrators to identify potential participants for your study.

3. When first meeting your research participants, provide them with a brief overview of your study. Be sure that they understand what the purpose of your study is, why they have been invited to participate, and whether they will receive any compensation for their participation.

DIFFICULTIES RECRUITING KEY PARTICIPANTS

Despite clarity in your sampling approach, you quickly discover that recruiting participants is not as straightforward as you once thought. For instance, you invited the Deputy Superintendent for Teaching and Learning to participate in your study. As the Deputy Superintendent supervises principals throughout the district, you assumed she would offer an incredibly useful perspective from the district. While she initially said yes to participate in your study, she declined at the last minute. "What now?" you think to yourself. You were banking on her participation, as you were hopeful that her perspective would help you understand how the district as a whole understands what it means for principals to be an instructional leader.

Over the next few days, you try to find another participant with as broad of a perspective as the deputy superintendent. You contact many of the central office staff on your list. All say yes to participating in your study. After conducting a few of the interviews, you still cannot help but wonder what you might have gleaned had you had the opportunity to interview the Deputy Superintendent.

Focus Questions:

1. What are some practical ways that you can ensure some level of success in recruiting participants for their study?

2. How might you broaden perspectives in a dataset when senior leaders in an organization are unable or unwilling to participate?

4. After informing the participant of their rights as a research participant, be sure to obtain an Informed Consent Form (see Chapter 4 for additional details on this process).

5. Remember that if you are intending to include minors in your study, you must acquire consent from their guardians/parents prior to inviting them to assent (see Chapter 4 for a more detailed discussion of this process).

6. Provide the participant with a copy of the informed consent for their reference.

7. Recognize that participants are free to leave the study at any time, and thus it is often helpful to maintain a list of potential participants who can replace any individuals who leave the study—particularly if you need a specific number of participants in the study.

COLLECTING QUALITATIVE DATA

Beyond selecting participants for your study, carrying out a research study also involves making choices about how you design various data collection activities. In qualitative research, this often involves deciding what questions you will ask (if conducting an interview or focus group), what you will observe and how often (if making observations), and what documents or artifacts you will collect (if collecting artifacts and/or documents). Of course, there are other considerations for those who may be focusing on collecting classroom talk or Internet-based data. We highlight some of the more common data sources in practitioner-scholarship, and certainly encourage you to continue reading and studying about the collection of additional qualitative data sources.

Interviews and Focus Groups

The process of conducting qualitative interviews has been described in detail elsewhere (Kvale & Brinkmann, 2009; Roulston, 2011); it is important, however, for practitioner-scholars to keep three basic considerations in mind. First, what is the aim of the interview? While it may be tempting to treat every interview as an opportunity to engage in ongoing, open-ended conversations, the reality is that it is useful to design the interview to assure that you generate useful data while respecting your research participants' (often limited) time. Therefore, as you develop your interview protocol, keeping the main purpose of the interview in mind is *essential*. For example, if your aim is to use the interview data to understand what the participant thinks about a newly adopted professional development curriculum, your interview questions should be connected to the curriculum and/or the experiences they have had with the curriculum. In such an interview, you would perhaps not want to ask the participant questions that relate to their perspectives about and experiences with the process of structuring professional development generally, as this would lead you down a potentially unrelated path. The following list highlights a few additional, initial questions to consider as you begin developing your interview protocol.

1. What's the aim or purpose of the interview?

2. Who will participate in the interview?

3. Which research question(s) does the interview address?

4. How much time will you spend with the participant?

5. Where will the interview be conducted?

6. Will you audio- or video-record the interview?

7. Will you take notes?

8. How familiar will the participant be with the topic?

9. Are the questions that you plan to present clear?

10. Are the questions closed-ended?

11. Are the questions leading or biased?

12. How might you redesign your questions to assure that they are open-ended and *not* open-ended?

Second, you need to consider whether your interview approach will be structured, semi-structured, or unstructured. In a structured interview protocol, the practitioner-scholar asks pre-determined questions that are explicitly listed in a predefined script. The practitioner-scholar rarely deviates from the list of questions that were prepared in advance. Typically, each question is asked in the order it appears on the protocol.

Adler and Clark (2003) noted that, "structure in an interview can limit the researcher's ability to obtain in-depth information on any given issue," as "using a standardized format implicitly assumes that all respondents understand and interpret questions in the same way" (p. 281). As such, a semi-structured interview protocol is often incredibly useful for the purposes of eliciting in-depth understandings of a phenomenon of interest. A semi-structured interview protocol provides the practitioner-scholar with more flexibility. The questions presented in the interview protocol serve as a general guide but the practitioner-scholar often introduces them as topics, ideas, or comments require. Further, the practitioner-scholar would certainly ask additional open-ended, clarifying questions. This approach is often used as it provides the practitioner-scholar with the flexibility to conduct the interview in a more conversational manner, and also allows for unexpected understandings to emerge. From the Field 7.3 provides an example of a semi-structured interview protocol from a qualitative case study that "sought to understand how the small schools movement of school reform . . . was able to overcome historical school reform barriers by engaging in systems thinking and forming and maintaining true learning organizations" (Buehler, 2006, p. iv).

The final type of interview, an unstructured interview, is the least structured and generally feels the most like a conversation with the research participant. In an unstructured interview, the practitioner-scholar engages the participant in a conversation without previously structuring the questions she or he will ask. This approach is useful when the practitioner-scholar intends to use the interview as an opportunity to explore the participant's thinking, experiences, or even life history.

Relatedly, it may be necessary to consider whether or not to use a focus group interview protocol, in which a practitioner-scholar interviews multiple participants (four to six participants) at once using a common protocol. Focus group protocols are similar to interview protocols in that they are often based on a set of key topics or semi-structured questions that are asked openly to all of the participants or selectively to one participant at a time. Focus groups can be especially useful when conducting qualitative research with students, as it is often less intimidating for a young student to participate in a focus group with their peers rather than being interviewed one-on-one by a researcher. At the same time, there are certainly drawbacks to this approach. For instance, some students may be less willing to talk about a sensitive topic in the presence of their peers. It is important to weigh these concerns in relationship to your research context and the overarching purpose.

Third, it is important to consider the design of the interview, specifically in relationship to the types of questions you will pose. There are several useful frameworks for developing your interview questions (see Carspecken, 1996), which are often good resources to consider. Generally, interview questions should be framed in an open-ended manner that allows the participants to share openly. The questions should be framed without bias or so that the participant does not think the researcher is looking for one specific answer or response. Relatedly, you must work to avoid leading the participant to a particular answer or idea. An example of a leading question is, "So, I imagine that you find the experience of teaching to be

FROM THE FIELD 7.3

An Example of a Semi-Structured Interview Protocol

Teacher Interview Protocol

Grand Tour Question:

1. Tell me what it's like being a teacher at this school.

Learning Organization:

2. What old ways of thinking did you have to challenge in order to make the changes you made?

3. What systems do you have in place to ensure that you continue to refine your programming?

4. How do you obtain feedback on the school's progress?

5. Give me an example of something you had to rethink once the school got started.

6. What were some of the lessons you learned as teachers while planning and implementing the small school?

7. How would you do things differently if you were starting over?

Systems Thinking:

8. How do you think this school has been able to approach education in a new way?

9. What aspects of the educational system did you have to take into account in order to make these changes?

10. Tell me about some of the factors that made this change possible.

11. What support did you receive from outside of the school to enable this change?

12. What were some of the barriers to change?

Change as Part of the Existing System:

13. How has remaining in the public school system impacted your ability to meet the goals of this school?

14. What factors do school reformers need to take into account when creating a new school inside a traditional school?

15. How did you see power relationships change through this process of change?

16. How have you been able to justify what you do in this school to skeptics?

Source: Buehler, 2006, p. 183

---

rather overwhelming, right? Could you talk about that?" First, the question, "I imagine that you find the experience of teaching to be rather overwhelming, right?" is closed and invites only a "yes" or "no" response. Second, the question leads the participant toward a particular answer or response, in this case, "feeling overwhelmed." The participant may not experience teaching as overwhelming, yet this particular question has given her no choice. Thus, generally, it is important to avoid leading questions and remember that interview questions should never be phrased as "yes" or "no" responses unless immediately followed with open-ended questions that allow you to explore the participant's response. Finally, interview questions should not be double-barreled; that is, they should not ask the participant to address two things at the same time. For instance, the question, "What has your experience been like as a first-year principal and what is your decision-making process like?" is inviting the participant to: (a) describe their experiences as a first year principal, *and* (b) discuss their decision-making process. Instead, it is better to simply ask single-barreled questions (such as "what has your experience been like as a first year principal?").

CONDUCTING THE INTERVIEW. While many of the considerations we have discussed thus far relate to designing the interview, there are also important considerations related to conducting the interview. First, it is important to present yourself professionally to the research participant(s). While it can be intimidating to participate in a research interview, you can reduce the participant's stress by presenting yourself as being transparent about your research focus and being responsive to the participant's needs. Second, you should always come prepared to the interview with a copy of your informed consent form, an audio or video recorder, extra batteries, a tablet, and a pen. Once the interview begins, it is never appropriate to leave for these materials or supplies. Third, as you carry out the interview, it is important not to share comments or thoughts from other participants, as this can lead participants to believe that you will also be sharing their thoughts or comments with other participants. This can make participants hesitant to share their feelings or views, as well as doubt the degree to which you intend to maintain their privacy.

Observations

In addition to interview protocols, practitioner-scholars who plan to conduct observations may also want to develop an observation protocol. Much like an interview protocol, an observation protocol helps the practitioner-scholar structure their data collection. Unlike an interview protocol, however, an observation protocol focuses specifically on what the practitioner-scholar will look for in the field, as well as how they will orient to their participants. Observation protocols should describe how the practitioner-scholar will enter the site, what specific types of interactions or exchanges will be of substantive interest, and how these relate to the study's research focus and question(s).

A key consideration for observations relates to the role that the practitioner-scholar assumes in relation to her/his research participants. There are two basic types of observations: (a) participant observations and (b) non-participant observations, recognizing that practitioner-scholars may adopt an observational role that is somewhere between these two extremes. In a participant observation, practitioner-scholars interact with their research participants while simultaneously observing for research purposes. For example, if observing a professional development session, the practitioner-scholar might participate as others do in the professional development activities. This approach to observation positions the practitioner-scholar inside of the activity or experience that they are observing, and can be really useful for generating an in-depth understanding. In contrast, a non-participant observation entails the practitioner-scholar minimizing her or his interactions with participants. Such an observation positions the practitioner-scholar outside the activity or experience that they are observing. As illustrated in From the Field 7.4, Honig (2006) provided a concise description of a non-participant observational approach she used in a study that examined the interactions between central office administrators and community-based organizations. Her approach is noteworthy as it refers not only to her own position as an observer but also her approach to recording the events she observed (verbatim transcripts), as well as the types of events (formal meetings) that she observed.

FROM THE FIELD 7.4

An Example of an Observational Approach in a Qualitative Study

In addition to interviews, between 1998 and 2000, I directly observed formal, meetings (approximately 160 hours) between representing of the school district central office . . . school/community sites, and others specifically convened to support implementation, such as directors of nonprofit youth-serving organizations and public youth-serving agencies. At these meetings, I wrote almost verbatim transcripts to capture the transfer of information and relationships between the central office and other meeting participants.

Source: Honig, 2006, p. 362

Read the full article at:
www.sagepub.com/lochmiller

As noted, it is often helpful for practitioner-scholars to develop a protocol that clearly identifies what they will observe. This protocol can serve as a form that you might fill in during the observation or a list of data points that you might watch for as you record the exchanges. In some cases, it may be helpful to audio or video record meetings, events, and other activities that you can use for later analyses. The following list illustrates some of the most important considerations to keep in mind when developing an observation protocol.

1. What is the aim or purpose of the observation?

2. What role will you assume (participant or non-participant)?

3. Will you allow your role to change during the observation if it becomes necessary?

4. What will you watch for during the event or activity?

5. In your observation notes, what will you record?

6. Will you record specific exchanges, exact statements, and/or describe the environment?

7. How frequently will you make entries in your notes?

8. Will you augment your written notes with audio or video recordings?

9. Are you trying to generate a verbatim account of the activity?

Documents

In addition to identifying what questions you will ask your participants, as well as what you will look for during your observations, it is also important to identify documents and other salient artifacts that could be helpful in your study. Thus, it is useful to develop a list of potential documents before you begin your research. Documents used in many education research studies include copies of a school improvement plan, meeting notes or agendas, or handouts that you collect in classrooms. For classroom-based research studies, the documents could also include copies of student work or learning activities.

As you begin collecting documents, it is important to consider how you will store and catalog the documents for your study. There is nothing more frustrating than completing your fieldwork and finding that you have a pile of documents that are completely disorganized. In our own research, we often prepare a short coversheet for each document that describes the document, the circumstances in which the document was used, and how we collected the document. This information is particularly helpful in large studies or simply as your dataset begins to grow.

Relatedly, it is important to consider how you will store the documents that you have collected. We recommend that you try to convert the documents you collect to an electronic format such as PDF. You can expedite the process by requesting copies of the documents directly from your research participants in an electronic format. We recommend making this request in writing or as part of a memo describing your plans for the field visit, while being cognizant of not unfairly placing time-intensive expectations on research participants. Ideally, participants should be given at least two weeks to prepare any documents you request, with you also offering to support the process or complete it in its entirety. If documents are not available in electronic form or are too large to scan to a PDF, we encourage you to maintain a three-ring binder, filing drawer, or record box to store the information.

As you collect your documents, it is important to maintain a list of all that you have collected, as well as clearly indicate the format in which you are saving the documents. This list will assist you in more easily recalling where the documents are stored and whether you have collected similar documents from other research participants and/or research sites. When compiling this list, it is also helpful to indicate which research question the document addresses.

Finally, given that you may collect documents containing student information, it is especially important that you store the documents securely. During your visit to a school or district for data collection, it is often appropriate to ask participants to load documents onto a USB drive or to send the documents to you via e-mail (if e-mail correspondence still maintains confidentiality). However, once the information is in your possession, you must take care to delete any identifiable information. This ensures that the identities of students, teachers, schools, or districts involved in the study are protected and that the participants' confidentiality is assured. Further, if you need some way to identify the source or location of the document, we encourage you to develop a coding sheet that assigns a non-descriptive label to the participant or site wherein the identity of the participant or site is stored separate from the document.

REFLECTIVE OPPORTUNITY 7.2

When making participant observations, practitioner-scholars often face a unique ethical dilemma.

1. Specifically, how do they account for the unexpected in the observation, particularly when individuals who are not familiar with their study, nor have consented to participate, enter the research environment? Should they exclude them from their notes? Should they immediately approach them and share the details of the study?

2. From your perspectives, what would be a way in which to ethically and thoughtfully respond to such a situation?

COLLECTING QUANTITATIVE DATA

Practitioner-scholars who conduct a quantitative research study often collect data using student assessments, research instruments, surveys, or by retrieving and analyzing numerical data contained in existing datasets. In this section, we briefly review each type of data and relate them to possible ways that you can use them in your own research.

Student Assessments

Given the world in which practitioner-scholars work, student assessment data is one of the most common forms of quantitative data available that can be collected for research. From Dynamic Indicators of Basic Early Literacy Skills (DIBELS) to Measures of Academic Progress (MAP) to state assessments of student learning, each of these data sources offer practitioner-scholars a wealth of information with which to conduct their research. The process for obtaining this information is usually straightforward and either involves working with your school district's assessment staff, your school principal, or another district colleague who has access to student-level information. The information you receive will depend upon the nature of your data request, as well as privacy rules. For example, you might request student-level information that includes DIBELS scores for each student in your school district. The district will release this information to you, provided the information is reported in a form that does not directly identify individual students. Thus, you might receive a data file that includes a randomly generated student identification number rather than the student's first and last name.

Classroom teachers can also use data from their own assessments to conduct quantitative research. For example, you could use classroom assessments generated by your grade level team or department to identify patterns or trends across students. If you have access or can acquire access to your district's student information, you might be able to include student characteristics (for example, gender, race/ethnicity, special education status, limited English proficiency status, free-or-reduced-price lunch status, among others) in your dataset. The only caveat when using classroom assessment data for your study is to determine whether (a) you have a sufficient number of records (such as student scores) to carry out your analysis, and (b) you have the permission of your students and their parents to use the data for research purposes.

Research Instruments

There are a number of existing research instruments that are available for collecting data directly from research participants. These instruments focus on issues such as classroom instruction, school climate, teacher professionalism, and leadership support among others. For example, if you were interested in studying the climate in your elementary school, you could obtain an existing research instrument that examines school climate. One such example, the Organizational Climate Description Questionnaire (OCDQ-RE), developed by Dr. Wayne Hoy, could be used to study various behaviors in schools that are associated with a healthy school climate. The instrument captures information from participants about their relationships with colleagues and support from administrators. As shown in Figure 7.1, the questionnaire is fully developed and thus easily used in a research study that you might undertake. Indeed, for the novice researcher, these instruments often serve as an excellent starting point for the development of a quantitative study.

Figure 7.1 Organizational Climate Description Questionnaire (OCDQ-RE)

OCDQ-RE

Directions: The following are statements about your school, Plase indicate the extent to which each statement characterizes your school.

	Rarely Occurs	Sometimes Occurs	Often Occurs	Very Frequently Occurs
1. The teachers accomplish their work with vim, vigor, and pleasure.	①	②	③	④
2. Teachers' closest friends are other faculty members at this school.	①	②	③	④
3. Faculty meetings are useless.	①	②	③	④
4. The principal goes out of his/her way to help teachers	①	②	③	④
5. The principal rules with an iron fist.	①	②	③	④
6. Teachers leave school immediately after school is over.	①	②	③	④
7. Teachers invite faculty members to visit them at home.	①	②	③	④
8. There is a minority group of teachers who always oppose the majority.	①	②	③	④
9. The principal uses constructive criticism.	①	②	③	④
10. The principal checks the sign-in sheet every moring.	①	②	③	④
11. Routine duties interfere with the job of teaching.	①	②	③	④
12. Most of the teachers here accept the faults of their colleagues.	①	②	③	④
13. Teachers know the family background of other faculty members.	①	②	③	④
14. Teachers exert group pressure on non-conforming faculty members.	①	②	③	④
15. The principal explains his/her reasons for criticism to teachers.	①	②	③	④
16. The principal listens to and accepts teachers' suggestions.	①	②	③	④
17. The principal schedules the work for the teachers.	①	②	③	④

Source: Obtained from http://www.waynekhoy.com/pdfs/ocdq-re.pdf, Used with permission from Wayne Hoy

Surveys

One of the most commonly used protocols for collecting quantitative data is a survey. Surveys, as we discussed previously, allow practitioner-scholars to collect information from participants about their views, experiences, or perceptions. Surveys are easily converted to quantitative data that are then analyzed using either descriptive or inferential statistics. When practitioner-scholars decide to use a survey in their research, it is important that they keep the following three points in mind. First, surveys should be developed in close consultation with the literature related to the research study. It is never appropriate to develop a survey that simply asks a range of questions that were haphazardly developed. Such surveys produce information that rarely aligns with specific research questions. Rather, practitioner-scholars who use a survey in their research should develop a survey instrument that is: (a) closely aligned with the purpose of their research study, and (b) that is connected to the existing research literature.

Second, in some instances it may be appropriate to use an existing survey instrument as a basis for your own survey. It is also acceptable to model your survey after one that already exists, provided you obtain permission from the original survey author/developer. Survey instruments can be found by reviewing published research studies. In some cases, survey instruments can be obtained from university-based research centers, ERIC, and other online resources as well.

Third, when developing a survey, it is especially important to think about the way that the survey will be deployed, and how the type of deployment may influence the time required to complete your study. For example, if you are conducting a paper-based survey that involves mailing the survey instrument to your research participants, it is important to allow sufficient time for the survey to reach the participants and then be returned to you. Similarly, if you are conducting an online survey, it is important to consider how long you will leave the survey open and how many times you will remind your participants about the survey. Generally, you should leave your survey open between two weeks and one month in order to allow at least one or two reminders to be sent to your participants. The following list highlights some key questions to consider when you prepare to develop and administer a survey.

1. How much time do you want the survey to require of your participants?

2. How many questions will the time constraints of your survey allow you to ask?

3. What format do you want the questions to have (Likert, matrix, open-ended, and so on)?

4. How will you deploy the survey (in-person, online, paper, phone, e-mail)?

5. How much time will you allow your participants to complete and return the survey?

6. How many times will you remind your participants about the survey?

7. What is the minimum number of responses you need (your response rate) to be able to decide when to close your survey?

8. How will you handle responses received after the survey closes?

9. Will you use a survey incentive or thank you? If so, what will you use?

10. How will you handle incomplete surveys?

Public-Use Datasets or Extant Data

While it may be tempting to collect your own information directly from participants, there are also a number of public-use datasets available for practitioner-scholars to use. For example, the National Center for Education Statistics (NCES) at the U.S. Department of Education provides a number datasets that practitioner-scholars can download freely and use in their analyses of student, school, and district-level issues. For example, if you wanted to examine changes in per-pupil funding for schools in your state to determine how changes were associated with increases or decreases in student enrollment, you could download this information from NCES. Additionally, there are also data available that focus on postsecondary institutions. Relatedly, the U.S. Census, the Annie E. Casey Foundation's Kids Count database, and many others offer convenient access to data that can be used. Further, many state departments of education offer similar datasets that focus specifically on state-level topics. Given the public nature of this information, typically no permission is needed to use this information in your study.

CONSIDERING TECHNOLOGY TOOLS TO SUPPORT DATA COLLECTION

There are a variety of technologies that can support you in collecting your data, ranging from digital-recorders for conducting interviews to online survey platforms (such as SurveyMonkey) for collecting survey data to cameras for collecting visual data. It is important to think carefully about the technologies that you use in your research, as they shape the types and form of data you generate and ultimately analyze.

There are many technologies that serve to streamline the data collection process, allowing you to more easily generate, store, and retrieve your data sources. For instance, if you are conducting online interviews, it is useful to know about the newest technologies that can support recording conversations that occur on Skype or other online communication platforms. In addition, many emergent technologies are creating possibilities for new types of data and therefore new spaces for research to occur (Paulus, Lester, & Dempster, 2014). For example, social media sites such as Second Life are relatively new online spaces that many researchers view as their primary research site.

The key is to become familiar with the technologies most relevant to your research needs, which can range from exploring what digital audio or video recorders best meets your needs to examining technologies that might be used to secure and store your data in online databases. As you make technology decisions for conducting your research, we encourage you to consider six key questions, as highlighted in the following list.

1. If you intend to record your data (interviews, focus groups, naturally occurring talk, and so on), what types of audio- or video-recording features do you need? Might there be any apps available to support your recording process?

2. If you intend to use an online survey platform, what types of features would you find useful?

3. To what extent will the technology help you organize and be able to retrieve data for your analysis?

4. To what extent does the technology used to complete your research relate to your analytic tools (for example, ATLAS.ti or SPSS)?

5. To what extent does the technology allow you to share information, if working on a collaborative project?

6. What are the potential limitations of the technology tool(s) selected to carry out the research?

SUMMARY

In this chapter, we introduced you to some of the key considerations for conducting or carrying out your research study. First, we discussed the various ways to conceptualize and think through sampling in both a qualitative and quantitative study, as well as issues related to accessing research sites and recruiting participants. Second, we also shared about key ideas related to collecting qualitative data, particularly in relationship to preparing and conducting interviews, making observations, and collecting artifacts and documents. Third, we offered a brief discussion related to some of the key concerns for collecting quantitative data, with a specific focus on student assessments, research instruments, surveys, and extant data. Finally, we encouraged you to consider which technologies would support you in carrying out your research, particularly in relation to collecting and storing data.

KEY TERMS

Convenience Sample 141

Focus Group Interview
   Protocol 151

Non-Participant Observation 153

Nonprobability Sampling 143

Participant Observation 153

Population 140

Probability Sampling 143

Purposeful Sample 141

Sample 140

Semi-Structured Interview
   Protocol 151

Simple Random
   Sample 144

Snowball Sampling
   (or chain referral sampling) 142

Stratified Sampling 144

Structured Interview Protocol 150

Systematic Sampling 144

Unstructured Interview 151

1. What are the primary differences between a sample and a population?

2. How might you describe the various types of qualitative sampling strategies? How might you distinguish them from one another?

3. What are the different forms of quantitative sampling strategies? Why might you use one sampling strategy over another?

4. What are some of the key considerations for developing an interview, observation, and document-collection protocol?

5. What are some of the critical considerations for collecting quantitative data?

6. How might technological tools support you in carrying out your research? What tools might be most useful considering your interests and research focus?

CHAPTER EXERCISES

1. You are interested in conducting a qualitative study exploring the experiences of first-year teachers working in a rural school district. What sampling strategy might you propose to use and why?

2. Conducting interviews effectively involves preparation and practice. Considering your research focus, develop a semi-structured interview protocol and conduct a mock interview with a colleague. Record the interview. At the conclusion of the interview, invite your colleague to share any suggestions they might have related to your questions and interviewing style. Also, spend time listening to your interview in order to identify ways in which you might more effectively engage in the interview process.

3. If you are planning to conduct a survey for your study, what are the steps involved in designing, piloting, and deploying a survey instrument? Create a timeline or map that outlines the process of carrying out your survey study. This illustration should show not only what the steps in the process will be, but also the timing of each step (months, days, and so on).

4. Visit your state department of education website and/or school district's website and locate publicly available data files. What types of analyses might you conduct with this information? How might this information be linked to other data you collect? What do you need to make these links? Create a table that identifies the variables available to you that might be used to support a quantitative analysis highlighting the differences in student achievement.

LEARNING EXTENSIONS

There are several useful resources for thinking about how best to carry out your research, particularly in relation to collecting qualitative data and completing a survey study. A useful place to begin if you are planning to conduct qualitative interviews is with Roulston's (2011) book, *Reflective Interviewing: A Guide to Theory and Practice*. Spending time reading about the theory that grounds qualitative interviewing is important, as is thinking through practical concerns. If you intend to make observations, Emerson, Fretz, and Shaw's (2011) book, *Writing Ethnographic Field notes*, offers both theoretical and practical considerations. Writing from an ethnographic perspective, the authors discuss what it means to engage in ethnographic observations, as well as how to participate, observe, and take notes while engaged in fieldwork. Finally, if you intend to use a survey instrument to collect data, we encourage you to explore Rea and Parker's book (2014), *Designing and Conducting Survey Research: A Comprehensive Guide*, which offers a discussion around designing questionnaires and survey questions, as well as the analysis process.

Sharpen your skills with SAGE edge!

edge.sagepub.com/lochmiller

SAGE edge for Students provides a personalized approach to help you accomplish your coursework goals in an easy-to-use learning environment. You'll find action plans, mobile-friendly eFlashcards, and quizzes as well as videos, web resources, and links to SAGE journal articles to support and expand on the concepts presented in this chapter.

8

COMPLETING QUALITATIVE DATA ANALYSIS

ANALYZING QUALITATIVE DATA

Assuming that you conducted a qualitative case study to explore the perceptions of central office administrators in relation to the instructional leadership practices of school principals, you find yourself awash in data that include interviews, focus groups, observations, and documents. Looking at this pile of data, you wonder how you will make sense of and ultimately come to understand the data that you have collected. It seems insurmountable! Yet, you know that you must proceed if you hope to understand how the central office administrators you carefully interviewed perceive and define school principals' instructional leadership.

INTRODUCTION

The opening vignette positions you where many practitioner-scholars find themselves after completing their data collection for a qualitative study—awash in data with no clear path forward. In Chapter 5, we introduced you to six different qualitative methodologies and noted how each brings with it particular assumptions about the research focus, research question(s), and data sources. Similar to qualitative methodologies more generally, when considering qualitative data analysis it is important to keep in mind that there are many different approaches to analyzing qualitative data. Indeed, it is beyond the scope of this textbook to introduce you to *all* of the approaches to qualitative data analysis. However, we do aim to introduce you to one of the mainstay approaches to analyzing qualitative data: thematic analysis.

In this chapter, we first introduce you to some of the overarching aims and purposes of qualitative data analysis, and briefly highlight the varied approaches to analyzing qualitative data. Then, we

Learning Objectives

By the end of the chapter, you will be able to:

- Describe the aims and purposes of qualitative data analysis.

- Illustrate the overarching steps of a thematic analysis.

- Summarize the types of transcripts.

- Discuss the various types of transcription software.

- Describe the different types of coding and their functions.

- Explain how to move from codes to themes.

- Summarize how validity has been conceptualized in qualitative research.

- Identify the role of computer-assisted qualitative data analysis software in qualitative data analysis.

present qualitative data analysis as an iterative process, and discuss the steps of analysis in detail. Specifically, we describe the process of: (1) preparing your data for analysis, (2) becoming familiar with your data, (3) transcribing your data, (4) memoing your data, (5) coding your data, (6) moving from codes to categories to themes, and (7) creating a coding map. We then briefly discuss issues related to validity and quality in qualitative research. Finally, we share how computer-assisted qualitative data analysis software can support qualitative data analysis.

DEFINING QUALITATIVE DATA ANALYSIS: AIMS AND PURPOSES

Historically, data analysis in qualitative research has been viewed as mysterious. However, there has been a recent boom in articles and books describing how to do qualitative data analysis, with some calling for publically disclosing the analysis process (Anfara, Brown, & Mangione, 2002). Generally, there is a recognition that the analysis process needs to be clearly described so that outsiders can evaluate how a practitioner-scholar went about interpreting their data and empirically grounding their conclusions.

The purpose of qualitative data analysis is to bring meaning and some type of order to the data (Anfara et al., 2002). The aim of most approaches to qualitative data analysis is to inductively interpret the data, with findings being grounded in the actual dataset. For instance, rather than just writing that a major finding generated from a case study of first-year principals was that they felt a sense of isolation, a practitioner-scholar would illustrate this by including quotes from actual interviews and the interpretation of these quotes. This would highlight how the practitioner-scholar came to their conclusions, with these conclusions grounded in the words of the participants; that is, the actual data.

Indeed, qualitative data analysis does not mean *one* thing; instead, it encompasses a variety of approaches linked to particular research traditions, fields, and qualitative methodologies. For instance, From the Field 8.1 highlights how a qualitative data analysis was described in a discourse analysis study (Lester, 2014). From the Field 8.2 offers a different perspective, showing how an analysis was described for an ethnographic study (Gallo, 2014). Taken together, these provide two examples with which to illustrate the breadth of analytic traditions in qualitative research.

As illustrated in From the Field 8.1 and From the Field 8.2, there are both inherent similarities and differences between discourse and ethnographic analysis, which can be said of most approaches to qualitative data analysis. As you make decisions about your approach to qualitative data analysis, it is critical to keep in mind that qualitative data analysis strategies are linked to: (a) your methodology, (b) your research focus, and (c) your research questions. Ultimately, the way you carry out your analysis should inform how you also present your findings in your final research report/paper (see Chapter 12 for a discussion of writing up your research).

Miles and Huberman (1994) suggested that there were some commonalities across qualitative approaches to analysis. As highlighted in Chapter 2 as well, they noted six "analytic moves" that are common across approaches to qualitative data analysis, including:

An Example of a Description of Data Analysis Within a Discourse Analysis Study

Throughout the analysis process, three analytic questions sensitized my process: (a) What is the discourse functioning to do/perform? (b) How is the discourse constructed to do this? and (c) What conversational resources are employed to perform this interactional activity? (Potter, 2004; Wood & Kroger, 2000). In alignment with the assumptions of DP, I attempted to "avoid 'reading into' the data a set of ready made analytic categories," allowing instead for that which I found "interesting" to be sensitized by what the participants made relevant (Edwards, 1997, p. 89). I completed a seven-step analysis process, which included (1) intensive listening and viewing of the recorded therapy sessions and waiting room conversations (Wood & Kroger, 2000); (2) transcription of the recorded data (Potter & Wetherell, 1987), using a modified Jeffersonian transcription style (Jefferson, 2004; see Appendix A in the Supplemental Materials); (3) repeated readings of the transcripts, which were synchronized with the audio or video file, allowing me to stay close to the data (Paulus, Lester, & Dempster, 2014); (4) a refined, "more intensive" study of the discourse patterns (Potter & Wetherell, 1987, p. 167); (5) generation of interpretations; (6) sharing of emergent findings with the participants to generate new analytical directions and insights; and (7) reflexive reporting of findings.

More specifically, I began the analysis with listening and relistening to the audio and video recordings,

listening at least two times to each recorded therapy session. Throughout this step, I recorded notes in relation to those sections of the data that I found most striking (Rapley, 2007). Next, I transcribed the data, orienting to the transcription process as being "a constructive and conventional activity" (p. 166) and positioning it central to the analysis. Then, I read and reread all of the synchronized transcripts in their entirety, searching for and identifying patterns (e.g., constructions of competence) and conversational features (e.g., turn-taking organization). As I worked across the data set, I labeled segments of the talk in relation to concepts drawn from discourse theory and conversation analysis. Initially, I created lists/ descriptions of common language features within selected excerpts of the talk, organizing and identifying patterns across the data related to specific conversational features of focus (e.g., turn-taking organization). I labeled selected excerpts with this developing list/description of common features. Next, after identifying patterns and variability across the data, as well as attending to the sequential relationships within the interactions, I formed tentative explanations about the functions of various discursive features used within the data set and began to write up the findings. Throughout, with a commitment to publicly disclosing my analysis process, I followed the suggestions of Anfara, Brown, and Mangione (2002) and developed a mapping of my analysis process, as shown in Appendix B in the Supplemental Materials.

Source: Lester, 2014, pp. 182–183

Copyright © 2014 by the American Psychological Association. Reproduced with permission. Lester, J. N. (2014). Negotiating abnormality/normality in therapy talk: A discursive psychology approach to the study of therapeutic interactions and children with autism. *Qualitative Psychology*, 1(2), 178–193. The use of APA information does not imply endorsement by APA.

- Affixing codes to a set of field notes drawn from observations or interviews

- Noting reflections or other remarks in the margins

- Sorting and sifting through these materials to identify similar phrases, relationships among variables, patterns, themes, distinct differences among subgroups, and common sequences

An Example of a Description of Data Analysis Within an Ethnographic Study

My ethnographic analyses follow Emerson, Fretz, and Shaw (1995) and Heath and Street (2008), iteratively drawing patterns from the hundreds of field notes, video logs, and transcribed interviews. During data collection I read through my corpus of data quarterly to bring together emergent themes, which I typed into conceptual memos (Heath & Street, 2008). After I completed data collection, my analysis included open coding using the qualitative data software program Atlas.TI. During this phase of analysis I continually adjusted my coding scheme to reflect central themes and wrote additional memos that highlighted connections and inconsistencies I noticed among the data. The larger project resulted in 60 codes including themes such as "fatherhood," "literacy practices," and "translanguaging." The data in this article come from a subset of categories that emerged around immigration and schooling, such as "documentation," "immigration," "police,"

"separation," "literacy," "linguistic creativity," and "translation." As I analyzed these data I looked to understand the subtle and overt ways that immigration practices were shaping students' lives and learning and the ways that teachers recognized the effects of these practices. I also began to notice an abundance of hybrid language practices as families navigated new obstacles in the face of harsh immigration practices. Although there are non–immigration-linked instances in which children also engage in hybrid languaging and learning, such as everyday translation at the store or making sense of an obscure homework assignment, I began to notice how challenges created by immigration practices increased opportunities and necessities for such hybridity. I began to wonder how similar practices were utilized or recognized in students' classrooms and their potential to support students' classroom learning.

Source: Gallo, 2014, p. 485

 Read the full article at:
www.sagepub.com/lochmiller

- Isolating these patterns and processes, commonalities and differences, and taking them out to the field in the next wave of data collection

- Gradually elaborating a small set of generalizations that cover the consistencies discerned in the database

- Confronting those generalizations with a formalized body of knowledge in the form of constructs or theories. (p. 9)

In this chapter, we offer a general description of the qualitative analysis process, specifically focusing on the process of producing a thematic understanding of a qualitative dataset—a process often referred to as thematic analysis. Many of the analytic steps we discuss here can be found in part within a variety of approaches to qualitative analysis.

CARRYING OUT QUALITATIVE DATA ANALYSIS

As highlighted in Chapter 5, qualitative research is an inductive endeavor, wherein the practitioner-scholar is viewed as the primary research instrument. Patton (1980) noted that, "inductive analysis means that the patterns, themes, and categories of analysis come from the data; they emerge out of the data rather than being imposed on them prior to data collection

DETERMINING YOUR ANALYTIC APPROACH

Before you begin to analyze your data, you decide that you need to see how other researchers have undertaken this important step. You begin by downloading several published case studies that were recently conducted. These studies are not all aligned with your topic, but provide various examples that show you how you can complete your data analysis. In one study, you see that the researcher analyzed the data using a thematic analysis. This approach allowed him to identify cross-cutting themes that broadly described how the participants in his study described their thoughts and ideas. In another study, you find that the researcher analyzed the data to construct a theory that explains conceptually how participants in the study interacted with other members of the school leadership team. This made sense to you as the study was described as a grounded theory study. Finally, in another study you note that the author referred to his analysis as "iterative" but did not provide further details. You were left with many questions. Looking at the examples, you realize that your interest as a researcher is primarily to

generate cross-cutting themes from the interviews that you conducted with central office administrators in your case study. You want to show how the perspectives are related and unrelated to one another. Moreover, you want to show how the perspectives they offered are in some way connected to your conceptual understanding of what it means to be an instructional leader at the school level. Thus, from your review of the literature, you realize that you are likely to complete your analysis using a thematic analysis rather than some other analytic approach. Further, you realize that your analytic approach aligns well with your methodological approach.

Focus Questions

1. How might you assure that your approach to analyzing the data is clear and transparent for outside readers?

2. What might be some of the challenges inherent to carrying out a thematic analysis?

and analysis" (p. 306). At the same time, what emerges out of the data is directly linked to your interpretation of it and the methodology, research questions, theoretical framework, and subjective positions you bring to the data (Srivastava & Hopwood, 2009). This analytic process, then, demands a commitment to being reflexive, as noted in Chapter 5. In addition, as you carry out a qualitative analysis, it is helpful to think about it as an iterative process. It is therefore an ongoing process that involves returning again and again to the data, new questions and connections that arise through the analysis, and the theoretical perspectives and methodology informing the study. Miles and Huberman (1994) described the analysis process as "interactive" and "cyclical," noting that the analysis of qualitative data often drives a researcher back to collect additional data, for instance (p. 12). Figure 8.1 illustrates one way to think about this iterative process.

While qualitative data analysis can certainly be conceived of as nonlinear, we also believe it is important to recognize the value of taking a systematic approach, particularly in how you describe the approach to analysis. Being systematic does not mean that you discount the value of being flexible and open to the sometimes messy process of doing qualitative data analysis; rather, it means that you are prepared to chronicle your analysis process for others and able to ground your findings in your dataset.

Figure 8.1 The Iterative Qualitative Data Analysis Process

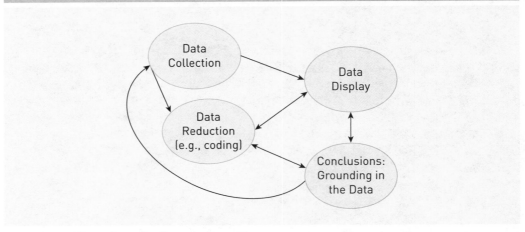

Source: Adapted from Miles and Huberman, 1994, p. 12

We next discuss several steps central to carrying out a thematic analysis, an approach to analysis that allows you to move from broad understandings of your data to identifying themes across the dataset. While we present the analytic process in a step-by-step way, we acknowledge that these steps quite often occur in an iterative fashion.

Preparing and Organizing Your Data for Analysis

After collecting qualitative data, practitioner-scholars are often left wondering what to do with the data. How do you prepare them for analysis? How do you store the data? Where do you store the data? How do you keep track of multiple interviews, focus groups, and documents? Where do you store your observational notes? There are many questions to consider as you begin preparing your data for analysis. We offer a few key considerations.

First, it is important to begin preparing and organizing your data throughout your data collection process. We *strongly* recommend that you do not wait until you have collected all of your data to begin thinking about how to organize your dataset. Rather, we recommend establishing an organizational system prior to beginning data collection. Things to consider include:

- Label data clearly. It is helpful to label your data based on the data type, participant pseudonym, and date of data collection (for example, "Interview_Teacher Susan 1_August 21, 2013). You may want to include other identifiers in your file name, while assuring that you maintain the participants' confidentiality even at this stage. Labeling your data and setting up a clear folder system will ultimately save you time and decrease the chances of losing data.

- Develop a data table. Creating a master data table that clearly lists out each data source will assist you in staying organized, and provide you with a resource to easily reference when writing about your data sources. Within this table, we suggest that you include items such as data type (for example, interview versus focus group), the name or pseudonym of the participant(s), the date when the data was collected, and other relevant descriptive details, such as the length of the interview, the role of the participant (for instance, principal), or other relevant demographic information. In addition, if you are working on a research team, it is also important to indicate who collected the data.

- Store data in a secure place. While it is tempting to store data on sites such Dropbox, you need to think carefully about the security of such storage sites, which is particularly true when storing sensitive data. In fact, many Institutional Review Boards do not allow for data to be stored on sites like Dropbox; rather, they require that you store your data on a password-protected computer hard drive and/or external drive. We recommend that, whatever you do, you assure that your data is securely and privately stored, and that you store it in multiple locations. There is nothing worse than losing data due to a computer crash! To avoid this, keep multiple copies of your data files.

Second, a frequently overlooked aspect of preparing and organizing data is ethics. For instance, should you list out participants' real names in your data table or assign pseudonyms even as you begin to organize your data? At what stage in the research process should you develop and apply pseudonyms to your research sites? We suggest that you take early steps to make your data confidential. One early step to take is to develop a master list of participants linked to their assigned pseudonyms. The same can be done for your research site(s). For instance, you might assign names to school sites or specific communities. Once you establish this list and securely save it, all of your other research files should use these pseudonyms. This will simply add an additional layer of security to your data set.

Becoming Familiar With Your Data

During and after you have completed data collection, it is important to spend time getting to know your data more intimately. Prior to transcribing data, it is helpful to spend time listening and relistening to your audio recordings and/or viewing your video recordings. As you do this, there are several general analytic questions to consider, as listed here. Keeping a record of your responses to these questions is useful, as you can refer back to this as you progress through the analysis process.

REFLECTIVE OPPORTUNITY 8.1

You will be faced with numerous ethical considerations as you organize and prepare your data for analysis.

1. Considering the resources you already have available to you, where might be the best place to store your data? Personal computer? Password-protected hard drive?

- What are the key messages in the dataset that stand out for you?

- How do your data sources relate and inform your research focus?

- How might your theoretical framework(s) shape how to make sense of your data?

- Are there any claims or statements that raise questions about your theoretical or conceptual framework(s)?

- How do the statements, views, and perspectives of your participants differ from your own assumptions of the phenomenon of interest?

- In what ways do the claims and/or perspectives of the participants converge or diverge from one another?

- After reviewing your data, what additional questions do you have?

- Where do you see gaps in your dataset? Should additional data be collected?

While this first step of analysis may seem to simply add time to the process, we view it as invaluable, as it allows you to stay close to your data. Further, early familiarity with the data allows you to foresee any potential challenges you may face during the transcription process, which we discuss next.

Transcribing Your Data

Transcription is an important part of the analysis process. While transcription can be easily conceived of as something that you do to prepare your data for analysis, we view transcription as central to the analysis process. Why? First, when you transcribe your recorded data you make important analytic decisions. Will you transcribe everything? Will you only transcribe the portions of an interview that you believe are most relevant to your research question(s)? Throughout the transcription process, you make choices, which are closely related to your methodology and theoretical perspective (Kvale, 2007). Beyond this, the transcription process involves a great deal of interpretation (Ochs, 1979). A transcript is not simply a pure representation of what was stated in an interview or focus group; rather, the moment you transform your data from an audio or video file to a written transcript, you engage in interpretation. For instance, you have to think about how you will transcribe certain utterances. Should you transcribe words like "um" or ignore them? Should you transcribe laughter or crying? As you make these decisions, you must also consider the consequence. What is lost and gained in the creation of your transcripts?

Related to these decisions, you must also determine what type of transcript you are going to produce. There are many different approaches to transcribing and therefore varied types of transcripts. The type of transcript you decide to create is connected to your methodology and the purpose of your research. Paulus, Lester, and Dempster (2014) identified four transcription types, including: (a) verbatim, (b) Jeffersonian, (c), gisted, and (d) visual. While it is beyond the scope of this textbook to describe each transcript type in detail, we offer brief definitions of each and encourage you to explore Paulus and colleagues' (2014) writing around this.

First, a verbatim transcript entails typing everything you hear (in the audio recording) or see (in the video recording). You would therefore type out all utterances and even stay true to the dialect used by the participant. When creating a verbatim transcript from video data, you would also transcribe all of the nonverbal communication (such as yawning). The idea behind a verbatim transcript is that you capture everything that occurred (verbally and nonverbally) in the original recording. Obviously, this is not really possible, as there is no way to capture *everything*. However, if you are particularly interested in studying all that was uttered, this type of transcript is preferred.

Second, a Jeffersonian Transcript is a transcript that uses symbols to represent conversational features of the interaction, such as places where there is overlapping speech or the length of a silence or gap in speech. If you create this type of transcript, you would first need to create a verbatim transcript. Then you would apply symbols that represent details of the interaction. The symbols are often referred to as Jeffersonian symbols, as they are drawn from a transcription system developed by Gail Jefferson (2004). There are other systems of transcription symbols that you might use (for example, see Du Bois, 1991). A Jeffersonian transcript is often associated with discourse analysis studies that are informed by conversation analysis. Conversation analysis is a qualitative methodology that focuses on the sequential organization of talk or language use (Sacks, 1992). Table 8.1 highlights some of these transcription symbols and the aspects of the interaction that may be focused upon.

Third, a gisted transcript is a transcript that gives you the gist or overall sense of the audio or video file. In other words, it highlights the main points of the audio or video recordings without providing all of the nuanced details of each utterance. There are different types of gisted transcripts, including a condensed transcript. A condensed transcript, which is a type of gisted transcript, is a transcript that does *not* include unnecessary words (such as "ums"). In a condensed transcript, you keep the participants' exact words, but you do not add any additional details as you would in the verbatim or Jeffersonian transcript. We have found that a condensed transcript is quite common among practitioner-scholars, particularly when they are working with interview or focus group data as part of a case study.

Table 8.1	An Abbreviated List of Jeffersonian Symbols
Symbol	Meaning or Explanation
↑	Upward arrows represent marked rise in pitch.
↓	Downward arrows represent a downward shift in pitch.
> <	Text encased in greater than and less than symbols can be heard as faster than the surrounding speech.
< >	When turned greater than and less than symbols encase speech, the speech can be heard as stretched or slower than the surrounding speech.
(7)	Numbers in parentheses indicate pauses timed to the nearest second. A period with no number following (.) indicates a pause that can be heard, yet too short to measure.
eat	Underlining represents a sound or word(s) uttered with added emphasis.
EAT	Capital letters represent that something was said loudly or shouted.

Source: Jefferson, 2004

Fourth, a visual transcript provides a broad strokes description of what was shared or occurred in the audio or video file, as well as images (for example, pictures or still shots from video data) that represent the participant's actions. This type of transcript would be particularly useful for those who are interested in visual analysis (see Rose, 2012, for more information)—an approach to qualitative analysis that is beyond the scope of this textbook.

Indeed, transcription requires time and lots of it! Thus, an important aspect of transcription is the actual process of completing the transcription. What starts out as a 1-hour interview can quickly turn into a 30-or-more-page document. How might you create transcripts with relative ease? While you may be tempted to use a professional transcription service, we suggest that doing the transcription yourself helps you to get to know your data. Even if you use a professional transcription service, it will be important to go through your transcripts carefully to assure that they are accurate and align with your approach to analysis. We suggest listening to the recorded files and reading the transcriptions simultaneously in order to do this. In the end, the transcription process allows you to stay close to your data and even develop some initial analytic ideas related to your next steps.

You may want to invest time in learning to use a transcription software package, which serves to support the process of moving from an audio or video file to a written transcript. Paulus and colleagues (2014) outlined four transcription software packages (Express Scribe, Audio Notetaker 3, InqScribe 2.2.1, and F4/F5) that are useful for supporting the transcription process. Investing time and money in a transcription software package allows for you to systematize the transcription process. The main features of these four packages are highlighted in Table 8.2.

Table 8.2 Transcription Software Features		
Software	**Features**	
Express Scribe	• Free version (does not expire)	
	• Mac/PC compatibility	
	• Supports both audio and video data	
	• Fee-based version supports foot pedal use	
	• Hotkey control playback	
	• Integrates with word processing systems	
	• Works with voice recognition software	
Audio Notetaker 3	• 30-day fully functional free trial version (with site license options)	
	• Mac/PC compatibility	
	• Supports audio data only	
	• Supports foot pedal use	
	• Audio represented visually with colored bar segments for navigation, editing, and organizing	
	• Works with voice recognition software	
InqScribe 2.2.1	• 30-day fully functional free trial version with academic discounts	
	• Mac/PC compatibility	
	• Supports audio and video data	

	• Supports foot pedal use
	• Can insert time codes for transcript/media file synchronization
	• Can create macros (snippets) for repeated words and phrases
	• Works with voice recognition software
F4/F5	• Free version with limited functionality
	• Mac/PC compatibility
	• Supports audio and video data
	• Supports foot pedal use (in pro version)
	• Hotkey to control playback, add timestamps and other shortcuts
	• Integrates with word-processing programs and with other computer-assisted qualitative data analysis software
	• Does not work well with voice recognition software

Source: Adapted from Paulus et al., 2014, p. 108

Memoing Your Data

Many qualitative researchers spend time memoing their data. A memo is a written reflection of your data, often linked directly to some aspect of your data. Simply put, a memo is a "conversation with ourselves about our data" (Clarke, 2005, p. 202). Writing memos "should be a creative activity" and "should be suggestive; they needn't be conclusive" (Dey, 1993, p. 89). For instance, you might attach a memo to a section of an interview transcript focused on a new principal's experience of evaluating teachers. Perhaps you note the way that the principal described the process of evaluating teachers and highlight your initial thoughts around how his statements might be interpreted through the lens of your theoretical framework. From the Field 8.3 shows a memo that was linked to an interview of a school leader in Colombia, South America. The memo focused on making some suggestive links between the school leader's practices and sensemaking, which is a theoretical perspective drawn from organizational sciences that describes how actors within organizations make sense of events (Weick, 1995). Note that the memo was clearly labeled and included a date, allowing for the practitioner-scholar to keep their interpretations organized chronologically.

REFLECTIVE OPPORTUNITY 8.2

As you transcribe your data, it is important to think carefully about how you might protect your participants' identities even as you transcribe. Participants may reference other people, state where they or others live, or provide other identifying information. You need to think carefully about how you will transcribe this information.

1. Will you anonymize your data as you transcribe or clean the data after the analysis is complete?

2. What are the benefits and drawbacks related to your choice?

An Example of a Memo That Was Written in Relationship to a Portion of a Transcribed Interview

Title: Potential links to sensemaking perspectives

Date: 12/5/15

In this quote of the interview, the principal seems to acknowledge an external impetus that leads them to a new understanding of the challenge in their school. In particular, the example shows how the principal sees her current actions related to the implementation of the Leader in Me curriculum as being different from the implementation of the International Baccalaureate program. The principal's recognition of this illustrates the extent to which she engaged in sensemaking. This would be an interesting passage to return to when considering external stimuli.

Some qualitative researchers memo all of their data prior to coding and others do it concurrently, even adding memos about the actual codes and the coding process. Generally, practitioner-scholars should use memos as a way to record their analytic ideas and emerging findings. As such, you can envision the memoing process as something that may take place throughout the analysis process, and used to set the stage for deeper analysis through coding.

Coding Your Data

As briefly noted in Chapter 2, coding is the process of attaching a short word or phrase to specific portions of your data. A code is simply a text-based label that gives meaning to a segment of your data. Much like painting a house, coding involves multiple layers. The first layer of codes is designed to prime your dataset much like you would prime your house to prepare it for painting. This layer involves identifying broad passages, ideas, or statements of substantive interest. The next layer of coding involves applying color to those broad passages, which relates in some way to your interpretations or to the meanings that you want to attach to the dataset. The final layer is often about fine tuning or focusing on details that allow you to bring together your interpretation. This final layer is the most abstract and general, and in a thematic analysis results in producing themes.

There are many different purposes for codes, ranging from codes designed to describe some aspect of the data to codes designed to summarize, condense, or reduce your data. Relatedly, there are different types of codes (Saldaña, 2009), including in-vivo, descriptive, and a priori. Descriptive codes describe in a word or phrase the main topic of a segment of the data. For example, "curriculum development" could describe the process in which teachers engaged while developing a new math curriculum. Similarly, "principal feedback" might refer to the ways in which principals described giving feedback to classroom teachers about their practice. In-vivo codes refer to the actual word or phrase used by the participant. For instance, a principal says in an interview, "I engage in instructional leadership by being classroom-focused, meaning I provide detailed feedback to teachers based on my observations of them." Perhaps a practitioner-scholar uses the phrase "classroom-focused" as an in-vivo code to describe more broadly how practitioners engage in instructional leadership and provide feedback to classroom teachers.

A priori codes are predetermined words or phrases that are directly linked to the research literature and/or specific theories informing your work. If sensemaking is the theoretical framework that you are using to inform your interpretation of the data, then you might use the word "sensemaking" as an a priori code to describe those instances in which you see a principal or teacher leader engaging in behaviors that you want to characterize as sensemaking based on your understanding of the related literature. The key assumption of an a priori code is that you, as a practitioner-scholar, have carefully read and reviewed the existing literature and formulated an understanding of practice based on that literature. Table 8.3 shows a coded interview, with the participant pseudonym listed in the left-hand column, the coded interview passage in the center column, and descriptive codes listed in the right-hand column.

As you develop your codes, it is important to think carefully about the definitions that support those codes. Defining your codes systematizes the way that you use your codes. Indeed, the way you use a code might change as you carry out the analysis, but you should chronicle how your understanding changes. Table 8.4 provides an example of a segment of a code list with definitions of each code used in a case study of a principal preparation program.

Finally, as you code your data, we encourage you to remain reflexive about the process. Saldaña (2009, pp. 50–51) offered several questions to consider during the coding process, as highlighted in the following list. We encourage you to record your responses to these questions as you progress through the analysis process.

- Is the coding method(s) harmonizing with your study's conceptual or theoretical framework?

- Is the coding method(s) relating to or addressing your research questions?

- Are you feeling comfortable and confident applying the coding methods to your data?

- Are the data lending themselves to the coding methods (that is, are the codes appropriate for field notes, appropriate for interview transcripts, and so on)?

Table 8.3 Interview Passage Coded With Three Descriptive Codes

Participant Pseudonym	Interview Passage	Descriptive Codes Applied
Program Director	Well, they're very coy about it. I mean every time we ask that question, it's like, "We'll see." Clearly it can't happen now because we weren't able to—it's not in the budget. We're doing a whole new way of doing budget this year because of et cetera, et cetera. So maybe it can happen next year, et cetera. So how I'm navigating it is looking for grant money and trying to put a little bit of pressure through the state capital, through the superintendent. That kind of backfired when [Person A] met with [Person B] and talked about the fact that the grant was running out and that we'd made a proposal for phase two and that we hadn't heard anything, et cetera.	CHALLENGES KEY STAKEHOLDERS SUSTAINABILITY

Table 8.4 An Example of a Segment of a Code List With Definitions

Code	Code's Definition
Admissions	Participant description of the admissions process, requirements, or metrics used to admit students into the program.
Alignment With District Context	Evidence of alignment between the principal preparation program context and the district's administrative context (that is, how is the principal preparation program providing activities or learning that are directly aligned with district's practices or procedures?).
Alignment with Standards	Participant's comments regarding the alignment of principal preparation program activities with the state or national leadership standards.
Apprenticeship Activities	Activities or responsibilities that were assigned to the apprentice during their program experience.
Competency Assessments	Participant comments concerning the program's use of competency assessments.
Course Objectives	Participant- or document-based statements, which define the course objectives.
Curriculum Development	Participant's description of the process used to develop the curriculum for the program.
Definition of Turnaround Leadership	Participant recollections or references that relate to turnaround leadership, either as the program or the participants define it.
Design Features	Specific considerations or choices about the design, function, or scope of program as perceived by participants.

- Is the coding method(s) providing the specificity you need?
- Is the coding method(s) leading you toward an analytic pathway (for example, toward the construction of categories)?

Moving From Codes to Categories and Categories to Themes

Qualitative data analysis involves moving from individual statements to interpretations that are more abstract but directly related to or address your research questions. Codes correspond to individual fragments of data that, on their own, tell us very little. Coding is the first step in the qualitative analysis process. In essence, codes are much like individual puzzle pieces—they are disconnected and unrelated pieces of a much bigger puzzle that must be brought together if we are to understand the full picture. Codes might refer to participant characteristics, individual participant experiences, events, or activities. Each of these may have meaning but until we relate them in some way they remain quite disconnected.

Categories thus take us a step further than codes in that they begin to relate and add meaning to the individually coded passages. Categories bring together various coded passages and assign meaning about their relationship, differences, similarities, or interactions. For example, if we coded a series of interviews from principals about their participation in a recent professional development workshop, we might bring these coded passages together into one category if we were to find that principals generally appreciated or valued a particular activity, topic, or presentation.

Categories serve as the basis of our themes. Themes are broad, analytically driven statements about your data. Unlike codes, which refer directly to our data, and categories, which bridge our data with our analytic interpretations, themes are almost entirely based on our analytic interpretation of the data. Themes thus bring together various categories. To return to our example, if we identified a series of categories that related to a particular aspect of a principal's experience in a professional development program, we might characterize these experiences broadly with a thematic statement. If principals identified the value of problem-based learning, we might articulate the value they placed on this type of learning in a thematic statement, such as, "Principals assessed value of problem-based learning activities in a professional development workshop." This statement captures broadly the underlying coded passages that relate to various aspects of the professional development experience, as well as the categories that refer to these coded passages. The thematic statement effectively captures both codes and categories by bringing them under a single, understandable umbrella that is aligned with our research questions and reflective of our study's theoretical framework. The process of moving from the level of code to theme is illustrated in Figure 8.2.

Making an Analysis Map

It is important to make your analysis process visible for others. From extensive memoing to thoughtful coding, you should aim to generate an audit trail of your decision-making process. An audit trail is a paper-based or electronic account of each of your analytical decisions, from how you defined and described each code to the way in which you moved from codes to categories to themes. Generating a clear account of each analytic decision is critical for maintaining transparency and quality within your analysis process.

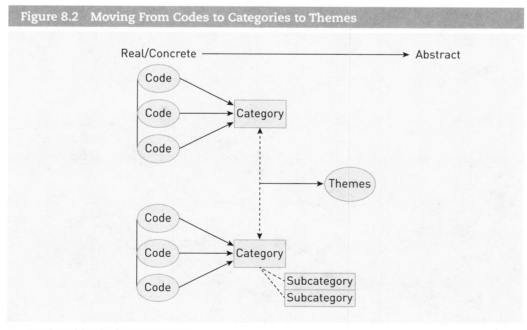

Figure 8.2   Moving From Codes to Categories to Themes

Source: Adapted from Saldaña, 2009, p. 12

In addition, Anfara and colleagues (2002) highlighted the value of producing a coding map that lists the codes applied to the data and the actual process of moving from codes to categories to themes. An analysis map provides an abbreviated summary of how you moved from codes to themes or final findings. The purpose of this map is to build transparency around your analysis process, while also illustrating in an explicit way one aspect of your analytical decision-making process. Figure 8.3 provides an example of a portion of a coding map from a dissertation study focused on the perceptions of a middle school principal as a caregiver (Stein, 2008). The study was designed as an exploratory descriptive case study and included a thematic analysis of interviews, observations, and documents. Within Figure 8.3, one of the themes ("caring leadership") is listed in relation to three categories, as well as the codes that were initially applied to the data.

Knowing When Your Analysis Is Complete

When carrying out qualitative data analysis our students often ask us: "How do I know when I'm done?" Our response to this question is often: "It depends." Each qualitative analysis requires practitioner-scholars to work a different length of time. Thus, it is difficult to affirmatively say when a qualitative analysis is complete. Nonetheless, there are some clear indications for when to end a study (Lincoln & Guba, 1985), including exhaustion or saturation of codes and categories and evidence of clear patterns or regularities in your understanding of the data. Saturation can be defined as the point in data collection and analysis (which often occur simultaneously in qualitative research) at which no new information and understanding is generated. Reaching a point of saturation includes having adequately applied codes from across your coding scheme to segments of your data, articulating several potential categories, and identifying tentative themes. Saturation does not imply a particular number of codes, categories, or themes. Rather, it suggests that your findings are robust and fully

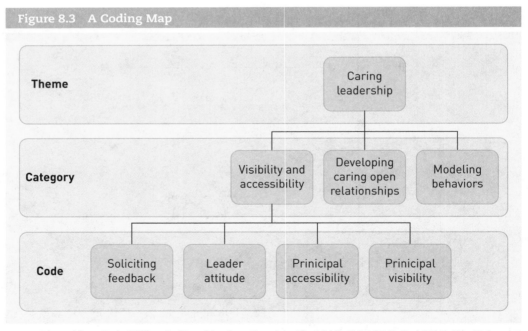

Figure 8.3   A Coding Map

Source: Adapted from Stein, William L., "Searching for a Caregiver: The Middle School Principal." PhD diss., University of Tennessee, 2008. http://trace.tennessee.edu/utk_graddiss/510

COMPLETING QUALITATIVE DATA ANALYSIS

After selecting your analytic approach, you begin the work of analyzing your data. Your analysis begins with transcription and loading your transcribed data into a qualitative data analysis software package. Your next step is to read through the data and note those passages that appear relevant to your study. Given your interest in studying the perspective of central office administrators as it relates to their understanding of school-level instructional leadership, you note those passages in which the central office administrator refers to principals' work. As you read through your data, you note that central office administrators make numerous references to "supervision" and "evaluation." They also make numerous references to "teachers" and "classrooms." This, you think, is an important understanding about principals' instructional leadership and thus you flag these passages by applying a code. After reading through the data, you then return to those coded passages. You focus specifically on the passages that appear to articulate how the central office administrators think about or understand the principal's work as an instructional leader. In re-reading these passages, you note that you regularly flagged passages that appeared to describe the principal going into a classroom and supervising teachers. For example, central office administrators offered countless examples of principals entering classrooms and offering teachers informal feedback about their instruction. This makes you pause. Does this mean that central office administrators think that instructional leadership is primarily about supervising teachers? Could it mean that supervision is central to their understanding of what principals as instructional leaders do? You decide to create a memo that captures these hunches or initial understandings. You also

decide to re-code some of the passages so that the codes are better related. These, you think, will serve as the basis for your categories.

First, you create a new code that consolidates all of the references to a principal entering a classroom. You refer to this as "location of instructional leadership." Next, you create another code that consolidates all of the actions that central office administrators take when engaging in instructional leadership. You refer to this code as "instructional leadership actions." Next, you re-read the passages of text that you coded previously and find that they suggest that the central office administrators you interviewed tended to view instructional leadership as a classroom-based endeavor. Rarely did the administrators you interviewed mention the other responsibilities that principals as instructional leaders have. For example, they did not talk about working with the parent or school community. This, you think, is important and explains well their understanding of what principals as instructional leaders do. "They place great priority on our supervision of teachers," you think to yourself. This leads you to formulate your first thematic statement from your study: Instructional Leadership as a Classroom-Based Endeavor. This statement captures the categories you constructed previously and also relates well to the research question you hoped to explore.

Focus Questions

1. How might your early understandings of the data guide your qualitative data analysis?

2. What might be the approach you take to developing categories?

grounded in the dataset. This means that each abstract claim you make (theme) can be illustrated through multiple data fragments (quotes). In fact, you will likely display your findings by offering a series of quotes and detailed interpretations of these quotes as they relate to the overarching theme(s).

A less sophisticated way of describing this process is to say that your analysis is done when you have something important to say that can be illustrated with quotes from multiple data sources. By "important" we mean that it addresses your research question(s), illuminates relationships in your conceptual and theoretical framework, and in some way adds to your understanding of practice. As is true of each aspect of the analysis process, it is important to chronicle your decision-making processing around when you conclude your analysis.

ISSUES OF VALIDITY IN QUALITATIVE RESEARCH

Validity in educational research has often been discussed in relationship to whether research is 'bad' or 'good'. Thus, validity has often been associated with the quality of a given research study. In qualitative research, the concept of validity has a rich and checkered history, with many different perspectives on how to define it and its place in the qualitative research process (Onwuegbuzie & Leech, 2005). Creswell and Miller (2000) noted that qualitative researchers have often referred to validity with varying terms, including authenticity, goodness, adequacy, trustworthiness, validation, and credibility, to name just a few. Traditionally, validity in qualitative research has been defined as the degree to which a practitioner-scholar's account aligns with or matches the participants' reality (Eisner & Peshkin, 2000). This, however, is a perspective that is contested and not always well received across some qualitative methodologies. More generally, validity deals with concerns related to truth, the establishment of truth, and how we come to justify our truth claims.

It is well beyond the scope of this textbook to discuss the nuances of and ongoing debates that surround validity in qualitative research. Nonetheless, for the purposes of practitioner-scholarship, we have found it useful to think about validity in terms of trustworthiness, which is the degree to which your data collection, analysis, and presentation of findings are presented in a thorough and verifiable manner. Several strategies to pursue trustworthiness include: member-checking, engaged time in the field, audit trails, triangulation (as discussed in Chapter 5), and peer debriefing. We provide definitions of each of these in Table 8.5 below.

Table 8.5   Strategies for Establishing Trustworthiness in Qualitative Research

Strategy for Establishing Trustworthiness	Definition	
Member-checking	The process of a practitioner-scholar sharing their emergent findings with participants to elicit their feedback and perspectives on them.	
Engaged time in the field	The extent of time that a practitioner-scholar spends collecting data, interacting with research participants, and becoming familiar with the research site/context.	
Audit trails	A paper-based or electronic account of each of a practitioner-scholar's decisions, from how they went about defining and describing their study to how they coded their data, and so on.	
Triangulation	A validity procedure wherein a practitioner-scholar seeks to establish evidence across multiple lines of data (see Chapter 5 for further information).	
Peer debriefing	The process of a practitioner-scholar working with a colleague(s) who is a critical friend of the research study and willing to ask questions related to their process, biases, and next steps.	

You are likely to see many of the validation strategies highlighted in Table 8.5 in the methods section of a published qualitative research study. And, in the event that you do not see one or more of these strategies described in some way, you may question the quality of the study. Tracy (2010) linked some of these strategies with the broader tenets related to producing a quality, qualitative research study. Specifically, she identified eight criteria, including: (a) worthy topic, (b) rich rigor, (c) sincerity, (d) credibility, (e) resonance, (f) significant contribution, (g) ethics, and (h) meaningful coherence. She linked these criteria to particular practices or strategies. Table 8.6 offers a summary of these criteria in relationship to the means or practices used to meet a particular criterion.

Table 8.6   The Eight "Big Tent" Criteria for Quality in Qualitative Research

Criteria for quality (end goal)	Various means, practices, and methods through which to achieve
Worthy topic	The topic of the research is • Relevant • Timely • Significant • Interesting
Rich rigor	The study uses sufficient, abundant, appropriate, and complex • Theoretical constructs • Data and time in the field • Sample(s) • Context(s) • Data collection and analysis processes
Sincerity	The study is characterized by • Self-reflexivity about subjective values, biases, and inclinations of the researcher(s) • Transparency about the methods and challenges
Credibility	The research is marked by • Thick description, concrete detail, explication of tacit (nontextual) knowledge, and showing rather than telling • Triangulation or crystallization • Multivocality • Member reflections
Resonance	The research influences, affects, or moves particular readers or a variety of audiences through • Aesthetic, evocative representation • Naturalistic generalizations • Transferable findings

(Continued)

Table 8.6 (Continued)	
Criteria for quality (end goal)	**Various means, practices, and methods through which to achieve**
Significant contribution	The research provides a significant contribution • Conceptually/theoretically • Practically • Morally • Methodologically • Heuristically
Ethical	The research considers • Procedural ethics (such as human subjects) • Situational and culturally specific ethics • Relational ethics • Exiting ethics (leaving the scene and sharing the research)
Meaningful coherence	The study • Achieves what it purports to be about • Uses methods and procedures that fit its stated goals • Meaningfully interconnects literature, research questions/foci, findings, and interpretations with each other

Source: Tracy, 2010, p. 840

Throughout the analysis process, it is important to consider criteria related to quality and strategies that support you in establishing trustworthiness. By thinking about these issues early on in your research process, you create the possibility of producing a study that makes a quality contribution to your field and practice.

REFLECTIVE OPPORTUNITY 8.3

Many qualitative researchers engage in member-checking at multiple points during their data-analysis process. Interactions with research participants about your findings are invaluable opportunities to deepen your understanding of the phenomenon of interest. However, it is important to consider how to respond when participants disagree with your findings.

1. How should their perspectives shape your findings?

2. What should you do if their feedback fundamentally challenges one of the assumptions in your study's findings?

ESTABLISHING TRUSTWORTHY QUALITATIVE FINDINGS

Beginning with your thematic statement, instructional leadership as a classroom-based endeavor, your next task is to begin thinking about how you will establish trustworthiness in your findings. There are numerous ways to do this, but you decide that you will begin with two strategies. First, you review the data you coded to identify quotes that thickly describe the central office administrator's perspective. You select quotes that are representative of the theme. For example, you select one quote in which a central office administrator describes her experience conducting classroom observations and learning walks with a recently appointed school principal. You select another quote that described a principal creating a simple checklist to monitor how often he visited classrooms and offered feedback to teachers. These quotes, you think, illustrate well the tendency of central office administrators to think that instructional leadership occurs primarily at the classroom level. Next, you write up your findings related to this theme and include the quotes you have selected from across the data set. After writing up your findings, you then take them back to the central office administrators who you interviewed and ask them to read and offer feedback and further insight on the findings. Only two of the central office administrators are able to meet with you.

This process, which is referred to as member-checking, provides your participants with an opportunity to verify that you have accurately interpreted their words and ideas, and to offer additional insights and/or counter perspectives. In one case, you find that the central office administrator concurs with your initial findings and the findings resonate with his daily experiences and interpretation of them. In the other, you find that your interpretation is accurate but you left out important details from the quote. The central office administrator encourages you to include these details and, in turn, you revise the quote so that it is accurate. Collectively, this process aims to ensure that your findings are trustworthy and that you have taken the care necessary to ensure that your findings thoughtfully represent your participant's ideas and perspectives.

Focus Questions

1. What are some of the validation strategies that you view as central to the qualitative research process?

2. Why might it be valuable to engage in member-checking in a way that elicits counter-perspectives from your participants?

TECHNOLOGY THAT SUPPORTS QUALITATIVE DATA ANALYSIS

There are a growing number of software packages that support the analysis of qualitative data. Across these packages, it is important to keep in mind that they do not do the analysis for you, rather they support you in carrying it out. It is helpful to allot time to learn how to use a computer-assisted qualitative data analysis (CAQDAS) package. CAQDAS refers to software packages designed and used to support the analysis of qualitative data. Ultimately, we suggest that using CAQDAS may keep you more organized as you move through your analysis, and allow you to track your decision-making process in a visible way. Most major CAQDAS packages include memoing and coding features, as well as features that allow you to make visual displays of your data. At present, three popular CAQDAS packages are ATLAS.ti, MAXQDA, and NVivo. These three packages have many similar features, yet have unique interfaces and are built with slightly different assumptions (such as the structure of coding). There are also useful packages that are designed to support specific types of analysis. For instance, Transana is particularly useful when analyzing video data.

We highlight next four software features that are useful for qualitative data analysis, including the: (a) quotation features, (b) memo feature, (c) coding feature, and (d) visualizing/display feature. These features represent only a sampling of those found in most CAQDAS packages. We selected ATLAS.ti to focus on because it is the CAQDAS package that we both use in our own research. If your college or university provides access to ATLAS.ti or another qualitative software package, you can find more information about that package on the company's website. Further, if you decide to invest in a CAQDAS package, it is important to spend time exploring some of the differences between the CAQDAS packages prior to spending time and money on one package. The University of Surrey's CAQDAS Project offers some useful online resources for making decisions around which CAQDAS will meet your analytic needs.

Quotation Feature

When using ATLAS.ti, rather than jumping straight into the coding process, you can spend time familiarizing yourself with your data by creating "quotations." A quotation is simply a segment of your data that might be of interest to you in your future analysis. You can create these quotations within transcript files or you can create quotations directly to your audio or video files. In Figure 8.4, a quotation was created in an interview transcript, as noted by the grey bar to the right of the interview transcript.

Memo Feature

After you create quotations, you may want to add memos to the quotations that you created, linking your initial thoughts to the dataset. You may also want to create memos

Figure 8.4   A Quotation of Interview Data in ATLAS.ti

002 003	*Interviewee:*	I started teaching international ESL after university, and so did that for about four and a half to five years, and then I went back to England to do my PTC, and worked in England for a year, and then I came here. So this is my first international school teaching primary overseas but I taught English overseas before, so…
004		
005	*Interviewer 1:*	Is it your first school in which PYP is?
006	*Interviewee:*	Yeah.
007 008	*Interviewer 1:*	So how were you first exposed to PYP when you arrived here?
009 010	*Interviewee:*	We had a few bits of training, like little sessions with Angela and that kind of thing. But it was a bit kind of there you go, like, you know, *[inaudible]*. But in a way, I think that's kind of – for PYP, it's almost a bit good because it is that kind of way with the kids, like you learn for yourself. So that's why *[inaudible]*. *[Laughter]*. So that's why I did.

Source: ATLAS.ti Scientific Software Development Gmbh - Berlin

that are linked to other portions of the data, either directly to your audio/video files or transcribed data. ATLAS.ti also allows you to create memos that are not linked to any data, but are saved as part of your project file. These memos are referred to as "free memos" because they are not attached or linked to a particular part of your dataset. A practitioner-scholar may create a free memo that captures the overall focus of their research. Figure 8.5 shows a "free memo" that was stored within a project file and captured the big ideas related to student focus group data.

Coding Feature

The coding feature in ATLAS.ti allows you to select and directly code textual data, as well as audio, video, and visual data. Coding your data in ATLAS.ti enables you to retrieve passages of text from across documents, thereby increasing the richness of your understandings and claims given that they are drawn from multiple data points. Codes can be easily merged into categories, with these decisions all being easily documented within ATLAS.ti. Figure 8.6 shows how descriptive codes were applied to a passage of a transcript from interview data.

Visualizing/Display Feature

The visualizing tools within ATLAS.ti (referred to as the "Network View") are quite useful, particularly as you identify relationships among codes and move from codes to categories to themes. For example, after you have completed your first cycle of coding, you will likely spend time making sense of the relationships among various codes. Are the codes referring to the same

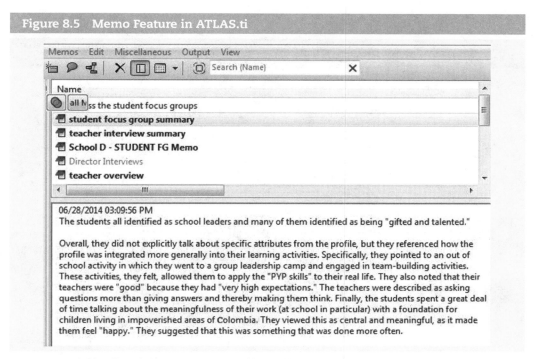

Figure 8.5 Memo Feature in ATLAS.ti

Source: ATLAS.ti Scientific Software Development Gmbh - Berlin

Figure 8.6 Coding in ATLAS.ti

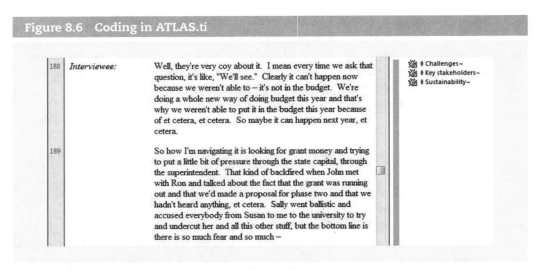

Source: ATLAS.ti Scientific Software Development Gmbh - Berlin

thing? How are they related? Are they associated with one another? Are two or more codes components of a broader concept or category? In ATLAS.ti, you can label the relationships and develop visual understandings and displays of your data. We have found this to be a particularly useful feature for creating categories and eventually moving to the level of theme. Figure 8.7 offers an example of this, wherein four descriptive codes are displayed in order to facilitate a better understanding of their relationships.

Figure 8.7 Visual Display (or Network View) of Codes, Categories, and Themes in ATLAS.ti

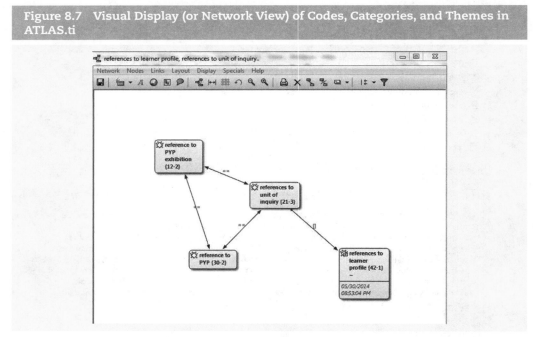

Source: ATLAS.ti Scientific Software Development Gmbh - Berlin

SUMMARY

In this chapter, we introduced you to some of the basics of qualitative data analysis, specifically focusing on how to generate themes. We also highlighted how issues related to validity and quality have been conceptualized in qualitative research. Additionally, we presented examples of the ways in which technologies can support the qualitative data analysis process. Indeed, this chapter offers only a brief overview of some of the general features of qualitative data analysis, which encompasses an array of approaches. Thus, as you progress in your research practices, it is important to study in detail the analytic approach associated with your methodology.

KEY TERMS

Analysis map 178
A priori codes 175
Audit Trail 177
Categories 176
Code 174
Coding 174
Condensed Transcript 171

Conversation Analysis 171
Descriptive Codes 174
Gisted Transcript 171
In-vivo Codes 174
Jeffersonian Transcript 171
Memo 173
Quotation 184

Saturation 178
Thematic Analysis 168
Themes 177
Trustworthiness 180
Verbatim Transcript 171
Visual Transcript 172

QUESTIONS TO CONSIDER

1. What are the primary aims of qualitative data analysis?

2. How would you describe the process of completing a thematic analysis?

3. What are the different types of transcripts? What are their purposes?

4. Why might you use transcription software to support the transcription process?

5. What is the purpose of coding in qualitative data analysis?

6. How might you move from code to theme when carrying out qualitative data analysis?

7. How has validity been conceptualized in qualitative research?

8. What is the role of computer-assisted qualitative data analysis software in qualitative data analysis?

CHAPTER EXERCISES

1. A useful way to become versed in qualitative data analysis is to become familiar with how researchers talk and write about qualitative data analysis. Take some time to search a key journal in your field (such as the *Journal of School Leadership* or *Education Administration Quarterly*) for two to three published qualitative studies. Then, go to the section of the article focused on data analysis, which is typically found in the methods section. Take note of: (a) how the analysis process is described (or not), (b) the level of detail provided in the description of data analysis, (c) details you felt were missing, and

(d) how the overarching methodology shaped (or not) the analysis process.

2. The transcription process is an important aspect of your analysis. Indeed, it is time-consuming and requires practice and patience. Thus, record 10 minutes of an interaction with a colleague and create a verbatim transcript. What did you find challenging? What surprised you about the experience? What might you do differently when transcribing data from your research project?

3. It is often helpful to engage in a practice or collaborative analysis session with colleagues or an adviser familiar with the qualitative data analysis process, as this allows you to acquire feedback and guidance. As such, select a data source from your research project and meet with colleagues and/or an adviser to discuss how you would proceed in making sense of the data. Invite your colleagues and/or adviser to offer suggestions and participate in an initial reading of your data, also writing collaborative memos related to initial impressions.

4. If you plan to use CAQDAS throughout your qualitative data analysis process, it is helpful to begin by exploring one or more of the CAQDAS packages. Go to one of the major three packages' websites (http://www.atlasti.com; http://www.qsrinternational.com; http://www.maxqda.com/) and download the free trial version. Explore the package and play with some of the main features. As you do so, consider how these features might shape how you make sense of and come to understand your data.

LEARNING EXTENSIONS

There are a plethora of useful resources related to analyzing qualitative data. While it is often useful to read books and articles that discuss analysis in relation to your selected methodology, there are a handful of books focused on qualitative data analysis at a more general level. For those interested in exploring this topic further, we suggest starting with Saldaña's (2009) book, *The Coding Manual for Qualitative Researchers*, which focuses on different approaches to coding. In addition, the classic book, *Qualitative Data Analysis: A Sourcebook*, written by Miles, Huberman, and Saldaña (2014), is an invaluable resource for new and seasoned qualitative researchers. Finally, if you are intending to engage in qualitative data analysis, we strongly encourage you to become familiar with technologies that might support your process. In the book, *Digital Tools for Qualitative Research*, Paulus and colleagues (2014) illustrate how digital tools can be used throughout the qualitative research process, including data analysis.

Sharpen your skills with SAGE edge!

edge.sagepub.com/lochmiller

SAGE edge for Students provides a personalized approach to help you accomplish your coursework goals in an easy-to-use learning environment. You'll find action plans, mobile-friendly eFlashcards, and quizzes as well as videos, web resources, and links to SAGE journal articles to support and expand on the concepts presented in this chapter.

9

COMPLETING QUANTITATIVE DATA ANALYSIS

ANALYZING QUANTITATIVE DATA

Over the past year, you and your colleagues have grown increasingly concerned about fourth grade student performance in reading and math. While you have not yet analyzed any data, you strongly believe that the problems you are observing begin before the students arrive in your classroom. You want to confirm this prior to moving ahead with any improvements in your school's approach to reading and math. Thus, you and your colleagues decide to collect data from your school's student information system and from your school's online gradebook. Collectively, you think these data points will help you to make sense of student performance. Being vaguely familiar with quantitative research, you realize that it might be useful to extract information from your school's student information system about the student's gender, race/ethnicity, free-or-reduced-price lunch status, and their eligibility for special education and language assistance services. With all of these data on the way, you wonder where you should begin!

INTRODUCTION

As illustrated in the opening vignette, quantitative data analysis is used to analyze numeric data. The purpose of quantitative data analysis is to use descriptive and inferential statistics to assess patterns, trends, and relationships in data. As a practitioner-scholar, you may worry that you need to have a vast understanding of statistics in order to analyze quantitative data or that this type of research involves the use of complicated formulas and sophisticated software that is beyond your understanding. While in this chapter we do assume that you have some basic knowledge of statistics, our hope is that by the end of this chapter you develop a greater understanding of how to carry out quantitative data analysis. At the same time, we strongly encourage you to view this chapter as the start of your ongoing study of quantitative data analysis.

Learning Objectives

By the end of the chapter, you will be able to:

- Describe the aims and purposes of quantitative data analysis.

- Illustrate the overarching steps in quantitative data analysis.

- Compare and contrast descriptive and inferential statistics.

- Demonstrate when to use descriptive or inferential statistics.

- Compare and contrast different inferential statistics.

- Summarize how to handle missing or incomplete data.

- Discuss the role of computer software in conducting quantitative data analysis.

In fact, if you have not already, it would be valuable to complete both basic and more advanced statistics courses, particularly if you intend to carry out a quantitative research study. Such courses would provide you with an important theoretical and practical foundation and thus enable you to understand when and why to use specific statistical tests. More practically, with the current educational climate focused on data-driven decision-making, becoming skilled in quantitative data analysis will support you in your work as an educator, not simply as a practitioner-scholar.

We position this chapter as a discussion of the *basic concepts* related to quantitative data analysis, and acknowledge that there is much more that you need to consider as you move forward in your work. We begin the chapter by presenting the quantitative data analysis process, highlighting the importance of preparing your data and identifying variables. We also point to some of the basics related to descriptive and inferential statistics, which broadly describe the two types of statistics that you might carry out in a quantitative study. We also briefly consider how to deal with missing data, validity and reliability, and the uses of technology in the quantitative data analysis process.

QUANTITATIVE DATA ANALYSIS: A CYCLICAL APPROACH

As illustrated in Figure 9.1, quantitative data analysis can be thought of as a cycle—through which each step brings you closer to a deeper understanding of your dataset.

Much like we presented the process of analyzing qualitative data, we suggest that the process of analyzing quantitative data unfolds over time. First, quantitative data analysis begins by preparing the dataset. Preparing the dataset includes standardizing values, identifying and managing missing data, and in some cases, keypunching responses—concepts that we discuss in greater detail below. Second, practitioner-scholars should spend time familiarizing themselves with their dataset by identifying the variables in the dataset that they will use for analysis. Third, practitioner-scholars often begin their analysis by calculating simple descriptive statistics to familiarize themselves with patterns, trends, and frequencies in the data. Finally, practitioner-scholars frequently select and run additional inferential statistical tests to determine how variables relate to one another and whether one variable predicts or influences another. Practitioner-scholars often identify relationships among variables prior to conducting additional inferential statistics. This process often helps a practitioner-scholar identify underlying relationships that may potentially influence inferential statistics. We describe each of these steps in greater detail below.

Preparing the Dataset

First, you should have a plan for structuring your dataset and noting any specific assignments that you make to variables. A quantitative dataset is simply the data that you will use to complete your analysis that may have been obtained from a survey or questionnaire, a student information system, an in-class assessment, or any type of protocol that allows you to collect numeric data. A variable is an element in the dataset to which you have assigned some value or meaning that is relevant to your study. Assignments refer to values that you give to the variables in the dataset. For example, if you have conducted a survey and the responses you entered are numeric responses, you must decide which numeric response relates to which survey item (for example, strongly agree = 5, agree = 4, neither agree nor disagree = 3, disagree =2, or strongly disagree =1).

Figure 9.1 The Quantitative Data Analysis Cycle

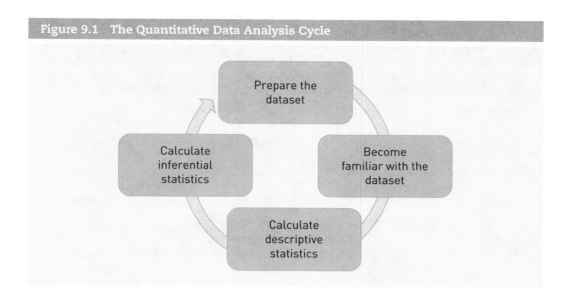

Second, you must prepare your dataset for analysis. This process involves standardizing values for each variable, ensuring that all variables are entered correctly and that missing variables are appropriately handled. We discuss how to deal with missing data later in this chapter. Standardizing values is the process of ensuring that variables with the same value are treated similarly. For example, this means that all scores from an in-class assessment are entered as percentages or numeric values rather than traditional letter grades. In the process of preparing your dataset for analysis, we also recommend that you take time to develop a codebook, which is an inventory of the individual variables in your dataset and their respective values. As illustrated in Table 9.1 below, this inventory or codebook need not be sophisticated but it should be clear and allow you to determine what each value in your dataset means.

If you are using surveys or questionnaires, the process of preparing your dataset might also include keypunching your surveys into a Microsoft Excel spreadsheet or SPSS worksheet. Keypunching is the process of entering values into an electronic format that supports analysis. For many practitioner-scholars, however, this process will be simplified as they are likely to use an online survey system (such as SurveyMonkey).

It is important to keep in mind that you will need to describe your data as part of your research methods. This description should include what data you collect, which variables were included in the dataset, what values were assigned to those variables, and any adjustments or manipulations you made. From the Field 9.1 provides an example of how researchers describe their dataset.

IDENTIFYING TYPES OF VARIABLES. Before beginning any quantitative data analysis, it is important to spend time thinking critically about the types of variables involved in your study, as this will inform the type of inferential statistical test you run. Quantitative studies generally include an independent and dependent variable. As noted in Chapter 6, an independent variable is a variable that does *not* depend on any other variable and thus may be considered a predictor variable. In an experimental research study, for example,

Table 9.1 Illustrative Codebook for a Study of Student Achievement in Reading and Math			
Variable	Description		Values
Student ID	Identification number assigned to each student		001–599
Gender	Student gender		0 = Male 1 = Female
Race/Ethnicity	Student race/ethnicity		1 = Asian 2 = Black 3 = Hispanic 4 = Caucasian
FRL Status	Free-or-reduced-price meal eligibility as of October 2013		1 = Paid meals 2 = Reduced 3 = Free
LEP Status	Eligible for language support services		0 = No 1 = Yes
Special Education Status	Eligible for special education services		0 = No 1 = Yes
Reading Assessment	Reading assessment score as of Spring 2013		0–100
Math Assessment	Math assessment score as of Spring 2013		0–100
Teacher ID	Student's classroom teacher as of Spring 2013		1 = Judy 2 = Sally 3 = Brian 4 = Josh

a practitioner-scholar manipulates the independent variables to try to change a behavior or outcome. A dependent variable depends on other variables and is thus thought of as an outcome variable. For instance, a practitioner-scholar may be interested in exploring the effect of an instructional strategy for reading on students' reading comprehension. In this case, the independent variable is the instructional strategy, and the dependent variable is the students' reading comprehension. Finally, an extraneous or confounding variable refers to any variable that is not the independent variable but could potentially impact the dependent variable. These variables might be related to the situation in which an experiment was conducted (for example, room temperature or time allocated for the study), factors that might be related to the participants in the study (for example, prior educational experiences or family characteristics), factors associated with the experiment itself (such as instructions provided to study participants), and unintended factors that influence how participants in the experiment might experience the study (they may become tired, anxious, and so on).

Beyond being independent, dependent, or extraneous, variables can also refer to specific types of measures, which are generally described as categorical or continuous. Categorical measures broadly refer to categories (for instance, men or women). There are three types of categorical

An Example of How Researchers Describe a Dataset

We analyzed the Beginning Postsecondary Students (BPS) Longitudinal Study data set, which is available from the U.S. National Center for Education Statistics (NCES) through a restricted data license (Wine, Heuer, Wheeless, Francis, & Franklin, 2002). The 1996/2001 waves of this study followed a nationally representative sample of first-time U.S. undergraduates for six years, including transfers from one institution to another. The data set includes both students who entered college directly after high school and those who delayed entry for any number of years, provided that the start of the cohort period (fall 1995) was their first attempt in higher education. Its two-stage sampling design is suited for an analysis of institutional effects because it contains observations on several students with potentially different background characteristics, per institution.

We limited the sample to entrants to four-year colleges (excluding for-profits) who participated in the final (2001) wave of the study. Because we were interested in modeling reasonably timely graduation from college, the six academic years represented in this data set made for an appropriate window to measure baccalaureate degree completion. We then combined the BPS student-level data with collected characteristics drawn from the Integrated Postsecondary Education Data System (IPEDS) database. The latter contains information provided by college administrators about the SAT distribution of the college, the socio-demographic characteristics of the student body, as well as tuition and cost measures. The BPS student data are provided with weights that adjust for sampling and differences in response rates and attrition; we used these in all models.

Source: Heil, Reisel, & Attewell, 2014, pp. 918–919

Read the full article at:
www.sagepub.com/lochmiller

measures, including binary variables, nominal variables, and ordinal variables. Binary variables refer to categorical measures that are dichotomous (such as male or female). Nominal variables refer to a categorical measure that has three or more categories (for example, student's race/ethnicity). Ordinal variables are categorical measures that have a defined order (such as first, second, or third place).

Continuous variables are those variables that are assigned any value between a minimum and maximum, such as a test score or your height. There are two types of continuous variables: interval and ratio. Interval variables are numeric scores or values for which an absolute zero can be defined. For example, 97.5 percent or $1,011 both represent interval variables, as a practitioner-scholar can define an absolute zero in both cases. A ratio variable is similar to an interval variable except that the scores are based on a scale. For example, a student's ACT score would represent a ratio variable as the scores are based on a scale that gives each score meaning.

These distinctions matter because the types of variables included in your dataset inform which type of statistical test you can use to analyze your data. Thus, we recommend that practitioner-scholars engaged in quantitative data analysis begin their analytic efforts by listing each variable in their study, identifying whether the variable is independent or dependent, and then determining which level of measurement that variable relates to. This information will become invaluable as you move into more complex analyses.

Descriptive Statistics: Identifying Patterns, Trends, and Frequencies

For many practitioner-scholars, the first step in their data analysis is to identify patterns, trends, or frequencies in their data, which are referred to as descriptive statistics. This step essentially involves using descriptive statistics to become familiar with the dataset. Indeed, frequencies are perhaps the easiest way to understand how data are distributed. Frequencies are simple counts that refer to the number of times something has occurred. Frequencies are often useful in determining the composition of the dataset, identifying baseline patterns in the data, and noting differences across variables. For example, if we were analyzing data about third grade students' reading and math achievement, it would be helpful to know how many male and female students we have in the dataset and what proportion of the students qualify for free-or-reduced-price lunch, receive language support, or come from each classroom. From the Field 9.2 highlights how researchers discussed the descriptive statistics of their data from a study of the principal skills that were correlated most highly with school outcomes.

Two important considerations within description statistics include: (a) measures of central tendency, and (b) measures of variability. We consider each of these next.

MEASURES OF CENTRAL TENDENCY. Measures of central tendency provide practitioner-scholars with an opportunity to determine how scores or values relate to the mean. The mean is the most common measure for assessing scores and is simply the arithmetic average of all of the scores or values. The median, on the other hand, is the midpoint in a distribution of scores or values. For example, if you observed five scores—20, 23, 25, 27, and 29—the median score would be 25. The mode is the most frequently occurring score. For example, if you observed six scores—20, 20, 40, 37, 23, and 39—the mode would be 20 as it occurred more than any other score. Collectively, these measures provide practitioner-scholars with an opportunity to assess how scores in the *entire* distribution relate to each other. For most purposes, the mean is the best measure of central tendency.

FROM THE FIELD 9.2

An Example of How Researchers Talk About the Descriptive Statistics of Their Dataset

Table 1 shows descriptive statistics for all variables used in the analyses, with the exception of principal and assistant principal ratings, which we describe later. The 244 schools in our sample serve 33% Black students, 57% Hispanic students, and 68% students eligible for subsidized lunch, numbers very similar to those for all 314 regular schools in M-DCPS. School grades range from 1 (F) to 5 (A) and average almost a 4 (B). Teacher satisfaction averages 3.3. Climate grades from parents are on an 8-point scale (C–, C, C1, B–, B, B1, A–, A); grades of F, D–, D, D1, and A1 were also options but not observed as mean ratings. On average, parents graded schools at 5.6, approximately a B1.

Source: Grissom & Loeb, 2011, p. 1097

Read the full article at:
www.sagepub.com/lochmiller

MEASURES OF VARIABILITY. While practitioner-scholars are often concerned with determining how scores or values relate to the mean, there are also times when practitioner-scholars are interested in determining how scores vary. Measures of variability describe the spread of the scores or values. The range is one of the most simplistic measures of variability in that it simply describes the difference between the lowest and highest score or value. For example, if the highest score a student in a classroom earned is 85 and the lowest score a student in a classroom earned was 36, the range of scores in the class would be 49. While the range provides us with an overarching understanding of the scores or values we observed, it does not provide us with an understanding of the variation between the scores or values we observed and the mean. For this, we need to calculate the variance, which is the amount of spread among scores. There are two types of variance: population variance and sample variance. Population variance considers the spread of all scores for all members of a given group. For example, population variance would consider the scores of every fourth grade student in your school. Sample variance, on the other hand, would consider a subset of the students. To continue our example, this might mean only those fourth grade students in your school who were eligible for free-or-reduced-price lunch.

The standard deviation provides another measure of the variation in a set of scores. The standard deviation is the square root of the variance of a set of scores. The standard deviation is used with interval or ratio data and is the most stable measure of variability. The primary advantage of calculating the standard deviation is that it provides a standardized score that can be compared to other scores. In other words, the standard deviation provides you with a standardized way of determining which scores are normal (that is, falling within one standard deviation of the mean) or are considered larger (falling two or more standard deviations above or below the mean). For example, students in a fourth grade classroom who score more than one standard deviation above the class mean on a reading assessment might be considered to have performed exceptionally well on that assessment while students who score more than one standard deviation below the class mean might be considered to have performed less well. In both cases, the students' performance is assessed relative to the class mean.

The normal distribution underlies each of these concepts as it generally describes the distribution of scores or values. The normal distribution (or normal curve) illustrates how the majority of values or scores you observe are located near the mean, as shown in Figure 9.2. As illustrated in the figure, the majority of scores cluster near the center of the curve. Scores to the right of the mean are typically higher or of greater value, with scores to the left of the mean being lower or of lesser value. It bears noting that standard deviations can be overlaid on the normal distribution, as well. While a score that is within one standard deviation of the mean is typically found near the mean, a score that is two or more standard deviations above or below the mean is found closer to either tail. The tail refers to the most extreme portion of the normal distribution where the fewest scores are likely to be found.

The normal distribution is particularly important for practitioner-scholars, as it provides a picture with which to visualize how the distribution of your data looks in relation to scores or values that are normally distributed. In essence, then, the normal distribution provides practitioner-scholars with a way to compare their data to determine if their data are positively or negatively skewed. Skew refers to the degree to which scores or values cluster above or below the mean. As illustrated in Figure 9.3, scores that are positively skewed are typically below the mean and thus closer to the y-axis. Scores that are negatively skewed are typically above the mean and thus further from the y-axis.

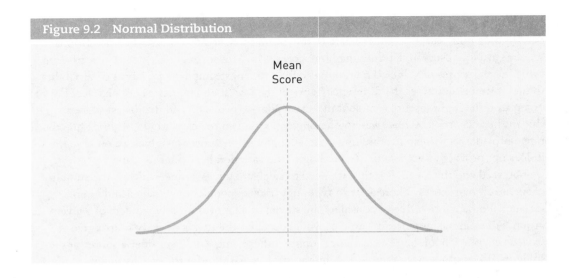

Figure 9.2 Normal Distribution

Mean Score

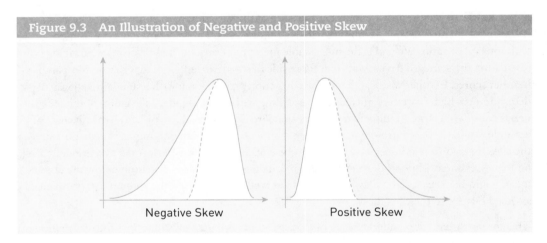

Figure 9.3 An Illustration of Negative and Positive Skew

Negative Skew

Positive Skew

Understanding the normal curve, as well as the skew of the curve, is important as it ultimately relates to the shape of your data and the underlying distribution of scores. For instance, Figure 9.4 shows a histogram of scores from a dataset with the normal curve overlaying it. As illustrated, the scores are normally distributed as the majority of scores cluster around the mean. It is important to know whether or not your data are normally distributed because of the assumptions you will then be able to make about your dataset and therefore which statistical tests you can use. We discuss some of these statistical tests in greater detail later in this chapter.

Graphing the Data In addition to describing descriptive statistics numerically, it can sometimes be helpful to illustrate these statistics graphically. For example, if you wanted to illustrate the racial/ethnic composition of students in your sample, you might calculate the frequencies and percentages for each racial/ethnic group and graph them using some type of chart, such as a pie chart, as shown in Figure 9.5. Similarly, it may be of interest to illustrate the reading and math scores for each student by classroom, which you could

Figure 9.4   Distribution of Scores Relative to the Normal Curve

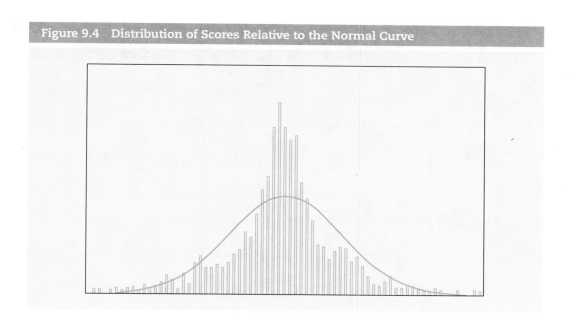

Figure 9.5   Example of a Pie Chart for Displaying Descriptive Data About the Number of Students Enrolled

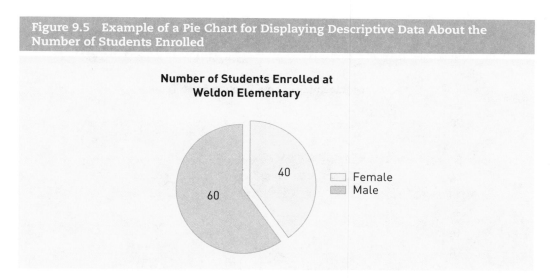

do using a histogram as illustrated in Figure 9.6. If you wanted to show how your students' reading and math achievement changed over time, you might use a line graph to illustrate these changes, as highlighted in Figure 9.7. Regardless of the graphic or visual you use, you must first calculate descriptive statistics to create them.

Selecting and Running Inferential Statistics

Inferential statistics enable practitioner-scholars to generalize their interpretation of quantitative data to a larger population. Thus, unlike descriptive statistics, inferential statistics allow practitioner-scholars to make inferences about the population as a whole, predict how variables

Figure 9.6 Example of a Histogram for Displaying Descriptive Data About the Number of Students Enrolled by Race/Ethnicity

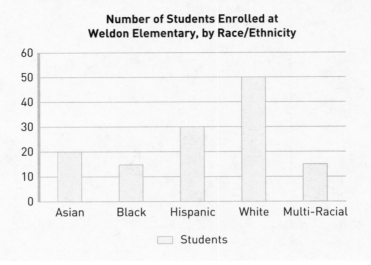

Figure 9.6 Example of a Histogram for Displaying Descriptive Data About the Number of Students Enrolled by Race/Ethnicity

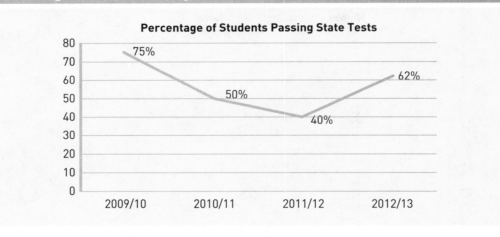

Figure 9.7 Example of a Line Graph for Displaying Descriptive Data About the Percentage of Students Passing the State Test Over Time

will interact or relate, and assess the degree to which these interactions predict particular outcomes. There are numerous inferential statistics that can be used by practitioner-scholars. It is the beyond the scope of this textbook to adequately describe them all. Instead, we focus on some of the tests that a practitioner-scholar is most likely to encounter as they read published educational literature, as well as embark on their own research. We briefly define what these tests are and what types of data or variables are required to complete them.

HYPOTHESIS TESTING. Given one of the aims of inferential statistics is to predict whether variables relate to one another or contribute to some type of change, many of these tests

STARTING WITH DESCRIPTIVE STATISTICS

After collecting information from your district's student information system, you begin your analysis by calculating the mean, median, and standard deviation for students' reading and math scores. In addition, you calculate frequencies and percentages to identify how many students were included in the dataset and what their characteristics were. In calculating these descriptive statistics, you determined that the average score for the third grade reading assessment was 84.3 percent and for the math assessment it was 69.2 percent. For female students, you found that the average score was 85.2 percent in reading and 71.3 percent in math. For male students, you found that the average score was 82.9 percent in reading and 59.6 percent in math. While

you need more information, these results highlight that there *may* be differences between third grade reading and math achievement based on gender. When you compare the average scores for male and female students across the classrooms in your study, you find that male students consistently score lower in reading and math.

Focus Questions

1. How might these initial hunches guide your quantitative data analysis?

2. What might your next step be in determining whether the differences in reading and math achievement are significant?

require practitioner-scholars to formulate a hypothesis and test whether that hypothesis is valid or not. There are two types of hypotheses. A null hypothesis states that there will be no difference between two groups, a set of scores, or as a result of a specific intervention. In short, a null hypothesis simply says that nothing happened. For example, one might say, "principal participation in professional development will *not* influence student achievement." An alternative hypothesis states that there will be a difference between two groups, a set of scores, or as a result of a specific intervention. Thus, the alternative hypothesis reflects the practitioner-scholar's view that a meaningful difference exists. Alternative hypotheses can be framed as directional statements, meaning that practitioner-scholars can make an assumption about the nature of the effect (for example, that it will be positive or negative) or leave open the possibility that either effect may have occurred. From the Field 9.3 highlights how researchers presented a hypothesis within the context of a published research study.

To understand hypothesis testing, it is also important to revisit the normal distribution. As stated previously, the normal distribution is simply an illustration that describes how scores distribute from the mean. As illustrated in Figure 9.8, the normal distribution also enables you to determine when you will or will not reject your null hypothesis—and thus claim that there was a meaningful difference between scores observed. For the purposes of hypothesis testing, it is important to set the significance level (or alpha level) that you will use to inform your decisions about the null hypothesis. The significance level is the maximum risk you are willing to take that your results are attributable to chance. In most education research studies, practitioner-scholars use a .05 alpha level. In fact, when you hear researchers refer to statistically significant findings, they are frequently referring to findings that have met the alpha level they have set (usually .05). This level

FROM THE FIELD 9.3

An Example of Hypotheses in a Published Research Study

In the empirical phase of this investigation, we tested two hypotheses. The first involved the original finding that the collective properties of academic emphasis, efficacy, and faculty trust are the composite elements of academic optimism (Hoy et al., 2006). Therefore, our first hypothesis was that academic emphasis, collective efficacy, and faculty trust in parents and students would form a general latent construct labeled academic optimism. Our second hypothesis went beyond the original work of Hoy and his colleagues (2006). To extend previous work, we proposed a test of the relationship between academic optimism and achievement, hypothesizing student academic achievement would be a function of academic optimism after control for SES, urbanicity (population density), and previous student achievement.

Finally, we expected that SES and previous achievement would be directly related to both academic optimism and student achievement and that both would make indirect contributions to achievement through academic optimism. Hence, our third hypothesis was that SES and previous student achievement would make direct contributions to student achievement, as well as indirect contributions through academic optimism.

Source: Hoy, Tarter, & Woolfolk Hoy, 2006, pp. 432–433

Read the full article at:
www.sagepub.com/lochmiller

Figure 9.8   Normal Curve Distribution as Related to Null and Alternative Hypotheses

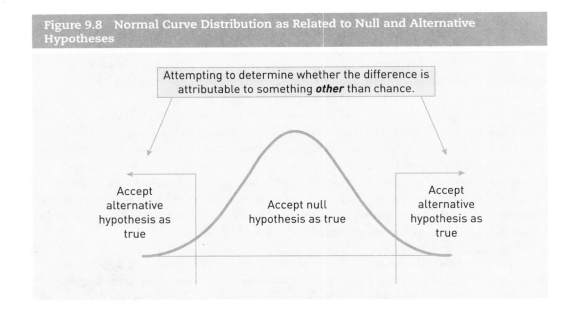

Attempting to determine whether the difference is attributable to something *other* than chance.

Accept alternative hypothesis as true

Accept null hypothesis as true

Accept alternative hypothesis as true

---

suggests that if you ran an experiment, 5 out of 100 times the result of the experiment would be attributable purely to chance.

The level of significance you assign in your study aligns with the tails on the normal distribution. The tails of the normal distribution are an area in which you can reasonably conclude that the

FORMULATING HYPOTHESES

Given that you and your colleagues are interested in determining what predicts fourth grade reading achievement, you realize that you need to formulate a hypothesis to test your assumptions. Looking over the descriptive data that you have collected, you decide that your first hypothesis will be: "Third grade students who scored at or above grade level will achieve at higher levels on the fourth grade reading assessment." This hypothesis will thus require you to conduct a one-tailed test to determine whether scores are, in fact, higher for students who performed at or above grade level in

reading in third grade. Your null hypothesis will thus be: "Third grade students who scored at or above grade level will not achieve at higher levels on the fourth grade reading assessment."

Focus Questions:

1. How might your formulation of the alternative hypothesis influence which tests you are able to conduct?

2. How could these hypotheses be reformulated to consider other variables?

differences in your scores were attributable to something other than chance and thus it is safe to accept your alternative hypothesis.

TYPE-I AND TYPE-II ERROR. Quantitative researchers invest considerable effort in trying to reject the null hypothesis with confidence. Whether or not we accept or reject the null hypothesis is important when using inferential statistics as they are related to Type-I or Type-II error. A practitioner-scholar makes a Type-I Error when he or she accepts that the alternative hypothesis is true but in actuality it is not. Type-I error is particularly concerning as it effectively states that something (an effect, a difference, and so on) happened when it did not. A practitioner-scholar commits a Type-II Error when he or she accepts the null hypothesis as being true, when in reality there was an effect. Type-I and Type-II Errors are particularly important when conducting experimental research, as the purpose of this type of research is to state that a cause-and-effect relationship exists. For example, let's consider a practitioner-scholar who conducts an experimental study to determine the effect of alternative approaches to math instruction on students who are considered at risk for failure. The practitioner-scholar compares the achievement before and after the new instructional method was introduced. She analyzes her results and determines that there was in fact an improvement in student achievement and makes a recommendation to expand the instructional method to serve more students in her school. Upon further analysis, however, the practitioner-scholar finds that she has committed a Type-I error in her analysis, as there was in actuality no significant effect on math achievement. This scenario is particularly concerning given that additional students have been introduced to an instructional strategy that may not effect student achievement. This type of situation is particularly concerning as it could introduce students, in this example, to an instructional strategy that was perhaps not actually effective. Thus, it is important for practitioner-scholars to be cognizant of the potential for Type-I and Type-II error.

REFLECTIVE OPPORTUNITY 9.1

It is important to consider Type-I and Type-II Error, recognizing that there are significant ethical issues related to these types of error.

1. Provide an example related to both Type-I and Type-II Error in which an ethical concern may arise. Explain how you might address this through either your research design or through your analysis process.

CALCULATING INFERENTIAL STATISTICS

As we stated previously, to calculate inferential statistics practitioner-scholars must be able to identify both the independent variable(s) and dependent variable(s) in their study. Additionally, practitioner-scholars must be able to determine whether the independent and dependent variables are continuous (that is, a ratio or interval variable) or categorical (a nominal or ordinal variable). Practitioner-scholars must also determine whether their data are parametric or non-parametric. Parametric data refers to data that are normally distributed (that is, adheres closely to the normal distribution). Non-parametric data refers to data that are *not* normally distributed and thus require the practitioner-scholar to use different statistical tests than they would otherwise (for example, a practitioner-scholar would use a Mann-Whitney U test instead of a t-test to assess differences between two groups).

It is also important for you to consider some additional questions as you make decisions around your statistical tests. Both Field (2009) and Rudestam and Newton (1992) provided guidance to practitioner-scholars as they consider which inferential statistics to calculate. As illustrated in the following list, this guidance rests on the broad purpose of your study, the number and kind of independent variables you have included in your study, the number and kind of dependent variables you have included in your study, and whether your data are normally distributed—and are thus parametric or non-parametric.

- Do you plan to compare or relate variables in your hypotheses or research questions?

- How many independent and dependent variables do you have?

- Will you be controlling for any factors that might influence your results?

- How will your independent variable(s) be measured?

- How will your dependent variable(s) be measured?

- Are the scores in your dataset normally distributed?

Your responses to these questions will inform which statistical test you select to use. As illustrated in Table 9.2, there are a number of statistical tests that you can use to both compare groups and

Table 9.2 Types of Inferential Statistics and Their Relationship to Variables

Statistical Test	Purpose	# Independent Variables	# Dependent Variables	Type of Independent Variable	Type of Dependent Variable	Parametric Data?
t-Test	Compare groups	1	1	Categorical	Continuous	Yes
ANOVA	Compare groups	1+	1	Categorical	Continuous	Yes
Mann-Whitney U	Compare groups	1	1	Categorical	Continuous	No
Kruskall-Wallis	Compare groups	1+	1+	Categorical	Continuous	No
Friedman's Chi-Square	Compare groups	2+	2+	Categorical	Continuous	No
Chi-Square	Compare categories within groups	1	1	Categorical	Continuous	No
Pearson Correlation	Relate variable	1	1	Continuous	Continuous	Yes
Multiple Regression	Relate variables	2+	1	Continuous	Continuous	Yes
Spearman Rho	Relate variable	1	1+	Categorical	Categorical	No

Source: Cresswell, John W., *Educational Research: Planning, Conducting, and Evaluation Quantitative and Qualitative Research, 4th Edition,* © 2012. Reprinted and Electronically produced by permission of Pearson Education, Inc., New York, New York

relate variables. Similar to what we have signaled previously, the test you use ultimately depends on knowing how many independent and dependent variables are included, what type of variable they are, and whether the data are normally distributed and are thus parametric.

Identifying Relationships and Differences Between Variables

Many research questions require that you use more sophisticated approaches to determine how variables in your dataset are related and how strong these relationships are. The Pearson Correlation (r) is a statistical test that indicates whether there is a relationship between two variables. The Pearson Correlation is based on a scale from 1.00 to –1.00. A correlation coefficient of 1.00 indicates that two scores are perfectly and positively related. A positive relationship indicates that as one variable increases the other variable will increase. A correlation coefficient of –1.00 indicates that two scores are perfectly related but they are negatively (or inversely) related. A negative (or inverse) relationship indicates that as one variable increases the other will decrease. Pearson correlations are helpful for practitioner-scholars as they provide an opportunity to describe the relationships between variables before engaging in further, more sophisticated analyses. In a correlational study, a Pearson correlation can be used as the primary statistic for the study itself.

A FEW OF THE MOST COMMON STATISTICAL TESTS

Although there are a number of statistical tests, each with their own variations to serve different needs, practitioner-scholars often rely on four basic statistical tests. These include the t-test, analysis of variance, regression, and the chi-square. We describe each of these tests here, presenting a short introduction.

t-Test

The most basic inferential statistical test is a t-test. The t-test is particularly useful when comparing scores or values from two groups. For example, a practitioner-scholar might use a t-test to determine whether there is a statistically significant difference between male and female student scores on a classroom assessment. A significant difference would indicate that male students performed at a different level than female students. A result that was not significant would indicate that the achievement differences were not significantly different. In this example, the student's gender is a categorical independent variable. The student's test score is a continuous dependent variable.

Analysis of Variance (ANOVA)

An analysis of variance (ANOVA) is an equally useful test that compares groups. However, unlike a t-test, which is restricted to two groups, an ANOVA can be used to compare two or more groups. For example, a practitioner-scholar might use an ANOVA to compare reading and math scores from four different schools or classrooms. A statistically significant difference would allow the practitioner-scholar to identify whether students from School A performed differently than students at Schools B, C, or D. In this example, each of the four schools serve as the categorical independent variable while the student's test score serves as the continuous dependent variable.

Simple Linear Regression or Multiple Regression

Simple Linear Regression or Multiple regression is used when a practitioner-scholar seeks to relate scores or values. In particular, it allows you to predict the value of an independent variable from the known values of one or more dependent variables. A regression is used when both independent and dependent variables are continuous and the data are parametric. Regression rests on the assumption that there is a linear relationship between variables and is particularly useful for practitioner-scholars as it can be used to predict values from other values that we know. For example, if we know that there is a positive relationship between the number of hours of direct instruction in math a student received in third grade and their score on the fourth grade math assessment, we could determine how many hours of direct instruction are needed in order for a fourth grade student to achieve a passing score. In this example, the student's test score serves as a continuous dependent variable, while the number of hours of direct instruction serves as a continuous dependent variable.

Multiple regression is an extension of simple linear regression (Berry & Feldman, 1985; Schroeder, Sjoquist, & Stephan, 1986). It allows practitioner-scholars to predict the value of an independent variable from the known values of two or more dependent variables. For example, if we wanted to know if other variables influenced student performance on the fourth grade math assessment, we might use a multiple regression to determine the extent to which each of these variables contributed to the student's performance. For example, we might seek to determine whether and to what extent the student's age or performance in reading influenced their performance in math. Multiple regression is particularly useful as it allows you to compare how these factors influence the independent variable.

Chi-Square

A chi-square is a statistical test used when the practitioner-scholar seeks to determine whether there is a statistically significant difference between data that are reported in the form of frequency counts, percentages, or proportions. A chi-square is used when a practitioner-scholar seeks to determine whether distributions of categorical variables (for instance, male or female, elementary or secondary) differ from one another. More specifically, the chi-square is used to determine whether there is a difference between observed and expected values. The chi-square does not provide an indication of the strength of the relationship between categories; rather it can only be used to indicate whether there is or is not a relationship. For example, we might use a chi-square to determine whether our projections between number of students actually enrolling in Advanced Placement and General Education courses matches our projections. In this example, the chi-square would allow us to determine whether our actual enrollment differs from projected enrollments. Similarly, we might use a chi-square to ask whether male students are more likely to get detention than female students. In both examples, the chi-square is useful in answering questions that are effectively framed as "yes or no" questions.

IDENTIFYING MISSING OR OUT-OF-RANGE VALUES

As you begin assessing your dataset, you may find that there are missing or out-of-range values in the data that, if left unaddressed, may impact the results of your analysis. Indeed, as Peugh and Enders (2004) noted, "missing data are a common problem in quantitative research studies. Standard statistical procedures were developed for complete datasets, so missing values represent a considerable nuisance to the analyst" (p. 525). Missing data pose particularly significant challenges to practitioner-scholars using inferential statistics.

The research literature indicates that there are numerous approaches that you can take to address missing data. We note three of the more common approaches to dealing with missing data. The first, list-wise deletion, involves deleting entire records from the dataset. This approach is often used in studies with large samples. In studies with smaller samples, pair-wise deletion might be preferred. Pair-wise deletion involves excluding incomplete or missing variables only from those analyses where the variables are meaningful. For example, a record that was missing a student's age would be excluded from those analyses where age was a meaningful variable. Finally, mean imputation might be used when variables cannot be deleted entirely or excluded partially. In these instances, the mean of the scores is entered in place of the missing score or value. While these are common strategies for handling missing data, and are suitable for most studies conducted by practitioner-scholars, there are more sophisticated techniques that should be considered.

One question remains: How much can I use these approaches without affecting my analysis? Depending on what approach you use, George and Mallery (2001) indicated that you may be able to substitute up to 15 percent of the values in your dataset without affecting your analyses. While we recommend a much lower threshold (5 percent), this range should enable you to fully manage missing or out-of-range values in preparing for analysis.

🔗 **LINK TO PRACTICE 9.3**

SELECTING AMONG INFERENTIAL STATISTICS

With your dataset complete and descriptive statistics generated, the next step in your analysis is to select the appropriate inferential statistic. To make the appropriate selection, you realize that it is often helpful to revisit the codebook that you established at the beginning of your analysis to determine whether your independent and dependent variables are continuous or categorical. It can also be helpful to revisit this codebook to determine how many dependent variables you have included in your analysis. At this stage, selecting the correct inferential statistic depends both on the research questions you intend to ask as well as the type of variables that you have to work with. You find that you are using a continuous dependent variable (student achievement scores) and several categorical independent variables (student gender, race/ethnicity, free-or-reduced-price lunch status,

and so on). Given your primary interest is to compare student achievement across groups, you decide to use an ANOVA to compare the groups. Unlike a t-test, which is limited to just two groups, an ANOVA will allow you to compare two or more groups for each variable. This affords you the flexibility you need to make the comparisons and ultimately determine whether there were statistically significant differences across the groups.

Focus Questions:

1. Had your analysis included both a continuous independent and dependent variable, how might this have changed the selection of an ANOVA?

2. What are the potential difficulties of comparing multiple groups in a study of this kind?

REFLECTIVE OPPORTUNITY 9.2

Missing data pose a significant challenge to practitioner-scholars, and are certainly something that cannot be ignored. Yet, the ways in which a practitioner-scholar addresses missing data will inevitably come with ethical considerations.

1. What might be some of the ethical challenges associated with entering or addressing missing data?

2. How might you mitigate these challenges?

RELIABILITY AND VALIDITY IN QUANTITATIVE RESEARCH

In quantitative research, discussions around reliability and validity have most often occurred in relation to the development and administration of instruments (such as tests, surveys, and so on). Broadly, reliability refers to the consistency of measurement or the degree to which your measure is replicable across multiple administrations. Put simply, reliability is the ability of an instrument to achieve the same measure regardless of the number of times it is administered (Kirk & Miller, 1986). It is important to note that reliability is not measured; rather it is estimated based on the development and administration of the instrument. The estimate is based on the similarity of scores, across multiple administrations, given to the same person under similar conditions.

While authors such as Cronbach (1971) and Messick (1989) discussed validity in relation to the validity of interpretations rather than simply validity of instruments, the conversation around validity still often centers on the use of a test. Validity is described as the degree to which the inference drawn from a score is accurate. In short, validity is the ability to say that a score represents what you think it does (Golafshani, 2003). It is important to note that there are also different types of validity. Construct validity, for instance, refers to the congruence between your ideas and the way that you measure them. Content validity refers to the degree to which a test measures what it intends to measure. Criterion validity, alternatively, is the extent to which a test score accurately reflects some type of performance indicator. Sample validity is the extent to which a sample represents the population. Collectively, some have argued that these types of validity ensure that the measures you include in your quantitative study accurately reflect what you intend to study.

TECHNOLOGY THAT SUPPORTS QUANTITATIVE DATA ANALYSIS

For many practitioner-scholars, the need to calculate statistics by hand is daunting. Fortunately, there are many tools available to support you in completing quantitative data analysis. One of the most popular tools is SPSS, a software package that provides practitioner-scholars with a multitude of statistical features and data management resources. SPSS is available at most colleges or universities and can be purchased relatively inexpensively given campus-based software licensing agreements. Most important, the SPSS environment is similar to Microsoft Excel; thus, many practitioner-scholars generally find it easy to learn. Figure 9.9 provides an example of the user interface of SPSS.

Figure 9.9   The SPSS User Interface

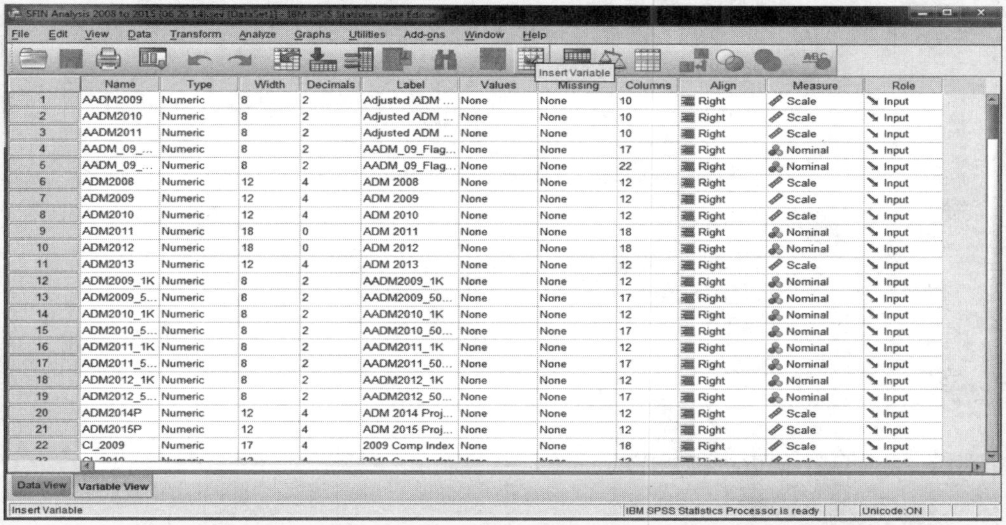

Source: SPSS © Copyright IBM Corporation

While we cannot cover all of the features available in SPSS, it is important to highlight a few of the most useful. First, SPSS provides robust tools to manage data and prepare your data for analysis. SPSS offers practitioner-scholars the ability to quickly compute descriptive statistics that can be used to assess the overall quality of the dataset.

Second, SPSS can be used with a variety of forms of data. For example, many commercial software systems now allow users to directly export files into SPSS. Similarly, SPSS imports files from Microsoft Excel and other common office programs. Given that many school districts and schools use student information systems that export information as Microsoft Excel files, this makes importing data for analyses using SPSS relatively straightforward.

Third, for practitioner-scholars engaged in studies that involve significant data manipulation or management, SPSS provides access to syntax—a programming language that allows practitioner-scholars to record each of their decisions regarding data management. Syntax is particularly useful in that it allows practitioner-scholars to share their data management decisions with a peer and/or adviser. This provides opportunities to check each other's work, as well as to catalog data decisions in ways that contribute to improved reliability and validity in research studies. Figure 9.10 highlights what SPSS syntax looks like.

Finally, the SPSS environment has been widely described in introductory statistics textbooks (e.g., Field, 2009; Weinberg & Abramowitz, 2008). Thus, there are ample resources available to guide your use of SPSS—even at the most basic level. Given many practitioners benefit from an applied introduction to statistics, the ability to learn more about statistical concepts within a software package is likely very helpful.

Figure 9.10 Example of Syntax in SPSS

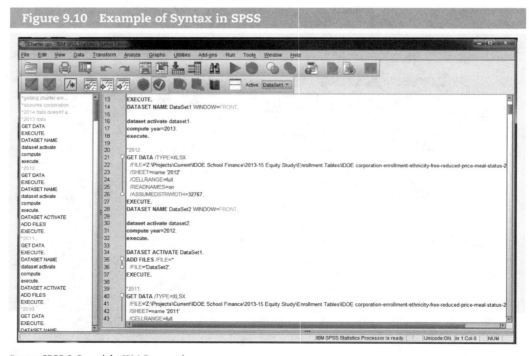

Source: SPSS © Copyright IBM Corporation

REFLECTIVE OPPORTUNITY 9.3

Compare the quantitative data analysis process with qualitative data analysis. As you do so, reflect upon ethical challenges that may arise.

1. Are there any ethical issues that you feel are unique to quantitative data analysis?

2. Are there any ethical issues that you feel are unique to qualitative data analysis?

3. How might these similarities and differences inform your research process?

SUMMARY

In this chapter, we introduced you to the basic concepts related to quantitative data analysis. First, we highlighted the importance of becoming familiar with your dataset, pointing also to the need to develop a codebook. Second, we discussed the importance of differentiating among the different types of variables. Third, we shared some of the basic considerations for carrying out descriptive statistics and inferential statistics. Fourth, within our discussion of inferential statistics, we noted some of the common statistical tests that you may consider in your research. We also briefly shared the importance of considering Type-I and Type-II Error, as well as missing data. Fifth, while concepts like validity and reliability are talked about in varied ways in both qualitative and quantitative research, we also mentioned some of the important considerations around these two concepts. Finally, we concluded by noting the importance and relevance of learning about and using software packages, such as SPSS, when conducting a quantitative data analysis.

KEY TERMS

Alternative Hypothesis 199
Analysis of Variance (ANOVA) 204
Assignments 190
Binary Variables 193
Categorical Measures 192
Chi-Square 205
Codebook 191
Construct Validity 207
Content Validity 207
Continuous Variables 193
Criterion Validity 207
Dataset 190
Extraneous or Confounding
    Variable 192
Frequencies 194
Interval variables 193
Keypunching 191

List-Wise Deletion 205
Mean 194
Mean Imputation 205
Measures of Central Tendency 194
Measures of Variability 195
Median 194
Mode 194
Negatively Skewed 195
Nominal Variables 193
Non-Parametric Data 202
Normal Distribution 195
Pair-Wise Deletion 205
Parametric Data 202
Pearson Correlation (r) 203
Positively Skewed 195
Population Variance 195
Range 195

Ratio Variable 193
Reliability 206
Sample Validity 207
Sample Variance 195
Significance Level 199
Simple Linear Regression or
    Multiple Regression 204
Skew 195
SPSS 207
Standard Deviation 195
Standardizing Values 191
Syntax 207
t-Test 204
Type-I Error 201
Type-II Error 201
Validity 207
Variance 195

QUESTIONS TO CONSIDER

1. What are the aims and purposes of quantitative data analysis?

2. How would you describe the overarching process of conducting a quantitative data analysis?

3. What are the differences between descriptive statistics and inferential statistics?

4. What are some of the inferential statistical tests that might be used when carrying out a quantitative study?

5. How might you determine which inferential statistical test to use?

6. What are some of the ways that you might handle missing data?

7. How might software packages like SPSS be used when conducting a quantitative data analysis?

CHAPTER EXERCISES

1. A useful way to become more familiar with quantitative data analysis is to study how researchers write about their analyses. Therefore, take time to search a journal in your field (such as *Education Administration Quarterly*) for two to three published quantitative studies. Then, go to the section of the article focused on data analysis, which is typically found in the methods section. Take note of: (a) the way in which the author(s) described the statistical procedures used, (b) the variables identified, and (c) how they conducted their analysis.

2. If you plan to use SPSS for your quantitative data analysis, it is useful to spend time exploring the features that are available. If you have access to a university computer lab with SPSS, practice using SPSS with a dataset to which you have access. UCLA's Institute for Digital Research Education has a helpful page devoted to SPSS, offering pertinent resources for exploring what SPSS might offer you (http://www.ats.ucla.edu/stat/spss/).

3. Identify the independent and dependent variables in the following two statements:

   a. Do students perform better in math and science if they participate in afterschool math and science clubs?

   b. What are the effects of a phonics-based versus whole-language-based reading program on students' verbal comprehension?

4. A researcher is interested in comparing the differences in student achievement between male and female students. Assuming the researcher wanted to make this comparison across four different schools (School A, School B, School C, and School D), which inferential statistical test might they use to make these comparisons and why?

LEARNING EXTENSIONS

As previously noted, we strongly encourage you to complete both an introductory and advanced level study of statistics if you plan to complete a quantitative research study. One additional way to expand your study is to begin reading books written around statistical analyses, as well as the use of software packages like SPSS to support your analytical work. A useful book to begin with is Creighton's (2007) book, *Schools and Data: The Educator's Guide for Using Data to Improve Decision Making.* This book provides a straightforward introduction to statistics, which is situated in the world of practice. Next, you may want to explore additional writings around statistics specifically, perhaps exploring books such as *Understanding* *Statistics in Behavioral Sciences*, written by Pagano (2004). Pagano's book provides a clear introduction to both descriptive and inferential statistics. Finally, Field's (2009) book, *Discovering Statistics Using SPSS*, introduces you to more advanced aspects of quantitative data analysis, as well as the ways in which SPSS might support your research process.

Sharpen your skills with SAGE edge!

edge.sagepub.com/lochmiller

SAGE edge for Students provides a personalized approach to help you accomplish your coursework goals in an easy-to-use learning environment. You'll find action plans, mobile-friendly eFlashcards, and quizzes as well as videos, web resources, and links to SAGE journal articles to support and expand on the concepts presented in this chapter.

10

INTRODUCING MIXED METHODS RESEARCH AND ANALYSIS

CONTEMPLATING A MIXED METHODS RESEARCH STUDY

Given all of the recent attention on teacher evaluation policy, you find yourself wondering how teachers in your school district perceive the evaluation processes as impacting their practices. You are particularly interested in knowing whether classroom teachers think these evaluation processes are informing or shaping their instruction. In other words, are teachers teaching differently because of the way that they will be evaluated? You decide that this topic is important and that you want to undertake a study. Yet, you realize that your interests in this topic do not fit neatly in either a purely qualitative or purely quantitative methodology. Rather, you would like to study this topic using both. Thus, you find yourself contemplating the development of a mixed methods research study.

INTRODUCTION

In the opening vignette, we present a scenario that is becoming increasingly relevant to practitioner-scholars. In this vignette, we show how a contemporary problem of practice may require the use of mixed methods to be fully understood. Indeed, we find it essential that practitioner-scholars thoughtfully explore mixed methods research as an option given the inherent ambiguity and complexity of the problems faced in schools. These problems do not consistently lend themselves to a purely qualitative or quantitative methodology and thus require practitioner-scholars to consider methodologies that allow them to blend methods.

In this chapter, we introduce you to mixed methods research and the analyses associated with it. In particular, we highlight the definition of mixed methods research and take care to discuss some of the

Learning Objectives

By the end of the chapter, you will be able to:

- Define mixed methods research.

- Describe the basic assumptions of mixed methods research designs.

- Compare a qualitative-leading and a quantitative-leading mixed methods research design.

- Identify the basic characteristics of the mixed methods research models, including: convergent parallel design, explanatory sequential design, exploratory sequential design, embedded design, multiphase design, and transformative design.

- Discuss the differences between a fixed and an emergent mixed methods research design.

- Formulate the steps of carrying out a mixed methods research study.

- Summarize how mixed method analysis draws upon qualitative and quantitative analytic practices.

related characteristics. We note how these characteristics have developed over time and serve to distinguish mixed methods research from other research traditions (qualitative and quantitative). Next, we present two broad orientations to mixed methods research and then discuss specific models that have been developed within the mixed methods community. We then describe how to carry out a mixed methods research study and complete the analysis. In conclusion, we discuss a web-based application that supports mixed methods analysis.

DEFINING MIXED METHODS RESEARCH

Previous researchers have defined mixed methods research as "the class of research where the researcher mixes or combines quantitative and qualitative research techniques, methods, approaches, concepts, or language into a single study" (Johnson & Onwuegbuzie, 2004, p. 17). There have also been a variety of terms used to refer to mixed methods research, including multi-methods, multiple methods, and mixing methods (O'Cathain & Thomas, 2006). In this textbook, we define mixed methods research as a pragmatic orientation to research in which the practitioner-scholar draws upon the strengths of qualitative and quantitative research methods to wholly describe and study the research topic, phenomenon, or experience. Our definition thus acknowledges that it is not simply that mixed methods research is blended or mixed. Rather, it recognizes that the researcher makes an informed choice to use both types of data because, from their perspective, that is how they will fully understand their research topic of interest.

For practitioner-scholars, many of their research interests or questions do not fit neatly in either a qualitative or quantitative research design. Instead, questions presented by practitioner-scholars often "bridge" both quantitative and qualitative research methodologies and thus require that they adopt a mixed methods approach. For example, a practitioner-scholar might be interested in surveying students about their experience in schools, but also wants to know more specifically about an individual student's story. This desire often requires a practitioner-scholar to adopt a mixed methods research design, whereby they draw upon both qualitative and quantitative paradigms to address their research questions. From the Field 10.1 provides an example of a mixed methods study of teachers' commitment to environmental education. We highlight this abstract as it demonstrates how qualitative and quantitative approaches point to different aspects of teachers' commitment.

As Johnson and Ongwuebuzie (2004) noted, "The goal of mixed methods research is not to replace either of these [qualitative or quantitative] approaches but rather to draw from the strengths and minimize the weaknesses of both in single research studies and across studies" (pp. 14–15). This description of mixed methods is instructive for a simple reason: it avoids the notion that either qualitative or quantitative research is inherently better. Rather, it positions qualitative and quantitative research methods as equally useful in mixed methods research and thus creates the opportunity to blend two equally valued methodological traditions. In simpler terms, mixed methods research is a pragmatic approach to educational research. It strives to address the complexity of educational challenges using the full spectrum of data available. Indeed, it strives to bridge the gap between research methodologies in order to fully understand and make sense of practice (Onweugbuzie & Leech, 2006).

FROM THE FIELD 10.1

An Abstract of a Mixed Methods Study

This article argues that a mixed methods approach is useful in understanding the complexity that underlies teachers' commitment to environmental education. Using sequential and concurrent procedures, the authors demonstrate how different methodological approaches highlighted different aspects of teacher commitment. The quantitative survey examined significant factors that determine teachers' commitment, whereas the qualitative approach used a soft systems methodology to expand understanding and to explore ways of increasing teacher commitment to environmental education. Results indicate a complex range of factors affecting commitment, and different layers of reality discovered by the different methods provide a holistic understanding of teacher commitment to environmental education. The article also demonstrates how a mixed methods approach can serve the dual role of confirming and elaborating findings.

Source: Sosu, McWilliam, & Gray, 2008, p. 169

CHARACTERISTICS OF MIXED METHODS RESEARCH

Fundamentally, mixed methods researchers claim that combining qualitative and quantitative methods results in greater confidence in one's results/findings (Dixon-Woods, Agarwal, Young, Jones, & Sutton, 2004), compensates for weaknesses inherent in a single research design (Bryman, 2008), and results in a more complete dataset and therefore results/ findings (O'Cathain & Thomas, 2006). In education, mixed methods research is growing in popularity. This growing popularity has been linked to the increasing emphasis on evidence-based research. More particularly, the evidence-based movement has tended to privilege quantitative research designs (O'Reilly & Kiyimba, 2015), with the genesis of mixed methods research being primarily quantitative in scope. Perhaps not surprisingly, educational researchers have increasingly been called upon to use methods that allow for replication of their results/ findings (Makel & Plucker, 2014). This call has, at the same time, spurred increased interest in the use of mixed methods research, as it is viewed as one way to strengthen the perceived weaknesses of single research designs.

Researchers have attempted to describe the underlying principles of mixed methods research. Johnson and Turner (2003), for example, noted the fundamental principle of mixed methods research, which implies that researchers who adopt mixed methods designs do so in a way that maximizes the strengths and minimizes the weaknesses of any particular methodology. We highlight four additional considerations that have been central to the development of mixed methods research designs.

First, mixed methods researchers assume that qualitative and quantitative approaches are compatible. This is an important point, as this has been a long-debated issue. Early on in the development of mixed methods research designs, there were concerns around the compatibility of combining qualitative and quantitative methods. In the 1970s and 1980s, many qualitative

CONSIDERING A MIXED METHODS STUDY

Given your interest in understanding how teachers in your school district perceive new teacher evaluation criteria as impacting their practice, you see that a purely qualitative or purely quantitative study is not likely to allow you to fully address the topic. While the thought of talking to a few teachers about their experience is interesting to you, there is also part of your interest that wants to look across the district to see how teacher perspectives vary by type of school, demographics of the students served, and also by their professional characteristics. At the same time, you think it is important to talk with teachers about their experiences to understand better what the new teacher evaluation criteria mean to them. You recognize that a survey study would allow you to obtain a broad perspective but a qualitative study—particularly one including the use of interviews or focus groups—would enhance your understanding. Thus, you decide to pursue a mixed methods design that will begin with a survey of teachers in the school district and conclude by asking selected teachers to participate in focus groups. This approach, you hope, will allow you to balance your desire for a broad understanding of teacher perspectives with a specific understanding from teachers with particular characteristics.

Focus Questions

1. To what extent might you risk minimizing the qualitative findings or quantitative results in a mixed methods study?

2. What are some of the logistical challenges you may face by completing a study that includes both survey and focus group data?

researchers expressed concerns regarding the mixing of epistemological perspectives. There were concerns that qualitative and quantitative approaches could not be combined because they were based on fundamentally different paradigms. This paradigm debate resulted in some researchers suggesting that mixing methods was not possible because you could not combine a constructivist paradigm with a positivist paradigm, for instance. Kuhn (1962) and others argued that paradigms have their own language and way of making sense of the world and therefore two different paradigms were incompatible. Methodological purists promoted a concept referred to as the incompatibility thesis, wherein the mixing of qualitative and quantitative approaches was positioned as impossible (Howe, 1988). Many researchers, however, grew frustrated with what they viewed as a constraining position, and argued for a pragmatic or practical approach to combining qualitative and quantitative methods.

Second and relatedly, mixed methods research is fundamentally based in pragmatic perspectives. Within the pragmatic movement, researchers claim that a practical approach should and can be taken, which allow for a practitioner-scholar to use whatever methods seem appropriate for their research purposes (Yancher & Williams, 2006). As such, pragmatism is typically described as the philosophical basis for mixed methods research (Johnson & Onwuegbuzie, 2004).

Third, mixed methods research is often described as being driven by research questions (Newman & Benz, 1998; Tashakkori & Teddlie, 1998). In addition, developing mixed methods research questions has been described as challenging, as it requires mixed methods research questions to be developed and reformulated at different points during the research process (Onwuegbuzie &

Leech, 2006). For instance, the research questions may be reformulated during data analysis or data interpretation, or even after the research report/paper has been written.

Fourth and finally, mixed methods research requires the practitioner-scholar to have an integrated understanding of qualitative and quantitative research methods. When conducting a mixed methods research study, the practitioner-scholar needs to have a great deal of familiarity with both qualitative and quantitative research traditions. Some have argued that the need for dual competency can be solved through research teams wherein one individual has expertise in one research tradition and another individual brings expertise from another research tradition. Regardless of the approach that you take, it is important to consider your level of competency prior to delving into a mixed methods study.

MIXED METHODS RESEARCH DESIGNS

There are three basic mixed methods research designs, which have been described elsewhere as QUAL-Quan, QUAN-Qual, and QUAN-QUAL (Creswell, 2012). Broadly, these designs characterize whether the mixed methods study relies primarily on qualitative, quantitative, or on a mix of data. For instance, the QUAL-Quan design emphasizes and foregrounds qualitative research, whereas the QUAN-qual emphasizes and privileges quantitative research. The QUAN-QUAL model is described as giving equal weight or emphasis to both the quantitative and qualitative research design.

Sometimes this description of mixed methods is found to be a bit ambiguous or unclear. In this textbook, as in our own work with practitioner-scholars, we refer to these designs more simply as a qualitative-leading mixed methods research design and a quantitative-leading mixed method research design. We have purposefully excluded the balanced designs given the difficulty that practitioner-scholars often have in crafting a truly mixed or balanced research topic. Further, we have found that most practitioner-scholars tend to employ either a qualitative-leading or quantitative-leading mixed methods research design.

In a qualitative-leading mixed methods research design, the practitioner-scholar develops a study that involves a qualitative problem of practice and relies primarily on qualitative data to investigate this problem. In such a study, quantitative data is used to expand upon the qualitative findings. For example, if a practitioner-scholar proposed a case study that relied primarily on interviews with school staff who were involved in the student assignment process at their school, they might undertake a study that used interviews to explore the perspective of classroom teachers who are directly involved in the assignment process and then use a survey to acquire the perspectives

REFLECTIVE OPPORTUNITY 10.1

Mixed methods research results in inherent tensions between research traditions. For example, how do you navigate the tension between reporting aggregate results from a quantitative analysis and individual responses from a qualitative analysis? What dilemmas might this lead to?

DECIDING ON A QUALITATIVE- OR QUANTITATIVE-LEADING DESIGN

Given your decision to use a mixed methods research design for your study of teacher perspectives regarding the influence of new evaluation criteria on practice, your next decision is whether you want the qualitative or quantitative data to lead your study. Given your primary interest is to identify how teacher perspectives vary, you decide that you will begin your study with a survey of classroom teachers in your district. This will allow you to capture the broad perspectives of teachers that motivated your study initially. This means that your study will be quantitative leading. The primary benefit of this approach, you feel, is that it will help you identify where to focus your attention in terms of the focus groups you want to conduct with teachers. You think

that it might be possible to identify groups of teachers who have differing views on the impact that the new evaluation criteria are having and use these results to inform how you select teachers to participate in the focus groups. In short, you see the qualitative data collection as being primarily informed by the quantitative results you obtain through your study.

Focus Questions

1. How might you ensure that the questions you pose in the focus groups are aligned with your quantitative results?

2. What might you do if the qualitative findings disconfirm or challenge the quantitative results?

of the process from the entire school staff. The survey might present questions that reflect the understandings she or he obtained through the interviews with the staff who were directly involved in the assignment process. Alternatively, the survey might ask questions designed to confirm or disconfirm the participants' understandings of the process. In this mixed methods design, the practitioner-scholar allows the qualitative data to lead her or his discussion of the research problem, while relying on the quantitative data to expand upon or challenge the qualitative perspectives he or she obtained.

In quantitative-leading mixed methods research designs, a practitioner-scholar relies on quantitative data to formulate their understanding of the research problem, while using qualitative data to deepen, enlighten, or explore particular ideas, concepts, or concerns. In a quantitative-leading design, the practitioner-scholar formulates his or her research problem broadly so as to maximize the value of the quantitative data. For example, if a practitioner-scholar began by surveying classroom teachers in their school about the student assignment process, they might use interviews to probe more deeply into the teachers' perspectives about the assignment process that appeared to be problematic.

MODELS OF MIXED METHODS RESEARCH

There are six basic models used in conducting mixed methods research. These models have been developed to guide your decision-making about when and how to phase in qualitative and quantitative approaches in a mixed methods study. These models are still being developed and continue to evolve as researchers use them in their research in new ways. It is important to note that these models serve as images of possibility, and do not necessarily offer step-by-step guidance on how to carry out a mixed methods study.

Convergent Parallel Design

In a convergent parallel design, the practitioner-scholar carries out a qualitative and quantitative study simultaneously, as illustrated in Figure 10.1, and then mixes the findings/results during the analytic phase.

In this design, the practitioner-scholar is most interested in linking and associating findings from the qualitative and quantitative components of the study so that they result in a coherent narrative. For example, as part of a qualitative case study, a practitioner-scholar might interview classroom teachers about the expectations being placed on them by new teacher evaluation criteria. At the same time, the practitioner-scholar might survey principals to understand how they perceive the new evaluation criteria influencing classroom teachers. During the analysis, the practitioner-scholar would then try to relate the findings from these individual study strands.

Explanatory Sequential Design

The explanatory sequential design is completed in two phases in which the practitioner-scholar begins by collecting quantitative data and then concludes by collecting and analyzing qualitative data. Figure 10.2 illustrates this design.

In an explanatory design, quantitative data and a quantitative research problem drive the focus of the study. The practitioner-scholar, therefore, uses their interpretation of the quantitative results to inform how and to what extent qualitative data are used. The explanatory sequential design is thus equivalent to a quantitative-leading design. For example, a practitioner-scholar who is interested in studying how teachers perceive new teacher evaluation criteria influence their classroom instructional practice might begin by conducting a survey of classroom teachers across a school district to identify salient cross-cutting perspectives and then conduct interviews with a subset of classroom teachers who fit particular characteristics identified by the survey. These

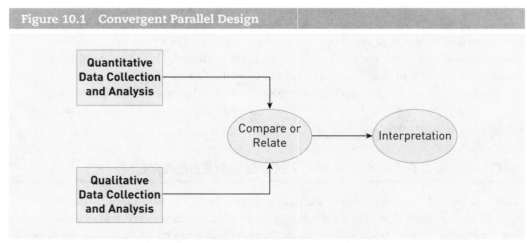

Figure 10.1   Convergent Parallel Design

Source: Adapted from Creswell & Plano Clark, 2011, p. 69

Figure 10.2 Explanatory Sequential Design

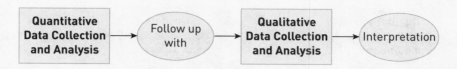

Figure 10.2 Explanatory Sequential Design

Source: Adapted from Creswell & Plano Clark, 2011, p. 69

teachers might, for instance, have a certain number of years of experience or have participated in particular professional development activities and thus have a unique perspective to share on the implementation of the teacher evaluation criteria that is distinct from other survey respondents. We highlight an abstract from a study that used an explanatory sequential design in From the Field 10.2.

Exploratory Sequential Design

The exploratory sequential design prioritizes qualitative data, as illustrated in Figure 10.3.

This design is thus equivalent to a qualitative leading design. In an exploratory sequential study, the practitioner-scholar uses their interpretation derived from the qualitative data to inform which

FROM THE FIELD 10.2

Example of an Explanatory Sequential Design

The purpose of this study was to increase the science education community's understanding of the experiences and needs of girls who cross the traditional categorical boundaries of gender, race and socioeconomic status in a manner that has left their needs and experience largely invisible. A first of several in a series, this study sought to explore how African American girls from low SES communities position themselves in science learning. We followed a mixed-methods sequential explanatory strategy, in which two data collection phases, qualitative following the quantitative, were employed to investigate 89 African-American girls' personal orientations towards science learning. By using quantitative data from the Modified Attitudes toward Science Inventory to organize students into attitude profiles and then sequentially integrating the profile scores with year-long interview data, we found

that the girls' orientations towards science were best described in terms of definitions of science, importance of science, experiences with science, and success in science. Therefore, our mixed method analysis provided four personality orientations which linked success in school and experiences with science to confidence and importance of science and definitions of science to value/desire. In our efforts to decrease the achievement gap, we concluded there should be more emphasis on conceptual understanding and problem-solving skills, while still being cognizant of the danger of losing the connection between science and society which so often plagues achievement-focused efforts. Our continued efforts with this group of girls will center on these instructional techniques with the goal of addressing the needs of all science learners.

Source: Buck, Cook, Quigley, Eastwood, & Lucas, 2009, p. 386

 Read the full article at:
www.sagepub.com/lochmiller

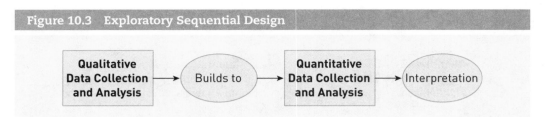

Figure 10.3   Exploratory Sequential Design

Qualitative Data Collection and Analysis → Builds to → Quantitative Data Collection and Analysis → Interpretation

Source: Adapted from Creswell & Plano Clark, 2011, p. 69

quantitative variables she or he will integrate into their study. For example, a practitioner-scholar who begins a qualitative case study by conducting interviews with classroom teachers to determine how they perceive new evaluation criteria impacting their classroom instructional practice might specifically collect quantitative data about the amount of time that teachers engage in different instructional strategies. This data would thus allow the practitioner-scholar to add to his or her interpretation of the teachers' qualitative interviews. We highlight an example of an exploratory sequential design in From the Field 10.3.

Embedded Design

Unlike the explanatory or exploratory sequential design, which effectively privilege quantitative or qualitative methods, an embedded design does not privilege either research tradition. Instead, an embedded design treats both research approaches equally and thus in theory does not introduce qualitative or quantitative data in phases, as shown in Figure 10.4.

For example, a practitioner-scholar who wishes to conduct a qualitative case study of teachers' perspectives regarding the impact of new teacher evaluation criteria might introduce some type of intervention to determine whether particular supports or guidance influenced their perspectives. This design would thus involve introducing a quasi-experiment into the otherwise qualitative study from the very start.

FROM THE FIELD 10.3

Example of an Exploratory Sequential Design

Elementary school children between 9 and 12 years of age were interviewed on what they believed to be the causes of learning difficulties and were invited to take part in the analysis of the data. We achieved this with Trochim's concept mapping approach that combines qualitative and quantitative data analyses. Study results indicated that children were more knowledgeable than expected. Although each participant gave relatively few ideas, they collectively generated a list of 42 unique statements, which they categorized into a meaningful structured conceptualization. Results showed that children were competent and reliable participants in the concept mapping process. Educational, research, and methodological implications are discussed.

Source: Nowick, Brown, & Stepien, 2014, p. 69

Read the full article at:
www.sagepub.com/lochmiller

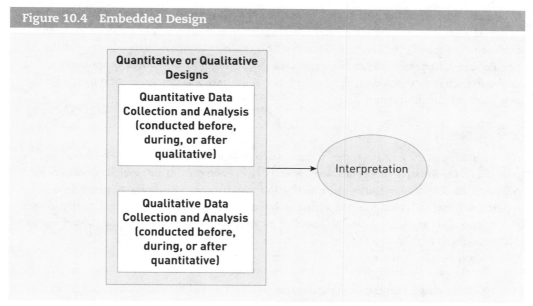

Figure 10.4   Embedded Design

Source: Adapted from Creswell & Plano Clark, 2011, p. 70

For a practitioner-scholar, the embedded design is likely difficult to execute because it requires an ongoing effort to balance two distinct research traditions within and across all aspects of the study. The problem statement, for example, should attend to both research traditions. Similarly, research questions should be formulated in such a way that qualitative and quantitative elements of the study are clearly defined. We feel this adds a level of complexity that practitioner-scholars, indeed all researchers, will likely find challenging.

Multiphase Design (Multi-Study)

In a multiphase design, the practitioner-scholar essentially carries out separate qualitative and quantitative studies, as illustrated in Figure 10.5, and then relates the results/findings from these individual studies.

This design is particularly popular when focused on the evaluation and improvement of individual programs. For instance, a practitioner-scholar might survey classroom teachers in a school district

Figure 10.5   Multiphase Design

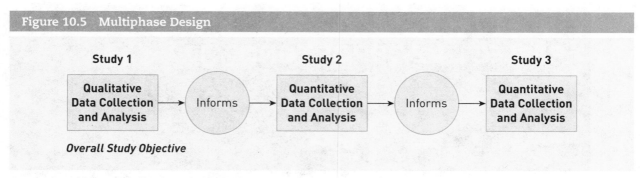

Source: Adapted from Creswell & Plano Clark, 2011, p. 70

to determine how existing professional development is currently supporting the implementation of new teacher evaluation criteria. After this, the practitioner-scholar may conduct qualitative case studies of specific programs to illuminate how those programs reference or address the new criteria. Ultimately, the practitioner-scholar would bring together their quantitative and qualitative interpretations into a single discussion of professional development supports for the new teacher evaluation criteria.

Transformative Design

A transformative design is a mixed methods design in which the practitioner-scholar adopts a transformative theoretical lens, which draws upon critical and socially oriented perspectives. This design is less concerned with the particular positioning of qualitative or quantitative methods than it is concerned with the use of a theoretical perspective that allows the practitioner-scholar to attend to issues of power, privilege, oppression, and discrimination. Mertens (2009) highlighted three characteristics that are typically associated with transformative mixed methods research designs, including:

1. Underlying assumptions that rely on ethical stances of inclusion and challenging oppressive social structures.

2. An entry process into the community that is designed to build trust and make goals and strategies transparent.

3. Dissemination of findings in ways that encourage use of the results/findings to enhance social justice and human rights. (p. 5)

Collectively these assumptions distinguish a transformative design from other mixed methods designs in that there is a clear mandate to use the results/findings of the mixed methods study to impact and potentially change practice. As such, we see the transformative design as a potential link between mixed methods research and action research, particularly participatory action research. Further, this design allows practitioner-scholars to uncover and more fully illuminate the existing inequities and inherent injustices in schools and districts. For example, a practitioner-scholar who is interested in understanding how policies related to teacher evaluation are in some way reinforcing inequitable access to highly qualified teachers for students living in impoverished neighborhoods might adopt this design. Specifically, a practitioner-scholar may survey all teachers in a school district to determine how they perceive

REFLECTIVE OPPORTUNITY 10.2

In purely survey research studies, you often promise your participants confidentiality in their responses.

1. How might this promise of confidentiality be impacted in a mixed methods study when you know that you would like to conduct interviews

with a subset of participants who completed the survey?

2. How might this change the consent process?

3. What ethical issues may arise?

the new evaluation criteria consider (or not) issues of poverty, and then follow up with teachers and other community members in high-poverty schools to develop and carry out a participatory action research study that could result in some type of positive change.

SELECTING A FIXED OR EMERGENT MIXED METHODS DESIGN

It is also important to distinguish between whether your mixed methods research design will be fixed or emergent. Fixed designs establish how data will be used at the beginning of the study. In a fixed design, practitioner-scholars decide which parts of the study will depend on qualitative data and which will depend on quantitative data. They often map the types of data to specific research questions in their study and focus on different types of data at different stages in their research design. Fixed designs are thus systematic inquiries, which purposefully introduce qualitative and quantitative data collection. These studies are often designed in phases whereby the practitioner-scholar focuses on one type of data and then moves to another type of data. It is not uncommon, for example, for a practitioner-scholar to propose a phased study in which they complete either the qualitative or quantitative portion of the study first.

In contrast, emergent designs introduce qualitative and quantitative data into the study as is necessary to address or respond to specific research questions. This approach is often used when a second type of data is added to the study in response to emergent findings (Morse & Niehaus, 2009). Such designs are among the most pragmatic research designs, as they introduce data into the study as specific needs or concerns arise. For example, if you were conducting a case study and found that your qualitative data led you to ask questions about the population as a whole, it might be appropriate to introduce quantitative data (such as a survey) in order to address these concerns. Similarly, if the data you obtained on a survey raised questions about the extent to which students' perceptions about school influenced their willingness to attend school, you might conduct interviews or focus groups with students to be able to better articulate these understandings. The primary distinction between an emergent design and fixed design is that the introduction of additional types of data was not planned in advance.

BEYOND SELECTING A MIXED METHODS MODEL

Deciding to use a mixed methods research design is about far more than simply picking one of the mixed methods models described above. In reality, mixed methods research is similar to qualitative and quantitative research designs in that you must strive for a high degree of alignment among your research purpose, research question(s), conceptual and theoretical frameworks, and the underlying methodological assumptions of your study. Maxwell and Loomis (2003) indicated that a researcher's considerations about a mixed methods design should be informed by five elements of the study, including: (a) purpose, (b) conceptual framework, (c) research questions, (d) research methods, and (e) validity considerations.

When considering a mixed methods research design, particularly whether the study will be qualitative-leading or quantitative-leading, the practitioner-scholar should focus on the purpose of the study to determine what type of data the study should be based on. For studies that are highly descriptive or have an inherently broad focus, it is likely more appropriate to adopt a quantitative-leading design. This design allows the practitioner-scholar to take advantage of the strengths of quantitative research, particularly surveys. In studies that are exploratory or narrowly focused, it is likely more appropriate for the practitioner-scholar to adopt a qualitative-leading design. Relatedly, it is also important for a practitioner-scholar to consult their conceptual or theoretical framework. If the purpose of the mixed methods study is to validate or confirm a particular theoretical framework, this approach would likely encourage the use of a quantitative-leading design. In contrast, a study that uses a conceptual or theoretical framework as a general explanation of potential relationships or interactions might be best suited for a qualitative-leading design. Given the close relationship among the research purpose, conceptual framework, and research questions, it is not surprising that explanatory or exploratory research questions would lend themselves to a qualitative-leading design, while descriptive or definitive research questions would likely lend themselves to a quantitative leading design. As should be clear, whatever mixed methods design you select must be closely related to the broader purposes of the research in much the same way as a purely qualitative or quantitative design would be.

CARRYING OUT A MIXED METHODS STUDY

Researchers have previously described how to carry out a mixed methods research study (see Onwuegbuzie & Leech, 2006, for a useful discussion of this). We highlight here a simplified process of carrying out a mixed methods study that is intended to guide you through the major steps. We note 11 steps:

1. Clarify the goals and research objectives.

2. Establish research questions.

3. Determine why a mixed methods design is appropriate.

4. Determine what research tradition (qualitative or quantitative) will drive the design, if this is the case.

5. Decide whether data collection will be phased (that is, collecting qualitative first or collecting quantitative first) or blended (collecting qualitative and quantitative data simultaneously).

6. Revisit the research questions.

7. Collect the data using appropriate methods.

8. Complete analysis so that it is consistent with a phased or blended design (for example, analyze qualitative data first or quantitative data first, or analyze both types of data simultaneously).

9. Revisit the research questions.

10. Identify the intersections of the qualitative and quantitative findings/results.

11. Develop a coherent presentation of the findings/results that draws upon the data in relation to the selected mixed methods research design.

It is important to note that one of the steps in carrying out a mixed methods research study is to continually revisit and potentially reformulate your research questions based on your growing understanding of how the qualitative and quantitative research traditions relate (or need to relate) in order to address your research questions. This process is not unlike what we discussed in Chapter 2 in relation to the research process more generally; however, in a mixed methods study reformulating your research questions is a particularly important step (Onwuegbuzie & Leech, 2006). We view the process of revisiting your research questions as being directly informed by your mixed methods analysis, which we discuss next.

MIXED METHODS ANALYSIS

Mixed methods analysis requires that researchers draw upon qualitative and quantitative data analysis procedures. As Creswell and Plano Clark (2011) noted, there are similar steps involved in analyzing qualitative and quantitative data. These steps broadly relate to the preparation, analysis, and interpretation of the data. In mixed methods analysis, you must focus on the important task of bringing these analytic strategies together in order to conduct a mixed methods analysis.

In mixed methods data analysis, a practitioner-scholar may undertake qualitative and quantitative data analysis concurrently or sequentially. Thus, unlike a purely qualitative or quantitative research study, a mixed methods researcher must have an understanding of the analytic procedures in *both* research approaches, as well as how these analytic procedures relate to and strengthen each other. In addition, the mixed methods researcher needs to be aware of the inherent challenges that may arise when mixing multiple approaches to analysis. Each approach to analysis brings with it particular assumptions, which may or may not be easily compatible.

Creswell and Plano Clark (2011) highlighted the similarities between qualitative and quantitative data analysis, as related to mixed methods research. Their discussion suggested that both approaches proceed along similar lines, but involve different ways of thinking about setting up and analyzing your data. Table 10.1 provides a brief overview of the similarities between qualitative and quantitative analytic procedures.

Table 10.1 Basic Steps in Qualitative and Quantitative Analysis		
Steps in the Analytic Process	Quantitative	Qualitative
Prepare the data for analysis	• Code data by assigning numeric values • Prepare the data for analysis in a computer software package (e.g., SPSS or Microsoft Excel) • Recode the values as necessary • Create a code book to identify and track the meaning of the coded variables	• Organize documents and other data sources • Transcribe audio and video data • Load the data into a software package (e.g., ATLAS.ti, NVivo, MAXQDA, etc.)

(Continued)

Table 10.1 (Continued)		
Steps in the Analytic Process	**Quantitative**	**Qualitative**
Explore the data	• Inspect the data for missing, incomplete, or incorrect values • Conduct descriptive analyses to obtain a basic understanding of the data • Check for trends, distributions, or relationships	• Read through the data, noting important or salient passages • Establish a coding sheet • Create initial memos to note important or salient points about the data
Analyze the data	• Choose an appropriate statistical test • Analyze the data to answer specific research questions	• Code the data • Memo the data • Assign labels to codes • Group codes into categories • Establish themes
Represent and interpret the results/findings	• Represent the results as statements • Provide results in tables • Explain how the results address the research question • Compare the results with the literature	• Prepare thematic statements • Identify supporting or salient quotes • Explain how the themes address the research questions • Relate or compare the findings to the literature
Validate the data and results/findings	• Compare results with previous applications of the survey or instrument	• Use triangulation strategies • Use member checking

Source: Adapted from Creswell & Plano Clark, 2011, pp. 205–206

Beyond the basic steps in qualitative and quantitative research, mixed methods research includes additional considerations that allow the practitioner-scholar to integrate qualitative and quantitative findings into a coherent narrative. Onwuegbuzie and Teddlie (2003) noted seven steps, which we have adapted and rearranged for practitioner-scholarship.

1. *Data reduction*—which involves narrowing quantitative results to those that can be directly and meaningfully linked to qualitative findings. For example, this might involve excluding unrelated survey response items that cannot be connected to corresponding qualitative interview questions.

2. *Data transformation*—which involves transforming qualitative data into quantitative data. For example, you may analyze transcripts using a content analysis approach that results in quantifying the number of times that participants make references to experiences, programs, and so on.

3. *Data correlation*—which involves correlating quantitative data (for example, percentage of students eligible for free-and-reduced-price lunch, student achievement data) with qualitative data that have been transformed into quantitative data (for example, frequencies derived through

content analysis of interview transcripts). For example, you may take the frequencies that you derived through a content analysis of interviews and relate those to the percentage of students who passed the state assessment to determine whether there is a positive or negative relationship between the number of references to "prepping for the test" in interviews and the number of students who passed the state assessment.

4. *Data consolidation*—which involves blending data obtained from two separate studies into a single dataset. For example, data consolidation might involve selecting data from two independent studies to create a new mixed dataset. This might include drawing upon survey data from a quantitative study and a series of focus group transcripts from a qualitative study.

5. *Data comparison*—which involves comparing data from different data sources. This step often occurs after a dataset has been consolidated. For instance, this might involve looking at the responses obtained from a single question posed during a focus group and comparing those responses to a specific survey item about a related topic.

6. *Data integration*—which involves bringing qualitative and quantitative data into a coherent whole. We characterize this as "weaving" your data together through your findings into a coherent narrative.

7. *Data display*—which involves identifying meaningful ways to visually represent your qualitative and quantitative findings/results. This may involve you creating charts or graphs, rubrics, or other textual representations of your findings/results.

These steps illustrate different mixed methods analysis strategies that a practitioner-scholar might pursue in order to bring coherence and clarity to the presentation and discussion of the qualitative and quantitative data. You should not interpret these steps as all being required in order to conduct a mixed methods analysis; rather, they are possibilities that you should use to inform your decision-making process.

Analyzing Data in a Fixed or Emergent Mixed Methods Research Design

When a practitioner-scholar adopts a fixed design, she or he will also typically use a phased analysis. A phased analysis involves completing your qualitative or quantitative analysis separately. In the first phase, you would analyze the qualitative data you collected in your study to identify broad, overarching themes. This process involves reading the interview transcripts and other qualitative data, applying qualitative codes, generating categories, and ultimately articulating specific thematic statements. In the next phase of the analysis, the practitioner-scholar would then turn to analyzing his or her quantitative data. These data might include extant data retrieved from a student information system or public website or survey data obtained through the administration of a survey. In this phase of the mixed methods analysis, you might calculate descriptive or inferential statistics. These statistics would then be related to the qualitative findings in order to offer further validation or support.

Unlike a fixed design, in which the researcher decides up front how qualitative and quantitative data will be used in a mixed methods study, analysis in an emergent design takes a less structured approach. Different data types are introduced in response to specific findings. For example, you may introduce quantitative data based on the findings of your qualitative data analysis. This introduction is not pre-planned; rather it is in response to your emergent findings. When analyzing data in an emergent mixed methods design, it is therefore likely that the practitioner-scholar will rely on qualitative data to lead the initial analysis and determine the next steps. Qualitative data and its analysis better support the emergent nature of this type of design, as qualitative research designs are inherently emergent and intentionally flexible. As themes emerge from the analysis of qualitative data, for instance, you may decide to introduce quantitative data in response to the qualitative themes that help you to elaborate or expand upon your current understanding. Fundamentally, analysis within an emergent mixed methods design is flexible and responsive to emergent findings.

Regardless of the approach you take to mixed methods analysis, your analytic decisions will be informed by both qualitative and quantitative analytic strategies. Thus, your level of familiarity with such strategies is crucial. In addition, as you progress in your mixed methods analysis, we encourage you to remain thoughtful and reflective about your decision-making process. To support this reflection we offer several important questions to consider when completing a mixed methods analysis.

- How might the introduction of qualitative findings address the presumed weaknesses of quantitative research results alone?

- How might the introduction of quantitative findings address the presumed weaknesses of qualitative research findings alone?

- How might the findings/themes from the qualitative analysis be expanded upon through the use of quantitative data?

- What questions might be better understood if quantitative data are paired with qualitative data in the study and vice versa?

- How might qualitative findings have additional applications for practice should they be paired with quantitative data and vice versa?

- In what ways might qualitative data allow for broader interpretations of the quantitative results?

- How might quotes or insights from qualitative data provide additional context for quantitative results?

- How might the voices of those who are underrepresented in the quantitative data be heard more loudly if qualitative data were introduced?

- How might qualitative findings be more generalizable with the addition of quantitative data?

- In what ways might you assure that your findings/results address issues related to validity/trustworthiness?

DATA ANALYSIS IN A MIXED METHODS STUDY

Given your interest in understanding how teachers perceive that new teacher evaluation criteria influence their practice, you decide to conduct a mixed methods study that will employ a fixed design. In the first phase of the study, you plan to conduct interviews to determine what teachers feel are the most significant impacts on their practice. Your interviews will ask the teachers to share their thoughts about the new evaluation criteria, as well as to describe the impact that these criteria are having on their practice. After conducting your interviews, you will then conduct a survey of classroom teachers throughout the district to determine whether the perspectives you found in their interviews are common across the district.

Through your interviews with teachers, you find that teachers feel that the new criteria are narrowing their practice in significant ways. Instead of taking risks or being creative with their instruction, teachers perceive that the new criteria are forcing them to use more direct instruction. Teachers offer numerous explanations for this trend, but largely note that the potential of being evaluated "while teaching" is driving them to engage in instructional strategies that are more direct and less student-centered. Further, you note that teachers across content areas view the impact of the teacher evaluation criteria differentially. Reading and math teachers are largely amenable to the new criteria while science, arts, music, and other non-core teachers are somewhat more concerned. Finally, you note that novice teachers appear more supportive of the criteria than older teachers.

Recognizing these three themes, you construct a survey that: (a) aims to determine the extent to which teachers report that they are engaging in direct instruction versus student-centered activities; (b) allows for comparison of teacher responses across subject areas; and (c) includes questions that allow you to tease out potential differences in teacher perspectives based on the number of years they have taught. The survey is thus designed to build from your qualitative analysis of your interviews and provide an opportunity to look across the district's teachers to determine how the findings you derived from your qualitative analysis hold up.

After administering your survey, you find that teachers across the district largely feel compelled to engage in more direct instruction given the new evaluation criteria. Contrary to the interviews you conducted, you find that teachers in different content areas do not appear to feel that the criteria impact them differently. Rather, all teachers who completed the survey appear equally concerned. Finally, consistent with your interviews, you find that novice teachers across the district are more comfortable with the new criteria than the more experienced teachers.

Focus Questions

1. What strategies might you build into your research design to check the accuracy of these contrasting findings?
2. As you consider how to report your findings, how might you work across both datasets to illustrate both the confirming and disconfirming findings?

REFLECTIVE OPPORTUNITY 10.3

Considering that mixed methods research involves both qualitative and quantitative research practices, you will inevitably face ethical challenges common to both research traditions.

1. How might you reconcile the ethical challenges that arise across the varied research approaches?

TECHNOLOGY TO SUPPORT MIXED METHODS ANALYSIS

When completing your mixed methods analysis, you are likely to use one or more of the technologies discussed in Chapter 8 (such as ATLAS.ti) or Chapter 9 (such as SPSS). In fact, many of the computer-assisted qualitative data analysis software packages now support certain aspects of mixed methods analysis, with built-in features allowing you to import data from SPSS or Excel. Dedoose is a web-based service that is specifically designed to support the management and analysis of qualitative and mixed methods research data. This web-based application allows practitioner-scholars to work across computers, making it possible to analyze data at home or work. Dedoose is an affordable option in that you can purchase access on a monthly basis, rather than having to make a major investment up front. While we do not highlight all of the features of this package here, we do note, as shown below in Figure 10.6, that Dedoose allows you to conveniently see the frequencies of coded passages and thus to interpret them using descriptive statistics.

In addition, Dedoose allows you to easily export the frequencies of coded passages and underlying document characteristics to Microsoft Excel so that you can use the more advanced quantitative analysis functions to calculate descriptive and inferential statistics. With qualitative data converted to a quantitative format, it allows you to link data generated in Dedoose to extant data (such as student achievement, demographics, and so on) and perform more advanced statistical analyses. Collectively, these features support the integrated nature of mixed methods analysis.

Figure 10.6   Dedoose User Interface and Associated Coding Frequencies

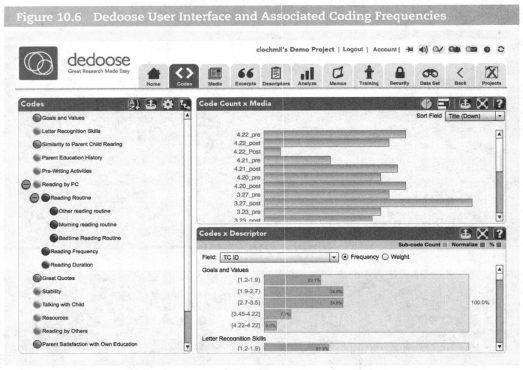

Source: Dedoose.com

SUMMARY

In this chapter, we discussed the definition and basic characteristics of mixed methods research. We also highlighted the various models of mixed methods research studies that are commonly employed by practitioner-scholars. Further, we presented the process of analyzing mixed methods data. Finally, we pointed to the potential uses of Dedoose in supporting mixed methods research.

KEY TERMS

Convergent Parallel Design 218
Dedoose 230
Embedded Design 220
Emergent Design 223
Explanatory Sequential Design 218

Exploratory Sequential
  Design 219
Fixed Design 223
Incompatibility Thesis 215
Multiphase Design 221

Qualitative-Leading Mixed Methods
  Research Design 216
Quantitative-Leading Mixed Methods
  Research Designs 217
Transformative Design 222

QUESTIONS TO CONSIDER

1. How would you define mixed methods research?

2. What are the basic assumptions or characteristics that underlie mixed methods research designs?

3. How do you know whether your mixed methods research design is qualitative-leading or quantitative-leading?

4. What are the similarities and differences among the mixed methods research models?

5. What is the primary difference between a fixed versus an emergent mixed methods research design?

6. How do you know when to use a fixed versus an emergent mixed methods research design?

7. What are the steps for carrying out a mixed methods research study?

8. How is mixed methods analysis dependent upon qualitative and quantitative analytic strategies?

CHAPTER EXERCISES

1. Develop a proposal for a qualitative-leading mixed methods study. First, describe the mixed methods model that you will draw upon. Second, describe the purpose and objective of your study and the initial research questions. Finally, discuss how you will collect and analyze your data, indicating whether these processes will be phased or concurrent.

2. Develop a proposal for a quantitative-leading mixed methods study. First, describe the mixed methods model that you will draw upon. Second, describe the purpose and objective of your study, as well as the initial research questions. Finally, discuss how you will collect and analyze your data, indicating whether these processes will be phased or concurrent.

3. Develop a T-chart and indicate the strengths and weaknesses of mixed methods research based on your understanding after reading this chapter. After identifying the strengths and weaknesses, develop a rationale for why you would or would not use a mixed methods research design to study your research topic of interest.

4. Locate a mixed methods research article in the *Journal of Mixed Methods Research* related to your area of interest. Using the article you locate, take note of the: (a) type of data collected, (b) analytical approaches employed, and (c) ways in which the data sources were used to support the findings.

With growing attention being given to mixed methods research in education, there are an increasing numbers of books and articles focused on how to carry out mixed methods research, as well as discussions of the challenges of this particular research approach. A useful place to begin your study is Creswell and Plano Clark's book (2011), *Designing and Conducting Mixed Methods Research*. This book provides a helpful overview of the history of mixed methods research, as well as detailed descriptions of the models of mixed methods research. Additionally, we encourage you to spend time exploring the *Journal of Mixed Methods Research* to identify potential models or examples that you could use in your research.

Sharpen your skills with SAGE edge!

edge.sagepub.com/lochmiller

SAGE edge for Students provides a personalized approach to help you accomplish your coursework goals in an easy-to-use learning environment. You'll find action plans, mobile-friendly eFlashcards, and quizzes as well as videos, web resources, and links to SAGE journal articles to support and expand on the concepts presented in this chapter.

11

INTRODUCING ACTION RESEARCH

SEEING A NEED FOR ACTION RESEARCH

Throughout the school year, you and your colleagues have worked hard to improve your fourth grade professional learning community (PLC). At each meeting, you and your colleagues discuss how you make decisions, affirm your shared commitments about instruction, and also identify (using data) where you plan to go next. This process has been rewarding and yet you fully realize that there are a few teachers in your PLC who are not active participants. Thus, you feel the need to develop a new decision-making model that will require engagement from all stakeholders. How should you start this process? What should you do so that all of your colleagues see this as a challenge? Indeed, your informal conversations suggest that some of your colleagues think that, "everything is fine" and "nothing needs to change." This lack of engagement, however, frustrates you and many of your colleagues. Unfortunately, the colleagues who are most resistant are also veteran teachers, while you are only in your second year of teaching.

INTRODUCTION

As illustrated in the opening vignette, research studies often emerge directly from your work as a practitioner-scholar. Indeed, throughout this textbook, we aim to make consistent links between your daily work and the research process. In this chapter, we highlight action research, which we view as a primarily qualitative research methodology that provides a framework to systematically examine problems or challenges within practice-based settings. Action research has grown in popularity in recent years and has become a common methodology used by many educators, particularly classroom teachers and principals.

Learning Objectives

By the end of the chapter, you will be able to:

- Describe the characteristics of action research and participatory action research.

- Identify the different types of action research.

- Formulate the various criticisms of action research.

- Outline and describe the action research cycle.

- Assess the unique ethical considerations of action research.

- Summarize the ways in which a website or blog might be used in the context of an action research study or a participatory action research study.

In this chapter, we begin by presenting an overview of action research, highlighting the different types of action research and the criticisms related to action research. We specifically discuss the unique purpose of action research, as well as the circumstances that emerge as practitioner-scholars undertake such a study. Here, we also offer a brief description of participatory action research. We then present the five steps that typically occur when completing an action research study. These steps are similar to the steps of the research process, generally, but focus specifically on: (1) defining a relevant research topic; (2) identifying current understandings of the topic; (3) developing and (4) implementing an intervention; and (5) assessing whether the intervention had an impact. We next briefly consider some of the unique ethical considerations for action research. We conclude the chapter by illustrating how blogs and other online communication tools might serve as a support to practitioner-scholars engaged in this type of research.

OVERVIEW OF ACTION RESEARCH

Action research has become a compelling alternative to traditional (basic) research designs. Practitioners have long argued that traditional (basic) research is not well suited to, nor easily consumed, by individuals working in classrooms, schools, and districts. Kennedy (1997), for example, noted that classroom teachers have often critiqued education research for lacking both authority and persuasiveness within the context of their classroom practice. In addition, classroom teachers have argued that research questions posed by many researchers are unappealing to individuals working in schools, and that findings from research studies are difficult to apply in schools. Finally, they have critiqued the ability of education systems to implement researchers' ideas given both the pace of education reform, as well as the unique constraints under which schools and districts operate.

Action research has become a popular alternative because it lends itself well to immediate application and implementation in classrooms, schools, and school districts. Action research has been used by teacher educators, classroom teachers, school principals, and district administrators to embed the research process within their daily practice. While action research has gained considerable popularity in recent years, it is important to emphasize that action research, much like qualitative or quantitative research, is an umbrella term that describes different approaches to research that all seek to make an immediate connection to practice.

Definition of Action Research

In this textbook, we define action research as an orientation to education research in which a practitioner-scholar selects a problem, challenge, or issue drawn from their practice and uses the research process to identify and implement a possible solution or response. Central to action research is an *inquiry cycle* that rests on five steps: (1) identifying a problem of practice or relevant research topic; (2) identifying current understandings of the topic; (3) developing an intervention; (4) implementing the intervention in practice; and (5) assessing whether the intervention impacted the individuals or organization.

Though similar to traditional approaches to research, the inquiry cycle underlying all action research studies is unique in that it is highly situated and typically not intended to be generalized

Given that action research is highly situated, it is important to recognize that action research findings are typically not intended to be generalized to other professional settings. As you reflect upon this issue, consider the following two questions:

1. If you are a classroom teacher or school administrator reading someone else's action research study, why might it be unethical to simply re-administer the same intervention or use the same strategies with your students?

2. Prior to implementation of an intervention used in someone else's action research study, what might you do first to assure that your application of the findings is situated in your own context?

to other settings. When practitioner-scholars engage in an action research study they are doing so for the purpose of understanding and responding to a local challenge that may or may not be found in other schools or with other groups of students. It is imperative that you, as a practitioner-scholar, consider this when undertaking an action research study.

As Stringer (2014) noted, "Fundamentally, action research is grounded in a qualitative research paradigm," with the purpose being ". . . to gain greater clarity and understanding of a question, problem, or issue" (p. 36). It is quite common for practitioner-scholars to use interviews, observations, documents, and other qualitative data sources in their action research studies. For example, classroom teachers often use examples of student work or curricular materials as primary data sources in action research studies. However, action research studies need not consider only qualitative data sources. In fact, it is possible to use quantitative data in action research. A school administrator, for example, may include school-wide discipline data in an action research study to describe the behavioral patterns of students, as well as to establish the school's responses to these patterns over time. A classroom teacher may conduct a survey with his students' parents about their perceptions of in- and out-of-school reading activities. Nonetheless, it is far more common for an action research study to be qualitative in scope.

Types of Action Research

As we noted previously, action research is an umbrella term that covers a range of approaches. Calhoun (2002) described action research as being primarily focused on individual teacher research, collaborative action research between teachers or administrators, and school-wide action research involving a combination of school-level stakeholders. Other researchers have also described these as action research aimed at the classroom level (Mertler, 2014), participatory action research (McIntyre, 2008), and action research that is aimed at the organizational level (Stringer, 2014). Indeed, McNiff (2013) suggested that one of the threats to the development of action research as a field relates to the abundance of "loose words" that variously describe action research applied to different settings, contexts, and educational problems. Even as we began developing this chapter, we struggled with our own assumptions about the particular meaning(s) of action research and how best to present it as one of the many methodologies available to practitioner-scholars.

Thus, it is fair to say that there are a number of approaches to action research, much like there are a number of approaches to qualitative or quantitative research. For example, Stringer (2014) describes a model of action research whereby an individual engages in a three-step process: *Look, Think, Act*. In the "Look" phase of an action research study, "participants define and describe the problem to be investigated and the general context within which it is set" (p. 74). In the "Think" phase of an action research study, the practitioner-scholar analyzes and interprets "the . . . ." situation to extend their understanding of the nature and context of the problem" (p. 74). Finally, in the "Act" phase, the practitioner-scholar, and sometimes the participants, "formulate solutions to the problem" (p. 74). As should be clear, a central aim of Stringer's approach is to formulate comprehensive understandings of problems derived from and that live within practice. This process may or may not involve participants other than the practitioner-scholar.

In contrast, participatory action research sets out to engage research participants as co-researchers. Participatory action research is a methodological approach that builds on the traditions of action research, and specifically "aims to identify a socially relevant problem within a community and then develop and implement a plan of action" (Koo & Lester, 2014, p. 1). In this approach, community members are positioned as co-researchers and are part of identifying, investigating, and proffering solutions to relevant social issues. Participatory action research also gives attention to social issues that perpetuate social inequities and has a particular intention to address and potentially eradicate such inequities (Rodríguez & Brown, 2009). McIntyre (2008) identified four "tenets" that she suggested underlie all participatory action research projects, including:

1. A collective commitment to investigate an issue or problem;

2. A desire to engage in self- and collective reflection to gain clarity about the issue under investigation;

3. A joint decision to engage in individual and/or collective action that leads to a useful solution that benefits the people involved; and

4. The building of alliances between researchers and participants in the planning, implementation, and dissemination of the research process. (p. 1)

Fundamentally, participatory action research is often described as "research of the people, by the people, and for the people" (Park, 1997, p. 8), as it orients to research as being mutually developed, carried out, and disseminated.

There are many examples of participatory action research studies in education. For instance, in From the Field 11.1, a general description of McIntyre's (2008) participatory action research study in an inner-city school is presented.

Much like the action research process, as discussed below, participatory action research often entails a cyclical research process and begins by: (1) questioning a particular social issue of relevance to the participants; (2) reflecting upon and exploring the identified social issues; (3) collaboratively developing an action plan; and (4) implementing and refining the action plan. Typically, there is also a great deal of attention given to how understandings about the social issue will be shared with key stakeholders in the larger community.

Example of a Participatory Action Research Study in Education

From 1997 to 2000, I engage in a PAR [participatory action research] project at the Blair Elementary and Middle School, an inner-city public school in Bridgeport, Connecticut. Although located in one of the wealthiest counties in the United States, Bridgeport has a disproportionate share of the problems that affect many urban communities throughout the country—for example, high criminal activity, unemployment and low-wage jobs, underresourced schools, and racial isolation.

In 1997, I was introduced to Mrs. Leslie, a sixth-grade teacher at the Blair School. She invited me to present my idea about a PAR project to her 24 African American, Jamaican, Puerto Rican, Dominican, and Haitian students (12 boys and 12 girls). I told the young people a little bit about myself: my experiences growing up and teaching in Boston schools, my journey from classroom teaching to teaching in a university, and my desire to collaborate with them in exploring what it meant for them to live in a Bridgeport community. After a lively discussion about how we would engage that exploration, the young people decided to participate in the project.

Over a 3-year period, a group of graduate students from the university where I worked, a shifting population of young adolescents, and I met together once a week for an average of an hour and a half per group session. Together, we participate in a range of project-related activities aimed at furthering the young people's goal of informing their community about the effects of violence on themselves, their schools, and their environment.

Source: McIntyre, 2008, p. x

Criticisms of Action Research

It is important to keep in mind that action research, much like any other research methodology, is subject to criticisms from various research communities. A common, though fading, charge of action research is that it lacks the methodological rigor needed to qualify it as a true research methodology. Further, some individuals suggest that action research cannot be considered research because it is too firmly planted in the world of practice and thus not adequately concerned with the generation of new educational theories or perspectives. As McNiff (2013) noted, action research is frequently diminished by classically trained researchers as simply "telling stories" (p. 6). We suggest, however, that action research is one of many valid research methodologies for practitioner-scholars to consider when seeking to study their own practice or the practices within their own organization.

One response to these criticisms is that action research is *not* devoid of qualitative or quantitative research methodologies. Rather, action research is dependent on such methodologies. Underlying every action research study, there is a carefully designed qualitative or quantitative study that employs many of the same methodological and analytical approaches that you would find in traditional (basic) research. The same consideration should be given to formulate a compelling research problem, develop coherent research questions, and articulate a clear and well-planned analytic strategy. Absent these qualities, it is easy to see how action research might be misrepresented, misunderstood, and perhaps even fairly critiqued.

SELECTING AN ACTION RESEARCH TYPE

Given your interest in improving your PLC, you decide to undertake an action research study that will look carefully at the decision-making process in your PLC. While you at first thought of conducting your action research study with your colleagues as co-researchers and thus employing a participatory action research approach, you instead decide that you will use Stringer's (2014) *Look-Think-Act* model. You feel that this model is best suited for your study, as your goal is to understand why your colleagues feel as though decisions are being made without their input and what you (in collaboration with your colleagues) can do to improve the decision-making process. You also realize that the participatory action research model is one that focuses more specifically on critical social issues and you have not conceptualized your topic as such.

Further, you are unsure whether your colleagues would be interested in being involved as co-researchers, which presents you with some ethical concerns. Given these challenges, you are not comfortable conducting a study involving your colleagues as co-researchers, as it would potentially undermine your goal of understanding the current decision-making processes.

Focus Questions

1. What types of data might you collect in order to better understand how your colleagues view the current decision-making process?

2. What are some of the ethical challenges you may face as you work closely with your colleagues to understand the decision-making process?

THE ACTION RESEARCH CYCLE

The action research process rests on an inquiry cycle, as illustrated in Figure 11.1.

As Stringer (2014) highlighted, this cycle ". . . provides the means to systematically investigate and design more effective solutions to the complex array of issues at work in any social setting" (p. 5). This inquiry cycle rests on five steps. First, action research calls upon you as a practitioner-scholar to identify a problem of practice that can be studied and addressed. For instance, if you are a principal, you may use an action research approach to explore the potential barriers to implementing a new decision-making model. Second, action research involves the systematic collection of data potentially through both qualitative and quantitative means. So, as a principal interested in studying your new decision-making model, you may want to carry out interviews with your teacher leaders and conduct an anonymous survey with all teachers at your school about their views on the decision-making process. Third, action research involves careful analysis of the data to address underlying causes or explanations for the phenomenon of focus. As such, after collecting and analyzing interview and survey data, you may find that novice teachers in your school are more comfortable offering their opinions than are veteran teachers. Fourth, action research involves developing interventions or responses to the phenomenon of focus. Thus, in the example here, you might create a new decision-making model in which you include opportunities for *both* novice and veteran teachers to participate in decision-making and voice their perspectives openly. Finally, action research requires practitioner-scholars to assess whether the intervention had an effect. Thus, after implementing your new decision-making

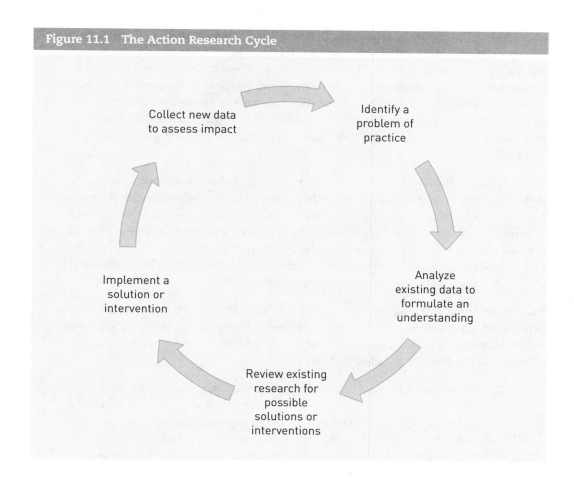

Figure 11.1 The Action Research Cycle

Collect new data to assess impact

Identify a problem of practice

Analyze existing data to formulate an understanding

Review existing research for possible solutions or interventions

Implement a solution or intervention

model, you may conduct another anonymous survey of all teachers in your building to determine whether the decision-making climate had changed.

Identify a Problem of Practice for an Action Research Study

Similar to the other research methodologies we have discussed, practitioner-scholars who engage in action research should begin by identifying a problem of practice that can be studied. Unlike other research methodologies, however, these problems of practice are often found exclusively in your classroom, school, district, or community. For example, as a classroom teacher you might find that many of your students are struggling with a particular reading concept year after year. This might be an appropriate issue for which to use action research if your primary aim is to improve student performance on this concept. Similarly, if you are a school leader and have observed increasing numbers of behavioral issues in several classrooms, it might be appropriate to identify a particular response to a behavioral concern to see if the response influences the behavioral patterns you have observed.

What is a good action research topic? This question is perhaps one of the most challenging to answer for practitioner-scholars who are beginning their first action-research study. Johnson (2008) highlighted three potential areas where a practitioner-scholar might focus their action research study: (a) instructional practices, (b) unexplained problems, or (c) an emerging area of interest. Mertler and Charles (2011) expanded on these topics to include the classroom environment, instructional materials used within teachers' work, strategies for classroom management, student achievement, grade or assessment practices, and communication with parents and colleagues. Each of these topics is directly tied to your work as a practitioner-scholar. Indeed, as Mertler (2014) noted, "since personal and professional experience are so central to . . . action research, possible topics for investigation might be anything about which you are curious" (p. 39).

While Mertler's (2014) words accurately reflect the breadth of action research topics generally, we suggest that practitioner-scholars consider the following characteristics when selecting a research topic. First, as Mertler suggested, action research topics should be inherently grounded in the practitioner-scholars' practice. The topic should serve as an opportunity to study, reflect on, and improve your practice as a practitioner-scholar. Ideally, your practice should change as a result of the action research study. In fact, this is the primary goal for conducting an action research study—changing practice to improve teaching, learning, or leading.

Second, action research topics should be clearly bounded within the context of a classroom, department, school, district, or a particular community. The action research study should live in your classroom, school, or community, and as such, the same study may not be as relevant or applicable to another setting. As Stringer (2014) noted:

> Action research . . . is based on the proposition that generalized solutions, plans, or programs may not fit all contexts or groups to whom they are applied and that the purpose of inquiry is to find an appropriate solution for the particular dynamics at work in a local situation. . . . Generalized solutions must be modified and adapted in order to fit the context in which they are used. (p. 5)

This proposition relates to research in two important ways. First, it presumes that action research studies may not be generalizable; that is, their findings may be so unique or contextually bound that the only way that another practitioner-scholar might be able to interact with these findings is to view them as a description of a particular practice. Second, it presumes that action research studies both reflect the local context, as well as seek to influence it. Action research is thus dynamically situated in the local (lived) context and therefore should be integrally embedded in your daily work as a classroom teacher, school administrator, or district leader. From the Field 11.2 highlights an example of how an action research study focused on introducing iPad technology to help students with developmental disabilities was described as being located within a very particular context.

Given the embedded nature of action research, it is essential that the topic for an action research study be clearly identified, particularly when the study employs some form of intervention. A key question for a practitioner-scholar employing an action research design with an intervention is to be able to succinctly answer: How does this differ from my every day practice? Thus, it may be helpful to think of this as "limiting the topic" (Mertler, 2014, p. 39); in other words, narrowing the topic so that it can be studied within the context of an action research study and distinguished from your daily practice.

Description of a Setting of an Action Research Study

The high school in which the presented study took place is a part of a private Jewish college in Sydney's eastern suburbs that serves over 1800 students in years Kindergarten–12. The special education department operates under the title of EST [education support team], and consists of one psychologist, five teachers, and two teacher aides. The EST supports the students academically and socially through the use of Individual Education Plans (IEPs), modified curricula, specialized teaching, counseling, and life skills training. Although the school has since implemented a one-on-one student laptop program and extended its iPad program to music classes, at the time of this study, students had access to Information and Communications Technology (ICT) only through the use of classroom desktops and computer labs. The lack of portability of this technology limited the opportunities that students had to employ it in their studies.

Source: Cumming, Strnadova, & Singh, 2014, p. 155

 Read the full article at:
www.sagepub.com/lochmiller

Third, the problem or topic should be of current and future interest to you and/or your colleagues. One of the key features of an action research study is its relevance to practice. As illustrated in Table 11.1 below, the topics selected for an action research study are often descriptions of a common, everyday problem that teachers, administrators, and other educators face. Note that each of the problems is formulated as an action statement and not as a more typical research problem statement. Further, each of the problems is tightly scoped; that is, the research activities are completed in a specific setting for a specific purpose with the aim of improving a particular practice.

Analyze Existing Data to Develop an Explanation

Once you have established a topic for your action research study, it is important to begin your action research study by examining existing data to develop a potential explanation. The data you use at this stage of the action research study may come from a variety of sources. For example, if you intend to focus your action research study on students' motivation to read chapter books, you might begin by reviewing recently completed reading logs from your students. These logs may have been collected as part of an assignment or reading unit and not originally intended for use as part of an action research study. Nonetheless, these reading logs become an important source of information for developing an understanding of the problem and to begin identifying potential explanations that can be used to formulate an intervention. Similarly, you might conduct a short, in-class survey of students to identify the amount of time they are reading at home, whether or not they are reading with a parent, and how frequently they read a chapter book when they are not in school. Both sources of data provide you with an initial understanding of the problem and thus allow you to begin formulating a response based on the data rather than your hunches alone.

Given the embedded nature of action research, we strongly encourage you to use data sources that are already accessible within your classroom or school during this initial stage. We also encourage you to reflect on your practice at this stage to identify what you are currently doing. For example,

Table 11.1 Illustrative Action Research Study Topics

Location	Study Topic
Classroom	• Reviewing a classroom-based language mentoring program that helps students who are learning English • Exploring strategies that help students become independent learners within the context of a scripted curriculum • Examining whether grouping strategies improve cooperative learning in a third grade classroom • Exploring the importance of character education in a middle school education program • Reviewing strategies to integrate fine arts in social studies curriculum • Using interactive notebooks to help students improve their achievement • Using student facilitation to improve family involvement in classroom activities
School	• Improving relationships among novice and veteran classroom teachers in a high-poverty elementary school • Reviewing how professional development on data use informs response-to-intervention strategies • Exploring strategies to improve parent participation in the school's parent-teacher organization • Reviewing student discipline practices and their association with specific behavioral patterns in fifth grade • Improving relationships on a fourth grade instructional team • Reviewing the decision-making processes among math teachers in an urban high school
District Central Office	• Improving responsiveness in a school district's teaching and learning department • Reviewing decision-making protocols between the superintendent and school board • Enhancing relationships between a new school board member and the district's board chair

if you are studying student motivation in reading, a reflective question you may wish to ask yourself might be: "How do my actions as a classroom teacher potentially impede or influence my student's motivation to read?" This question provides you with an opportunity to reflect on your responsibility for your students' current behavior and to identify personal behaviors that you could change that might potentially improve your students' motivation. Indeed, we see the link between a practitioner-scholars' current practice and their understanding of the problem in an action research study as being inherently related. One of the strengths of an action research study is that it provides you with meaningful opportunities to reflect on your practice and thus become a more reflective and thoughtful practitioner.

Develop an Intervention or Response

After reviewing the data, your next task is to develop an intervention or response. An intervention is a central component of an action research study and should be a carefully developed part of the overall research effort. An intervention is simply an action that you take to address the challenge or problem as you define it. Interventions may range from adjusting how you teach a particular part of a lesson to providing specific instructional activities for students who are struggling with a particular concept to developing a new decision-making model to be used within your school or district. The intervention should be developed in response to your analysis of the data and should directly respond to the findings from your analysis. For example, if data from your classroom indicate that students are struggling to understand compound fractions, your intervention should seek to address their struggles.

There are three important considerations when developing an intervention for an action research study. First, the intervention you select should be rooted in published literature, while also taking into account your professional judgment. While it may be tempting to simply rely solely on your professional judgment as a classroom teacher or school administrator, action researchers should always consult the literature to identify practices that have been shown to work with students, groups of students, or in specific educational settings. These practices can be found in any number of published educational journals, as noted in Chapter 3's discussion of the literature review, and ensure that what you do in your action research study has some basis in existing research. In effect, the purpose of an action research study is to put research to use and thus it is imperative that you identify interventions that have already been tested or explored (at least to some extent).

Second, the intervention you select should be clearly defined and distinct from your everyday practice. A pre-test or baseline should be collected or measured to document the outcomes prior to the intervention. The intervention should be introduced after this documentation is complete and used only for a specific amount of time (for instance, a school-year, semester, or trimester).

Third, outcomes after the intervention should be collected or measured to determine whether the intervention had any effect. The length of time the intervention is used should be rooted in the existing research, which would describe when the intervention is expected to be most effective and under what conditions it has been shown to have the most impact on students and/ or their learning.

What, then, are possible interventions that you might explore in an action research study? The interventions should typically be rooted within your daily work. For example, if you are interested in improving your students' motivation to read chapter books, you could introduce an incentive structure that recognized the number of books a student reads over time; you could increase the students' opportunities to select books from a defined list that are age appropriate; you could engage parents in helping instill positive reading examples at home; or you could launch an afterschool reading club that provides opportunities for students to read, discuss, and engage in arts-based activities connected to the readings. Each of these interventions are clearly defined and can have an outcome specifically associated with them. Moreover, they are interventions that can be studied in the empirical literature prior to identifying which intervention you employ.

We recognize that these interventions are classroom-based and that they may not work as well for a practitioner-scholar who leads a school or works in a district central office. Thus, what are interventions that could be introduced if you are in such a leadership role? If you are a building principal who is interested in improving parent participation in your school's parent-teacher organization, for example, you might focus your interventions on removing the barriers that customarily prevent parents from attending school events. For example, you might partner with a local employer who employs a large number of your parents to hold the parent-teacher organization meeting onsite during the employees' lunch hour. Similarly, you might work with the same employer to market and/or encourage parents to attend family events at the school through the employer's newsletters or internal communications. Both

REFLECTIVE OPPORTUNITY 11.2

Ethical considerations are particularly important in action research studies given both the situated nature of the research process (that is, it is occurring in your own classroom—where boundaries associated with research ethics may be less clear) and the immediate impact that your study may have on students (for example, an immediate change in curriculum could potentially have an immediate impact on students). Thus, we encourage you to consider the following questions when carrying out an action research study:

1. How will you ensure that your participants feel comfortable indicating that they do not want to participate in your action research study?

2. What measures will you take to create opportunities for participants to voice their perspectives on the interventions that are being used?

3. What will you do if a participant indicates that they are not comfortable being subjected to a particular intervention?

interventions seek to improve parent participation and thus could reasonably be studied in an action research study that is situated at the school or district level.

Systematically Collect Qualitative and Quantitative Data

After identifying the problem of practice for your action research study and implementing an intervention, you should begin collecting data in a systematic way. Ideally, you should collect data before you introduce the intervention so that you have clearly established a baseline for your participants' performance prior to the intervention being implemented. Much like other research methods we describe in this textbook, action research studies employ many of the same data collection techniques (such as interviews, observations, and surveys) and should adhere to the same standards as a traditional (basic) research study. Further, the same care should be taken to ensure that qualitative and quantitative data align with the overarching research questions and are guided by a specific protocol or design, and that all research decisions are fully catalogued or detailed. Indeed, a common critique of action research is that its emphasis on practice gives way to sloppy data collection. This is something that can be fully avoided by being systematic and thoughtful throughout the action research process.

As illustrated in Table 11.2, we suggest that you develop a multilevel data collection strategy whereby you are collecting information about the students, your practice as a practitioner, and the environment in your classroom, school, district, and/or community. As illustrated below, student-level data could include examples of student work and recent assessments as well as perception data gathered through surveys or interviews. Perception data refers to data that center on the perceptions or perspectives of the participants. At the level of practice, we suggest that you record your thoughts and reflections in journals so that you maintain a record of your practice and note how your thinking about your practice evolves as the action research study takes place. Finally, you should also collect data about your classroom, school, district, and/or community. This might include lesson plans, notes from a peer observation, and/or copies of forms and other documents

Table 11.2　Multilevel Data Collection in an Action Research Study

Level	Types of Data Collected
Student	Examples of student work (e.g., reading logs, reflections about chapter books) Assessment data (e.g., reading quizzes, tests) Perception data (e.g., surveys about reading behaviors at home)
Practice	Reflections and journal entries about your practice
Classroom	Examples of lesson plans or class assignments Notes from a peer observation
School	Student achievement data Teacher perception data (e.g., surveys about the implementation process of a new curriculum) School improvement planning document Copies of the master schedule
District	District achievement data Perception data (e.g., surveys about decision-making experiences at the school and district level) School district strategic plan District curriculum materials

that you use to monitor your students' behaviors. Much of this information should be collected *before* you implement the intervention so that it forms a baseline with which you can compare students' or others' performance after the intervention has been introduced.

Analyze Data to Identify Potential Explanations

As we mentioned previously, action research draws on many of the same analytic procedures used in qualitative research (see Chapter 8) and quantitative research (see Chapter 9). Practitioner-scholars who undertake an action research study often analyze their data to identify patterns that explain how the problem identified in the action research study emerged and what the problem may be related to. For qualitative data, this approach is similar to thematic analyses, whereby the practitioner-scholar identifies broad, emergent themes from their data. For example, a theme such as the "role of parental support in reading motivation" might emerge if interviews with students make recurring references to a parent's role in supporting their reading behaviors at home.

Assess the Impact of the Intervention or Response

A critical question for practitioner-scholars who engage in action research is whether an intervention worked. While action research studies do not permit practitioner-scholars to make claims about causation (that is, that the intervention led to a specified outcome), these studies do permit practitioner-scholars to draw inferences about the relationship among the intervention and the observable outcomes. The nature of the intervention lends itself to either a qualitative or quantitative analysis. For example, if your intervention is primarily interested in improving student achievement, it is likely that you will employ a quantitative analysis to determine whether the intervention worked. If, however, your intervention was primarily related to the perspectives of classroom teachers or a process in the school (for example, decision-making practices), your

⚓ LINK TO PRACTICE 11.2

CONDUCTING AN ACTION RESEARCH STUDY

After selecting Stringer's (2014) action research model, you next begin formulating your action research problem statement. Your primary interest is in improving the decision-making process in your PLC; however, your PLC has only three members and is thus quite a small sample size. Thus, you decide to focus your study on all of the teachers in your school and plan to explore the following questions: "How do elementary teachers participating in PLCs perceive that decision making occurs? What could be done to improve the decision-making process throughout the school and in grade level PLCs specifically?" Your focus on all PLCs allows for your colleagues to be more open and will ultimately give you data that allow you to fully understand the views of your colleagues.

Consistent with Stringer's model, your aim is primarily to define the problem as you and your colleagues perceive it and then to take actions to improve it. To this end, the *Look* phase of your study will begin with an anonymous survey of the teachers in your school. The survey provides baseline data about the teachers' views and also offers them an opportunity to share their views regarding factors that prevent them from feeling that their voice is valued. In addition, you collect meeting minutes from each of the PLCs to examine what decisions were made in the past school year and who was involved. Finally, you observe PLC meetings in two additional grade levels apart from your own to document the ways in which decisions are made.

Taken together, your data suggest that veteran teachers in each of the PLCs make most of the decisions and that novice teachers tend to feel less safe. As one teacher wrote in their survey, "I feel like the principal only listens to the teachers who have been here the longest, and so we all sort of default to them as our leaders." Indeed, after analyzing the data, you realize that senior teachers dominate conversations in PLCs and tend to discourage novice teachers from sharing their views—perhaps unintentionally. Thus, in the *Think* phase of your study, you realize that this "old versus young" dynamic partly explains the difficulties reaching consensus in the PLCs. It also explains why so many teachers with whom you interact—mostly novice teachers—feel left out of the decision-making process.

While the problem is clearer, you now face an interesting challenge. How should you implement changes so that all of your colleagues feel that their voice is valued in the decision-making process? In this *Act* phase of your study, you decide that you will begin first by sharing the results/findings of your study with the entire school. You see this as an opportunity to educate your colleagues about the issues. Further, you will use this opportunity as a way to encourage your principal to provide training for classroom teachers in the area of PLC facilitation. From your vantage point, you think that making your veteran colleagues aware of the views of the novice teachers, as well as helping them gain the skills needed to engage in a more collaborative decision-making process, will be beneficial for all. You plan to conduct a follow-up survey in six months to determine whether your efforts have improved the decision-making processes.

Focus Questions

1. What are the ways in which you might create a research environment in which all individuals feel safe sharing their perceptions with you regarding the decision-making process currently employed in the PLC?

2. What are some of the ethical concerns that might arise as you begin sharing your early findings with your colleagues?

REFLECTIVE OPPORTUNITY 11.3

Action research studies often unearth previously unknown disagreements or concerns within a school staff, leading to ethical challenges for the practitioner-scholar. Consider the following three questions as you reflect upon how you might navigate these challenges:

1. How might an action research study, which potentially identifies the concerns of one school-based employee group (such as novice teachers), expose or potentially introduce conflict within a school?

2. How might you, as a practitioner-scholar, thoughtfully mitigate the fallout from action research findings?

3. What are the ways in which you might involve all participants in making sense of and thoughtfully responding to an action research study's findings?

analysis will likely be qualitative in nature. Chapters 8 and 9 discuss the analytic approaches for both qualitative and quantitative data and provide you with more detail regarding the analytic process that you will need to use.

UNIQUE CONSIDERATIONS FOR ACTION RESEARCH

Given the unique nature of action research, it is important that you consider issues related to reflection, your role as a researcher, and research ethics when undertaking an action research study. First, when you conduct research in a familiar setting with participants with whom you are very familiar, it is imperative that you engage in reflection throughout the research process. As your familiarity with the research setting will influence how you think about the study, your participants, and your analysis, it is imperative that you continuously reflect upon how your own biases, assumptions, and/or perspectives might shape what you are seeing (or not seeing) as a researcher. Chronicling your thinking and even inviting feedback from colleagues, supervisors, and university advisers is wise.

A further consideration relates to the way(s) that your position as a classroom teacher or school administrator might shape how participants respond to your study. In research terms, we refer to this as your role as a researcher. Your role as a researcher, particularly as it relates to your power and authority over your research participants, is a very important consideration in action research, especially as you may be working with individuals who may not feel comfortable expressing their desire *not* to participate in your study. For instance, if you are conducting a study in your own classroom with your students, you, as the researcher and teacher, have considerable power over your participants. Your role as a teacher will influence how students talk about their experience in your classroom and this will influence what data you collect. Thus, if your goal is to identify what students are experiencing as students in your classroom, it may be important to consider how your role and position influences your students and what steps you can take to mitigate this. For example, if you are using interviews in your study, you might ask a trained colleague to conduct the interviews so that students do not feel intimidated or threatened when they speak about their experiences in your classroom. The key is to think about your data-collection process in relation to your role as a researcher who has many identities; that is, you are not solely a researcher, but also a practitioner.

The final consideration relates to research ethics. As we highlight throughout this textbook, research ethics involves far more than successfully completing an Institutional Review Board application. Indeed, as Mockler (2014) noted, ethics in action research acutely considers how we treat research participants, how we make sense of the data we collect, and the care with which we report our research results/findings. The final point around reporting your research results/findings is particularly important in action research. While one of the hallmarks of action research is that the research report/paper is written in an accessible and practical way, it should maintain the confidentiality of research participants. We suggest that many of the approaches taken in other types of research apply to action research. For example, using pseudonyms, avoiding providing too much background information about individual students, and withholding some identifiable characteristics are important steps that you can take to ensure confidentiality. As you complete your action research study, it is critical to be thoughtful about how you engage with research ethics and continually check in with your participants regarding their experience as research participants in your study.

USING TECHNOLOGY IN ACTION RESEARCH

We view technology as an important tool in action research studies. In particular, the use of blogs or websites can be used to catalog the research process, document your thoughts about the research, and share findings and ideas with your colleagues. Blogs (or web-logs) can be defined as "easy-to-update websites characterized by dated entries displayed in reverse chronological order" (Stefanc, 2006, p. 230). You can think about a blog as an online journal or diary, wherein "persistent conversations" can occur and "be referenced months or years later" (Paulus, Lester, & Dempster, 2014, p. 15). Further, blogs can be publically shared or kept private, depending on the purpose. For instance, From the Field 11.3 highlights how blogs were used in an action research study of iPad uses with students with developmental disabilities.

We suggest that there are three primary reasons to use a blog when completing an action research study. First, blogs help you create a digital record of the action research study. Maintaining clear records of your unfolding thinking and reflections is critical throughout the research process. A blog is one space wherein you might chronicle certain aspects of your research process, while also potentially inviting the participation of others. Thus, second, blogs are one means by which to collaborate and share with others. In action research, it is often helpful to find systematic ways to share your research findings with your larger community. One way to do this is via a blog. However, it is also important to keep in mind that in doing so, you want to be thoughtful about what types of information you publically disclose. It is simply good practice to assure that the identities of research participants remain private, whether writing on a blog or elsewhere. Third, blogs have been frequently described as tools for reflection and the practice of researcher reflexivity (LaBanca, 2011), a concept we discussed in Chapter 5.

There are a variety of free blogging platforms, such as WordPress or Blogger, that provide practitioner-scholars with a powerful forum to capture their thinking about the action research process. Blogger can be easily integrated into your Google e-mail service and Gmail. Such blogs can be kept private or shared publically, depending on the nature of the action research project, as highlighted in Figure 11.2. Deciding whether to maintain a public versus a private blog is a critical decision, as this requires that you also examine the sensitivity of your study and any potential reasons for not making your ideas and research process public.

Description of the Use of a Blog in an Action Research Study

The teacher blog was used before and during the implementation of the iPads. In Term 1, the teachers used the blog to share research and news articles about iPad and technology use in classrooms, as well as to share apps that they found that they felt would be beneficial for teaching and learning integration. In Terms 2–4, they used the blog to share their experiences, and post pictures of students using the iPad in their classes. Posting on the blog was voluntary; therefore there were different rates of posts from each teacher. Teacher MD posted 10 times and MC posted 9 times, but the other teachers only posted once or twice. When asked about this during the focus group, the teachers explained that once the iPads were implemented, they found it to be "just one more thing to do," and unnecessary, since they were sharing information with each other informally in the teachers' lounge and formally during their biweekly team meetings. They thought it would be helpful for potential readers of the blog (possibly teachers collaborating at a distance) though. Overall, the blog was a space for teachers to share their experiences with implementing iPads and using the devices as an instructional tool. Thus the blog presents another source of data, which was used in triangulation with interviews and focus group. All sources of data were analyzed following the inductive content analysis approach.

Source: Cumming, Strnadova, & Singh, 2014, pp. 163–164

 Read the full article at:
www.sagepub.com/lochmiller

If you are collaborating with two colleagues, you may want to only share your blog site with them. In fact, you may all contribute to the blog site, interacting through the course of your study. On the other hand, you may want to maintain a public blog site, wherein you invite colleagues and the general public to read about and comment on your research process. Figure 11.3 provides an example of how a practitioner-scholar might maintain a public blog site chronicling their action research study. The practitioner-scholar might make weekly entries or reflections highlighting where they are at in the inquiry cycle, as well as noting their next steps.

Similarly, Figure 11.4 presents an example of how a researcher used a website as a space for chronicling a participatory action research study, as well as more broadly sharing the study's findings.

Figure 11.2 Public Versus Private Settings in Blogger

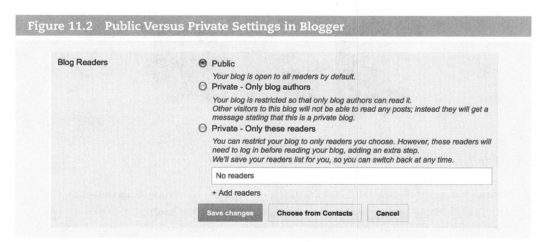

Source: Blogger.com

Figure 11.3   An Example of an Action Research Study Blog

Action Research: Examining the PLC

Tuesday, March 24, 2015

Week One: Reflections on Identifying a Problem of Practice

I've been thinking quite a bit about how I might focus my action research study. I'm really interested in exploring the Professional Learning Community (PLC) in our school building. We've had so many issues lately related to decision-making and the PLC seems a place where this is made visible. I think this likely is impacting the climate of the school generally, at least among the staff. I'm starting to think that perhaps I could carry out an action research study, with the aim of better understanding how decision-making is understood within the PLC.

Posted by Jessica Nina Lester at 8:55 AM   No comments:

M□ ⅀ ♥ ❏ ♥ 8·1 Recommend this on Google

About Me

▢ Jessica Nina Lester
View my complete profile

Blog Archive

▼ 2015 (1)
  ▼ March (1)
    Week One: Reflections on
    Identifying a Problem of ...

Maybe a true collective, where power is equally shared and voices equally valued can never really be achieved. But we can reach for that. We can work toward it. And we can talk openly and honestly about our successes and our failures in those struggles.

And that's better than nothing, right?

So here, on these pages, is an effort to make ourselves known, in our own words. Mrs. James introduces herself and talks a bit about her goals and her thoughts on the project and on her SSS students.

The SSS students get a chance to introduce themselves – in their own words, as well as to reflect on the process and the project – in their own words.

And Meagan takes an opportunity to introduce herself and as openly and honestly as possible to lay out her positionality in relation to this project, as well as her thoughts on how it went.

About Mrs. James   About the Students   About Meagan

Source: http://researchforempowerment.com/

As Figure 11.3 and 11.4 illustrate, blogs and other online communication tools provide practitioner-scholars with a powerful resource to conduct an action research study. Moreover, consistent with the goal of action research (that is, to improve practice), blogs create meaningful opportunities to link the practitioner-scholar's research with their work as a practitioner.

REFLECTIVE OPPORTUNITY 11.4

While using a blog to chronicle your research process is a practical and useful way to make your research process transparent, it can also lead to ethical dilemmas. Take a few moments to consider the following questions:

1. What are some concrete things you might do to protect your participants' identities when making a blog post?

2. Why might you choose to maintain a public versus a private blog?

3. What are some of the ways in which the public nature of blogs or websites may impact the bounded nature of your action research study?

SUMMARY

In this chapter, we provided you with an opportunity to consider action research, and, to a lesser extent, participatory action research. We highlighted the inquiry cycle associated with an action research study. In particular, we described how you move from a problem of practice to an action research design. We concluded the chapter by illustrating how technology such as blogs or websites is a useful tool for practitioner-scholars seeking to chronicle their practice in an action research or participatory action research study, as well as to invite colleagues and the community as a whole into the research process.

KEY TERMS

Blogs 248

Intervention 242

Participatory Action Research 236

Perception Data 244

Web logs 248

QUESTIONS TO CONSIDER

1. What are the unique characteristics of action research studies?

2. What are some of the unique characteristics of participatory action research studies?

3. How might you determine which type of action research study to use?

4. What are the key criticisms of action research and how might you respond to them?

5. What are the steps in the action research cycle? Provide an example for each.

6. What are some of the ethical dilemmas that you might face in an action research study? How might some of these issues be unique to the nature of action research?

7. How might blogs or websites be used in an action research study?

CHAPTER EXERCISES

1. Similar to Table 11.1, construct a list of potential problems of practice specific to your professional context that could be practically studied through action research.

2. Assume that you are a classroom teacher or school administrator who is interested in improving practice at your school. Using the action research inquiry cycle described in this chapter, develop an action research study that would enable you to carefully examine and make recommendations about improving classroom instruction. Specifically, identify a problem of practice, explain what data you would need to collect to establish a baseline understanding of the problem, explain how you would analyze these data, and describe how you would develop an intervention based on your understanding of the data. Finally, explain how you would assess the impact of the intervention you developed and implemented.

3. McIntyre (2008) offered four tenets of participatory action research, as described earlier. As you think about your own professional context and the possibility to engage in participatory action research, identify: (a) a social issue/problem that your school community may have a joint commitment to investigating; (b) how you might collectively engage in critical reflection and practically investigate the issue; (c) what types of collective activities might assist you in coming to a useful solution as a group; and (d) how you might build alliances among the individuals and groups involved in the study.

4. Using a free online blogging platform such as Blogger or Wordpress, set up a blog that chronicles some aspect of your current work. Use this site much like a journal or diary to record your practice, reflective questions, challenges, and hunches. After recording your thoughts and ideas over the course of several weeks, begin to consider them in relation to the literature. This will allow you to begin using your blog as a space to develop an action research study. You may also want to invite colleagues to participate, particularly if you envision pursuing a collaborative action research project.

LEARNING EXTENSIONS

McIntyre's (2008) book, *Participatory Action Research*, provides a general overview of participatory action research. It highlights three dimensions of participatory action research projects, using two example projects to illustrate the key ideas. Stringer's (2014) book, *Action Research*, is a useful resource for practitioner-scholars seeking an action research model that emphasizes problem identification. This particular model is widely used by school administrators as part of their efforts to improve classroom instruction and student achievement. The model has also been widely used in master's theses and doctoral dissertations as a conceptual framework.

Sharpen your skills with SAGE edge!

edge.sagepub.com/lochmiller

SAGE edge for Students provides a personalized approach to help you accomplish your coursework goals in an easy-to-use learning environment. You'll find action plans, mobile-friendly eFlashcards, and quizzes as well as videos, web resources, and links to SAGE journal articles to support and expand on the concepts presented in this chapter.

PART III

PRODUCING RESEARCH
TO IMPROVE PRACTICE

The third and final part of the textbook considers how you might go about writing up and sharing your research with a broader audience. This section also offers a general review of the research process, while returning to the problems of practice presented in Part I. Within Part III of the textbook, the connection to your daily work is revisited, with the aim being to highlight how your daily practice might inform research and research might inform your daily practice.

12

WRITING THE RESEARCH

WRITING UP YOUR RESEARCH FINDINGS

After completing your research study, analyzing your data, and generating initial findings you are now ready to begin writing up your results/findings. At first, you are not sure how to begin writing and are not even clear about what a research report/paper should look like. You have often found the writing process to be intimidating, and this task is especially difficult given it is your first research study. What audience should you write for? How should you present your findings? What data should you use to support your claims? How should you tie your research to the existing literature? How should you structure your research report/paper? What comes first in your research report/paper? You recognize that these are all important considerations as you begin the writing process. Further, you realize that the way you write up your research will shape how others view and interpret your research study. As such, you understand that thinking about the writing process is an important step in the research process.

INTRODUCTION

As illustrated in the opening vignette, writing is central to the research process. Writing is required as you develop your research proposal, carry out your research, complete your analysis, and ultimately share your research findings. Thinking through the writing process is important, particularly in that academic writing requires a particular way of thinking and writing. Indeed, it is the particularity of academic writing that often proves challenging for practitioner-scholars. Academic writing is structured and at times quite technical. Thus, for many practitioner-scholars, academic writing feels much like learning to speak a foreign language. However, we assure you, once you have become familiar with the process, writing can be very enjoyable.

Learning Objectives

By the end of the chapter, you will be able to:

- Describe the main considerations for academic writing.

- Compare the various types of research reports.

- Explain the importance of considering your audience.

- Discuss the importance of using language carefully when writing research reports.

- Summarize the differences between qualitative and quantitative research reports.

- Identify technology tools that can be used to support writing up your research.

In this chapter, we discuss the main tenets of the academic writing process. In doing so, we highlight some key considerations and also share the basic structure of qualitative and quantitative research reports/papers. We give particular attention to the general differences between writing qualitative findings and quantitative results, recognizing that those who write mixed methods research studies must consider how to combine these two approaches to writing. We conclude by pointing to some technologies that can support your writing process.

ENGAGING IN THE ACADEMIC WRITING PROCESS

At its core, academic writing is about building an argument for the purpose of having a scholarly conversation with a particular audience—an audience who is typically associated with the field(s) in which you locate your research and who would be interested in your research activities. For instance, if you are studying instructional leadership behaviors by school principals or teachers thinking about curriculum, you are likely going to be writing for those who study the principalship or those who focus on the preparation and development of classroom teachers. In addition, as you engage in the academic writing process, you must keep in mind that your writing process is fundamentally about building an argument—the goal is for your research to contribute to the conversation. As a researcher, you must ground your argument in the interpretation of your data. With clear and concise writing, your aim is to invite the reader into the details of your study in a way in which they understand the nuances of your research process and see evidence for your argument. While the process of doing this varies from study to study, across your writing it will be critical to consider: (a) the type of report/paper you are generating, (b) your specific audience, (c) how your language choices shape your overarching message, and (d) your manuscript style (for example, APA versus MLA).

Determining the Type of Report or Paper

After you have completed your study, your research can be reported in different forms. For example, if you are a master's or doctoral student, your research will most likely be presented as a thesis or dissertation. A thesis or dissertation is an academic assignment that demonstrates to your graduate adviser and supervisory committee that you have mastered both the content that you studied and the research process. A thesis or dissertation tends to be a lengthy document because it requires that you show mastery on multiple levels ranging from the construction of a scholarly argument to the theoretical and technical development of your research methodology and methods. In contrast, a conference paper tends to be shorter and only shares a portion of a larger study. For instance, if your dissertation focused on the role that human resource staff assumed in supporting principals and classroom teachers, you might present a conference paper that highlights one aspect of your findings (for example, how central office administrators created tools to help the principals implement human resource initiatives). You might then revise this conference paper further and submit it as a formal journal article, which would subject your research to peer review and allow your findings to be consumed by a broader audience. Some practitioner-scholars may report their findings to their school or district in the form of a technical or policy report that seeks to inform decision making and practice. For instance, if you conducted your research around a specific intervention for students, district and school administrators may well be interested in your findings given the applicability to decision making within the district. As such, you may decide to disseminate your research in an easily consumable format that uses minimal jargon and focuses primarily on key findings and implications of greatest relevance to the stakeholders.

Considering Your Audience

Given the variety of forms that your writing can take, it is important to keep your audience in mind as you write. A good place to begin is to decide whether you are writing for a predominately practitioner audience or an academic audience. While it is certainly possible that you will be writing for multiple audiences, most often you need to select a primary audience, as this will impact the style in which you write your research report/paper. Your primary audience includes those individuals and/or organizations that you need to consider as you develop your research report/paper and who are most likely to be impacted by your research. Your secondary audience includes those individuals and/or organizations who might benefit from your research report/ paper, but who you did not design your comments to address directly.

To illustrate this point, it is useful to consider how various journals are designed to reach different audiences. Practitioner-oriented journals, such as *Phi Delta Kappan* or *Educational Leadership*, are popular journals that primarily aim to reach practitioners. Both of these journals are editorially reviewed (not peer-reviewed) and tend to publish shorter, highly accessible articles on current education topics of interest. Quite often, practitioner-scholars share broad insights drawn from a research study in these publication outlets, recognizing that the goal of such journals is not to share the nuances of a research study but to focus on the links to practice. From the Field 12.1 provides an excerpt from an article published in *Phi Delta Kappan* around teacher-leaders. Note how the tone is informal and conversational, as the writing is designed to be accessible to a broad audience.

As illustrated in From the Field 12.1 and 12.2, who you are writing for impacts how you convey your ideas, and, more generally, the writing style that you adopt. Even as a consumer of research, you have likely noted that some writing appears to use extensive jargon, or appears only accessible to a select audience. While academic writing is often viewed as minimally accessible and full of jargon, we encourage you to write in a clear and concise way regardless of your audience. As a practitioner-scholar, you should aim to develop a research report/paper that is both readable and broadly accessible. Your aim is not only that a fellow researcher can read your research but that one of your colleagues down the hall can read your research as well.

Making Thoughtful Language Choices

Part of maintaining accessibility is to think carefully about the words you choose to use and how you choose to use them. The language choices you make will impact not only the readability and accessibility of your research report/paper, but also the degree to which others view your work as grounded and sound. Indeed, it is important to familiarize yourself with the writing traditions within your field, while also recognizing that you may adopt other styles in hopes of being even more sensitive in your writing. Specifically, we encourage you to be precise and clear in your writing, which includes avoiding colloquial phrases (e.g., "practically all of the participants") and

An Example of a Publication Written for a Practitioner-Based Audience

Sometimes we are so accustomed to the way things are that we can't imagine a different way of doing things. For example, in 1927, one of the Warner brothers made a famously wrong prediction: "Who the hell wants to hear actors talk?"

When it comes to defining teacher leadership, how much do we limit ourselves by assuming that the way teachers work today must always be the way teachers work? Most of us assume that schools must be managed from the top down, so a teacher's job must be to implement and support whatever federal, state, and district leaders decide. We assume teachers are in charge of classroom management but not whole-school management.

We assume that if teachers want to progress professionally they must become administrators and leave their passion for teaching students behind. We assume "teacher voice" means having input in or being the face of someone else's ultimate decision. We assume teachers don't want to define these arrangements differently, and neither does anyone else.

In this context, educators and advocates have created and embraced professional learning communities (PLCs), hybrid roles, and teacher-led professional development. In some places, teachers can individually become curriculum specialists or project and team leaders. Teachers can even pursue a teacher leader certification to qualify them for such roles. These are excellent teacher leadership opportunities.

But limiting the scope of teacher leadership to opportunities that fit within current assumptions also limits teachers' potential to use their leadership positions to choose or invent fundamentally different approaches to schools and schooling. Twenty years from now with the perspective of hindsight, we might want to kick ourselves for this.

In contrast, From the Field 12.2, which is drawn from a case study about leadership practices in seven different nations published in a peer-reviewed journal, targets an academic audience. Note how the style is more formal, technical, and closely grounded in the research. Unlike From the Field 12.1, the text offers more details that help the reader to understand more fully the context of the research.

Source: Farris-Berg, 2014, pp. 31–32, Reprinted with permission of Phi Delta Kappa Internationa, www.pdkintl.org. All rights reserved.

Read the full article at:
www.sagepub.com/lochmiller

the continual use of jargon. You must also consider: (a) how to use language sensitively; (b) your use of pronouns; and (c) the manuscript style that you adopt.

USING LANGUAGE SENSITIVELY. Using language with sensitivity and care is a central consideration in academic writing, as language creates particular images and perspectives about the world, and about groups of people more specifically. How researchers come to describe people and places has tremendous consequences, and, therefore, as a practitioner-scholar, you must be reflective of how you use language. More generally, it is important to think about how you describe people, and avoid language that results in people losing their individuality (for instance, "the elderly") and/or being directly equated with a particular condition (for example, "learning disabled students"). In academic writing, it is generally expected that you use people first language, wherein you put the person first (for example, saying "child with dis-abilities" rather than "disabled child" (American Psychological Association, 2010). Further, whenever possible it is important to

FROM THE FIELD 12.2

An Example of a Publication Written for an Academic Audience

Increased public accountability has had a major impact on the work of principals across nations since the 1988 Education Reform Act (ERA) in England. ERA included a framework of national curriculum goals and standards, high-stakes accountability and open enrollments that used neoliberal market approaches to reward schools for increased student counts. Since the early 2000s, schools in the USA have operated under similar accountability pressures because of required and publicly reported annual testing as per No Child Left Behind (NCLB) and Race to the Top (RttT) mandates. Under this test-driven regime, schools that persistently fail to make adequate yearly progress face consequences including reconstitution and administrator/teacher loss of employment. In Norway and Sweden the accountability movement is more recent, but developments in educational policy and reform are nevertheless raising expectations about school performance. For example, though Swedish schools still rank high in international studies such as PISA, there is an on-going political discussion about that nation's quality of education based on indications that students are not doing as well as in the past. The governing alliance of conservative parties introduced a State Inspection Agency, as well as so-called "free schools," that are free from local school board control, but still required to follow the national curriculum. Embracing both a democratic "citizenship" mandate and the traditional knowledge mandate has placed new demands and expectations on Swedish principals. Similar tensions exist in Denmark, where for the

past 20 years the government has decentralized certain administrative responsibilities to local school authorities, including personnel management and numerous day-to-day financial tasks while, simultaneously, re-centralizing certain instructional tasks by prescribing more detailed adherence to national standards through accountability and evaluation tools like national tests and quality reports. For many Danish principals, these neoliberal managerial competencies are in tension with traditional Danish democratic purposes of schooling known as Bildung (Gurr et al., 2011a).

The Australian schools of the future program (Department of Education, 1993) is a relatively long-standing approach to self-governance focused on the decentralization of numerous school functions including selection of staff, control over the budget, the articulation of goals in a school charter and the design of a framework for accountability. Victoria was a forerunner in this approach and by 1997 it had been extended to all schools, making Australia's decentralization policies among the most far-reaching worldwide. In the USA, decentralization has always been relatively commonplace with each state maintaining an autonomous educational system, with many states then delegating considerable authority to the local school districts in their jurisdiction (Jacobson, 2005). In contrast, educational governance in Cyprus has long been highly centralized and bureaucratic and only recently has the Ministry begun to promote more local involvement in educational strategic planning.

Source: Ylimaki & Jacobson, 2013, pp. 7–8

give participants an opportunity to self-identify—that is, self-describe. As a practitioner-scholar, you should seek to avoid all pejorative and prejudiced language. Further, it is important to avoid using "one group (often the writer's own group) as the standard against which others are judged" (American Psychological Association, 2010, p. 72). For instance, you may be tempted to compare research participants to a standard that is based on your own experiences and perspectives. This is an important temptation to avoid, as you want to illustrate for a reader that you came to your research aware of your own biases (as much as possible). Quite often, insensitive language finds its way into research reports/papers perhaps unknowingly or out of habit; thus, we encourage you to: (a) remain thoughtful and critical about your word choices and (b) invite colleagues and others to review your work with a critical eye towards language use.

USING PRONOUNS. Your use of pronouns (such as I, me, we, they, these, those) is an important consideration in academic writing. It is important to use pronouns in a way that minimizes ambiguity (American Psychological Association, 2010). For example, rather than writing, "these tests" you might write, "the math tests." Your aim is to make the referent of the pronoun crystal clear. In addition, you need to think carefully about the point of view from which you write. Will you write from a first-person point of view or a third-person point of view? First, consider the norms of your field. Second, consider the expectations of a particular methodology. Historically, quantitative researchers have often used a third-person point of view in their writing, reflecting the way in which objective reporting has been conceived. In contrast, qualitative researchers commonly write from a first-person point of view, as they make clear that they are the research instrument. See, for example, From the Field 12.3, in which Gallo (2014) describes her qualitative research process from a first person point of view.

It is important to note, however, that there is variability in how point of view is taken up across methodologies, and thus critical for you to become familiar with the norms and expectations specific to a given methodology.

Third, it is generally recommended that you use personal pronouns rather than write in the third person, particularly when describing your research (American Psychological Association, 2010).

FROM THE FIELD 12.3

An Example of Writing From a First Person Point of View in a Qualitative Study

I collected all data in the languages used by participants. For example, all interviews and playback sessions with fathers were conducted in Spanish, whereas all interviews with teachers were conducted in English. Children sometimes had monolingual interactions and also translanguaged in English and Spanish (Garcıá, 2009), which I would reciprocate. For example, if they spoke to me in Spanish or English I would respond in Spanish or English, and if they translanguaged, drawing upon resources in both languages in a single interaction, I would do the same. One exception was in interactions with parents and children—no matter the language children addressed me in, I would respond in Spanish so that their parents could understand.

Source: Gallo, 2014, p. 482

 Read the full article at:
www.sagepub.com/lochmiller

⚓ LINK TO PRACTICE 12.1

ENGAGING IN THE ACADEMIC WRITING PROCESS

Having recently submitted the first draft of your manuscript to your adviser, you find yourself now awash in feedback about your research and how you went about writing about it. Points that you thought were clear appear to have been questioned with comments such as, "Define this term more clearly," "What does this mean?" and "Explain this further." Simple terms, like "instructional leadership" or "achievement gap," which you and your colleagues use on a daily basis, are now being questioned. While you view yourself as a fairly strong writer, you find the academic writing process to be frustrating. This frustration prompts you to reach out to your adviser to ask for more guidance.

You and your adviser meet and talk through her feedback. She explains that what you are experiencing is normal and simply part of learning to write for an academic audience. "Terms that are used by practitioners," she shares, "need to be clearly defined, supported, and linked to the literature." You realize that you cannot assume that your audience is as familiar with your ideas as your colleagues might be. She encourages you to be more precise in your writing. For example, she encourages you to use the same terms throughout your manuscript rather than introducing new terms that refer to the same concept. She says this will help your reader better understand and remember what you're talking about. "These minor tweaks," she says, "will strengthen your argument and add clarity to the presentation of your findings." After meeting with her, you realize that this process takes time and energy, but is worth the effort. In some ways, it is similar to learning a new language—the academic language.

Focus Questions

1. How might you keep track of the specific definitions of terms that you are using in your research report/paper?

2. What resources might you use to help you understand how to present research in an "academic tone" or "academic voice"?

Thus, rather than writing, "the authors reviewed the literature related to teacher retention," you should state, "we reviewed the literature related to teacher retention."

Finally, it is important to avoid using what is often referred to as the "editorial we." When you use "we", it should only be in reference to yourself and your co-authors. Rather than writing, "we know that teachers who leave the field point to a variety of reasons," you might write, "researchers have noted that teachers who leave the field point to a variety of reasons." Again, your goal is to be clear and concise.

USING APA MANUSCRIPT STYLE. Educational research most often uses an APA manuscript style. APA manuscript style offers standard rules and procedures for writing in a scholarly way, and covers issues ranging from word choice to verb tense to minimizing bias in writing to how to structure a manuscript (American Psychological Association, 2010). Specifically, the APA style manual offers "explicit style requirements but acknowledges that alternatives are sometimes necessary" (American Psychological Association, 1994, p. xxii). As a practitioner-scholar in the field of education, it is important to become familiar with APA manuscript style, as this will likely be the style that you adopt.

REFLECTIVE OPPORTUNITY 12.1

As both a consumer and producer of research, an important ethical concern relates to honestly reporting the research process. Honest reporting entails avoiding any data fabrication or data massaging, as well as assuring that what you share is accurate and represents your own ideas and efforts.

1. What are some steps that you might take as a consumer of research to evaluate the degree to which a researcher honestly reports the research process?
2. What are some steps that you, as a practitioner-scholar, might take to assure that you engage in honest reporting?

THE BASIC STRUCTURE OF A RESEARCH REPORT

When you begin thinking about the structure of a research report, it is important to understand that qualitative and quantitative research are frequently presented in slightly different ways. Qualitative research is typically presented as part of an integrated narrative that begins by establishing a context for the research, presents a thorough review of the literature, moves to discussing the research methodology and methods, and finally presents the findings of the research. A qualitative research report/paper concludes by discussing the study's findings within the context of the existing literature base. Quantitative research is presented as a structured narrative in which the researcher begins by establishing what is currently known about the issue that was studied, describes his or her hypothesis and research questions, presents the methods and analytic techniques that were used in completing their research, and ultimately presents the results of various statistical tests before relating these results to the existing literature base. The order of a manuscript partly reflects the exploratory and contextually situated nature of qualitative research compared with the confirmatory and often more positivist approach taken in quantitative research. Mixed methods research often requires you to combine these approaches in ways that allow you to integrate your research narrative so that qualitative findings and quantitative results are given equivalent attention in your research report. Figure 12.1 illustrates the main sections of a qualitative and quantitative manuscript. Next, we discuss some of the individual sections of a research report in greater detail.

Writing the Introduction

The purpose of the introductory section of your research report/paper is to explain what the purpose of your study is, as well as to situate your study within a broader context. Practitioner-scholars thus often begin by presenting background information or other details that educate the reader about the importance of the study or give a rationale that supports why the study was needed. In a qualitative study, the introduction further serves as an opportunity for the researcher to problematize the study, meaning to present the research topic as a challenge that merits scholarly examination. Put simply, qualitative researchers often use the introduction of their research report/paper to raise awareness or concern that justifies the need for the study in more critically oriented qualitative research. In less critically oriented qualitative research, the introduction serves as an opportunity to contextualize the problem by describing the policy,

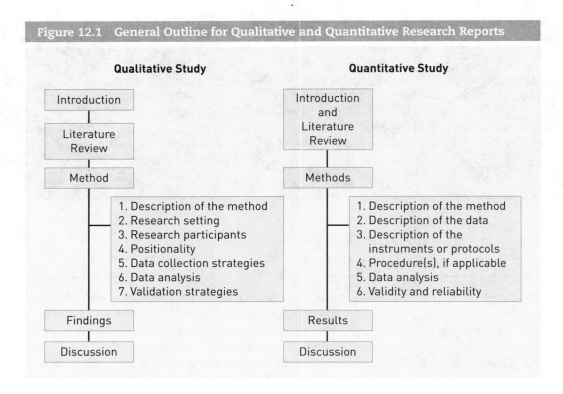

Figure 12.1 General Outline for Qualitative and Quantitative Research Reports

Qualitative Study

Introduction

Literature Review

Method

1. Description of the method
2. Research setting
3. Research participants
4. Positionality
5. Data collection strategies
6. Data analysis
7. Validation strategies

Findings

Discussion

Quantitative Study

Introduction and Literature Review

Methods

1. Description of the method
2. Description of the data
3. Description of the instruments or protocols
4. Procedure(s), if applicable
5. Data analysis
6. Validity and reliability

Results

Discussion

institution, practice, or individuals involved. The introduction in a qualitative research study typically ends with a list of the research questions that will be examined, which is preceded by a clear, succinct statement of the research problem.

Quantitative research studies often differ slightly in that the introduction and literature review may be blended and serve as an opportunity for the researcher to identify what is currently known. This acts to identify the current truth about the research problem. In the introduction, the practitioner-scholar presents background information, constructs an argument for their study, and identifies a theoretical perspective before presenting the research problem or research questions. The background serves as a justification for the study and provides evidence that the current study builds on the existing literature base. In a quantitative study, it is key that the reader understands these connections clearly upfront, as they are likely to inform the presentation of the research design, analysis, and ultimately the results/findings.

Writing the Literature Review

In Chapter 4, we discussed the process of conducting a literature review. At this stage, the challenge is less about finding the resources than about bringing the various references you collected into a coherent narrative. The literature review section of a qualitative or quantitative study may function slightly differently. In some qualitative studies, the purpose of the literature review is to contextualize the study in the larger literature base and make clear the researchers' theoretical and/or conceptual orientation. By the end of the literature review in a qualitative report/paper, you should have given the reader a clear understanding of the context for the research, as well as clearly stated your theoretical or conceptual ideas.

The literature review in a quantitative study may function slightly differently. The primary purpose of the literature review in a quantitative study is to summarize previous research and relate this work to the theoretical perspective that informed the analysis. Quantitative literature reviews thus spend less time contextualizing the research than providing clear links between the current research and the study that was completed. In quantitative research, this may include a hypothesis or set of hypotheses, as it is not uncommon to present the literature review in a way that builds support for your hypotheses.

Regardless of whether the literature review is written for a qualitative or quantitative study, it is essential that the review incorporates a healthy balance of summary, critique, and synthesis. Practitioner-scholars often assume that the purpose of a literature review is simply to summarize the existing research. While this is an important first step in the review, it is not sufficient. Rather, it is equally important that you spend time in your literature review critiquing the research that has been presented previously, as well as relating various results/findings to each other. Critiquing a research study does not mean simply rejecting its findings. Rather, it means reviewing the study to identify gaps, missed opportunities, or findings that warrant further explanation. Critiquing literature in the literature review is intended to expand on the existing research while providing a rationale for the study that you conducted.

Similarly, it is important that your writing for a literature review move beyond simply summarizing or critiquing the existing research. Your review should also relate various studies to each other. This process is referred to as synthesizing existing research. This process is critical as it helps the reader of your research paper/report to understand where potential gaps exist, as well as make sense of the argument for why your study is needed and important. For example, if you conducted a literature review that focused primarily on teacher leadership behaviors, you would want to note salient connections across the studies you reviewed, as well as various disconnects or gaps that you feel require further examination. Thus, the importance of synthesizing various previous studies is to help the reader understand how you made sense of the existing literature, and why and how your study contributes to the existing literature in a meaningful way.

Writing the Methods Section

The methods section is intended to present your approach to completing the research study in clear and comprehensive terms. Your methods section is not intended to be a work of creative writing. Rather, your methods section is intended to be a clear reporting of the steps that you took to complete your study. While the format for a methods section in a qualitative and quantitative study differs, the basic aims are the same. By the end of the methods section, your reader should understand very clearly how you completed your study, and which methodology(ies) informed your research process. In the methods section, you state clearly your approach to the research, who you included as participants, why you included them, and what you did to collect your data. Further, the methods section should also describe in detail how you analyzed your data.

Throughout the methods section, it is especially important that terms be clearly defined and that the various steps in the research process be explained in a clear manner. Without such clarity, your readers will struggle to understand how you conducted your study and thus may question the trustworthiness and/or validity of your findings. The methods section is critical in that it gives your reader a glimpse into your mind as you designed your study, carried out your research, and ultimately developed your findings.

Within the methods section, it is particularly important to note the various assumptions that you made throughout the research process. In a qualitative study, this might involve noting how you approached your participants, handled your own positionality, or described your emerging interpretations of the data. In a quantitative study, this might involve noting what assumptions you made about the variables in your study, how the variables were related to each other, and in what ways you manipulated or adjusted the dataset. These details are particularly important as they provide the reader of your study with an opportunity to look critically at your analytic process. In From the Field 12.4 and From the Field 12.5, we provide sample methods sections to illustrate the clarity with which your research design and method should be presented, as well as the types of details that make this possible.

FROM THE FIELD 12.4

An Example of a Methods Section From a Qualitative Research Study

Study Design

To investigate our questions regarding coaches' learning, we draw on data from a 4-year qualitative case study of the partnerships between a third-party support provider and two urban, and one rural/suburban school districts. Portions of the data collected for that study are utilized for this analysis.

The Overarching Study

In the fall of 2004, we initiated a qualitative, comparative case study of instructional reform efforts in one urban school district located near Seattle and, in the fall of 2005, extended research activities into two additional school districts (one in Washington and one in California), all of which partnered with the same support organization (Gallucci & Boatright, 2007; Gallucci & Swanson, 2008; Van Lare, Yoon, & Gallucci, 2008). One of the benefits of qualitative study designs is the flexibility to pursue relevant lines of inquiry as they emerge (Wolcott, 1990). As we studied how districts "learned" to improve instruction in the context of their external partnerships, our data collection and analysis revealed a problem—that of understanding and supporting coaches' learning—that was both pertinent to the practice of our study participants and noticeably under-researched. Initial reading of the data collected for the larger research project had also prompted our thinking

about the Vygotsky Space as a potentially useful heuristic. We developed a focused case study of one coach's professional learning activities and the organizational supports that appeared to support his learning using this analytic model.

A Case of Coach Learning

We analyzed the experiences of one coach (called Dan in this article) because he was the focal coach at one middle school research site and we had a robust account of his experiences from December 2006 through February 2008. The fact that we had 14 months of observational data about his learning and that he was articulate about the meaning of these experiences made his case an instrumental one (Stake, 1995) for examining the broader problem of how coaches learn to do their work. The deep analysis of a single case allowed rich detail and nuance that might have been lost if we had generalized across multiple or comparative cases. Our purpose was to develop hypotheses based on Dan's in-depth case that would lead to future research regarding coaches' learning.

We had multiple opportunities to observe Dan's district make organizational changes aimed at supporting coaches' (and others') professional development as described below. Dan's case, therefore, maximized our potential to discuss coach learning, as well as the organizational contexts pertinent to his experience. We did not consider that his case was typical of all cases of coach learning. As Stake (1995) explained, "Good instrumental case study does not depend on being able to defend the typicality" of the case (p. 4). The single case is important primarily in terms of what can be learned from it that may inform a larger problem (Wolcott, 2005).

The Context

We chose Dan's information-rich case from data collected in the Ridgeview School District in Ridgeview, Washington (all names used in this article are pseudonyms). The district had invested in a variety of professional development structures in the context of their reform activity; therefore, it provided a relevant context for exploring our questions regarding organizational support for coaches' learning (see the Appendix, available as supplementary material for this article in the online version of the journal).

Ridgeview is a small but growing bedroom community outside of Seattle. The district serves a population of approximately 52,000, which is increasing as residents move further out of Seattle in search of affordable housing. Ridgeview is a primarily White, middle- and working-class community, but it houses significant pockets of poverty and increasing ethnic diversity. The district also serves students from a Native American reservation. The majority of students in Ridgeview are White (74%); other racial groups represented in the district include Hispanic/Latino students (8%), Native American students (8%–9%), Asian students (7%), and African American students (2%). In 2006–2007, 34% of Ridgeview's 11,800 students qualified for free and reduced-price lunch.

Ridgeview Junior High was the study's middle school of focus in the school district. It was selected using a purposeful "intensity sampling" strategy (Mertens, 1998) that ensured that research sites had strong ties to the instructional improvement work promoted by the district and supported by the third-party organization. One of three middle-level schools in the district, Ridgeview served 957 students in grades

eight and nine at the time of this study. The school's student population mirrored that of the district in terms of race and ethnicity, but approximately 18.9% of the student population received free and reduced-price lunch during 2006–2007. Within the school, the English department was recognized for its participation in district-driven reform efforts.

Literacy Coaching and Instructional Reform in Ridgeview

Literacy coaches existed in Ridgeview School District (in elementary schools only) even before the district launched a major instructional reform with the goal of improving student outcomes in reading and writing in 2004–2005. With the reform initiative, Ridgeview prioritized professional development aimed at school leaders, instructional coaches, and lead teachers. Relevant to this case, during 2006–2007, when our research began in Ridgeview, the district selected studio classrooms as school-based sites for professional learning related to literacy instruction (the teachers in these classrooms were called studio teachers). The studio sessions provided an opportunity for participants to learn in their school and classroom contexts under the guidance of an external consultant. The sessions included observations of lesson planning (that is, a lesson that the studio teacher, the literacy coach, and the consultant jointly selected), demonstration lessons and debrief sessions, and discussions about professional literature. Teachers, coaches, and principals participated in the sessions for one-half to a whole school day. The goal of this approach was to help teachers and coaches (both studio teachers and others) incorporate what they observed in these settings into their own practice. For most schools, "studio days," as they were referred to in the district, occurred 3 to 4 times per school year.

Also in the fall of 2006, Ridgeview expanded what had been an elementary school coaching model to their middle-level schools by assigning lead teachers as part-time coaches (the configuration looked slightly different at each school). At Ridgeview Junior High, two lead teachers were selected as half-time literacy coaches; they also continued half-time as language

(Continued)

(Continued)

arts teachers. Dan, our focal coach, had been a teacher for 14 years (9 in Ridgeview) and had served as the chair of the English department at Ridgeview. His principal identified him as a leader who had been an active participant in prior professional development activities at the school. In this article, our case example focuses on Dan's early learning as a coach at Ridgeview Junior High.

Data Collection

The analysis for this article stems from four interviews with Dan, four interviews with teachers at Ridgeview Junior High, two interviews with the Ridgeview principal, and three interviews with the external consultant who worked closely with Dan. In all cases, we asked school participants to describe their work and to reflect on their professional learning experiences (that is, what they thought they were learning and how they were learning it).

We also observed 41 events that included Dan's participation, such as professional development sessions at the school, department meetings, coaching activities and coach professional development sessions, classroom teaching, and district-level instructional leadership sessions that occurred for a period of 2 years. For this article, we focused primarily on events at Ridgeview Junior High. Handwritten field notes in the form of running narrative were gathered at all events. An attempt was made to record what occurred as well as who participated and in what ways. Multiple artifacts, such as instructional memos, calendars, professional development plans, and instructional materials, were collected.

Data from the broader study of district reform efforts in Ridgeview School District were used to build contextual understanding of Dan's case. Other relevant data collected in the district over a 3-year period included six interviews with three central office leaders, as well as observations of district-level professional development events. We used these data to learn about the district's reform goals and professional development plans, which informed our understanding of (1) what the district expected Dan to learn and (2) the factors that supported Dan's learning.

Data Analysis

We brought ideas regarding social practice and social theories of learning to our analyses for this article. Our aim was to generate hypotheses and questions about the nature of coaches' learning and how district or school organizational structures may support coaches' professional development from the viewpoint of one developing instructional coach. Therefore, what Dan learned about instructional coaching practice was relevant, as well as the process of how he learned and how he was supported in that learning.

Steps taken for this analysis included (1) an initial reading and open coding of all the relevant data (Emerson, Fretz, & Shaw, 1995), during which we noted instances of "learning" on the part of individuals (the focus here was on Dan's learning), aspects of participation in learning events, or evidence of support for professional learning; (2) the development of a code list based on our initial reading of the data and constructs derived from the Vygotsky Space; (3) focused coding of all the data; and finally, (4) the development of hypotheses regarding support for the professional learning of coaches drawn from our analysis of Dan's experiences. All interview data were coded using HyperRESEARCH (2004), a qualitative data analysis program. Observational data and documents were hand-coded. The data types informed one another in this analysis; for example, Dan described his learning in interviews, but our observational record of his participation in a variety of professional activities verified how his coaching practice changed over time. As a final step in our analysis, we provided an earlier version of this article to Dan and to his supervisor (an assistant superintendent) and asked them to check the validity of our findings and hypotheses (Merriam, 1998).

Source: Gallucci, Van Lare, Yoon, & Boatright, 2010, pp. 927–931

An Example of a Methods Section From a Quantitative Research Study

Methods

This was a non-experimental, correlational study designed to determine the relationship between parental involvement and reading achievement in sixth grade students. The study did not determine a causal relationship between the independent variable (parental involvement) and the dependent variable (reading achievement), but rather attempted to find a correlation between the two.

Data were collected in the form of surveys to measure parental involvement and the McLeod Reading Comprehension test to measure reading level. Descriptive statistics were used to compare the independent and dependent variables. The data were analyzed using the Pearson Product-Moment Correlation.

Procedures

Data Required

As previously stated, the level of parental involvement, referred to as x, was measured through the use of a Parental Involvement Survey developed by the researcher. As well, a survey was developed and administered to students in order to portray a more realistic view of actual parental involvement. The parent survey was sent home to the parents of fifty-seven, sixth grade students and was to be returned within one week. The student survey was given in class by an outside observer. No names were used on the survey; an outside observer coded them. The parent and student surveys were each scored by the researchers and then the scores averaged. This determined the parent involvement score. Reading achievement, referred to as y, was measured through the McLeod Reading Comprehension Test. Each student was given a reading level, roughly equivalent to a grade level, based on his or her performance on the McLeod test.

Study Sample

The subjects selected for this study were sixth-grade students from a middle school in East Central Washington. This sample was selected based on the convenience method as the researcher used all students in her Language Arts classes. Fifty-seven students participated. The other participants, parents and guardians, were selected for obvious reasons; their son or daughter was part of the study. The study took place during the 2001–2002 school year.

Data Collection

The parent involvement survey was sent to parents and guardians of fifty-seven students. The survey was sent home from school with each participant and then a follow-up call was made to all parents in an attempt to ensure a high return rate. A survey in Spanish was sent home with students whose home language was Spanish as well. The survey was to be returned to the classroom teacher with the student within one week of the send home date.

The student survey, as previously stated, was given in class by an outside observer. Students were given a survey with their code on it and asked to complete it. The surveys were then returned to the classroom teacher for scoring. The survey contained six questions with 4 choices as a possible response. The possible responses were never, almost never, sometimes, and frequently. Each response of *never* was worth 1 point, *almost never* 2 points, *sometimes* 3 points, and *frequently* 4 points, for a possible score of 24. The total from the student survey (out of 24) was added to the total of the parent survey (out of 24) and then an average was determined and used as the parent involvement score for each student.

The instrument used to measure each student's reading ability was the McLeod Reading Comprehension test. This is the test given to all incoming 6th and 7th grade students in many school districts to determine reading level. The McLeod

(Continued)

(Continued)

works as a cloze test, one in which students must use context clues and reading strategies in order to fill in missing words. It is a test for understanding. The test is a part of the CORE reading program. CORE is a teaching resource for grades kindergarten through eight and was developed by Bill Honig, Linda Diamond, and Linda Gutlohn. The test was given individually, and a quiet testing environment was used whenever possible.

Data Analysis

The data in this study were analyzed using the Pearson Product-Moment Correlation. The

Pearson is a statistical test used to determine if a relationship exists between two variables. The means for the independent and dependent variables were computed and compared to determine if a relationship existed between the two. When a high correlation is found between two variables, it indicates that an increase in one variable accompanies an increase in another that shows a direct relationship. When a negative correlation is found, it indicates that as the value of one variable increases, the other decreases and no relationship exists. As well, variables may be found to have week or moderate correlational relationships.

Source: Hawes & Plourde, 2005, pp. 53–54

 Read the full article at:
www.sagepub.com/lochmiller

FORMULATING ARGUMENTS AND PRESENTING FINDINGS

While each of the preceding sections of your research report/paper are important, none may be more so than the presentation of your qualitative findings or quantitative results. This section demonstrates the sophistication and thoughtfulness of your analysis, as well as the quality of your interpretation of the data. Thus, how you formulate your argument and present your findings matters. In general, as you approach the task of writing up your results/findings, it is important to consistently include the following components. First, you should begin each paragraph with a clear topic sentence that aligns with your main argument. For example, if you conducted a qualitative study and found that your participants generally perceived that the type of professional development they received shaped how they understood the district's math curriculum, you might want to formulate a topic sentence that says, "Teachers perceived that professional development shaped their understanding of the district's new math curriculum." This sentence is not only structured to address a key point raised by your research questions but it also identifies an important finding for your study. In the next sentence, it is important to identify one of the key points from your analysis. This point should build from the topic sentence and clearly identify what element of the dataset you are drawing from. For example, you might want to state something like, "Math teachers with fewer years of professional experience indicated that professional development positively influenced their understanding. Math teachers with more experience perceived that the professional development was helpful but did not necessarily impact their understanding of the new math curriculum." Following such a statement, it is particularly important to provide supporting evidence (such as illustrative quotes or statistics). As this example assumes a qualitative study and notes both the perspectives of novice and experienced teachers, it is important to highlight quotes from both of these groups in the supporting evidence you provide. One strategy might be to include a quote from a novice principal and another from an experienced principal that highlight how the two groups of teachers differ in their interpretation.

After presenting the evidence, it is important to present your interpretation of the quotes. Many practitioner-scholars begin their work by offering a quote, a passage from a document, or a summary from an observation and then move to the next point. It is imperative that before you move to your next point, you provide the reader with your interpretation. This helps the reader understand why the evidence was included. It also demonstrates the rigor of your analysis. Finally, given the detail of research results/findings, it is important to conclude your points with a statement that summarizes or connects the points you have made to your topic sentence, as well as to the broader research questions you are addressing. Figure 12.2 presents a general overview of the process of building an argument.

While the preceding example referred to a qualitative research study, the basic process of presenting quantitative results is similar. Instead of using quotes, however, practitioner-scholars use the results of descriptive and inferential statistical tests. When presenting quantitative research, it is important to include an additional explanation of the variables or key assumptions that you made when conducting the statistical test. For example, if you are presenting the results of an experimental study, it can be very helpful to remind the reader what your hypotheses were that informed the analysis. Similarly, it can be very helpful to remind your readers what your dependent and independent variables were, as this can help explain your results. Beyond these distinctions, the basic process of constructing a compelling research argument is the same.

Finally, as you develop your research argument, ensure that your research results/findings are represented by the various types of data that you collected and analyzed in your research. This is particularly true in qualitative research studies, which often include multiple forms of evidence, but may also be true for action research studies or mixed methods studies.

Figure 12.2 Constructing a Research Argument

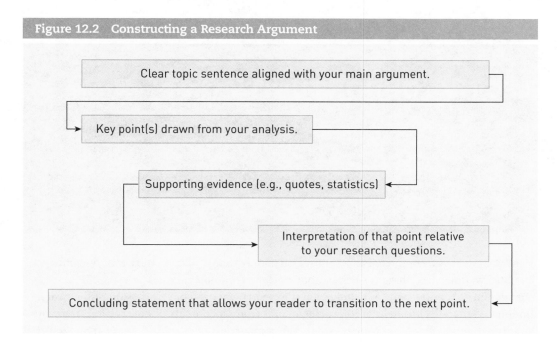

🔗 LINK TO PRACTICE 12.2

SELECTING DATA FOR YOUR ARGUMENT

After completing your analysis for a qualitative case study, you find yourself with a series of quotes describing the ways in which classroom teachers are currently implementing the district's new math curriculum. The quotes describe various perspectives, ranging from teachers who simply report having a positive experience to teachers who offer detailed critiques about the approach the district has taken to support the implementation. Three quotes are particularly helpful, you think, to describe a finding you have regarding the different ways in which teachers view the new curriculum, offering them ideas about teaching students who are not meeting standards. One teacher said simply, "The curriculum has provided me with new ideas about teaching numerical sense to students who are not meeting standard." Another teacher indicated, "The curriculum has offered me new ways to present numerical sense to students who are below standard, in particular the curriculum provides great examples of thinking problems that help them

understand magnitude. One example was great, as it used the number of fish in a fisherman's net. The teacher's guide suggested that I use paper fish and a net to demonstrate this to my students. I found that so helpful!" Finally, another teacher indicated, "The curriculum is prescriptive. It tells me exactly what to teach and how. I don't like that. It makes me feel like it is taking away my creativity as a classroom teacher." With these three quotes, you wonder how best to present an argument. The quotes are not all aligned (that is, the teachers do not offer uniformly positive reflections) and it makes you wonder whether you can present all of the quotes or not.

Focus Questions

1. How might you present a balanced representation of the teachers' perspectives?

2. What could you do, within the context of your written argument, to suggest that teachers offered or had different perspectives?

REFLECTIVE OPPORTUNITY 12.2

As you think about sharing your research findings, you will inevitably have to consider whether any of your findings might subtly reveal private information about your participants. While it is easy to think that issues related to confidentiality are not central to the writing process, this is a time in the research process where you need to be cognizant of any overlooked issues related to confidentiality. What might be some strategies that you could employ to assure that a research report/paper has been carefully evaluated for lapses in confidentiality?

For example, if you conducted a qualitative case study that involved interviews, documents, and observations describing how classroom teachers are implementing a new math curriculum, it is important to include each type of evidence in your discussion of the results/findings. Generally, it is helpful to provide quotes from documents or observations to create context, after which it is appropriate to provide supporting, challenging, or clarifying quotes. In quantitative research studies, using multiple types of data is typically not the concern.

Rather, the primary concern is to present various representations of your data (such as tables, charts, and graphs) and analyses to bolster your research claims.

TECHNOLOGIES TO SUPPORT WRITING AND DISSEMINATING RESEARCH

There are several technologies that serve to support your writing process. We highlight only one of these tools, and, more broadly, we encourage you to think creatively about how to create pathways for effective and efficient writing.

Technologies to Support the Writing Process

Throughout the research process, you will certainly engage in the writing process. While collecting data, for instance, you might make initial notes on your impressions of the data. As noted in Chapter 8, during the completion of a qualitative data analysis, you might write extensive memos. Thus, regardless of the stage you are at in the research process, identifying useful writing tools and strategies is essential. From basic computing to specialized software packages, there are a variety of technologies that can support the writing process. We highlight Scrivener, which we have found useful for when you begin developing your final research report/paper.

SCRIVENER. Scrivener is a word processing and project management tool that was developed to support the writing process, particularly for those who are creating lengthy documents. This tool is especially useful for organizing your ideas, taking notes, creating outlines, and developing an initial draft. Figure 12.3 shows the main interface of Scrivener.

Figure 12.3 Scrivener's Main Interface

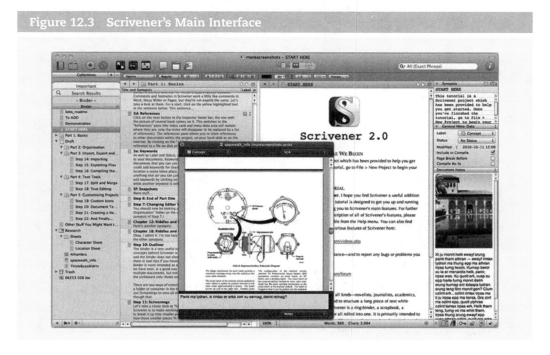

Source: http://www.literautreandlatte.com/scrivener.php

Scrivener offers multiple features that can support the writing process. For example, you can keep all of your relevant documents, including PDFs, web pages, and media files inside Scrivener. This allows you to work on your written document while also referencing key files, with the split screen showing the relevant file on one side and your research document on the other.

The "corkboard" feature is another particularly useful tool for those who prefer to organize their thoughts around several related ideas. This feature includes virtual index cards that allow you to create a summary of the key ideas discussed across multiple documents. For example, perhaps you have begun writing the sections of your research report in separate documents, with one document focused on the literature review, another document on the methodology and methods used, and another document focused on the results/findings. As you begin organizing and compiling the different parts of your paper, it might be useful to rearrange some of your ideas, with virtual index cards being a tool used to do so. This feature is much like a storyboard wherein you can move the cards around to create your story in a free-forming way. Figure 12.4 illustrates how the corkboard might be used when developing a research paper/report.

From synching your written documents with your iPhone or iPad to the outlining features, Scrivener offers a multitude of features to support the writing process. At present, there is a 30-day free trial version for both MAC and PC users, which we would recommend exploring prior to investing time and money into the package. Further, there are multiple YouTube video tutorials that offer examples of how others have used Scrivener to support their writing process.

Figure 12.4   The Corkboard Feature in Scrivener

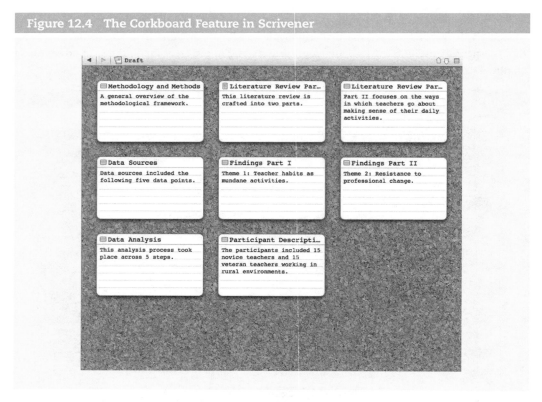

Source: http://www.literautreandlatte.com/scrivener.php

In this chapter, we introduced you to the basics of writing up your research study. First, we discussed some of the important considerations for engaging in academic writing, ranging from the use of sensitive language to pronoun usage to the place of APA manuscript style in the writing process. Second, we provided you with an overview of some of the unique characteristics of qualitative and quantitative research reports/papers. In doing so, we sought to highlight both the similarities and differences between qualitatively oriented versus quantitatively oriented research studies. Finally, we concluded by presenting a technology tool that you can use to support and organize your writing process.

KEY TERMS

APA Manuscript Style 260

People First Language 257

Primary Audience 256

Scrivener 271

Secondary Audience 256

QUESTIONS TO CONSIDER

1. How would you characterize the nature of academic writing? In other words, what about academic writing makes it academic?

2. What are the different purposes for the varied types of academic reports/papers?

3. Why is it important to consider your audience when developing a research report/paper?

4. When writing your research report/paper, what are some important considerations in regards to word choice?

5. What are some of the similarities and differences between qualitative and quantitative research reports/papers?

6. How might technological tools support you in writing your research report/paper?

CHAPTER EXERCISES

1. Locate one qualitative study and one quantitative study in a peer-reviewed journal. Read each article and note the similarities and differences among the: (a) structure of the article, (b) type of language used, and (c) way in which the argument is built.

2. Locate a recently completed dissertation in your area of study, which you can likely find through your college or university library system. First, review the table of contents, noting how the dissertation is structured. Second, determine whether the study can be described as a qualitative, quantitative, mixed methods, or action research study. Third, read through the results/findings chapter and note how the results/findings were developed.

3. Take a class paper that you have recently written about a topic that you are interested in and consider how you might further develop this paper into a manuscript for publication. In particular, identify how your argument may need to be restructured for publication, what additional references you may need, and what type of conclusions or implications you might make given your overarching argument.

4. Download the free trial of Scrivener (http://www
.literatureandlatte.com/scrivener.php) and practice
using it as a writing tool. Consider the following
questions: How might this tool require you to adjust
your writing process? What efficiencies might this
introduce into your approach to writing? How does
it compare to other tools that you currently use for
your writing? After considering these questions, make
a T-chart exploring the pros and cons of adopting
Scrivener.

LEARNING EXTENSIONS

Prior to embarking on proposal or research report/
paper writing, it is often helpful to review books and
publication manuals that have been written to support
you in developing a well-crafted description of your
research. A useful place to begin is with the *Publication
Manual of the American Psychological Association* (2010),
particularly in that educational research often adopts an
APA manuscript style. While a portion of the manual
considers the mechanics of writing and how to credit
sources, other sections of the manual discuss more
broadly the various types of manuscript styles, the
importance of using language carefully, and how to
display your research results/findings. Another useful
resource is Walliman and Buckler's (2008) book, *Your
Dissertation in Education*. This book walks the reader
through the process of planning, carrying out, and
completing a dissertation study. Further, it includes
a discussion of the ways in which to write about your
dissertation research and how to develop a research
proposal. Even if you are not planning to write a
dissertation in the near future, this text offers some
useful insights related to writing about a research study.

Sharpen your skills with SAGE edge!

edge.sagepub.com/lochmiller

SAGE edge for Students provides a personalized approach to help you accomplish your coursework goals
in an easy-to-use learning environment. You'll find action plans, mobile-friendly eFlashcards, and quizzes
as well as videos, web resources, and links to SAGE journal articles to support and expand on the concepts
presented in this chapter.

13

USING AND SHARING RESEARCH TO IMPROVE PRACTICE

SEEING THE PROCESS THROUGH

Having completed your study, you now feel a sense of relief and also a sense of pride. The research is done but more hard work remains. Given the results/ findings of your study, you are now poised to take your work forward— embedding your new understandings into your practice and sharing them with colleagues and others (for example, school board members, community members). You are committed to seeing the research process through to the end, with the hope of making a meaningful difference in your daily work and the life of your school. Recognizing this opportunity, your next and final task is to consider how the research you have completed can be used and thus linked to practice, as well as more broadly shared.

INTRODUCTION

As the opening vignette illustrates, throughout the research process, from identifying a research question to writing up your results/findings, you have undoubtedly focused on thoughtfully completing your research study. Now that your research is complete, you face an equally important task—particularly as a practitioner-scholar. This task relates to using your research to change practice, improve your classroom, school and/or district, or shape conversations about education or the policies that surround it. As a practitioner-scholar, the purpose of your research was likely never to sit idly on the dusty shelves of a university library. Rather, its purpose was to be brought to bear in classrooms, schools, and/or districts to improve the educational experiences provided to all students.

In this chapter, we revisit the meaning of practitioner-scholarship to reinforce the basic goals of this orientation to research, as well as the

Learning Objectives

By the end of this chapter, you will be able to:

- Demonstrate how your work as a practitioner-scholar intersects with the improvement of teaching and learning in your classroom, school, and/or district.

- Summarize the value of practitioner-scholarship as an invitation to reflect, refine, and renew practices in your classroom, school, and/or district.

- Identify concrete ways that research can be used and the forums that you can create to share your work.

- Recall the research process and useful methodologies.

- Discuss the salient connections between the problems of practice and their relevance to your work.

value that it has in relation to the daily work that occurs in schools. In particular, we conceptualize research as creating an opportunity for practitioner-scholars to reflect on, refine, and renew their practice. Then, we revisit the research process as we have presented it throughout the textbook in order to clarify once again its cyclical nature. Following this discussion, we revisit the problems of practice that served as a point of reference throughout the textbook. Finally, we highlight some of the ways you can share your research with a broader audience, and point to new technologies that might support this process. Given that the purpose of this chapter is intended to reinforce the links between research and practice, we do not present separate Links to Practice. Rather, we call upon you to identify various links between your practice as an educator and research throughout.

REVISITING THE MEANING OF PRACTITIONER-SCHOLARSHIP

Some researchers have suggested that much of the existing educational research is not well suited for practitioners. Specifically, these scholars have indicated that education research is generally not as useful or applicable to the work that occurs in schools (Burkhardt & Schoenfeld, 2003). In one study, Whitehurst (2003) surveyed state and district leaders and found that more than three quarters of the participating leaders indicated that education research was not useful, overly theoretical, and too academic in its orientation. While these criticisms should give traditional researchers reason to pause, they should also inspire and empower practitioner-scholars to begin and broadly share their research work. Indeed, we think these critiques are an invitation for you and other practitioner-scholars like you to conduct research that matters to the work occurring in classrooms, schools, and/or districts.

Policymakers and educators are clamoring for evidence-based practices that result in dramatic improvements in educational outcomes. As a practitioner-scholar, you can provide some of that information by sharing the findings/results from your research with your colleagues and other stakeholders, which may lead to incremental improvements. However, sharing information is only one part of the task. The other part, and perhaps the more important part, is to infuse what you have learned from your research into your practice. If you conducted a qualitative, quantitative, or mixed methods research study, it may not be entirely clear how you might integrate your research results/findings into your classroom, school, and/or district. But, rest assured, your research can be used to support improvements in your practice and the practices of your colleagues.

While practitioners often refer to a disconnect between research and practice, practitioner-scholars consistently see and make the connections needed to embed research in practice. In our estimation, the perception that there is a disconnect between research and practice often stems from the practitioner-scholar's own hesitation or reluctance to share their ideas with their colleagues. We thus encourage you not to take on this mindset. Your research is useful, and your research results/findings can empower significant changes in your own work, as well as your colleagues' work. As From the Field 13.1 highlights, there are numerous opportunities to introduce research into your practice—whether you are a classroom teacher or a school leader.

Informing Research With Practice

In our careers before we entered academia (one as an education consultant and the other as a high school principal), we encountered countless teachers and administrators who dismissed research as "too theoretical," too much embedded in the "ivory tower," or irrelevant to their local situations. These attitudes may stem from a perspective that assumes that what one reads in an article or a book will be directly applicable to a particular situation. If not, it is worthless. We hold a different view. We envision education leaders [and classroom teachers] understanding research and figuring out how specific aspects of research they have read can inform the decisions they need to make about instruction. Instead of adopting without question a recommendation made at the end of a scholarly article, the research informed leader asks, "How do this author's conclusions relate to what our teachers and students are doing?" In the process, teachers and principals examine information they already have about their students to determine where the similarities and differences are between their school and the research sites contained in the source(s) they have read. This is not a process of adopting or not adopting. It is a synthesis of what is known about one's school and what others have found who have studied similar and different educational circumstances.

Source: Bauer & Brazer, 2012, p. 29

From the Field 13.1 illustrates how the goal of research is not the wholesale adoption of new fads or ideas, but careful, thoughtful, and critical appraisal of research ideas in relation to current practice. We see research and your work as a practitioner-scholar as an opportunity to reflect, refine, and renew educational practices.

Research as an Opportunity to Reflect, Refine, and Renew

Some methods textbooks simply (and primarily) lay out the technical aspects of the research process. This is certainly important information that we have aimed to present throughout this textbook as well; however, we recognize that this technical information cannot be separated from your work as a practitioner, as your daily work in schools is central to the questions you pose and the ways you come to make sense of research. From the very beginning, our goal has been to change the orientation of this process to demonstrate in practically focused ways how researchers undertake and complete their work, as well as the practical steps that you can take to improve practice. Part of that improvement is to take the research you have completed to the level of implementation, and to begin using the ideas that you cultivated in your research to inform not only what you do as a practitioner but how you think about research. Thus, we see research as providing you with three distinct opportunities (alongside many others).

First, we see research as an opportunity to reflect on your practice, ideas, or beliefs as a practitioner. Research creates a space where you can thoughtfully consider how your previous understandings have shaped your work. In thinking about what other practitioner-scholars have found and/or what you have come to understand through your own research, you acquire new understandings about your practice and deeper explanations that are grounded in literature. Research provides you with opportunities to ask *how* and *why* practices in schools have come to exist as they have. For example, if you conducted a qualitative case study of classroom teachers and their experience with a new math curriculum, the study provides an opportunity to critically examine how curriculum shapes teachers' understandings of their work, as well as presents barriers to their work with students. Through this research, you might find that teachers' decisions are being adversely impacted by the curriculum because the curriculum requires teachers to follow pre-planned instructional activities. Such findings might enlighten your understanding about the current context of teaching in your district and invite you to consider how this context may or may not be shaping your own work. We list several reflective questions that you might consider once you have completed your research study.

1. To what extent do the results/findings of my research challenge my thinking about education, the purpose of schooling, and/or the role that I (as an educator) have in the community?

2. How has the research process encouraged me to think critically and intentionally about my practices? Their impact on students? Or their impact on my colleagues and schools?

3. To what extent are practices in my classroom, school, and/or district preventing improvement in student learning or achievement?

4. How do the results/findings of my study challenge me to revisit my instructional or leadership practices?

5. What questions or insights does my research present for my colleagues, administrators, parents, or stakeholders in our community?

6. In what ways has the research process changed my understanding of practice in my classroom, school, district, or education generally?

Second, when you begin integrating your research into your practice, it provides an opportunity to refine and improve your work. For example, if you conducted a case study of classroom teachers that were implementing a new math curriculum, your research provides an opportunity to engage in critically examining the practices in your school both from the perspective of classroom teachers, as well as the perspective of school administrators. If you found, for example, that teacher leader support was critical to the implementation of the new curriculum, such a finding might provide you (as a principal) with an opportunity to re-assess and re-evaluate how you have assigned staff in your building. Could you, for example, adjust the school's master schedule to create opportunities for teacher leaders to work with other teachers in implementing the curriculum? Might opportunities for collaboration be provided to support teachers in better understanding the new curriculum? In Table 13.1, we present examples of some of the ways that research might be used to refine current practices.

Third, when research-based ideas inform practices that are shared among your colleagues, research provides an opportunity to renew what we do as educators. This is perhaps the most powerful way that research can be used to influence schools, as it is only when new practices are adopted across classrooms, schools, and districts that they can impact large numbers of students.

Table 13.1 Using Research to Refine Current Practice

Classroom-Level Examples

- Following her qualitative case study of English Language Learning students in a nearby high school, a classroom teacher realizes that she needs to provide students with more information about college as many of the students in her research were not confident that they could attend college. In her classroom, she hangs posters of colleges and universities, introduces a college admissions essay writing assignment, and also works with the counseling center to introduce students to the importance of the SAT and ACT.

- As part of a qualitative study, an elementary teacher realizes that female students in his fifth grade classroom are less interested in science after he conducted a student survey and compared the responses by gender. Drawing upon literature he reviewed for his study, he introduces a series of new classroom activities that are designed to model for female students their role as architects, engineers, and scientists. He uses the presence of role models and writing assignments to inspire female students' interest in science.

- After completing an action research study with her colleagues to understand why male students were more likely to miss school, a teacher decides to meet one-on-one with parents and families of students who are chronically absent. She finds that students are often missing school because of issues with transportation. She works with other parents to setup a rideshare program to help get students to class when they do not have a ride.

School Examples

- As part of a qualitative case study, a middle school principal conducts a study of her school's classroom teachers to determine how they are cultivating caring relationships with students. To augment her study, she conducted focus groups with students to determine how students perceive these relationships unfolding and what, specifically, teachers do to demonstrate care. She finds that teachers who engage in respectful listening, show genuine interest in the students' lives, and maintain high standards for students are viewed as being the most caring by students. She designs a professional development session that highlights her results/findings and provides insights for teachers about the ways in which they can develop more caring relationships with students.

- As a part of a quantitative research study, an elementary school principal surveys parents who attend his open house to determine whether parents find the school responsive to their concerns about their children's education. The survey indicates that responsiveness seems to vary by grade level, with older grades being viewed by parents as less responsive. The principal summarizes the data and shares the information with his staff at a year-end staff retreat. He then groups teachers by grade level and invites them to discuss the data using a discussion protocol that focuses on the reasons for the parents' perceptions, as well as possible solutions. At the end of their discussion, he encourages the teachers to continue their discussions in their professional learning community (PLC) time throughout the year to develop and implement strategies that help parents feel that the school is responsive to their concerns.

(Continued)

Table 13.1 (Continued)

District Examples

- A central office administrator is interested in understanding how principals in his district perceive that the central office supports them in implementing new teacher evaluation criteria. He conducts a qualitative case study to explore principals' perceptions of the support they receive from the central office. He finds that principals see the superintendent's decision to assign each principal to a central office partner as a key step. The administrator shares this information with his colleagues in the district. The district decides to use this model for other initiatives.

- A doctoral student, who is also a school board member, is interested in the ways in which superintendents who identify as multi-racial experience leading school districts in predominately white communities. She conducts an ethnography with superintendents in three districts. She finds that the superintendents experience isolation, resistance, and fear in their leadership attributed to the communities that they serve. Recognizing the significance of her work, she partners with the state school board association to provide training to school board members on cultural competence and social justice. Her training helps school board members learn to navigate their own perceptions in light of the community they represent.

You might think that your work cannot have this impact. For example, you might be thinking, "But my study is so small or had so few participants—I don't see how it could make a difference." This is a feeling that many practitioner-scholars struggle with after completing their research; and while it may be true that your study was carried out in a specific context, with (only) a few participants, for a specific purpose, this does not mean that your study does not have value. That is why it is essential that you take the time to share your research with your colleagues—to empower them with the new understandings and information you have acquired. We highlight a few of the ways in which you might share your research with colleagues, and then offer additional, concrete suggestions in the following section.

- Share your research during a PLC or department meeting and design professional development activities that align with the topic of your study.

- Ask for an opportunity to present your research to district administrators (for example, superintendent or associate superintendent). Explain the importance of your research and bring the pertinent issues to their attention.

- Set up reading groups around research-related topics with your colleagues to deepen your understanding of key issues raised in your research, as well as to bring to your colleagues' attention the importance of the issues.

- Develop a blog, website, or other online source to share your research and begin building a virtual PLC to engage in thoughtful dialogue about the research topic. Where possible, link to other sites and resources to build capacity.

- Collaborate with faculty at your college or university to develop conference papers and publications aligned with your research and that serve to disseminate your research to practitioner and academic audiences.

TECHNOLOGIES TO
SUPPORT SHARING RESEARCH

There are numerous technologies that can be used to support the dissemination of your research results/findings. We suggest that it may be especially helpful for you to think beyond professional publications and consider alternative ways of presenting, sharing, and disseminating research. While traditional publication outlets (such as academic journals) are an important and meaningful place to share your work, accessibility can often be limited to those who are familiar with and/or have access to the publication. Popularizing or making research findings public has the potential to extend the reach of your research (Vannini, 2012). For instance, Lester and Gabriel (2012) shared findings from a qualitative study of school psychologists', parents', and students' experiences with special education meetings in the form of a community performance. While their findings were published in a traditional journal format as well (Gabriel & Lester, 2012), they expanded the audience for their work by holding multiple community performances to share findings and spark discussion among community members. There are other ways to disseminate your research, including through the use of blogs and websites, as well as digital storytelling (Paulus, Lester, & Dempster, 2014).

Blogs and Websites

There is a growing number of blogs and websites used for the purpose of sharing research findings. If you develop a blog for the purpose of sharing findings from a research study, you may want to do this in a way in which you encourage the public to offer comments regarding your study's results/findings and even future research directions. Similarly, you may decide to develop a website to share your research results/findings or the research process that you used. Some journals are even beginning to host blogs, with the aim of increasing the reach of their authors' research findings and perspectives. For instance, *Phi Delta Kappan* hosts a blog in which authors can share brief snippets and ideas from their current research, as shown in Figure 13.1.

When seeking alternative ways by which to present your research, it can also be helpful to look at fields beyond education. For example, in the field of health, websites have been widely used to disseminate research findings to a broader audience, including practitioners and policymakers. Some of these sites have received considerable recognition, as well. For example, healthtalk.org is an award-winning website with text- and video-based qualitative findings from a study of people's health experiences. The research team, a group at Oxford University's Department of Primary Care Health Services, described their goal as being to provide information that offers a range of perspectives on health experiences that might also be used to inform decisions about health based on research findings. Figure 13.2 provides an example from the site in which the researchers reported findings from interviews with 33 young people's experiences with drugs and alcohol.

Digital Storytelling

Digital storytelling refers to the use of a variety of media forms to share aspects of an individual or group story. This may be associated with narrative approaches to qualitative research, as discussed in Chapter 6. Broadly, digital storytelling can be used to represent your findings in a different format, which may result in greater accessibility for your research. A practitioner-scholar, for example, might develop a visual narrative that combines images, video, and voice when representing a participant's story (Lambert, 2006). One might also develop a digital story that represents the concerns of a

Figure 13.1   Phi Delta Kappan's Blog

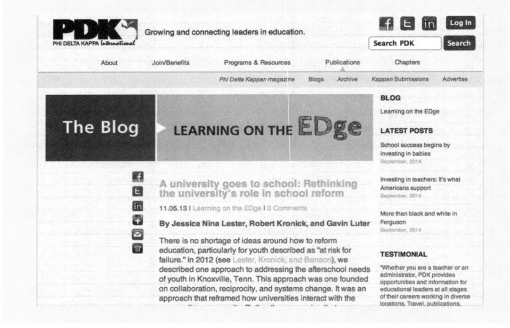

Source: Reprinted with permission of Phi Delta Kappa International, www.pdkintl.org. All rights reserved

Figure 13.2   Healthtalk.org's Website With Research Findings Presented as Video Narratives

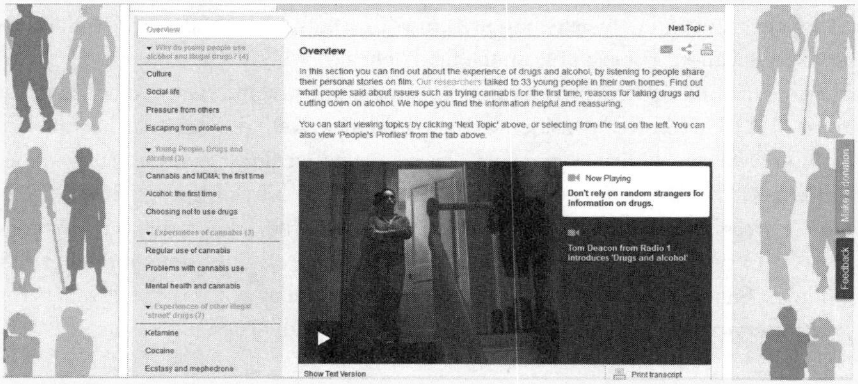

Source: Healthtalk.org

community or school, with the hopes of generating some kind of dialogue around the key issues. During the last few years, digital storytelling has become increasingly popular in education, with the collection and telling of stories being used by individuals, schools, and communities. For instance, the Center for Digital Storytelling holds workshops on digital storytelling and maintains a website with a

Figure 13.3   An Example of a Digital Story With Voice and Images

I Read Banned Books

This is a story about the struggles of reading teachers on book banning. Titles of books that are banned from being taught in American schools were also shown.

Source: see, http://digitalstorytelling.coe.uh.edu/example_stories.cfm, for additional examples

REFLECTIVE OPPORTUNITY 13.1

Disseminating your research in visible and public ways creates new possibilities for individuals who might want to learn about and from your research results/findings. At the same time, when making your work public, particularly on websites and in spaces like YouTube, you have to be thoughtful about maintaining participants' confidentiality. While participant confidentiality is an important consideration throughout your research process, it is especially obvious when you display your work in public ways.

1. What might be some of the ways that you can ensure that the approach you take to disseminating your research maintains participant confidentiality?

2. What might be some of the risks of disseminating your research via the Internet or in other more publically accessible ways?

collection of stories around central issues. Figure 13.3 shows a digital story about how reading teachers deal with the banning of books.

SUMMARIZING THE RESEARCH PROCESS AND THE METHODOLOGIES PRESENTED

Throughout this textbook, our focus has been on describing the research process while linking this process to everyday problems you may be facing in your classroom, school, and/or district.

Figure 13.4   The Cyclical Research Process

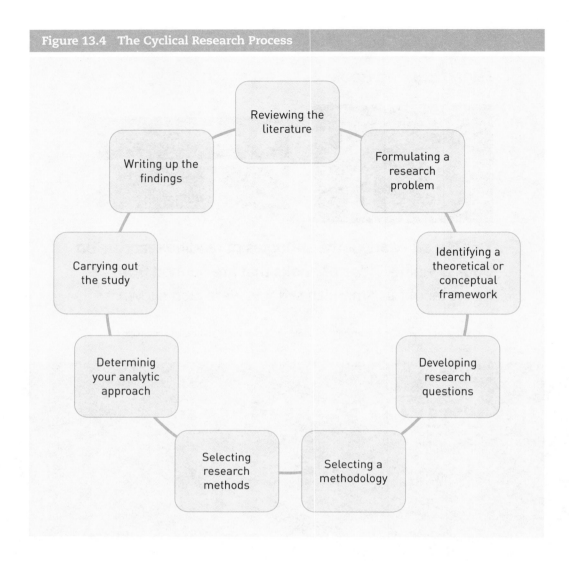

Now, in conclusion, we think it is important to briefly summarize the research process as we have described it so that you have a concrete understanding of the process from start to finish.

We begin by revisiting the research cycle, as represented in Figure 13.4.

It is useful to envision the research process as cyclical and recognize that it is often nonlinear and can even feel a bit messy. Nonetheless, quite often, many practitioner-scholars begin the research process by reviewing literature, and, through that process, identifying a research problem. Considering your unique context, we suggest that the research problem be aligned with a problem of practice, which we define as common, everyday challenges that inspire, frustrate, embolden, or drive you to support students and the learning community more broadly. Related to this, it is important to identify a theoretical or conceptual framework that informs your study and shapes not only the generation of

REFLECTIVE OPPORTUNITY 13.2

1. Across the research process, identify the most significant ethical concerns and/or challenges that are related to your research study.

2. In considering these challenges, identify ways that you could (a) address them and (b) design your research to prevent them from becoming significant concerns.

your research questions, but also serves to ground your analysis and interpretation. Next, it is critical to spend time developing meaningful research questions, with this process differing slightly when carrying out qualitative, quantitative, action research, or mixed methods research. As such, it is useful to spend time thinking carefully about your methodology and research methods.

As we noted in Chapter 1, we suggest that the selection of a research methodology should be intimately linked to a research paradigm(s) (such as positivism, post-positivism, and so on) and aligned with the theories that inform your research. Related to the four research traditions we highlighted within the textbook, we also noted that the varying research methods or procedures used for carrying out research are often aligned closely with particular methodologies. One key aspect for delineating your research methods is to identify and state explicitly the approach you will take to analyzing and interpreting your data. In this textbook, we also highlighted common qualitative and quantitative analytic approaches, which are both compatible with mixed methods and action research. Finally, we described the process by which practitioner-scholars carry out their research, and, quite importantly, begin writing and sharing their research.

RETURNING TO THE PLACE WE BEGAN: PROBLEMS OF PRACTICE

Underlying and informing the research process, we presented four problems of practice that we described as defining the current contours of the work that occurs in many classrooms, schools, and districts. Throughout the textbook, we have referred to these problems in various ways—presenting them within the context of Links to Practice, as references, and as examples. Now, in this final chapter, it is appropriate to offer insights on how these problems of practice can be developed as research topics and problems that, with your new understanding of the research process, you can take forward as research studies or as models for research studies that interest you.

The four problems of practice we introduced at the beginning of this textbook were rooted in the current work and challenges of educators. The first problem related to the challenge of promoting educational equity in student achievement. This challenge is inherently related to differences in student achievement results and has thus served as our anchor for references to quantitative research designs and methods. From basic descriptive statistics to more sophisticated inferential statistical designs, we see this topic as one that practitioner-scholars could pursue using data that they collect through various assessments or through secondary data sources that they acquire through student information systems, databases, and other existing information sources. Indeed, for practitioner-scholars who are interested in pursuing this line of research, there is a wealth of information that can be used with relatively little effort to collect it.

The second problem of practice that we introduced may, for many practitioner-scholars, seem out of reach. This problem relates to the challenges associated with implementing education policies. Throughout the textbook, we have referred to this problem of practice in various ways, most often noting the implementation of curriculum and new teacher evaluation practices. While these are not the only examples of education policies, we highlighted these to demonstrate how practitioner-scholars can conduct a qualitative research study or a mixed methods research study. In both cases, we sought to make policy-related research topics accessible to you, and to demonstrate that even as a classroom teacher or principal you can conduct research that informs and potentially influences the policy environment surrounding your classroom, school, and school district.

The third problem of practice we highlighted relates to reforming and improving educational organizations. We used the example of studying how central office administrators define principals' instructional leadership practice as an example, noting that greater understanding of the evolving principal's role can influence how support is provided to principals in their efforts to improve schools. We highlighted this problem as one that can be studied using qualitative methodologies, in particular a case study methodology. While other qualitative methodologies might be used, we argue that a case study approach is one that often resonates with practitioner-scholars.

Finally, we highlighted the problem of practice that is likely closest to your work as a practitioner-scholar, which relates to improving instructional and leadership practice. Throughout the textbook, we have framed this problem of practice as an opportunity to use action research, as well as other methodologies, to understand current practices and implement changes that result in their improvement. In presenting this problem of practice, we sought to make the research process relevant to your daily work and to show you how research can be used to improve your work even when the research process itself seems somewhat disconnected or detached.

Now that you have had an opportunity to learn more about the research process generally, we hope that you see how these problems of practice can be studied using various research methodologies and methods. Indeed, practitioner-scholarship is not dependent upon a single approach to research; rather, it calls upon you to thoughtfully consider the various approaches that you might take to research, as you engage in the critical *consumption* and *production* of research.

REFLECTIVE OPPORTUNITY 13.3

1. Looking at the four problems of practice discussed in this textbook, consider the ethical challenges related to each problem of practice and how these might influence the development of a research study.

SUMMARY

In closing, this textbook has provided you with an introduction to the research process, with a particular emphasis on the ways in which that process aligns with and helps you understand your work as a practitioner. Throughout the textbook, we have highlighted how the research process serves as an invitation to you— to better understand the students you serve, your work as an educator, the schools where you work, and the nature of the problems that both confront and challenge schools generally. We see this as an important invitation and one in which you, as a practitioner-scholar, have a vested interest. Indeed, this interest is essential to the long-term improvement of learning, teaching, schools, and districts.

KEY TERMS

Digital Storytelling 281

QUESTIONS TO CONSIDER

1. How might your work as a practitioner-scholar intersect with the improvement of teaching and learning in your classroom, school, and/or district?

2. What do you view as valuable about practitioner-scholarship?

3. What are some concrete ways that research can be used in everyday practices?

4. What are some of the forums that you might create to share your work?

5. What are some of the connections you have made between the problems of practice and their relationship to your current work?

CHAPTER EXERCISES

1. Write a brief statement describing your understanding of practitioner-scholarship and identify the ways in which your practice as a teacher or administrator shapes this understanding.

2. Identify a research topic based on one of the problems of practice discussed in this textbook. Develop a research question, select a research methodology, and describe how you would carry out the research study. In describing how you would carry out the study, consider how your understanding of practitioner-scholarship shapes the research design and your plan for carrying out the study.

3. Download an article related to a research topic you are interested in studying further. Read the article and note the ways in which you might approach the study differently. In particular, highlight the aspects of the study that seem inapplicable to your work and note how you would refine the study to make them more applicable.

4. Talk with colleagues in your department or PLC. Identify a potential research topic and plan a collaborative action research study. Use this as an opportunity to improve practice in your department or PLC. As you complete the study, consider how you can share your results/findings with colleagues in other departments to promote school-wide change.

As you continue to reflect upon the ways in which practitioner-scholarship might inform your everyday practices, you may find it useful to read more about how educators can use research to improve schools. Bauer and Brazier's (2012), book, *Using Research to Lead School Improvement: Turning Evidence Into Action*, offers a useful place to begin, as the authors present the connections between research and practice in clear terms directly related to everyday practices in schools. Vannini's (2012) book, *Popularizing Research: Engaging New Media Genres and Audiences*, is also a useful place to begin as you explore the varied ways by which you might share your research findings with broader audiences. His book provides multiple examples of how new media might be used to expand who gains access to research in meaningful and informative ways.

Sharpen your skills with SAGE edge!

edge.sagepub.com/lochmiller

SAGE edge for Students provides a personalized approach to help you accomplish your coursework goals in an easy-to-use learning environment. You'll find action plans, mobile-friendly eFlashcards, and quizzes as well as videos, web resources, and links to SAGE journal articles to support and expand on the concepts presented in this chapter.

GLOSSARY

Abductive Thinking: A way of thinking common to grounded theory wherein the practitioner-scholar explores the possible links and causation among phenomena.

Abstract: A brief summary of the contents of the article, typically placed at the beginning of an article.

Action Research: An orientation to education research in which a practitioner-scholar selects a problem, challenge, or issue drawn from their practice and uses the research process to identify and implement a possible solution or response.

Alternative Hypothesis: A type of hypothesis that states that there will be a difference between two groups, a set of scores, or as a result of a specific intervention.

Analysis of Variance (ANOVA): An inferential statistical test that compares two or more groups.

Anonymizing: The process of removing any identifiable characteristics from a dataset that could potentially (if the data were disclosed publicly) identify the participants in your study.

APA Manuscript Style: A set of standard rules and procedures for writing in a scholarly way, which covers issues ranging from word choice to verb tense to minimizing bias in writing to how to structure a manuscript.

Applied Research: Research that aims to understand a problem of practice and uses this understanding to address the problem of practice.

A priori codes: These codes are based on predetermined words or phrases that are directly linked to the research literature and/or specific theories informing your work.

Assent: Refers to the process wherein a minor agrees to participate in a research study.

Assignments: Refers to values that you give to the variables in the dataset.

Audit Trail: This refers to a paper-based or electronic account of each of your decisions, from how you defined and described each code to the way in which you moved from codes to categories to themes.

Basic Research: Research that aims to generate new knowledge and understanding about a topic of interest.

Bias: A concept that refers to a practitioner-scholar's or a study's tendency to ignore, overlook, or incorrectly interpret data collected in a study.

Binary Variables: Refers to categorical measures that are dichotomous (for example, male or female).

Blogs or **Web-Logs:** A website wherein a practitioner-scholar chronicles their experiences or thoughts either publically or privately.

Bracketing: A concept common to phenomenology that refers to suspending judgment about the phenomenon of interest in order that you might know how the object of study really is.

Bracketing Interview: A method common to phenomenology wherein the practitioner-scholar invites a trained colleague to interview them about their own experiences with the phenomenon of interest as a means of identifying their own biases and judgments.

Capacity: Refers to an individual's ability to understand and retain information, which becomes particularly important when sharing the purpose of a study with a potential participant.

Case: A concept common to case study methodology and defined as a bounded system in which there are a set of parts or operations that work together to create the whole.

Case Study: An approach to qualitative research in which a practitioner-scholar focuses on a detailed study of one or more cases within a bounded system.

Categorical Measures: Measures that broadly refer to categories (for example, men or women).

Categorical Variables: Variables that refer to a category (for example, male or female).

Categories: In thematic analysis, categories bring together various coded passages and assign meaning about their relationships, differences, similarities, or interactions.

Causal-Comparative Designs: A type of quantitative research design that is used when a practitioner-scholar wants to identify a reason for differences among the outcomes or behaviors of an individual or a group of individuals.

Chi-Square: A statistical test that is used when the practitioner-scholar seeks to determine whether there is a statistically significant difference among data that are reported in the form of frequency counts, percentages, or proportions.

Citation Management System: A software system that can be used to efficiently store and manage electronic documents

Closed-Ended Question: In a survey instrument, this type of question is one that forces the survey participant to select from among a series of pre-determined choices.

Code: This refers to a text-based label that gives meaning to a segment of your data.

Code: In qualitative data analysis, this is simply a flag or label that you apply to the text to associate it with a particular meaning.

Codebook: An inventory of the individual variables in your dataset and their respective values.

Coding: Refers to the process of attaching a short word or phrase to specific portions of your data.

Cohort Survey: Survey instruments that are designed to track changes in perceptions over time for a given group of individuals with similar characteristics.

Computer-Assisted Qualitative Data Analysis Software (CAQDAS): A software package that supports a researcher engaged in qualitative data analysis.

Conceptual Framework: Explains narratively or graphically the key factors and variables that are central to the research design.

Condensed Transcript: A type of gisted transcript that does not include unnecessary words (such as "ums").

Conflict of Interest: This occurs when a researcher may benefit financially from the research that she or he is conducting.

Consent: The process of informing and getting agreement from a research participant to participate in the study.

Construct Validity: Refers to the congruence between your ideas and the way that you measure them.

Constructivist Paradigm: A research paradigm that leads a practitioner-scholar to assume that there are multiple realities that can be studied, with the researcher deriving their own understanding of these realities by working with and through the participants' perspectives of a given phenomenon or problem of practice.

Content Validity: Refers to the degree to which a test measures what it intends to measure.

Continuous Variables: Those variables that are assigned any value between a minimum and maximum, such as a test score or your height.

Control Group: The group that does not receive the intervention in an experimental study.

Convenience Sample: The most straightforward approach to sampling in qualitative research, as it involves engaging individuals or sites that are most accessible to you as a researcher.

Convergent Parallel Design: A mixed methods research design wherein the qualitative and quantitative studies are carried out simultaneously.

Conversation Analysis: A qualitative methodology that focuses on the sequential organization of talk or language use.

Correlation Coefficient: A measure that describes the strength and direction of the relationship between two variables.

Correlational Studies: A type of quantitative study that enables practitioner-scholars to compare variables in two or more groups.

Criterion Validity: Refers to the extent to which a test score accurately reflects some type of performance indicator.

Critical/Feminist Paradigm: A research paradigm that leads to questions being raised about the power bases and inherent inequities that exist across race, gender, social class, sexual orientation, ethnicity, and language.

Cross-Sectional Surveys: Survey instruments that are designed to capture information from participants at a single point in time.

Database: A repository of information that can be accessed using queries.

Dataset: Refers to the data that you will use to complete your analysis.

Data Triangulation: A type of triangulation that is frequently highlighted in case study research, and is thought to be possible through the use of varied data sources, with evidence being gathered across time and space.

Dedoose: A web-based service that supports the management and analysis of qualitative and mixed methods research data.

Deductive Analysis: A type of analysis that occurs when a practitioner-scholar works from a series of premises to formulate a broader understanding or conclusion.

Dependent Variable: A variable that is dependent on other factors and thus thought to influence the outcomes that occur.

Descriptive Analysis: An analysis that summarizes the distribution of the data and thus presents to your reader a picture of what the data say.

Descriptive Codes: A word or phrase that points to the main topic of a segment of the data.

Descriptive Research: Research that provides important information about "what is" and thus provides opportunities to understand and critique existing practices in the education system.

Descriptive Statistics: Statistics that allow you to describe the distribution of the scores/values in a particular dataset.

Descriptive Studies: A type of quantitative study that is undertaken when the practitioner-scholar wishes to describe the characteristics of the data.

Digital Storytelling: The use of a variety of media forms to share aspects of an individual or group story.

Direct Consent: This type of consent is the preferred form of consent wherein the individual being asked to participate in a research study gives their consent directly to the researcher.

Discourse Analysis: Various qualitative approaches to a focused study of talk and texts.

Editorially Reviewed Source: A publication that has been reviewed by an editor for its substance and style, but not undergone peer review.

Embedded Design: A mixed methods research design that treats

both qualitative and quantitative research approaches equally and thus in theory does not introduce qualitative or quantitative data in phases.

Emergent Design: A mixed methods research design that introduces qualitative and quantitative data into the study as is necessary to address or respond to specific research questions.

Emergent Research Designs: Those research designs that adjust their methods even after data collection begins.

Emic Perspective: A perspective that considers things through the perspective of the participants.

Epistemology: A philosophical concept that refers to the idea of knowledge construction and centers around what we know and how we go about knowing.

Essence: A concept common to phenomenology that is used to describe a universally experienced phenomenon.

Ethnography: A qualitative approach to the study of cultural patterns and everyday practices and perspectives in natural settings.

Etic Perspective: An account of cultural patterns and practices based on the conceptual perspectives and frameworks of the researcher.

Experimental Designs: A quantitative research design that aims to identify a particular cause and effect.

Experimental Hypothesis: A hypothesis that describes the anticipated effect of an intervention on a specified outcome.

Explanatory Research: Research that enables researchers to generate

theoretical understandings of current practices, programs, processes, and policies.

Explanatory Sequential Design: A mixed methods research design that is completed in two phases in which the practitioner-scholar begins by collecting quantitative data and then concludes by collecting and analyzing qualitative data.

Explanatory Study: A type of quantitative study that aims to "test theories about how and why some attributes, behaviors, or phenomena are related as they are, or how and why the observed differences between pre-existing groups came to be" (O'Dwyer & Bernauer, 2014, p. 156).

Exploratory Sequential Design: A mixed methods research design that prioritizes qualitative data.

External Validity: A concept that refers to the degree to which the results of a study are generalizable.

Extraneous or Confounding Variable: Refers to any variable that is not the independent variable but could potentially impact the dependent variable.

Fabricating: Occurs when a practitioner-scholar makes up or creates data in order to support their results/findings.

Fixed Design: A mixed methods research design that establishes how data will be used at the beginning of the study.

Focus Group Interview Protocol: A guiding protocol wherein you interview multiple participants (approximately four to six participants) at once using a common interview protocol.

Frequencies: Simple counts that refer to the number of times something has occurred.

Generalizability: The ability to characterize or apply findings from a research study to the larger population.

Gisted Transcript: A transcript that gives you the gist or overall sense of the audio or video file.

Grounded Theory: A qualitative methodology that focuses on the development or construction of a theory that is grounded in a dataset.

Hypothesis: A theory-based prediction about the phenomenon you are studying.

Improvement-Oriented Research: Research that seeks to address practice and is concerned with identifying what could be if particular actions or reforms were adopted.

Incompatibility Thesis: A concept that refers to the position that the mixing of qualitative and quantitative approaches is not possible due to epistemological and ontological paradigm differences.

Independent Variable: A variable that does not depend on other factors and is thus manipulated by the practitioner-scholar to determine whether the variable causes measurable changes in a particular outcome.

Inductive Thinking: A type of thinking common to qualitative research in which you move from a specific to a broader understanding.

Inferential Statistics: Statistical tests that allow practitioner-scholars to make inferences about the population as a whole, predict how variables will interact or relate, and assess the degree to which these interactions predict particular outcomes.

Informed Consent: Refers to the process of informing the participant about his or her rights as a research participant.

Institutional Review Board (IRB): A group of individuals who are authorized by an institution, such as a university, to determine whether a proposed research study complies with federal and institutional research regulations and ethical professional standards.

Internal Validity: Refers to the practitioner-scholar's ability to say that the independent variable caused the changes in the dependent variable.

Interval or Ratio Variables: Numeric variables that are equally situated on some type of scale, with the primary difference between an interval and ratio variable being that an interval variable does not have an absolute zero while a ratio variable does.

Interval Variables: Numeric scores or values for which an absolute zero can be defined.

Intervention: An action that a practitioner-scholar takes to address the defined challenge or problem within an action research study.

In-vivo Codes: Codes that refer to the actual word or phrase used by the participant.

Jeffersonian Transcript: A type of transcript that uses symbols to represent features of the interaction, such as overlapping speech or the length of a silence or gap in speech.

Keypunching: The process of entering values into an electronic format that supports analysis.

List-Wise Deletion: Involves deleting entire records from the dataset.

Massaging: Occurs when a practitioner-scholar intentionally or unintentionally misrepresents their dataset.

Matching: In causal-comparative designs, practitioner-scholars often use matching to ensure that participants in comparison groups have similar characteristics.

Mean: The arithmetic average of all of the scores or values.

Mean Imputation: An approach to dealing with missing data that might be used when variables cannot be deleted entirely or excluded partially.

Measures of Central Tendency: Measures that provide you with an opportunity to determine how scores or values relate to the mean.

Measures of Variability: Refers to the spread of the scores or values.

Median: The midpoint in a distribution of scores or values.

Memo: A written reflection about your data, often linked directly to some aspect of your data.

Mendeley: A citation management system.

Mixed Methods: A research approach that combines qualitative and quantitative research methods to answer a research question of interest.

Mixed Methods Research: An approach to research that uses both qualitative and quantitative research methods to make sense of a research question and/or problem.

Mode: The most frequently occurring score.

Multiphase Design: A mixed methods research design wherein the practitioner-scholar carries out separate qualitative and quantitative studies.

Narrative Research: Encompasses a wide variety of qualitative approaches to the study of how people make meaning of their life through story.

Naturally Occurring Data: Data that exist regardless of the presence of a researcher.

Negatively Skewed: Scores that are typically above the mean and thus further from the y-axis.

Nominal Variables: Refers to a categorical measure that has three or more categories (for example, a student's race/ethnicity).

Non-Experimental Research: A type of quantitative research wherein the practitioner-scholar does not manipulate the variables, rather they attempt to make descriptive and inferential claims about the patterns, trends, or relationships within the dataset.

Non-Parametric Data: Refers to data that are *not* normally distributed and thus require the practitioner-scholar to use different statistical tests than they would otherwise.

Non-Participant Observation: An observation that entails you minimizing your interactions with participants and primarily engaging in observation.

Non–Peer-Reviewed Source: A publication that was not reviewed by a panel of expert reviewers.

Nonprobability Sampling: A type of sampling that includes the entire population in the research or entails selecting participants on the basis of nonrandom characteristics.

Normal Distribution: Illustrates the assumption that the majority

of values or scores you observe are located near the mean.

Null Hypothesis: A hypothesis stating that there will be no difference between two groups, a set of scores, or as a result of a specific intervention.

Objectivity: A concept that has been linked to the assumption that a truth or reality exists outside of the research process or the practitioner-scholar.

Ontology: A philosophical concept that refers to the nature of reality and the assumptions related to what exists.

Open-ended Question: In a survey instrument, this type of question offers participants the opportunity to provide a unique response.

Ordinal Variables: A variable that describes the rank of an individual or score relative to other scores.

Pair-Wise Deletion: This involves excluding incomplete or missing variables only from those analyses where the variables are meaningful.

Panel Study: In survey research, this is similar to a cohort study in that it looks at a group of participants; yet, unlike a cohort study, a panel study relies on the same group of participants for multiple survey administrations.

Parametric Data: This refers to data that are normally distributed (that is, adhere closely to a normal distribution).

Participant Observation: A form of observation wherein you interact with the research participants while simultaneously observing for research purposes.

Participant Triangulation: A type of triangulation that ensues when a pattern or theme is corroborated across multiple participants.

Participatory Action Research: A methodological approach that builds on the tradition of action research and specifically identifies a social issue with community participants to co-research and co-develop a solution.

Pearson Correlation (*r*): A statistical test that indicates whether there is a relationship between two variables.

Peer-Reviewed Source: A publication that is reviewed by experts in the field to ensure that standards have been met across the research process and a contribution is being made to the field.

People First Language: A writing style wherein you put the person first (for example, using "child with autism" rather than the "autistic child" label).

Perception Data: Data that center on the perceptions or perspectives of the participants.

Phenomenology: A qualitative methodology that applies a philosophical perspective to the study of human experience.

Plagiarism: The use of someone else's words, ideas, or thoughts.

Population: A collection of individuals or sites with similar characteristics that the researcher wants to know something about.

Population Variance: Considers the spread of all scores for all members of a given group.

Positively Skewed: Scores that are typically below the mean and thus closer to the y-axis.

Positivist Paradigm: A research paradigm that leads a practitioner-scholar to assume that they can identify a single truth about the phenomenon that they are studying.

Post-Positivist Paradigm:
A research paradigm that leads a practitioner-scholars to assume that a reality exists (similar to a positivist perspective), while acknowledging that this reality must be interpreted and thus can only be approximated because of one's limitation as a researcher.

Poststructuralist Paradigm:
A research paradigm that leads a practitioner-scholar to assume that there are multiple realities that individuals construct to give meaning to the universe and that there is not a truth (with a capital T) to be known.

"Post-test only" Design:
A quantitative research design that involves assessing performance after the intervention has been applied.

Practitioner-Scholar: An individual who aspires to study problems of practice in a comprehensive and systematic way.

Prediction Studies: A type of quantitative study that may contain a descriptive component but moves a step further in that it attempts to make claims about what might happen.

Predictive Research: Research that is designed to help practitioner-scholars anticipate changes in outcomes.

"Pre-test/Post-test" Design:
A quantitative research design wherein the practitioner-scholar assesses research participants before applying the intervention and then assesses the same participants after the intervention has been applied.

Primary Audience:
This includes those individuals and/or organizations that you need to consider as you develop your research report and who are most likely to be impacted by your research.

Primary Source: A publication that is written by the individuals who were directly involved in the events described and/or study being reported.

Probability Sampling: A type of sampling wherein you attempt to construct a sample that includes individuals who approximate the population.

Problems of Practice:
Common, everyday challenges that confront classroom teachers, teacher leaders, and school and district administrators.

Purposeful Sample: A qualitative sampling approach in which you select individuals or sites on the basis of specific criteria.

Qualitative-Leading Mixed Methods Research Design:
A mixed methods research design wherein the practitioner-scholar develops a study that involves a qualitative problem of practice and relies primarily on qualitative data to investigate the problem of focus.

Qualitative Methodologies:
An umbrella term that encompasses those methodologies that take an interpretative, inductive approach to the study of human experience and the social world.

Qualitative Research: Research approaches that typically study things in their natural environments and focus on exploring and understanding how people make sense of and experience the world in which they live.

Quantitative-Leading Mixed Methods Research Designs:
A mixed methods research design wherein a practitioner-scholar relies on quantitative data to formulate their understanding of the research problem while using qualitative data to deepen, enlighten, or

explore particular ideas, concepts, or concerns.

Quantitative Methodologies:
An umbrella term that encompasses those methodologies that take a deductive approach to the study of human experience and the social world, typically represented by numerical data.

Quantitative Research:
Research approaches that use numeric data to represent individuals, experiences, and outcomes and to identify, understand, and assess the strength of relationships between data points.

Quotation: In ATLAS.ti, this refers to a segment of your data that might be of interest to you in your future analysis.

Random Assignment: Refers to the process of assigning participants in a way that ensures each participant has an equal chance of being assigned to a group.

Randomized Control Trials:
A type of experimental research design that allows a practitioner-scholar to create experimental conditions in which they can test the efficacy of a specific educational intervention, curriculum, or program.

Range: Describes the difference between the lowest and highest score or value.

Ratio Variable: This type of variable is similar to an interval variable except that the scores are based on a scale.

Reflexivity: The process of intentionally accounting for the assumptions, biases, experiences, and identities that may impact the research study.

Reliability: Refers to the consistency of measurement or the degree to which your measure is replicable across multiple administrations.

Research: A systematic investigation designed to make sense of complex, everyday problems that impact classroom teachers, teacher leaders, and school and district administrators.

Research Design: The overall plan to study a problem of practice.

Researcher-Generated Data: Data that would not exist apart from the researcher's intervention or effort in generating them.

Researcher Triangulation: A type of triangulation that is believed to occur when multiple researchers work together to generate a complex understanding of the unit of analysis, with their perspectives converging around a particular pattern and thereby resulting in stronger evidence than a single researcher could produce.

Research Methodology: The stance or perspective that a practitioner-scholar adopts in order to understand a particular problem of practice.

Research Methods: The procedures that are used to carry out a research study.

Research Paradigm: A way of thinking about and making sense of the world centered around a shared set of assumptions about how the world works and how you can go about studying it.

Research Problem Statement: A statement that describes what your study will investigate.

Re-storying: The analytical process of gathering the stories told and restructuring them in relationship to time, place, plot, and so on.

Sample: This refers to the individuals or sites from the population who will be interviewed, observed, surveyed, or otherwise engaged in your research study.

Sample Validity: The extent to which a sample represents the population.

Sample Variance: Considers the spread of scores for a subset of the members of a given group.

Saturation: A concept that can be defined as the point in data collection and analysis at which no new information and understanding are generated.

Scrivener: A word processing and project management tool that was developed to support the writing process, particularly for individuals who are developing lengthy documents.

Secondary Audience: This includes those individuals and/or organizations who might benefit from your research report/paper, but who you do not design your comments to address directly.

Secondary Data Analysis: A type of non-experimental research that involves the re-analysis of a data set.

Secondary Source: A publication that is written by individuals who were not directly involved in the events described and/or study being reported.

Semi-Structured Interview Protocol: A protocol used in an interview wherein the questions are developed beforehand, but you ask them with flexibility.

Significance Level: The maximum risk you are willing to take that your results are attributable to chance.

Simple Linear Regression or Multiple Regression: Refers to statistical tests that are used to relate scores or values.

Simple Random Sample: A sample type wherein each participant has an equal chance of being included in the sample.

Single-Subject or Single-Case Experimental Research Design: A type of experimental research design that allows a practitioner-scholar to test the effect of an intervention on a single individual or a set of individuals who are considered one group.

Skew: Refers to the degree to which scores or values cluster above or below the mean.

Snowball Sampling (or Chain Referral Sampling): This type of qualitative sampling involves identifying one or more participants or sites initially and then allowing recommendations from participants to guide the further development of the sample.

Solomon Four-Group Design: A type of quantitative research design in which a practitioner-scholar uses four groups of participants, with two completing a "pre-test/post-test" design and two completing a "post-test only" design to determine whether the intervention had an effect.

SPSS: A software package that provides practitioner-scholars with a multitude of statistical features and data management resources.

Standard Deviation: The square root of the variance of a set of scores.

Standardizing Values: The process of ensuring that variables with the same value are treated similarly.

Stratified Sampling:
A quantitative approach to sampling used when you want to ensure that the characteristics of the individuals (and potentially sites) included in the sample are representative of the characteristics of the individuals (and sites) in the broader population.

Structured Interview Protocol:
An interview protocol wherein you ask pre-determined questions that are explicitly listed in a predefined script.

Survey Piloting: A process that involves presenting a draft survey instrument to prospective participants prior to administering the survey to the entire survey sample.

Survey Research: A type of quantitative research that is intended to capture the perspectives of participants at a moment in time or changes in their perspectives across a period of time.

Syntax: A programming language that allows you to record each of your decisions regarding data management.

Systematic Sampling: A type of sampling used in quantitative research that is similar to simple random sampling, but does not involve using a table of random numbers.

Thematic Analysis: An approach to qualitative data analysis that allows you to move from broad understandings/readings of your data to identifying themes across the dataset.

Themes: In qualitative data analysis, this refers to broad, analytically driven statements about data.

Theoretical Framework: The theoretical basis of a research study.

Theoretical Sampling:
A concept common to grounded theory wherein the practitioner-scholar samples "data to fill out the properties of an emergent conceptual category" (Charmaz, 2011, p. 363).

Theory Triangulation: A type of triangulation thought to occur when researchers apply different theories to a dataset to see how various concepts might help them understand their data more fully and increase evidence for the claims they are making.

Thick Description: A detailed account of a researcher's experience conducting fieldwork and making sense of local practices.

Third-party Consent: This type of consent occurs when someone other than the individual being asked to participate in the study gives consent on the participant's behalf.

Transformative Design: A mixed methods research design in which the practitioner-scholar adopts a transformative theoretical lens, which draws upon critical and socially oriented perspectives.

Treatment Group: The group that receives the intervention in an experimental study.

Trend Surveys: A survey instrument designed primarily to collect information from a group of participants over time.

Triangulation: The practice of using multiple data points to build a solid case for the claims you make.

Trustworthiness: Refers to the degree to which your data collection, analysis, and presentation of findings are presented in a thorough and verifiable manner.

t-Test: An inferential statistical test that is useful when comparing scores or values from two groups.

Type-I Error: A type of error that occurs when you accept that the alternative hypothesis is true but in actuality it is not.

Type-II Error: A type of error that occurs when you accept the null hypothesis as true, when in reality there was an effect.

Unstructured Interview: A type of interview in which you engage in a conversation without previously structuring the questions you will ask.

Validity: The degree to which the inference drawn from a score is accurate.

Variable: An element in the dataset to which you have assigned some value or meaning that is relevant to your study.

Variance: The amount of spread among scores.

Verbatim Transcript: A type of transcript wherein you type everything you hear (in the audio recording) or see (in the video recording).

Visual Transcript: A type of transcript wherein your transcript produces a broad strokes description of what was shared or occurred in the audio or video file, as well as images (such as pictures or still shots from video data) that represent the participant's actions.

Vulnerable Population:
A population that includes anyone that could be rendered powerless because of their current age, disability, or situation, and thereby potentially less capable of understanding the potential risks of participating in a study.

REFERENCES

Adelman, C. (2006). *The toolbox revisited: Paths to degree completion from high school through college*. Washington, DC: U.S. Department of Education, Office of Educational Research and Involvement.

Adler, E., & Clark, R. (2003). *How it's done: An invitation to social research* (2nd ed.). Australia: Thompson.

American Educational Research Association. (2002). *Ethical standards of the American Educational Research Association:* Cases and commentary. Washington, DC: Author.

American Educational Research Association. (2011). Code of ethics. *Educational Researcher*, 40(3), 145–156.

American Psychiatric Association. (2000). *Diagnostic and statistical manual of mental disorders* (4th ed.). Washington, DC: Author.

American Psychological Association (APA). (1994). *Publication manual of the American Psychological Association* (4th ed.). Washington, DC: Author.

American Psychological Association (APA). (2010). *Publication manual of the American Psychological Association* (6th ed.). Washington, DC: Author.

Anders, A. D. (2007). *Revisiting the panopticon: Educational narratives from incarcerated youth*. University of North Carolina, Chapel Hill: Unpublished dissertation.

Anders, A. D. (2011). Circuits of dominance in education and poverty: Control logic and counter narrative. *Urban Review*, 43(4), 528–546.

Anders, A., & Lester, J. (2011). Living in Riverhill: A postcritical challenge to the production of a neoliberal success story. In B. Portofino & H. Hickman (Eds.), *Critical service learning as revolutionary pedagogy: A project of student agency in action* (pp. 223–249). Charlotte, NC: Information Age Publishing.

Anfara, V. A., Brown, K. M., & Mangione, T. L. (2002). Qualitative analysis on stage: Making the research process more public. *Educational Researcher*, 31(7), 28–38.

Anyon, J. (2005). *Radical possibilities: Public policy, urban education, and a new social movement*. New York, NY: Routledge/Falmer.

Babbie, E. (1998). *The practice of social research* (8th ed.). Belmont, CA: Wadsworth Publishing Company.

Bach, H. (1998). *A visual narrative concerning curriculum, girls, photography etc.* Walnut Creek, CA: Left Coast Publishers.

Baldridge, B. J. (2014). Relocating the deficit: Reimagining black youth in neoliberal times. *American Educational Research Journal*, 51(3), 440–472.

Bandura, A. (1986). *Social foundations of thought and action: A social cognitive theory*. Englewood Cliffs, NJ: Prentice-Hall.

Barnes, S. B., & Whinnery, K. W. (2002). Effects of functional mobility skills training for young students with physical disabilities. *Exceptional Children*, 68(3), 313–324.

Bauer, S. C., & Brazer, S. D. (2012). *Using research to lead school improvement: Turning evidence into action*. Thousand Oaks, CA: SAGE.

Bell, S. E. (1988). Becoming a political woman: The reconstruction and interpretation of experience through stories. In A. D. Todd & S. Fisher (Eds.), *Gender and discourse: The power of talk* (pp. 97–123). Norwood, NJ: Ablex.

Berry, W. D., & Feldman, S. (1985). *Multiple regression in practice*. Thousand Oaks, CA: SAGE.

Biernacki, P., & Waldork, D. (1981). Snowball sampling: Problems and techniques of chain referral sampling. *Sociological Methods & Research*, 10(2), 141–163.

Blaikie, N. (2000). *Designing social research*. Cambridge, UK: Polity.

Bogdan, R., & Biklen, S. K. (2007). *Qualitative research for education: An introduction to theories and methods* (5th ed.). Boston, MA: Pearson Education.

Boote, D. N., & Beile, P. (2005). Scholars before researchers: On the centrality of the dissertation literature review in research preparation. *Educational Research*, 34(6), 3–15.

Bowers, A. (2010). Toward addressing the issues of site selections in district effectiveness research: A two level hierarchical linear growth model. *Educational Administration Quarterly*, 46(3), 395–425.

Bracht, G. A., & Glass, G. V. (1968). External validity of experiments. *American Educational Research Journal*, 5(4), 437–474.

Braddock, D. L., & Parish, S. L. (2001). An institutional history of disability. In G. L. Albrecht, K. D. Seelman, & M. Bury, (Eds.), *Handbook of disability studies* (pp. 11–68). Thousand Oaks, CA: SAGE.

Brophy, J. (1987). Synthesis of research on strategies for motivating students to learn. *Educational Leadership, 45*(2), 40–48.

Bryant, A., & Charmaz, K. (2007). Grounded theory in historical perspective: An epistemological account. In A. Bryant & K. Charmaz (Eds.), *The SAGE handbook of grounded theory* (pp. 31–57). London, UK: SAGE.

Bryman, A. (2008). S*ocial research method* (3rd ed.). Oxford, UK: Oxford University Press.

Buck, G., Cook, K., Quigley, C., Eastwood, J., & Lucas, Y. (2009). Profiles of urban, low SES African American girls' attitudes toward science: A sequential explanatory mixed methods study. *Journal of Mixed Methods Research, 3*(4), 386–410.

Buehler, A. E. (2006). A case study of successful small school reform: The construction academy as a fundamentally different enterprise. University of Tennessee: Unpublished dissertation.

Burkhardt, H., & Schoenfeld, A. H. (2003). Improving educational research: Toward a more useful, more influential, and better funded enterprise. *Educational Researcher, 32*(9), 3–14.

Cabrera, A. F., & La Nasa, S. M. (2001). On the path to college: Three critical tasks facing America's disadvantaged. *Research in Higher Education, 42*(2), 119–149.

Calhoun, E. J. (2002). Action research for school improvement. *Educational Leadership, 59*(6), 18–24.

Camburn, E. M., Rowan, B., & Taylor, J. E. (2003). Distributed leadership in schools: The case of elementary schools adopting comprehensive school reform models. *Educational Evaluation and Policy Analysis, 25*(4), 347–373.

Campbell, D. T. & Stanley, J. C. (1971). *Experimental and quasi-experimental designs for research.* Chicago, IL: Rand McNally.

Carspecken, P. F. (1996). *Critical ethnography in educational research: A theoretical and practical guide.* New York, NY: Routledge.

Charmaz, K. (2006). *Constructing grounded theory: A practical guide through qualitative analysis.* London, UK: SAGE.

Charmaz, K. (2011). Grounded theory methods in social justice research. In N. K. Denzin & Y. S. Lincoln (Eds.), *The SAGE handbook of qualitative research* (pp. 359–380). Thousand Oaks, CA: SAGE.

Clarke, A. E. (2005). *Situational analysis: Grounded theory after the postmodern turn.* Thousand Oaks, CA: SAGE.

Cohen, D. K., & Hill, H. C. (2001). *Learning policy: When state education reform works.* New Haven, CT: Yale University Press.

Collingwood, R. G. (1940). *An essay on metaphysics.* Oxford, UK: Clarendon.

Cook, T. D., & Campbell, D. T. (1979). *Quasi-experimentation: Design and analysis issues for field settings.* Chicago, IL: Rand McNally.

Cook, T. D., & Shadish, W. R. (1994). Social experiments: Some developments over the past fifteen years. *Annual Review of Psychology, 45,* 545–580.

Corbin, J. (2009). Taking an analytic journey. In J. M. Morese, P. N. Stern, J. Corbin, B. Bowers, K. Charmaz, & A. E. Clarke (Eds.), *Developing grounded theory: The second generation* (pp. 35–53). Walnut Creek, CA: Left Coast Press.

Coulter, S. E., & Lester, J. N. (2011). Finding and redefining the meaning of teaching: Exploring the experience of mid-career English teachers. *Journal of Curriculum and Instruction, 5*(2), 5–26.

Cozza, B., & Oreshkina, M. (2013). Cross-cultural study of cognitive and metacognitive processes during math problem solving. *School Science and Mathematics, 113*(6), 275–284.

Creighton, T. B. (2007). *Schools and data: The educator's guide for using data to improve decision making.* Thousand Oaks, CA: Corwin Press.

Creswell, J. W. (2012). *Educational research: Planning, conducting, and evaluating quantitative and qualitative research* (4th ed.). Boston, MA: Pearson.

Creswell, J. W., & Miller, D. L. (2000). Determining validity in qualitative inquiry. *Theory into Practice, 39*(3), 124–130.

Creswell, J. W., & Plano Clark, V. L. (2011). *Designing and conducting mixed methods research.* Thousand Oaks, CA: SAGE.

Cronbach, L. (1971). Test validation. In R. Thorndike (Ed.), *Educational measurement,* Vol. 2 (pp. 443–507). Washington, DC: American Council on Education.

Cumming, T. M., Strnadová, I., & Singh, S. (2014). iPads as instructional tools to enhance learning opportunities for students with developmental disabilities: An action research project. *Action Research, 12*(2), 151–176.

Datnow, A., Hubbard, L., & Conchas, G. Q. (2001). How context mediates policy: The implementation of single gender public schooling in California.

Teachers College Record, 103(2), 184–206.

Dee, T. S. (2007). Teachers and the gender gaps in student achievement. *Journal of Human Resources, 42*(3), 528–554.

Denzin, N. K. (1978). *The research act: A theoretical orientation to sociology methods* (2nd ed.). New York, NY: McGraw-Hill.

Denzin, N. K., & Lincoln, Y. S. (2005). *The SAGE handbook of qualitative research* (3rd ed.). Thousand Oaks, CA: SAGE.

Department of Education (1993), "Australian schools of the future," available at: http://download.audit. vic.gov.au/files/19971202-Special-Report-52-Schools-of-the-Future.pdf (accessed March 25, 2012).

Desimone, L. M., & Long, D. (2010). Teacher effects and the achievement gap: Do teacher and teaching quality influence the achievement gap between Black and White and high- and low-SES students in the early grades? *Teachers College Record, 112*(12), 3024–3073.

Dey, I. (1993). *Qualitative data analysis: A user-friendly guide for social scientists.* London, UK: Routledge.

Dillman, D. A., Smyth, J. D., & Christian, L. M. (2014). *Internet, phone, mail, and mixed-mode surveys: The tailored design method* (4th ed.). Hoboken, NJ: John Wiley & Sons, Inc.

Dixon-Woods, M., Agarwal, S., Young, B., Jones, D., & Sutton, A. (2004). *Integrative approaches to qualitative and quantitative evidence.* London, UK: Health Development Agency.

Du Bois, J. W. (1991). Transcription design principles for spoken discourse research. *Pragmatics, 1*(1), 71–106.

Edmonds, R. (1979). Effective schools for the urban poor. *Educational Leadership, 37*(1), 15–23.

Edwards, D. (1997). *Discourse and cognition.* London, UK: SAGE.

Edwards, D. (1999). Emotion discourse. *Culture & Psychology, 5*(3), 271–291.

Eisner, J., & Peshkin, A. (Eds.). (2000). *Qualitative inquiry in education: The continuing debate.* New York, NY: Teacher's College Press.

Elfers, A. M., Knapp, M. S., & Plecki, M. L. (2004). *Development and deployment of a "Fast Response" survey system in Washington State: Methodological notes.* Seattle: University of Washington, Center for the Study of Teaching and Policy. Retrieved from http://www.ctpweb.org.

Elfers, A. M., & Stritikus, T. (2014). How school and district leaders support classroom teachers' work with English Language Learners. *Educational Administration Quarterly, 50*(2), 305–344.

Ellerson, N. M. (2009). *Schools and the stimulus: How America's public school districts are using ARRA funds.* Arlington, VA: American Association of School Administrators (AASA). Retrieved December 10, 2011, from http://www.aasa.org/research.aspx.

Ellerson, N. M. (2010a). *Surviving a thousand cuts: America's public schools and the recession.* Arlington, VA: American Association of School Administrators (AASA). Retrieved December 10, 2011, from http://www.aasa.org/research.aspx.

Ellerson, N. M. (2010b). *Projections of national education job cuts for the 2010–11 school year.* Arlington, VA: American Association of School Administrators (AASA) Retrieved December 10, 2011, from http://www.aasa.org/research.aspx.

Emerson, R. M., Fretz, R. I., & Shaw, L. L. (1995). *Writing ethnographic fieldnotes.* Chicago, IL: University of Chicago Press.

Emerson, R. M., Fretz, R. I., & Shaw, L. L. (2011). *Writing ethnographic fieldnotes* (2nd ed.). Chicago, IL: University of Chicago Press.

Evans, K. (2011). *Suspended students' experiences with in-school suspension: A phenomenological investigation.* University of Tennessee: Unpublished dissertation.

Farris-Berg, K. (2014). A different model for school success: Empower teachers. *Phi Delta Kappan, 95*(7), 31–36.

Field, A. (2009). *Discovering statistics using SPSS* (3rd ed.). London, UK: SAGE.

Field, M. J., & Behrman, R. E. (2004). Ethical conduct of clinical research involving children: Committee on clinical research involving children. Washington, DC: National Academies Press.

Fowler, F. J. (2013). *Survey research methods* (5th ed.). Thousand Oaks, CA: SAGE.

Gabriel, R., & Lester, J. N. (2012). Teacher educators' varied definitions of learning disabilities. *The Review of Disability Studies: An International Journal, 8*(2), 4–19.

Gall, M. G., Gall, J. P., & Borg, W. R. (2007). *Educational research: An introduction* (8th ed.). Boston, MA: Pearson.

Gallo, S. (2014). The effects of gendered immigration enforcement on middle childhood and schooling. *American Educational Research Journal, 51*(3), 473–504.

Gallucci, C. (2008). Districtwide instructional reform: Using sociocultural theory to link professional learning. *American Journal of Education*, *114*(4), 541–581.

Gallucci, C., & Boatright, E. E. (2007). *Gaining traction through professional coaching: A partnership between the Center for Educational Leadership and Highline School District* (Interim Report No. 2). Seattle: Center for the Study of Teaching and Policy, University of Washington.

Gallucci, C., & Swanson, J. (2008). *Aiming high: Leadership for district-wide instructional improvement: A partnership between the Center for Educational Leadership and Norwalk-La Mirada Unified School District, Interim research report and case summary.* Seattle: Center for the Study of Teaching and Policy, University of Washington.

Gallucci, C., Van Lare, M. D., Yoon, I. H., & Boatright, B. (2010). Instructional coaching: Building theory about the role and organizational support for professional learning. *American Educational Research Journal*, *47*(4), 919–963.

Garcıá, O. (2009). *Bilingual education in the 21st century: A global perspective.* Malden, MA: Wiley-Blackwell.

Garet, M. S., Porter, A. C., Desimone, L., Birman, B. F., & Yoon, K. S. (2001). What makes professional development effective? Results from a national sample of teachers. *American Educational Research Journal*, *38*(4), 915–945.

Gay, L. R., Mills, G. E., & Airasian, P. (2012). *Educational research: Competencies for analysis and applications* (10th ed.). Boston, MA: Pearson.

Geertz, C. (1973). *The interpretation of cultures.* New York, NY: Basic Books.

George, D. & Mallery, P. (2001). *SPSS for Windows 10.0* (3rd ed.). Needham, MA: Allyn and Bacon.

Glaser, B. G. (1978). *Theoretical sensitivity.* Mill Valley, CA: Sociology Press.

Glaser, B. G. (1998). *Doing grounded theory: Issues and discussions.* Mill Valley, CA: Sociology Press.

Glaser, B. G., & Strauss, A. L. (1967). *The discovery of grounded theory.* Chicago, IL: Aldine.

Glass, G. V. (1976, November). Primary, secondary, and meta-analysis of research. *Educational Researcher,* *5*(10), 3–8.

Golafshani, N. (2003). Understanding reliability and validity in qualitative research. *The Qualitative Report*, *8*(4), 597–607.

Grissom, J. A., & Harrington, J. R. (2010). Investing in administrator efficacy: An examination of professional development as a tool for enhancing principal effectiveness. *American Journal of Education*, *116*(4), 583–612.

Grissom, J. A., & Loeb, S. (2011). Triangulating principal effectiveness: How perspectives of parents, teachers, and assistant principals identify the central importance of managerial skills. *American Educational Research Journal*, *48*(5), 1091–1123.

Grix, J. (2002). Introducing students to the generic terminology of social research. *Politics*, *22*(3), 175–186.

Gurr, D., Drysdale, J., Ylimaki, R., & Moos, L. (2011a). Preparing instructional leaders. In R. Ylimaki & S. Jacobsen (Eds.), *US and cross-national policies, practices, and preparation: Implications for successful instructional leadership, organizational learning, and culturally responsive practices* (pp. 125–152). Dordrecht, Netherlands: Springer.

Guthrie, J. W., & Peng, A. (2011). A warning for all who would listen— American's public schools face a forthcoming fiscal tsunami. In F. M. Hess & E. Osberg (Eds.), *Stretching the school dollar: How schools can save money while serving the students best* (pp. 19–44). Cambridge, MA: Harvard Education Press.

Hallinan, M. T. (1994). Tracking: From theory to practice. *Sociology of Education*, *67*(2), 79–84.

Hammersley, M., & Atkinson, P. (2007). *Ethnography: Principles in practice* (3rd ed.). New York, NY: Routledge.

Hart, C. (1998). *Doing a literature review: Releasing the social science research imagination.* London, UK: SAGE.

Hatch, J. A. (2002). *Doing qualitative research in education settings.* Albany: State University of New York Press.

Hawes, C. A., & Plourde, L. A. (2005). Parental involvement and its influence on the reading achievement of 6th grade students. *Reading Improvement*, *42*(1), 47–57.

Hay, C. (2002). *Political analysis: A critical introduction.* Basingstoke, UK: Palgrave.

Heath, S. B., & Street, B. V. (2008). On ethnography: Approaches to language and literacy research. New York, NY: Teachers College Press.

Heil, S., Reisel, L., & Attewell, P. (2014). College selectivity and degree completion. *American Educational Research Journal*, *51*(5), 913–935.

Hensley, M. K. (2011). Citation management software: Features and futures. *Reference & User Services Quarterly*, *50*(3), 204–208.

Hill, H. C., Rowan, B., & Ball, D. L. (2005). Effect of teachers' mathematical knowledge for teaching on student achievement. *American Educational Research Journal*, *42*(2), 371–406.

Honig, M. I. (2003). Building policy from practice: District central office administrators' roles and capacity for implementing collaborative education policy. *Educational Administration Quarterly, 39*(3), 292–338.

Honig, M. I. (2006). Street-level bureaucracy revisited: Frontline district central-office administrators as boundary spanners in education policy implementation. *Educational Evaluation and Policy Analysis, 28*(4), 357–383.

Honig, M. I. (2012). District central office leadership as teaching: How central office administrators support principals' development as instructional leaders. *Educational Administration Quarterly, 48*(4), 733–744.

Howard, T. C. (2010). *Why race and culture matter in schools: Closing the achievement gap in America's classrooms.* New York, NY: Teachers College Press.

Howe, K. (1988). Against the quantitative-qualitative incompatibility thesis, or, Dogmas die hard. *Educational Researcher, 17*(8), 10–16.

Hoy, W. K., Tarter, C. J., & Woolfolk Hoy, A. (2006). Academic optimism of schools: A force for student achievement. *American Educational Research Journal, 43*(3), 425–446.

Hoy, W. K., Tarter, C. J., & Woolfolk Hoy, A. (2006). Academic optimism of schools. In W. K. Hoy & C. Miskel (Eds.), *Contemporary issues in educational policy and school outcomes* (pp. 135–156). Greenrich, CT: Information Age.

Huberman, A. M., & Miles, M. B. (1984). *Innovation up close: How school improvement works.* New York, NY: Plenum.

HyperRESEARCH (Version 2.6.1) [Computer software.] Randolph, MA: Researchware, Inc.

Israel, M., & Hay, I. (2006). *Research ethics for social scientists.* London, UK: SAGE.

Jacob, S., Decker, D. M., & Hartshorne, T. S. (2011). *Ethics and law for school psychologists* (6th ed.). Hoboken, NJ: John Wiley & Sons.

Jacobson, S. (2005). The recruitment and retention of school leaders: Understanding administrator supply and demand. In N. Bascia, A. Cumming, A. Datnow, K. Leithwood, & D. Livingstone (Eds.), *International handbook of educational policy* (pp. 456–470). London, UK: Kluwer Press.

Jefferson, G. (2004). Glossary of transcript symbols with an introduction. In G. H. Lerner (Ed.), *Conversation analysis: Studies from the first generation* (pp. 13–31). Amsterdam, Netherlands: John Benjamins.

Jink, T. D. (1979). Mixing qualitative and quantitative methods: Triangulation in action. *Administrative Science Quarterly, 24*(4), 602–611.

Jochim, A. E., & Murphy, P. J. (2013, December). *The capacity challenge: What it takes for state education agencies to support school improvement.* Seattle, WA: Center for Reinventing Public Education.

Johnson, A. P. (2008). *A short guide to action research* (3rd ed.). Boston, MA: Allyn & Bacon.

Johnson, B., & Christensen, L. (2010). *Educational research: Quantitative, qualitative, and mixed approaches* (4th ed.). Thousand Oaks, CA: SAGE.

Johnson, R. B. & Onwuegbuzie, A. J. (2004). Mixed methods research: A research paradigm whose time has come. *Educational Researcher, 33*(7), 14–26.

Johnson, R. B., & Turner, L. A. (2003). Data collection strategies in mixed methods research. In A. Tashakkori & C. Teddlie (Eds.), *Handbook of mixed methods in social and behavioral research* (pp. 297–319). Thousand Oaks, CA: SAGE.

Jorgensen, M., & Phillips, L. (2002). *Discourse analysis as theory and method.* London, UK: SAGE.

Kanno, Y., & Cromley, J. (2013a). English language learners' access to and attainment in postsecondary education. *TESOL Quarterly, 47*(1), 89–121.

Kanno, Y., & Cromley, J. (2013b). *English language learners' pathways to four-year colleges.* Paper presented at the American Educational Research Association Annual Meeting (AERA), San Francisco, CA.

Kanno, Y., & Kangas, S. E. N. (2014). "I'm not going to be, like, for the AP": English language learners' limited access to advanced college-preparatory courses in high school. *American Educational Research Journal, 51*(5), 848–878.

Kazdin, A. E. (1982). *Single-case research designs: Methods for clinical and applied settings.* New York, NY: Oxford University Press.

Kennedy, M. M. (1997). The connection between research and practice. *Educational Researcher, 26*(7), 4–12.

Kerlinger, F. N. (1972). *Behavior research: A conceptual approach.* New York, NY: Holt, Rinehart, and Winston.

Kerlinger, F. N. (1986). *Foundations of behavioral research.* Fort Worth, TX: Harcourt Brace Jovanovich.

Kilbourn, B. (2006). The qualitative doctoral dissertation proposal. *Teachers College Record, 108*(4), 529–576.

Kirk, J., & Miller, M. L. (1986). Reliability and validity in qualitative research. Beverly Hills, CA: SAGE.

Knapp, M. S. (2008). How can organizational and sociocultural learning theories shed light on district instructional reform? *American Journal of Education, 114*(4), 521–539.

Knapp, M. S., Copland, M. A., Honig, M. I., Plecki, M. L., & Portin, B. S. (2014). *Learning-focused leadership in action: Improving instruction in schools and districts.* New York, NY: Routledge.

Koo, S., & Lester, J. N. (2014). Naming and un-naming a research study "participatory." *The Qualitative Report, 19*(23), 1–13.

Kromrey, J. D. (1993). Ethics and data analysis. *Educational Researcher, 22*(4), 24–27.

Kuhn, T (1962). *The structure of scientific revolutions.* Chicago, IL: University of Chicago Press.

Kuhn, T. S. (1970). *The structure of scientific revolutions* (2nd ed.). Chicago, IL: University of Chicago Press.

Kvale, S. (2007). *Doing interviews.* London, UK: SAGE.

Kvale, S., & Brinkmann, S. (2009). *Interviews: Learning the craft of qualitative research interviewing.* Thousand Oaks, CA: SAGE.

LaBanca, F. (2011). Online dynamic asynchronous audit strategy for reflexivity in the qualitative paradigm. *The Qualitative Report, 16*(4), 1160–1171.

Lambert, J. (2006). *Digital storytelling: Capturing lives, creating community.* Berkeley, CA: Digital Diner Press.

Lave, J., & Wenger, E. (1991). *Situated learning: Legitimate peripheral participation.* Cambridge, UK: Cambridge University Press.

Laverty, S. M. (2003). Hermeneutic phenomenology and phenomenology: A comparison of historical and methodological considerations. *International Journal of Qualitative Methods, 2*(3), 21–35.

Lee, J. (2002). Racial and ethnic achievement gap trends: Reversing the progress toward equity? *Educational Researcher, 31*(1), 3–12.

Lester, J. N. (2012). A discourse analysis of parents' talk around their children's autism labels. *Disability Studies Quarterly, 32*(4), Art. 1.

Lester, J. N. (2014). Negotiating abnormality/normality in therapy talk: A discursive psychology approach to the study of therapeutic interactions and children with autism. *Qualitative Psychology, 1*(2), 178–193.

Lester, J. N., & Barouch, A. (2013). Inviting the assent of children described as functionally nonverbal. In I. Paoletti, A. Duarte, I. Tomas, & F. Menéndez, *Practices of ethics: An empirical approach to ethics in social science research* (pp. 65–84). Newcastle-upon-Tyne, UK: Cambridge Scholars Press.

Lester, J., & Gabriel, R. (2012). Performance ethnography of IEP meetings: A theatre of the absurd. In P. Vannini (Ed.), *Popularizing research: Engaging new media, genres, and audience* (pp. 173–178). New York, NY: Peter Lang.

Lester, J. N., & Gabriel, R. (2015). Teaching the bodies of readers: A discourse analysis of instructional talk. Paper presented at the meeting of the American Educational Research Association, Chicago, Illinois.

Lincoln, Y. S., & Guba, E. G. (1985). *Naturalistic observation.* Thousand Oaks, CA: SAGE.

Lochmiller, C. R. (2012). Leading with less: Principal leadership in austere times. In B. G. Barnett, A. R. Shoho, & A T. Cyres (Eds.), *The changing nature of instructional leadership in the 21st century* (pp. 165–186). Charlotte, NC: Information Age Publishing.

Lochmiller, C. R. (2014). What would it cost to coach every new principal? An estimate using statewide personnel data. *Education Policy Analysis Archives, 22*(55), 1–16. http://dx.doi.org/10.14507/epaa. v22n55.2014

Lochmiller, C. R., Huggins, K. S., & Acker-Hocevar, M. A. (2012). Preparing leaders for math and science: Three alternatives to traditional preparation. *Planning and Changing, 43*(1/2), 198–220.

Loucks-Horsley, S., Love, N., Stiles, K. E., Mundry, S. E., & Hewson, P. W. (2003). *Designing professional development for teachers of science and mathematics* (2nd ed.). Thousand Oaks, CA: Corwin Press.

Luter, G., Lester, J. N., & Kronick, R. (2013). "Remember, it's a pilot": Exploring the experiences of teachers/staff at a university-assisted community school. *The School Community Journal, 23*(2), 161–184.

Lutz, C. A. (1990). Engendered emotion: Gender, power, and the rhetoric of emotional control in American discourse. In C. A. Lutz & L. Abu-Lughod (Eds.), *Language and the politics of motion* (pp. 69–91). Cambridge, UK: Cambridge University Press.

Luyten, H., Visscher, A., & Witziers, B. (2005). School effectiveness research: From a review of the criticism to recommendations for further development. *School Effectiveness and School Improvement, 16*(3), 249–279.

Machi, L. A., & McEvoy, B. T. (2009). *The literature review: Six steps to success.* Thousand Oaks, CA: SAGE.

Makel, M. C., & Plucker, J. A. (2014). Facts are more important than novelty: Replication in the education sciences. *Educational Researcher, 43*(6), 304–316.

Mangin, M. M. (2005). Distributed leadership and the culture of schools: Teacher leaders' strategies for gaining access to classrooms. *Journal of School Leadership, 15*(4), 456–484.

Mangin, M. M. (2006). Teacher leadership and instructional improvement: Teachers' perspectives. In W. K. Hoy & C. Miskel (Eds.), *Contemporary issues in educational policy and school outcomes* (pp. 159–192). Greenwich, CT: Information Age.

Mangin, M. M. (2007). Facilitating elementary principals' support for instructional teacher leadership. *Educational Administration Quarterly, 43*(3), 319–357.

Mangin, M. M., & Stoelinga, S. R. (Eds.). (2008). *Effective teacher leadership: Using research to inform and reform.* New York, NY: Teachers College Press.

Markham, A. (2006). Method as ethic, ethic as method. *Journal of Information Ethics, 15*(2), 37–55.

Mauthner, M., Birch, M., Jessop, J., & Miller, T. (Eds.). (2002). *Ethics in qualitative research.* London, UK: SAGE.

Maxwell, J. A. (2013). *Qualitative research design: An interactive approach* (3rd ed.). Thousand Oaks, CA: SAGE.

Maxwell, J. A., & Loomis, D. M. (2003). Mixed methods design: An alternative approach. In A. Tashakkori & C. Teddlie (Eds.), *Handbook of mixed methods in social and behavioral research* (pp. 241–271). Thousand Oaks, CA: SAGE.

May, P. J. (1992). Policy learning and failure. *Journal of Public Policy, 12*(4), 331–354.

Mazzoni, T. (1991). Analyzing state school policy making: An arena model. *Educational Evaluation and Policy Analysis, 13*(2), 115–138.

McDonnell, L. M., & Weatherford, M. S. (2013). Organized interests and the common core. *Educational Researcher, 42*(9), 488–497.

McIntyre, A. (2008). *Participatory action research.* Thousand Oaks, CA: SAGE.

McKee, H. A., & Porter, J. E. (2009). *Internet research: A rhetorical, case-based process.* New York, NY: Peter Lang Publishers.

McLaughlin, M., & Talbert, J. (2003, September). *Reforming districts: How districts support school reform.* Seattle, WA: Center for the Study of Teaching & Policy.

McNiff, J. (2013). *Action research: Principles and practice* (3rd ed.). New York, NY: Routledge.

Mead, S., Vaishnav, A., Porter, W., & Rotherham, A. J. (2010). *Conflicting missions and unclear results: Lessons from the education stimulus funds.* Washington, DC: Bellwether Education Partners. Retrieved December 10, 2011, from http://bellwethereducation.org/wp-content/uploads/2010/11/Bellwether_Conflicting-Missions-Unclear-Results.pdf.

Merriam, S. B. (1998). *Qualitative research and case study applications in education.* San Francisco, CA: Jossey-Bass.

Merriam, S. B. (2009). *Qualitative research and case study applications in education* (2nd ed.). San Francisco, CA: Jossey-Bass.

Mertens, D. M. (1998). *Research methods in education and psychology: Integrating diversity with quantitative & qualitative approaches.* Thousand Oaks, CA: SAGE.

Mertens, D. (2009). *Transformative research and evaluation.* New York, NY: Guilford.

Mertler, C. A. (2014). *Action research: Improving schools and empowering educators* (4th ed.). Thousand Oaks, CA: SAGE.

Mertler, C. A. & Charles, C. M. (2011). *Introduction to educational research* (7th ed.). Boston, MA: Allyn & Bacon.

Messick, S. (1989). Validity. In R.L. Linn (Ed.), *Educational measurement,* Vol. 3 (pp. 13–103). New York, NY: American Council on Education, MacMillan.

Mezirow, J. (1991). *Transformative dimensions of adult learning.* San Francisco, CA: Jossey-Bass.

Milanowski, A., & Kimball, S. (2004). The relationship between teacher performance evaluation scores and student achievement: Evidence from Cincinnati. *Peabody Journal of Education, 79*(4), 33–53.

Miles, M. B., & Huberman, A. M. (1994). *An expanded sourcebook: Qualitative data analysis* (2nd ed.). Thousand Oaks, CA: SAGE.

Miles, M. B., Huberman, A. M., & Saldaña, J. (2014). *Qualitative data analysis: A methods sourcebook* (3rd ed.). Thousand Oaks, CA: SAGE.

Mockler, N. (2014). When "research ethics" become "everyday ethics": The intersection of inquiry and practice in practitioner research. *Educational Action Research, 22*(2), 146–158.

Morgan, G. (1983). Toward a more reflective social science. In G. Morgan (Ed.), *Beyond method: Strategies for social research* (pp. 368–376). Beverly Hills, CA: SAGE.

Morse, J. M., & Niehaus, L. (2009). *Mixed methods design: Principles and procedures*. Walnut Creek, CA: Left Coast Press.

Moustakas, C. (1994). *Phenomenological research methods*. Thousand Oaks, CA: SAGE.

Newman, I., & Benz, C. R. (1998). *Qualitative-quantitative researcher methodology: Exploring the interactive continuum*. Carbondale: Southern Illinois University Press.

Noblit, G. W. (1999). *Particularities: Collected essays on ethnography and education*. New York, NY: Peter Lang Publishing.

Nolen, A. & Vander Putten, J. (2007). Action research in education: Addressing gaps in ethical principles and practices. *Educational Researcher, 36*(7), 401–407.

Nowick, E. A., Brown, J., & Stepien, M. (2014). Children's structured conceptualization of their beliefs on the causes of learning difficulties. *Journal of Mixed Methods Research, 8*(1), 69–82.

O'Cathain, A., & Thomas, K. (2006). Combining qualitative and quantitative methods. In C. Pope & N. Mays (Eds.), *Qualitative research in health care* (3rd ed.) (pp. 102–111). Oxford, UK: Blackwell Publishing.

Ochs, E. (1979). Transcription as theory. In E. Ochs & B. Schieffelin (Eds.), *Developmental pragmatics* (pp. 43–72). New York, NY: Academic Press.

Odden, A. R. (2012). *Strategic management of human capital in education: Improving instructional practice and student learning in schools*. New York, NY: Routledge.

O'Dwyer, L. M., & Bernauer, J. A. (2014). *Quantitative research for the qualitative researcher*. Thousand Oaks, CA: SAGE.

Office for Human Research Protections. Protection of human subjects: Title 45, Part 46. Available at: http://www.hhs.gov/ohrp/archive/humansubjects/guidance/45cfr46.html.

Onwuegbuzie, A., & Leech, N. (2005, March 10). A typology of errors and myths perpetuated in educational research textbooks. *Current Issues in Education* [online], 8(7).

Onwuegbuzie, A. J., & Leech, N. L. (2006). Linking research questions to mixed methods data analysis procedures. *The Qualitative Report, 11*(3), 474–498. Retrieved August 20, 2014, from http://www.nova.edu/ssss/QR/QR11-3/onwuegbuzie.pdf.

Onwuegbuzie, A. J., & Leech, N. L. (2007). Sampling designs in qualitative research: Making the sampling process more public. *The Qualitative Report, 12*(2), 238–254.

Onwuegbuzie, A. J., Leech, N. L., & Collins, K. M. (2012). Qualitative analysis techniques for the review of the literature. *The Qualitative Report, 17*, Article 56, 1–28.

Onwuegbuzie, A. J., & Teddlie, C. (2003). A framework for analyzing data in mixed methods research. In A. Tashakkori & C. Teddlie (Eds.), *Handbook of mixed methods in social and behavioral research* (pp. 351–383). Thousand Oaks, CA: SAGE.

Oreshkina, M. (2007). Teachers' experience of working with underachieving students: A comparative phenomenological study of teachers in South Africa, Russia, and the United States. University of Tennessee: Unpublished dissertation.

O'Reilly, M., & Kiyimba, N. (2015). *Advanced qualitative research: A guide to contemporary theoretical debates*. London, UK: SAGE.

Orr, A. J. (2003, October). Black-white differences in achievement: The importance of wealth. *Sociology of Education, 76*, 281–304.

Osterman, K., Furman, G., & Sernak, K. (2014). Action research in EdD programs in educational leadership. *Journal of Research on Leadership Education, 9*(1), 85–105.

Ostermann, A. C. (2003). Localizing power and solidarity: Pronoun alternation at an all-female police station and a feminist crisis intervention center in Brazil. *Language in Society, 32*(3), 251–281.

Pagano, R. R. (2004). *Understanding statistics in the behavioral sciences* (7th ed.). Belmont, CA: Wadsworth/Thomson Learning.

Park, P. (1997). Participatory research, democracy, and community. *Practicing Anthropology 19*(3), 8–13.

Pattall, E. A., Cooper, H., & Allen, A. B. (2010). Extending the school day or school year: A systematic review of research (1985–2009). *Review of Educational Research, 80*(3), 401–436.

Patton, M. Q. (1980). *Qualitative evaluation and research methods*. Beverly Hills, CA: SAGE.

Patton, M. Q. (2002). *Qualitative research and evaluation methods* (3rd ed.). Thousand Oaks, CA: SAGE.

Paulus, T. M., Lester, J. N., & Dempster, P. G. (2014). *Digital tools for qualitative research*. London, UK: SAGE.

Peugh, J. L., & Enders, C. K. (2004). Missing data in educational research: A review of reporting practices and suggestions for improvement. *Review of Educational Research, 74*(4), 525–556.

Polkinghorne, D. (1989). Phenomenological research methods. In R. S. Valle & S. Halling (Eds.), *Existential-phenomenological perspectives in psychology* (pp. 41–60). New York, NY: Plenum Press.

Polkinghorne, D. E. (2005). Language and meaning: Data collection in qualitative research. *Journal of Counseling Psychology, 52*(2), 137–145.

Potter, J. (1997). Discourse analysis as a way of analyzing naturally occurring talk. In David Silverman (Ed.), *Qualitative research: Theory, method and practice* (pp. 144–160). London, UK: SAGE.

Potter, J. (2004). Discourse analysis. In M. A. Hardy & A. Bryman (Eds.), *Handbook of data analysis* (pp. 607–634). London, UK: SAGE.

Potter, J., & Wetherell, M. (1987). *Discourse and social psychology*. London, UK: SAGE.

Price, J. N. (2001). Action research, pedagogy, and change: The transformative potential of action research in pre-service teacher education. *Journal of Curriculum Studies, 33*(1), 43–74.

Rapley, T. (2007). *Doing conversation, discourse and document analysis*. London, UK: SAGE.

Rea, L. M., & Parker, R. A. (2005). *Designing and conducting survey research: A comprehensive guide* (3rd ed.). San Francisco, CA: Jossey-Bass.

Rea, L. M., & Parker, R. A. (2014). *Designing and conducting survey research: A comprehensive guide* (4th ed.). Hoboken, NJ: Jossey-Bass.

Riessman, C. K. (1993). *Narrative analysis*. Newbury Park, CA: SAGE.

Rodríguez, L. F. & Brown, T. M (2009). Engaging youth in participatory action research for education and social transformation. *New Directions for Youth Development, 123*, 19–34.

Rose, G. (2012). *Visual methodologies: An introduction to the interpretation of visual materials* (3rd ed.). London, UK: SAGE.

Rosenwald, G. C., & Ochberg, R. L. (1992). Introduction: Life stories, cultural politics, and self-understanding. In G. C. Rosenwalk & R. L. Ochberg (Eds.), *Storied lives: The cultural politics of self-understanding* (pp. 1–20). New Haven, CT: Yale University Press.

Roulston, K. (2011). *Reflective interviewing: A guide to theory and practice*. Thousand Oaks, CA: SAGE.

Rudestam, K. E., & Newton, R. R. (1992). *Surviving your dissertation*. Newbury Park, CA: SAGE.

Rumberger, R., & Willms, J. D. (1992). The impact of racial and ethnic segregation on the achievement gap in California high schools. *Educational Evaluation and Policy Analysis, 14*(4), 377–396.

Sabatier, P. A. (2007). *Theories of policy process* (2nd ed.). Boulder, CO: Westview Press.

Sacks, H. (1992). *Lectures on conversation*. Oxford, UK: Blackwell.

Saldaña, J. (2009). *The coding manual for qualitative researchers*. Thousand Oaks, CA: SAGE.

Saldaña, J. (2014). *Thinking qualitatively: Methods of mind*. Thousand Oaks, CA: SAGE.

Salmon, M. H. (2007). *Introduction to logic and critical thinking*. Belmont, CA: Thomson Higher Education.

Sandelowski, M. (1995). Sample size in qualitative research. *Research in nursing and health, 18*(2), 179–183.

Sartain, L., Stoelinga, S. R., & Brown, E. R. (2011). *Rethinking teacher evaluation in Chicago: Lessons learned from classroom observations, principal-teacher conferences, and district implementation*. Chicago, IL: Consortium on Chicago School Research.

Schroeder, L. D., Sjoquist, D. L., & Stephan, P. E. (1986). *Understanding regression analysis: An introductory guide*. Thousand Oaks, CA: SAGE.

Senge, P. M. (1990). *The fifth discipline: The art and practice of the learning organization*. New York, NY: Doubleday.

Senge, P. M., Cambron-McCabe, H., Lucas, T., Smith, B., & Dutton, J. (2012). *Schools that learn (updated and revised): A fifth discipline fieldbook for educators, parents, and everyone who cares about education*. New York, NY: Random House.

Silverman, D. (2001). *Interpreting qualitative data: Methods for analyzing text, talk, and interaction*. London, UK: SAGE.

Solomon, R. L. (1949). An extension of control group design. *Psychological Bulletin, 46*(2), 137–150.

Sosu, E. M., McWilliam, A., & Gray, D. S. (2008). The complexities of teachers' commitment to environmental education: A mixed methods approach. *Journal of Mixed Methods Research, 2*(2), 16–189.

Srivastava, P., & Hopwood, N. (2009). A practical iterative framework for qualitative data analysis. *International Journal of Qualitative Methods, 8*(1), 76–84.

Stake, R. E. (1995). *The art of case study research*. Thousand Oaks, CA: SAGE.

Stake, R. E. (2005). Qualitative case studies. In N. K. Denzin & Y. S. Lincoln (Eds.), *The SAGE handbook of qualitative research* (3rd ed.) (pp. 443–466). Thousand Oaks, CA: SAGE.

Stefanac, S. (2006). *Dispatches from blogistan: A travel guide for the modern blogger*. Berkeley, CA: New Riders.

Stein, W. L. (2008) *Searching for a caregiver: The middle school principal*. University of Tennessee: Unpublished dissertation.

Strauss, A. L., & Corbin, J. (1998). *Basics of qualitative research: Grounded theory procedures and techniques* (2nd ed.). Thousand Oaks, CA: SAGE.

Stringer, E. T. (2007). *Action research* (3rd ed.). Thousand Oaks, CA: SAGE.

Stringer, E. T. (2014). *Action research* (4th ed.). Thousand Oaks, CA: SAGE.

Tashakkori, A., & Teddlie, C. (1998). *Mixed methodology: Combining qualitative and quantitative approaches.* Applied Social Research Methods Series (Vol. 46). Thousand Oaks, CA: SAGE.

Thapa, A., Cohen, J., Guffey, S., & Higgins-D'Alessandro, A. (2013). A review of school climate research. *Review of Educational Research, 83*(3), 357–385.

Tracy, S. J. (2010). Qualitative quality: Eight "big tent" criteria for excellent qualitative research. *Qualitative Inquiry, 16*(1), 837–851.

Trujillo, T. (2013). The reincarnation of the effective schools research: Rethinking the literature on district effectiveness. *Journal of Educational Administration, 51*(4), 426–452.

Valle, R. S., King, M., & Halling, S. (1989). An introduction to existential-phenomenological thought in psychology. In R. S. Valle & S. Halling (Eds.), *Existential-phenomenological perspectives in psychology* (pp. 3–16). New York, NY: Plenum Press.

Van Lare, M., Yoon, I., & Gallucci, C. (2008). *Orchestrating leadership in district-wide reform: A report for Marysville School District.* Seattle: Center for the Study of Teaching and Policy, University of Washington.

van Manen, M. (1990). *Researching lived experience: Human science for an action sensitive pedagogy.* Albany: State University of New York Press.

Vannini, P. (Ed.). (2012). *Popularizing research: Engaging new media, genres, and audience.* New York, NY: Peter Lang.

Vogt, W. P., Gardner, D. C., & Haeffele, L. M. (2012). *When to use what research design.* New York, NY: The Guilford Press.

Vygotsky, L. S. (1978). *Mind in society: The development of higher psychological processes.* Cambridge, MA: Harvard University Press.

Wallen, N. E., & Fraenkel, J. R. (2001). *Educational research: A guide to the process* (2nd ed.). Mahwah, NJ: Lawrence Erlbaum Associates.

Walliman, N., & Buckler, S. (2008). *Your dissertation in education.* London, UK: SAGE.

Watt, D. (2007). On becoming a qualitative researcher: The value of reflexivity. *The Qualitative Report, 12*(1), 82–101.

Wayman, J. C. (2005). Involving teachers in data-driven decision-making: Using computer data systems to support teacher inquiry and reflection. *Journal of Education for Students Placed at Risk, 10*(3), 295–308.

Weatherly, R., & Lipsky, M. (1977). Street-level bureaucrats and institutional innovation: Implementing special education reform. *Harvard Educational Review, 47*(2), 171–197.

Weick, K. E. (1995). *Sensemaking in organizations.* Thousand Oaks, CA: SAGE.

Weinberg, S. L., & Abramowitz, S. K. (2008). *Statistics using SPSS* (2nd ed.).

New York, NY: Cambridge University Press.

Whitehurst, G. (2003, April). *The Institute of Education Sciences: New wine, new bottles.* Paper presented at the annual meeting of the American Educational Research Association, San Francisco, CA.

Willis, J. (2007). *Foundations of qualitative research: Interpretive and critical approaches.* Thousand Oaks, CA: SAGE.

Wine, J. R., Heuer, E., Wheeless, S. C., Francis, T. L. & Franklin, J. W. (2002). *Beginning postsecondary students longitudinal study: 1996–2001. (BPS:1996/2001) methodology report (NCES 2002-171).* Washington, DC: U.S. Department of Education, Office of Educational Research and Improvement.

Winston, Jr., R. B. (1985, April). A suggested procedure for determining order of authorship in research publications. *Journal of Counseling and Development, 63*, 515–518.

Wirt, F. M., & Kirst, M. W. (1997). *The political dynamics of American education.* Berkeley, CA: McCutchan Publishing.

Wolcott, H. F. (1990). *Writing up qualitative research (Qualitative research methods,* Vol. 20). Newbury Park, CA: SAGE.

Wolcott, H. F. (2005). *The art of fieldwork.* Lanham, MD: Altamira Press.

Wolgemuth, J. R., Cobb, R. B., Winokur, M. A., Leech, N., & Ellerby, D. (2006). Comparing longitudinal academic achievement of full day and half-day kindergarten students. *Journal of Educational Research, 99*(5), 260–269.

Wood, L. A., & Kroger, R. O. (2000). *Doing discourse analysis: Methods for studying action in talk and text*. Thousand Oaks, CA: SAGE.

Woolgar, S. (1988). *Science: The very idea*. New York, NY: Routledge.

Yancher, S., & Williams, D. (2006). Reconsidering the compatibility thesis and eclecticism: Five proposed guidelines for method use. *Educational Researcher, 35*(9), 3–12.

Yin, R. K. (2009). *Case study research: Design and methods* (4th ed.). Thousand Oaks, CA: SAGE.

Yin, R. K. (2012). *Applications of case study research* (3rd ed.). Thousand Oaks, CA: SAGE.

Ylimaki, R., & Jacobson, S. (2013). School leadership practice and preparation: Comparative perspectives on organizational learning (OL), instructional leadership (IL), and culturally responsive practices (CRP). *Journal of Educational Administration, 51*(1), 6–23.

INDEX

NOTE: Page references to boxes, figures and tables are identified as (box), (fig.), and (table).